THE LIFE OF
Sir Arthur Conan Doyle

THE LIFE OF
Sir Arthur Conan Doyle

BY

JOHN DICKSON CARR

VINTAGE BOOKS

A Division of Random House

New York

FIRST VINTAGE BOOKS EDITION, August 1975

Copyright © 1949 by John Dickson Carr

All rights reserved under International and Pan-American Copyright Conventions. Published in the United States by Random House, Inc., New York and simultaneously in Canada by Random House of Canada Limited, Toronto. Originally published by Harper & Row, Publishers, Incorporated, in 1949.

Library of Congress Cataloging in Publication Data
Carr, John Dickson, 1905–
   The life of Sir Arthur Conan Doyle.
   Reprint of the 1st ed. published by Harper, New York.
   "Bibliographical archives": p.
   1. Doyle, Sir Arthur Conan, 1859–1930. I. Title.
PR4623.C3 1975   823'.9'12[B]   75–5535
ISBN 0–394–71608–6

Manufactured in the United States of America

CONTENTS

FOREWORD

"He had a horror of destroying documents, especially those which were connected with his past cases," writes Dr. Watson, "and yet it was only once in every year or two that he would muster energy to docket and arrange them. . . . Thus month after month his papers accumulated, until every corner of the room was stacked with bundles of manuscript which were on no account to be burned, and which could not be put away save by their owner."

Dr. Watson might have been speaking of his own creator. At Windlesham, all through the house as well as in the red-curtained study, this vast amount of material had accumulated at the time of Sir Arthur Conan Doyle's death in 1930. But in 1946 it was fully docketed and arranged. Therefore the biographer, most of whose material has never been published, must say a preparatory word.

This is a story of adventure, sometimes even of melodrama. To paint in full colours, to check the gallop, would be to misrepresent the man himself. But please do not imagine that, because this record has been presented like fiction, it is 'novelized' biography.

The facts cannot be helped. Things happened like that. When Conan Doyle speaks, he speaks in his own words out of letter, notebook, diary, authenticated press-cutting or letter about him. When the furniture of a room is described, or a scene takes place in the thunderstorm, or he scribbles a note on a theatre-programme, it is because there is documentation for such statements.

The dates of all important letters or documents—whose source will be found in the bibliography—have been included in the text. For far-off days (there are fifteen hundred letters to his mother), correspondence is the only true breath of life. Memories blur and grow tremulous. Even a man's autobiography hesitates as it gropes back. But *there,* shut up in old papers, is the living emotion; *that* was what he felt at the time, when the blood ran fast; that is the truth. Such letters were carefully saved by his mother, his brother Innes, his sister Lottie, his children, and above all by the late Lady (Jean) Conan Doyle.

We deal not altogether with far-off days. My greatest thanks must go to Mr. Adrian Conan Doyle, who for two years assisted me in a task which I could not have accomplished without his help; in almost equal measure, to Mr. Denis Conan Doyle and Miss Mary Conan Doyle.

Very heartily I wish to thank Mr. H. Sargeant, of the Central Library, Portsmouth, for the minute-book which enabled us to identify Dr. Watson; my old friend Mr. Reeves Shaw, who succeeded Greenhough Smith as editor of the 'Strand,' for the letters to Greenhough Smith; Mrs. Reginald Smith, whose husband was so closely associated with Conan Doyle at the firm of Smith, Elder & Co.; Dr. R. Cathcart Bruce and Dr. W. E. Carnegie Dickson, both of whom well knew Joseph Bell. Thanks must go also to Sir Home Gordon; Lieutenant-Colonel Arthur J. Woodroffe; Mr. C. W. Hearn; Mr. Ronald R. B. Bannerman of the British Embassy in Washington; Mrs. Barbara C. Windsor, niece of Major Arthur Grif-

fiths; Mr. G. J. Cubitt; Mr. J. Norris Evans; Mr. G.
Harcourt; Mr. Basil Gotto; Mr. Lionel Giles; Lord
Gorell; and to all those correspondents who have so
kindly given information and suggestions.

But behind them all stand the Archives, in which are
imprisoned the authentic voices of the past. If H. G.
Wells was pleased, or King Edward the Seventh laid
down the law at the dinner-table, or William J. Burns
suggested a detective-plot, we can hear them yet. We
deal, in the main, with a man's life between 1869 and
1919. I have had little more to do than to edit and
to arrange.

JOHN DICKSON CARR

THE LIFE OF
Sir Arthur Conan Doyle

I

HERITAGE:

The Golden Leopards

At Edinburgh, one summer afternoon in the year 1869, a gentleman approaching middle age sat at his water-colour painting in the small, scrubbed dining-room off the kitchen at number 3 Sciennes Hill Place. And he looked back over twenty years.

He was a tall man, with a silky beard stretching well down his waistcoat, heavy hair that curled across his forehead, and a manner retiring and apologetic for one of so distinguished appearance. His clothes, shabby-genteel, were as presentable as his wife could make them. Only in his eyes, as he glanced sideways towards the kitchen, could anyone see a humour and insight that penetrated far beyond the street door.

It was bad light for painting. Over Edinburgh, 'Auld Reekie' of the smoke and the east wind, a fine rain monotonously fell. But that was not the reason why the man in the long-skirted coat put aside his brush, being careful not to splash colour on Mary's best oak dining-room set. He could hear—through the partly open door to the next room—the thump-thump of the hearth-brush as his wife cleaned underneath the grate. These thumps punctuated her sentences as she laid down the law to their ten-year-old son Arthur.

"I am glad to find, my dear boy, that Hodder has *much* improved your French," said Mary. He could imagine her holding up the hearth-brush impressively.

"We will now, if you please, take up a subject of equal importance."

And so Charles Altamont Doyle looked back across his life.

He saw himself arriving from London, twenty years ago, at a railway-station set amid green fields. As the youngest son of a famous family, his prospects seemed good. He had been appointed deputy to Mr. Robert Matheson, head of Her Majesty's Office of Works at Edinburgh, beginning at a salary of £220 a year. Only beginning, mind you! Charles Doyle, by profession an architect, believed that his duties would be mainly architectural. It should leave him much free time to indulge his talent for painting, as his brothers were doing at home.

His brain teemed with designs sacred, designs comic, designs grotesque. Eagerly he explored Edinburgh, writing to his father long letters illustrated with pen-and-ink sketches. He was impressed by the grey Castle on its rock; fascinated by the tall toppling houses of the Canongate, "a sort of paradise to lovers of the picturesque if they had no noses"; but repelled by the outside of Holyrood Palace, which he likened to a prison or a madhouse.

The people he met (good Catholics, for the most part) liked this diffident young man as much as he liked them. Yet there were aspects of the Scots character which at first badly puzzled him.

He was not soon to forget his first New Year's Eve: when, after a deep solemnity of tea-drinking and religious conversation until midnight, all Edinburgh suddenly arose and got so stupendously drunk that by two o'clock the streets were impassable in a kind of witch's sabbath; and mysterious Highlanders, appearing in hordes out of nowhere, were still dancing reels in Mrs.

MacDonald's parlour. Charles, in some apprehension, had promised to escort two young ladies home.

"My dear sir," said his friend Mr. MacCarthy, calmly producing a life-preserver from his pocket, as though life-preservers were a part of any gentleman's attire like a beaver hat or a pair of tight trousers, "my dear sir, take this. I have another for myself."

"Hit them, you mean?"

"My dear sir, of course! Crack the skull of anyone who tries to charge us; and I have no doubt we shall see the ladies safely through it."

And then there was one really great occasion, late in August of '50, which roused all his patriotic fervour. It was true that most of the work, month after month of niggling detail and harassed preparation, fell on his own shoulders. At eighteen years old he was too excited even to notice. For the Queen and Prince Albert, with their children, were to visit Edinburgh.

From the roof of Holyrood Palace, where he had hurried to supervise the raising of the flag, Charles Doyle saw far away the steam of the approaching train. Scarlet-coated out-riders galloped ahead to clear the way. A vast crowd on the hill, flickering white with handkerchiefs, roared its welcome as the train drew in. Presently, when the royal carriages clattered into Palace Yard behind the glossiest of horses, Charles thought that young Queen Victoria "did not look well, being red in the face." But she jumped down from her carriage, without assistance, in lively fashion; and the echo of the cannon-salute still lingered from Castle rock.

Nevertheless, in those old days, Charles Doyle suffered from fits of homesickness he could not stifle. He longed to see his father, and his three brothers, and his sister Annette. Every letter from his brother Richard—

'Dicky' Doyle, the leading artist of *Punch*—carried Dick's drawling voice into loneliness.

"And how," he would inquire, "do you fare among the Sawneys?" Dick, the perfect man-about-town, kept up an elaborate pretence of believing that everybody in Scotland was descended from Sawney Bean, and still ate cannibal-meat in a cave.

"I daresay," wrote Dick, "you heard of Smith & Elder, through Mr. Williams, asking me to dinner to meet the Author of 'Jane Eyre,' who is a little delicate-looking but clever woman, about thirty, named Miss Brontë, and daughter of a clergyman in Yorkshire. Thackeray was also asked."

Or again, in the same letter:

"I think it was since you went to Scotland that Evans asked me to a Newsvendors' Benevolent Society Dinner, Chas. Dickens in the chair, who made an admirable speech, Luck, Phiz, Lemon, Leigh, &c., being present, which party and Mr. Peter Cunningham afterwards went with Dickens to the Rainbow Tavern in Fleet Street and partook of burnt Sherry and Anchovy toast until a late hour."

Paint and printer's ink and the lamps of the great world! Yet to Charles such letters had conjured up even more vividly the image of his straight-backed father, John Doyle.

John Doyle, king of political caricaturists, sat in state amid the polished oak panels and silver rose-bowls of number 17 Cambridge Terrace, Hyde Park. He looked so much like the old Duke of Wellington that he could not ride in the Park without being saluted. 'Lord John,' his sons called him, or 'the Guv'nor General'; but they seldom called him this to his face.

This John Doyle, of the Irish Catholic landed gentry, had come to England from an estate ruined by genera-

tions of penal laws against Catholics. His family was of
old Norman descent and had been granted estates in
Ireland in the first half of the 14th century. He was a
painter. When he arrived in England, he had just three
worldly possessions: a painting by Van Dyck, which he
refused to sell; some pieces of seventeenth-century family plate; and a mortar and pestle for compounding
home medicines. The world had changed much since
those incongruous objects adorned a bare room. Under
the pseudonym of H.B., he conquered London with the
sharp-pointed wit of his caricatures, done in wickedly
fastidious drawing, when other caricaturists were content
to depict public figures as bloated buffoons tumbling
downstairs. It would no more have occurred to John
Doyle to draw political opponents in this fashion than it
would have occurred to him to lay hold of one of his
own guests (say the late Sir Walter Scott), and pitch
him downstairs after an argument at dinner.

His wife, Marianna Conan, was dead. His four tall
sons—James, Richard, Henry, and Charles—he brought
up to use brush and pencil, just as he brought them up
to be devout Catholics. A stickler, the Guv'nor General!
Outsiders sometimes wondered that such an artistic sensitiveness, such a satiric smile, could lurk behind John
Doyle's stately bearing. In his work there was a touch of
the bizarre, which was to grow with such terrible effect
in the water-colours of his son Charles.

But Charles, in Edinburgh, found his homesickness
swept away. In the year 1855, Charles Doyle married
Miss Mary Foley.

The bride was just seventeen. Younger daughter of an
Irish Catholic widow, at whose house Charles stayed as
a paying guest almost from the first, Mary had been sent
away to a French school at the age of twelve. She returned, fully grown up, and turned his head. "Impu-

dent," he called her; vivacious she certainly was; small, grey-eyed, her fair hair parted in the middle and drawn behind the ears, every gesture full of Irish charm.

It must have astonished good Scots matrons to learn that the girl was a French scholar, and that her hobby was the study of heraldry. Odd tastes for a pretty face, but it welled up from the deepest springs of her nature: a fierce pride of lineage, surviving poverty and uttered almost with a vehemence of tears.

"The Doyles, I grant you," she would say, drawing herself up to her full height of five-feet-one, "are gentle-folk of ancient descent. But we, on the other hand, are descended from the feudal nobility."

And then:

"My mother, please observe, was born Catherine Pack. Her uncle was Major-General Sir Denis Pack, who led Pack's Brigade at Waterloo. And the seventeenth-century Packs, as everyone knows or ought to know, were allied in marriage with Mary Percy of Ballintemple, heir of the Irish branch of the Percys of Northumberland.

"In that wooden chest—don't interrupt me!—are the papers of our descent, generation by generation, for six hundred years; from the marriage of Henry Percy, sixth Baron, with Eleanor, niece of King Henry the Third."

Lineage, however, was small help to a young married couple who lived on Charles's £220 a year. Poverty sharpened its claws on a growing family. After the birth of their first child, a girl ("Mary is in an awful rage at your saying her baby is like any other babies!"), two more girls and a boy followed in successive years.

Though he laboured hard at the Office of Works—being clerk, architect, and practical builder as well—the young husband never seemed to make much outside money with his drawing. Charles Doyle would rather give away his paintings than offer his friends the intolerable insult of trying to sell them. If a London editor hedged for months in payment for a sketch accepted and used, Charles preferred to forget the whole matter rather than keep on dunning him.

He affected to treat all this humorously. But, when the question arose of getting him a Government position in London, he poured out his real feelings in a letter to his sister Annette.

"I have the greatest horror," he said, "of being herded with a set of snobs in the London Office, who would certainly not understand and probably laugh at the whole theory of construction, as also the technical terms in use among the builders here, to whom brick is an unknown quantity. The Accountant-General's office I simply could not stand. But if the present vacancy is anything in the way of composition, writing, or architectural work—where I would be left to myself, to do my best without any interference till I had done so—I would without hesitation accept the office."

To get the money he needed, Charles added rather wildly, he had all along cherished a vague idea of going out and digging for gold in Australia. It was a shrinking from the world; he never left Edinburgh.

Worst of all were the occasions when London friends, Brother Dick in his fine broadcloth and starched linen, or benevolent white-haired Mr. Thackeray, called to see how they were getting on. Then there must be a great pretence that nobody (least of all themselves) noticed the shabby house or the sagging sofa. Charles felt abject for the sake of Mary, swallowing her humiliation as she served up dinner. But it is possible that she minded less than he. For, in addition to being the daughter of Catherine Pack, she was also a Foley of Lismore: the fighting damn-your-eyes Irish who cared not twopence for anybody's opinion.

Charles worried about her health. Sometimes, he had complained, she looked as though a puff of wind would blow her away. Nevertheless she managed a succession of little houses—Nelson Street, Picardy Place, Sciennes Hill Place, Liberton Bank, and back to Sciennes Hill Place again—and bore two more children. Nothing had seemed to trouble her since the birth of their son, Arthur (the idol of her heart), at Picardy Place on May 22nd, 1859.

And so, ten years after the birth of that son and twenty years after he had come to Edinburgh, Charles Altamont Doyle put aside his paint-brush in the little, scrubbed room off the kitchen at Sciennes Hill Place. The voices of his wife and his son rose up with even greater distinctness above the patter of rain.

Though the door to the kitchen was partly closed, he could imagine Mary, with the hearth-brush in one hand and a glove full of cinders in the other; and the boy swinging his knickerbockered legs on the edge of the table. Brush and glove would hastily be put aside as Mary brought out of the cupboard large sheets of cardboard, cunningly drawn and painted by Brother James in London. What Mary said was:

"Blazon me this shield!"

The boy replied instantly and breathlessly, as one who knows his multiplication-tables well.

"Argent," he said, "a bend engrailed azure between two bucks' heads cabosed sable."

"And those are the arms of?"

"Needham, ma'am."

"Ah! Prettily done! Now blazon me *this* shield."

"Gules," said the boy, "a chevron between ten cinquefoils," he hesitated, and then rushed on confidently, "ten cinquefoils, four and two in chief argent."

"Yes. And those are the arms of?"

"Barklay, ma'am."

"Now this one, if you please; and take care to think before you speak."

"Or," the boy declared confidently, "on a bend gules a mullet between . . . between . . ."

There was a terrible silence.

"Arthur! And with this shield, too! What are you saying?"

"No, it's not a mullet! It's got six points; it's an estoile!" There was the noise of someone dancing excitedly on a stone floor. "Please, ma'am; let me change it! Or, on a bend gules an estoile between two crescents argent."

"Ah, that's better. And those are the arms of?"

"Thomas Scott of Nurley, ma'am."

"Thomas Scott of Nurley. Your great-uncle, my boy. Never forget it."

For that coat of arms, the star and crescent, told of nocturnal Border raids; and it told of more. The Scots of Nurley, in County Kilkenny, were a cadet branch of the Scots of Harden, who went to Ireland in the seventeenth century; they were kinsmen of Sir Walter Scott. Charles Doyle could imagine the boy's chest swelling with pride as Mary told him that. Upstairs the latest baby, named Caroline and called Lottie, squalled from her cradle. Annette, now nearly fourteen, hurried to Lottie's assistance, while small Constance pattered after her.

As for Arthur: "Well," as Charles had written to Dick only a few months ago, "I suspect Mary blows his trumpet enough." In truth she did. She adored the boy, who in turn adored her. When she was not scrubbing the floors, or bargaining with the butcher, or stirring the porridge while reading the *Revue des Deux Mondes* in her other hand, this little lady—both too young and too young-looking to wear a matron's white cap—told him endlessly of his illustrious ancestry, and traced it as far back as the Plantagenets. To the boy, listening round-eyed, the figure of Edward the Third at Crécy must have grown inextricably mixed up with Sir Denis Pack leading a brigade of Picton's division at Waterloo, or Admiral Foley at the Battle of the Nile.

She had a creed of behaviour, too, which she hammered at him while she pointed the porridge-stick. "Fearless to the strong; humble to the weak." "Chivalry towards all women, of high or low degree." Great golden names hung like banners in the little room; and, in both their imaginations, the knights thundered by.

Charles Doyle had once entertained the hope of bring-ing up his son to be a keen business-man and sound arithmetician: everything that he himself was not. This now seemed remote; the boy loathed arithmetic. His earliest admiration among authors, Captain Mayne Reid of the buffaloes and the Indians, had been put aside in favour of Sir Walter Scott; though the only book Arthur seemed to read, over and over, was *Ivanhoe.* He had, too, the appetite of an anaconda and an unquenchable thirst for getting into fights—which puzzled his father, and secretly delighted his mother, as the mud-stained victor swaggered home.

Such tendencies would have pleased old Michael Conan as well. They had named the boy Arthur Conan Doyle after this grand-uncle, fierce art-critic and editor of the 'Art Journal,' who now lived in the Avenue de Wagram at Paris.

"For we must not forget, Charles," Mary would say, "the strain of nobility on your side of the family." Then she would stamp her foot, furiously. "And why do you smile, Charles? Do you deny its truth?"

"Not at all, my dear. It is only that you are such a fearsome stickler for genealogy."

"And why not, pray? I have a duty. So have you. The Conans, after all, are descended from the ducal house of Brittany."

Great-Uncle Michael Conan, who sent the boy his first picture book of the Kings and Queens of France, was much amused with a literary composition executed by Master Arthur at the age of five. The composition concerned swords, guns, and pistols, with which a Bengal tiger was intrepidly pursued into a cave. Uncle Conan, too, had expressed decided views about the lad's education. "*Win* him," he roared, in this vexed question of arithmetic, "*win* him to multiplication, division, and the rule of three, and make him practically familiar with geography. I would soon familiarize him with maps."

For future education, Uncle Conan advised a Jesuit school. It was not, he warned, Charles and Mary, that he encouraged the Jesuits in their fanatical devotion to the 'per centra,' or all-for-the-soul, creed. "But in mere secular education they are, from experience and their employment therein, of the highest order of mind, unmatched."

Thus young Arthur, looking far from seraphic in this year 1869, came home in his first summer vacation from Hodder House, the preparatory school for the great Jesuit college at Stonyhurst. A year or two more, and he would enter Stonyhurst itself. Thank God, his father offered up a prayer in deep religious fervour, for that saving influence! Mary, with her quick sympathies and her stubborn mind, he sometimes suspected of being no true Catholic.

As for himself, Charles could now recognize—after

that last appeal to Dick, who was helpless—that he would gain no promotion. He would remain the man who could work in everyone's interest except his own.

In twenty years his salary at the Office of Works had risen from £220 to the princely sum of £250. True, his drawings sometimes brought him in as much as a hundred a year more. He had designed the fountain at Holyrood and the great window of Glasgow Cathedral. But where were the fine dreams now?

His own father, John Doyle, had died in January a year ago; not without a horrible fear on Charles's part that a journey to Edinburgh, taken in evil weather, might have hastened 'Lord John's' end. James assured him that this fear was nonsense; but there it was. He did not doubt that the house in Cambridge Terrace, with its memories of dancing and fencing lessons under a carved ceiling, would remain ever the same. Dick, after that old, old quarrel with *Punch*, had done no less well as a free-lance illustrator. James had published his *Chronicle of England,* illustrated by himself. Henry, close friend of the late Cardinal Wiseman, had only this year been appointed Director of the National Gallery of Ireland.

Good, affectionate fellows all! The Guv'nor General would have been proud of them!

More and more Charles Doyle's mind turned inwards for refuge. He loved fishing, because when you fished the nagging world let you alone. To his family he was becoming a dreamy, long-bearded stranger, with exquisite manners and an unbrushed top-hat. Each day he trudged the long walk from home to his office at Holyrood Palace and back again, to pat the children's heads absent-mindedly, as he might have stroked his pet cats. In painting he found his imagination turning from the comic and the elvish to the grotesque and even the terrible. On the easel before him now, in the rainy afternoon light, stood one such water-colour nearly finished. In eerie blue-and-white it flaunted thin-boned horrors, with rolling eyes, flinging up white arms and legs at broken angles as they capered through a church-yard after a terrified child who had just reached a Celtic cross.

It showed sweep and power, blown leaves before the devil. He would call it 'The Saving Cross.' Other such images, in pale colour and crooked line, thronged his mind. It might be a pity to dabble in this unsalable work, with poor bustling Mary having so much to do; but all the work in the world seemed of little use now.

Besides, it was so much pleasanter to go fishing.

II

ACADEMIC:

The Hidden Tutors

Arthur Conan Doyle, at Stonyhurst in Lancashire, sat down with a feeling of dignity to write a letter to his mother.

He was fifteen years old, in the second highest class at Stonyhurst, and growing at such a rate in both height and breadth as to cause Mr. Kellett not only anxiety but acute alarm lest he burst his clothes altogether.

Arthur himself was not concerned. He was not sartorially minded—except for pride in a noble new necktie, which he was always badgering his mother to send—and he had already pointed out that it didn't matter so long as his cricket-clothes still fitted him. His face broad but gaunt-featured, his brown hair plastered down with lime-cream supplied by The Ma'am, he settled himself to compose a worthy note.

"I hope," he wrote, "you all enjoy yourselves and have as fine weather as I have. On Shrove Monday we played the match, and we won a glorious victory. They got 111 runs and we got 276, of which I contributed 51. When I reside at Edinburgh, I would like to enter some cricket club there. It is a jolly game, and does more to make a fellow strong and healthy than all the doctors in the world. I think I could take a place in the eleven of any club in Edinburgh.

"I am getting very rich now, what with papa's and uncle's liberality. You must thank them from me. Perhaps since I have such abundance you will send me two shillings before June the 18th."

Here he paused, considering this last sentence. It was not quite right; it was what the Jesuit fathers would have called a non-sequitur.

"For on that day," he hastened to explain, "we go to Preston to see a great cricket match played there, and we will have to find our own dinners, I fear. I don't know whether I told you last letter about my success in schools, but I got second in schools this term, and did better in every respect than last term."

His years at Hodder House and at Stonyhurst, on the whole, were happy ones. He grew accustomed to being awakened, at six o'clock every morning, by the din of a policeman's rattle through the dormitory. He grew accustomed to the lack of hot pipes or fires in the Study Place, with a December wind whistling through cracks which (it was darkly hinted) had been deliberately knocked in the walls for the boys' discomfort.

Under the twin towers of Stonyhurst, rising in the country far from any town or railway-station, the Fathers kept iron discipline. Academic distinctions were rewarded by 'good' breakfasts or suppers, in the marble-floored hall with the musicians' gallery. Punishment, with a flat rubber weight called a Tolley, made the hands blacken and swell up to twice their size. In all his letters to his family Arthur never once mentioned punishment; this, dogged-mouthed, he kept to himself.

But he wrote excitedly of sport—of swimming, of cricket, of football, of hockey, of ice-skating—and he was always having to apologize for his handwriting when his mother sharply criticized it. One of his schoolmates, a Spanish boy who became the Marquis of Villa-vieja, has testified to his extreme untidiness and his powers of observation. The writing, he explained, was bad only because someone had accidentally jumped on his hand with a spiked shoe, or a fingernail became mysteriously dislodged at hockey, or he had somehow landed in the infirmary after 'a slight strain' caused by falling from the roof of the gymnasium.

There were notable events, too: like the Father Rector's Day.

On this occasion, when the boys went out with their skates after dark, they found the ice of the pond aglow under Chinese lanterns; torches, red and blue lights, flared against snow while a band played 'Rule Britannia.' The skating began after the boys had been provided with cigars and matches; the masters, on the bank, flung squibs and jumping crackers into this yelling turmoil; it ended, magnificently, when everyone drank the Father Rector's health in a tumbler of hot punch.

Best of all were the Christmas holidays, though few of the boys could go home. Over one Christmas festivity Arthur and three of his friends consumed:

"Two turkeys, one *very* large goose, two chickens, one large ham and two pieces of ham, two large sausages, seven boxes of sardines, one of lobster, a plate full of tarts and seven pots of jam. In the way of drink we had five bottles of sherry, five of port, one of claret and two of raspberry vinegar; we also had two bottles of pickles."

Which, taken in conjunction with the cigars, indicates considerable broad-mindedness on the part of the Fathers. This same Christmas produced notable concerts and amateur theatricals. On successive nights they saw 'The Road to Ruin,' a comedy in five acts, and " 'The Courier of Lyons,' or, 'The Attack on the Mail,' a melodrama and a jolly play (5 murders)."

Such fine entertainments, admittedly, were reserved for holidays. To pay for them were grey days in the

Lancashire drizzle, a grind of sing-song lessons. What troubled him—aside from his state of being chronically hard up, including a disaster when Uncle Dick sent him five shillings and he received only three-and-six—what troubled the untidy boy, making him fret and fume, was the intolerable dryness of these lessons.

Even history, which ought to have entranced him, made hard swotting. It was not at all like history as told to him by his mother, or in the novels of the great Sir Walter. (He lost *Ivanhoe*, which fell into a stream, but the others were fascinating if at times hard to understand.) This schoolbook history was like dry powder in the mouth; all dates and places, without any people; it had no more appeal to the imagination than the hated $x^2 + 2xy + y^2$.

Then came a day in '73, ever to be remembered, when his Uncle Michael Conan in Paris sent him a small book with gilt edges. It was called *Lays of Ancient Rome*, by a certain Lord Macaulay. He opened it; and the sun arose in splendour.

> Lars Porsena of Clusium
>   By the nine gods he swore
> That the great House of Tarquin
>   Should suffer wrong no more;
> By the nine gods he swore it,
> And named a trysting-day. . . .

He was swept away by the throb of the ringing lines, the crowding of pictures sun-clear in words, his own impulse to cheer aloud for the dauntless three who held the bridge. One verse leaped out at him.

> And how can man die better
>   Than facing fearful odds
> For the ashes of his fathers,
>   And the temples of his gods?

Here, put into flat words by one of these old Romans —a sporting crowd, too, since even the other side hurra'd for Horatius when he got safely back—was something he had been looking for. It fitted in so well with his mother's teaching back in Edinburgh, long before he had been in his teens.

Suppose, as had happened in Edinburgh, you saw a poor old woman with a market-basket being taunted and shoved into the gutter by a hulking bootmaker's boy? Here was no question of wanting to fight for its own sake. The question was: What would Ivanhoe have done? What would Edward the Third have done?

Why, clearly, Edward the Third would have called for a knightly spear-running. But, such matters being difficult to arrange in modern Edinburgh, Edward the Third would have waded in and given that bootboy the licking of his life. The fact that on this occasion Arthur lost the fight, due to being walloped over the skull by a green-baize bag containing a heavy boot, in no way affected the matter of chivalry involved.

And here was this tremendous Macaulay now. In search of more books by the same author, he found the *Essays*, which were really small histories, and the unfinished *History of England*. It was even more of a revelation; history came to life. It was romance, yet it was fact. Line after line of the *Essays* gave him a vague but pleasurable thrill he could not understand. The short, sharp sentences, clearly expounding; then the long phrase curling out in jewelled rhetoric to a whip-crack end; had there ever been such a writer as this?

In such a mood, at Christmas of 1874, he had the greatest adventure of his school days. Aunt Annette, his father's sister, invited him to spend three weeks in London, where his uncles would show him all the sights of the town.

His hand trembled with excitement when he wrote to Aunt Annette and Uncle Dick about final arrangements. It was fourteen below freezing, he said; but no ice-locked roads should prevent him from getting himself and his box to the nearest railway-station. His only fear was that they might not recognize him, now, if they met him.

"It is difficult to write a description of yourself," continued this fifteen-year-old, "but I believe I am 5 feet 9 inches high, pretty stout, clad in dark garments, and, above all, with a flaring red muffler round my neck."

Wrapped in the rugs of fellow-travellers, he arrived at Euston Station after three accidents on Lancashire railways. Aunt Annette, a stately middle-aged lady, recognized the red muffler with ease. He was to stay at Uncle Dick's studio in Finborough Road, where Aunt Annette kept house for Uncle Dick while their home in Cambridge Terrace was being redecorated. In the light and warmth of the studio, with its frieze of elves painted round the walls, he was having tea with Aunt Annette when Uncle Dick bustled in: rather bald now, but affable as ever and quite as free with pocket-money.

Those three weeks in London made a deep impression. Twice he went to the theatre with Uncle James—an imposing man, bearded to the cheekbones—and each time they had a box. Their first visit was to the Lyceum, to see Mr. Henry Irving in *Hamlet*.

"The play," Arthur wrote to his mother, "has continued three months, yet every night the house is crammed to suffocation by people wishing to see Irving act. Irving is very young and slim, with black piercing eyes, and acted magnificently."

The towering pillars of the Lyceum outlined against foggy gaslight, the black cabs and carriages a-spatter in six inches of half-frozen mud, made a background for these incredible crowds. The Lyceum was better than their visit to the Haymarket Theatre, perhaps because Arthur had previously seen the Haymarket play in Edinburgh. But he thought it a very funny comedy, and enjoyed it just as much. Mr. Sothern appeared in his original role of Lord Dundreary, with Buckstone as the shrewd, likeable Yankee, Asa Trenchard. The play was Tom Taylor's *Our American Cousin*. Arthur did not learn under what grisly circumstances that same comedy had been played, at Ford's Theatre, in Washington, one night just less than a decade before, when President Lincoln was assassinated in the state-box.

Meanwhile, he had this mighty capital to explore. He went first to Westminster Abbey, for a reason he refused to explain. He toured the show-places from St. Paul's to the Tower, where he stared in wonder at "67,000 Martini-Henry rifles and an enormous number of swords and bayonets"—O might and power of the British Empire!—"also racks, thumb-screws, and other instruments of torture."

His Aunt Jane, Uncle Henry's wife, he liked even more than Aunt Annette. Uncle Henry took him to see the Crystal Palace, Uncle Dick to Hengler's Circus. With a Stonyhurst friend he went to the zoo, where the seals kissed their keeper. Of particular fascination, he explained to his mother, was an expedition to see Madame Tussaud's Wax-Works. "I was delighted," he wrote, "with the room of Horrors, and the images of the murderers."

It is interesting to note that Madame Tussaud's, at this time and for ten years afterwards, was situated in Baker Street.

When Arthur returned to Stonyhurst, with the Matriculation examinations already looming up ahead, he warmed himself with a secret. His chief ambition in coming to London had been achieved. And nobody knew; not a soul. Though his heart poured with gratitude to his royally hospitable aunts and uncles, he would have died rather than mention it to them. It would have seemed foolish, and childish; even the Ma'am might not understand. But now he had realized his ambition. It was to go to Westminster Abbey, and stand at the grave of Macaulay.

Then his mood changed. He grew conscience-stricken because he had been enjoying himself in London, while his mother was saving half-pennies and doing without necessities at home. She had another small child to cope with: Innes, born in '73; at which time Arthur, considering the subject delicate, had written her a note of congratulation in French.

The least *he* could do now, in his last year at Stonyhurst, was to work until his brain burst to pass the Matriculation examinations. It was a formidable wall: English language, English History, French, Latin, and Greek Grammar, a book of Homer, Sallust's Catiline, Natural Philosophy, Chemistry, any French author, Algebra, Arithmetic, and Euclid. If you passed Matric, they automatically sent you up to sit for the Matriculation examination of London University. But, if you were plucked in one subject, you were plucked in all.

This wall grew still more formidable as the spring of '75 deepened into summer. Arthur was what he described as funky. "I think if I go up for the London examination I will pass easily enough," he said, "but my bugbear is this horrible trial examen here."

What he feared, undoubtedly, was some Machiavellian swindle on the part of the masters. When last year he had shown considerable talent for writing verse, and this year edited the school magazine, it seemed to him the Fathers were amazed to find he had any talents at all. The fact was, he thought, that they didn't respect him and they didn't like him.

Now here he was in error, as we know from correspondence between the Jesuit Fathers and his mother. They were aware of the boy's ferocious stubbornness; at the least suspicion that he was being intimidated, he would deliberately break rules so as to undergo the most savage punishment and show he could still look them in the eye afterwards. But his teachers both liked him and had the highest respect for his abilities. In fact they had already put him into Herr Baumgarten's German class, with special tuition because it was an advanced class, for a special project they had in mind.

In the rainy spring before Matriculation, when it was seldom possible to go outdoors, Arthur solaced himself with Macaulay. The picture of those old Roundheads of the seventeenth century, putting aside their buff-coats and lobster-tail helmets for the arts of peace, fired his imagination. Macaulay almost reconciled him to Oliver Cromwell, that bogey who cut off the King's head. Cutting off the King's head was beastliness, and always would be.

But what a leader, to the English of the time, this wide-jawed Cromwell must have seemed! He commanded the pikemen of an invincible army; he swept the seas of enemies when Blake's flag was often in a fourth-rater; he protected his co-religionists even in Catholic countries. "For a voice which seldom threatened in vain had declared that, unless favour were shown to the people of God, English guns should be heard in the Castle of St. Angelo."

The roll and rumble of that threat, Arthur reflected, could not have pleased the Pope very much. Indeed, it became increasingly clear that Macaulay (though always perfectly gentlemanly about it, of course) hadn't got much use for the Pope. Arthur, as a good Catholic, should have been disturbed by this.

His religious faith, and the duties it entailed, he had always accepted unquestioningly. It was the faith of his fathers, no more to be questioned, or even thought about, than a kind of sacred multiplication-table. Beyond that, its beauty and majesty appealed to him as a part of life. Only once had he been startled; and that was when an Irish priest thundered out, in public, that everybody who was not a Catholic would surely go to hell.

Now this pronouncement really shocked him. Never having considered the matter before, he was convinced there must be some mistake. But apparently there wasn't: among the Jesuits, at least. It haunted him to think of all the men he had read about, learned men and soldiers and statesmen, all writhing in flames. On this point he had been both consoled and worried to discover that his strong-headed, romantic mother thought that such priestly statements were all rubbish.

"Wear flannel next your skin, my dear boy," she cried, "and *never* believe in eternal punishment."

Meantime, he met the dreaded Matriculation examinations and passed them. Then, shivering with eagerness, he sat with thirteen other boys for the London examination. The packet containing the results arrived back from London on a blistering day in July, and was taken to the Rector's room. There was a quarter of an hour's silence, while the boys gnawed their fingernails and waited for news. Then they could stand it no longer. Let Arthur describe what happened:

"Pulling open the door of the playroom, regardless of the howls of the prefects, we dashed along the gallery, up the stairs, and along the corridor to the Rector's room. There were between forty and fifty of us; not all candidates, but many whose brothers or relations had gone up. There we crowded round the door, all pushing and yelling. The door opened and the Rector was seen inside, waving the packet over his head."

It has the passion of an epic; all that we ourselves have felt at such times; but everybody, including the headmaster, seems to have been remarkably emotional in 1875.

"Immediately a tremendous cheer rang along the gallery, and dozens of handkerchiefs were tossed in the air, for we knew the news must be good. When the up-roar had a little subsided, the old grey-haired prefect of studies got up on a chair and announced that of fourteen who had gone up thirteen had passed, the most that has ever passed since Stonyhurst was Stonyhurst."

The single plucked-one was not Arthur Conan Doyle. Arthur, on the contrary, not only passed but took Hon-ours. He himself was much more astounded than any-one else. To him some days later came Father Purbrick.

"How," asked Father Purbrick, "would you like to stay with us for a year longer?"

"Sir?"

"Oh, not here! How would you like to go abroad? There is a great school at Feldkirch, in western Austria, not far from Switzerland."

"Abroad, sir? Yes, sir! What for, sir?"

"Well, you're young for Philosophy yet. A year at Feldkirch would give you academic finish, to say nothing of perfecting your German, while you decide what you wish to do in the future. I will write to your parents about it, if you think they would consent?"

Hence in the autumn, fitted out with a new tweed suit, his hair again plastered down slickly under the short-peaked cap, Arthur shouldered his box and set forth into the world. There was weeping at home, though his own bearing seems to have been almost stately until exuberance burst out under the stimulus of the journey.

The town of Feldkirch lay in a green valley, watered by the River Ill, among cloudy mountains dark with fir-trees. Up there, six thousand feet up, hung the Pass of Arlberg, military key to the Tyrol from the west. A mediaeval fortress overshadowed the town and the massive Jesuit school. Here Arthur found a discipline far less strict than at Stonyhurst; the dormitories were 'artificially' heated; the food was good, the beer excellent. The students were mostly German boys from Catholic families, with some twenty English and Irish. Arthur took charge of them all.

His German grew fluent if a trifle erratic. When the boys went for their formal walks, three abreast, with one English boy to two Germans so that they should speak German, he plunged in and did his best. He talked to these Germans, for three hours on end, about the invincible power of the British Navy. He touched also on the glories of Stonyhurst; and, as his greatest effort in the entertainment-line, described how Captain Webb (*ein Engländer*!) swam the English Channel.

Best of all, he joined the Feldkirch band: his chosen instrument being the largest brass horn in existence. It resembled a piece of contemporary siege-artillery; it wound twice round him; and, when properly attacked, emitted a whump and boom like the approach of Judgment Day.

"That is my military-band cap on my head," he said proudly, explaining the details of a photograph he sent home; "and I have got on the very necktie"—his old passion—"which you bought for me down in Cockburn Street." As for the Bombardon horn: "Blowing it," he announced, "is splendid work for the chest." The comments of those who heard him practising are not recorded.

Though he had possessed neither the means nor the time to stop and see his Uncle Michael Conan in Paris, he sent Uncle Conan a whole sheaf of his poems written at Stonyhurst. The old critic, lips pursed, conned every word. As Christmas came, and blizzards made the Austrian mountains look like clouds, Uncle Conan wrote to Charles and Mary Doyle about this verse.

"There can be no doubt of his faculty for that accomplishment," roared Uncle Conan. "In each one of his more serious inspirations I found passages of thoroughly original freshness and imaginative refinement. It seems to me that he is in excellent spirits. His 'Feldkirch Newspaper' gives capital promise, and I suspect that it is his own from first to last."

This suspicion was correct. But writing the 'Feldkirch Newspaper,' or such lyrics as *The Infuriated Cabman* and *Figaro's Farewell*, were only the amusements of a schoolboy. It had already been determined at home that, when he left Feldkirch, Arthur should enter Edinburgh University and study medicine.

The suggestion came from his mother; Edinburgh had one of the finest medical schools in the world, and, after all, he would be at home. In this insistence she was abetted by a friend of the family, Dr. Bryan Charles Waller—a man learned and kindly, in religious matters an agnostic—who had begun to take a deep interest in the boy and for some years was profoundly to influence his life.

Arthur himself seems not to have cared one way or the other. It meant more science (why couldn't they make science as interesting as Jules Verne did?), and Mr. Lircom's science-lectures at Stonyhurst had been an affliction. But his mother wished it: that was final.

Besides, medicine might be fun. It would be a noble thing, one day, to stalk imposing and top-hatted into someone's sick-room; to listen to the symptoms, head inclined; and then curtly to give some diagnosis which should strike all hearers with wonder and gratitude.

During intervals of skating and tobogganing, he worked really hard. Dr. Waller sent him annotated chemistry-books, and the terrible *Roscoe* with its parabolas and ellipses. No romance now, except any which tended to practical knowledge.

But up there, over the Arlberg Pass, young Napoleon's eagles had suffered defeat when Masséna and Oudinot were driven back by the Austrians. Arthur began to read Napoleonic history, and commented on it to the people at home. His mother, fearing that these thickheaded Germans (he shared her opinion of them) might corrupt his knowledge of French, had sternly ordered him to write every letter in French. This, not unnaturally, confused him. It somewhat muddled his French grammar when he wrote her an essay grandly beginning:

"It is told of Alexander the Great that he said to Diogenes, 'If I were not Alexander, I should like to be Diogenes'; thus, it seems to me, if I were not an Englishman I should like to be a Tyrolese mountaineer." And ending abruptly with: "Continued in next."

One book he received, not in the line of self-improvement, might have upset the studies of anyone less dogged. The book not only impressed Arthur; it electrified him. He confessed in later years that no author, with the exception of Macaulay and Scott, so much shaped his tastes or his literary bent. The author was Edgar Allan Poe, and the first story he encountered was *The Gold Bug*.

"A good glass in the bishop's hostel in the devil's

seat—forty-one degrees and fourteen minutes—north-east and by north—main branch seventh limb east side —shoot from the left eye of the death's-head. . . ."

Or, flashing out of another story with even more stunning effect, in a room mysteriously lit by the rays of perfumed tapers:

" 'Dupin!' I said, completely unnerved, 'this hair is most unusual—this is no *human* hair.' "

Meanwhile, in the homely atmosphere of Feldkirch and among what Arthur called the aborigines, the thaw of 1876 put an end to skating. Spring dragged on with such incessant rains that he was able to point out, to his German friends, the superiority of the English climate. Then overnight came oven-hot summer, the valley alive with frogs. As one form of exercise the students, alpenstock on shoulder and singing German songs, marched forty-two miles in fourteen hours. Arthur's only complaint, a not infrequent one, was: "The Procurator will not issue *any* money to *any* person under *any* circumstances." And now it grew serious.

He would leave Feldkirch at the end of June. When he reached Edinburgh, he hoped to win a bursary, or Scottish scholarship; he believed with strong pride that he could at least distinguish himself in chemistry. By one of Messrs. Cook's economical arrangements, he estimated, he could do a rather complicated European tour on the way home, and visit his Uncle Michael Conan in Paris, all for the modest sum of five pounds.

Thus he reached Paris with a book on conic sections in his hand, Edgar Allan Poe in his head, and twopence in his pocket. After a dusty walk on a hot day, he found Uncle Conan sitting shirt-sleeved in the back garden of number 65 Avenue de Wagram. He knew, too, that he had found a friend. Uncle Conan, with his broad face and cropped grey beard, his arrogant narrowed eyes and the hair curling out aggressively over his ears, resembled one of his own ancestors: an Irish chieftain descended from the Dukes Conan of Brittany.

Like Mary Foley, he made the boy glow again with family pride. Of equal importance, he could sympathize. To him words were fireworks; he could understand his nephew's devotion to both these oddly contrasted tutors, Macaulay and Poe. Pounding his fist on the table, he would discourse on the merits of both: though the damned square-toed Whig, he said, had been rotten-wrong on so many points of fact, and the American with all his supreme art couldn't be trusted, by God, within miles of a bottle of brandy.

With Uncle Conan and his small wife, Aunt Susan, Arthur spent several glorious weeks. Training, instinct, descent, all gave him an affection for France; there was magic here. They passed much time in the garden; despite his bulk, Uncle Conan was weak in the legs and had to be attended by Aunt Susan. In the garden, towards twilight on a day shortly before his departure toward home, Uncle Conan gruffly approached family matters.

"This medical career of yours." The shaggy eyebrows drew together. "Five years, or even four. Won't it be something of a strain to your father and mother?"

"Yes, sir. But if I win this bursary, they tell me, it'll pay my expenses for a long time. And then, you see (at least, Dr. Waller explained it), you can hire yourself out as assistant to a real doctor, and make a bit like that, while you're still studying."

"Do you want to be a doctor?"

"Sir?"

"I said: Do you want to be a doctor?"

Of course he did, in a way. At least there was nothing else he wanted to do, or felt at all capable of doing. He would work hard, so help him! In Paris, with the street-lamps blooming amid the leaves of chestnut trees, his affection rushed back to a harsher city: to his grey-eyed and near-sighted mother, to his sisters, to his three-year-old brother, to his father looming tall and shadowy and rather shrunken in the background. Though he did not know it, it was the end of his boyhood.

Yes, he supposed, it was a good thing to study medicine.

III

ADVENTURE:

A Taste for Trouble

Young Dr. Conan Doyle—of Number 1 Bush Villas, Elm Grove, Southsea—crept out under cover of darkness to polish the brass plate affixed to the area-railing of his house.

It would never do to let the neighbours know he could not afford a maid-servant, especially in such a fashionable suburb of Portsmouth as this. The house of which he was so proud, three narrow storeys of sedate red brick, stood in a busy street near the junction of Elm Grove with Large Road, King's Road, and Park Street. At past midnight, however, there should be nobody to see him polishing the brass plate. Aside from getting into a fight with a navvy on his very first day in Portsmouth (the fellow was unchivalrously kicking his wife, and later became a patient), Dr. Conan Doyle's professional conduct had been flawless.

Any passer-by, on that September night in 1882, would have seen a frock-coated figure six feet two inches in height, seeming even taller by reason of its vast breadth, in weight fifteen stone when in training without an ounce of fat. Above starched collar and spreading tie loomed a large, young-looking, serious-minded face: hair parted and drawn across the forehead, with long sideburns and as yet only a modest line of moustache.

Much had happened since that autumn of '76 when

a gawky boy entered Edinburgh University and, in leisure evenings, petrified his family by reading Poe's tales aloud. He won the bursary. But there was a clerical error, and somebody else got the money. Arthur was determined, once he had got two years' medical knowledge, to compress each year's classes into half a year's. He could then at intervals go out as a medical assistant and earn a few odd pounds to help support his family.

At Edinburgh University there was little of what is called undergraduate life. You lived in lodgings; or at home, as Arthur did. You paid your fee, at choice, to hear the great men lecture. Otherwise professor and student had no contact whatever. Arthur, on holiday in the Isle of Arran during '77, was surprised to meet no less a personage than Dr. Joseph Bell. Since to Arthur it seemed impossible that so austere a man of science could himself be taking a holiday, the boy wondered what he was doing there.

But a parade of these professors, mostly with that streak of eccentricity which is the joy of student life, loomed always through bleak classrooms. There was Sir Charles Wyville Thomson, the zoologist who, in the wooden corvette H.M.S. *Challenger*, had dredged all the seas for new forms of animal life. There was squat Professor Rutherford, with his black Assyrian beard and his booming voice; the voice which could be heard echoing through the corridors as Professor Rutherford began a lecture before even entering the classroom. Best of all, perhaps because he showed the greatest personal kindness, Arthur remembered that same Joseph Bell of whom the world has heard so much.

He was a kindly soul, not quite like the formidable figure of legend, at this time in his early forties. But he had a dry sense of humour, with which he backed up his powers of deduction to impress the students that they must use eyes, ears, hands, and brain in making a diagnosis.

Very lean, with dexterous hands and a shock of dark hair standing up on his head like the bristles of a brush, he would sit behind his desk in a big bare room, with his dressers and students around. It was Arthur's duty to usher in the cases one by one.

"This man," Dr. Bell would declare in rich Scots, "is a left-handed cobbler." Then he would wait, with carefully concealed glee, for the puzzled looks of the students.

"You'll obsairve, gentlemen, the worn places on the corduroy breeks where a cobbler rests his lapstone? The right-hand side, you'll note, is far-r more worn than the left. He uses his left hand for hammering the leather."

Or again, with finger-tips together:

"This man is a French-polisher." Then, opening his eyes and rolling it out: "Come, now. Can't you smel-l-l him?"

The dryness of the tone, the look in the eye as he leaned forward, brought sheepish grins to the faces of the students. Dr. Bell, to whom everybody referred as Joe, lived in a house in Melville Crescent with a fine carved staircase which is there to this day. At this time he never thought of deductive powers in connection with crime, though we know that some fifteen years later he had a try at solving the Ardlamont mystery. He was a surgeon, tracking disease.

"The trained eye!" he would say. "A simple matter."

Not so simple, however, was Arthur's disturbed state of mind as he hacked away at his studies. Apart from work, he was always reading: books loaned by Dr. Waller, books from the library, books from the twopenny-tub. As between a meal and a book, it was often a book. Among rowdy students, who affected a grown-up cynicism and worshipped Professor Huxley from afar, laughter at the old theology was in the air.

All over Britain it was in the air. Arthur breathed it in the alcohol-smell of the dissecting room, where the human body hardly seemed a temple. Puffing at the amber-mouthed pipe he had bought at Stonyhurst, he looked back on Stonyhurst and saw much that now seemed not merely disquieting (as it had seemed then) but flatly ridiculous. Not only in the Catholic Church; in all churches as well.

Dr. Waller, the family friend and a hot-hearted agnostic, encouraged his gropings in a way he could appreciate. The doctor summed it up in a letter, after quoting from Emerson on self-reliance.

"Here," he wrote, "we put our finger on the weakness of all blind, vicarious trust in a hypothetical Providence, which forsooth is to help those who cannot or will not help themselves. Far truer and nobler is the teaching of the old proverb: Heaven helps those who help themselves. This manful inward life is what theology would fain kill by making us hold ourselves vile, sinful, and degraded, which is a pestilent lie and cuts at the root of all that is best in our natures: for take away a man's self-respect and you do much towards making him a sneak and a scoundrel."

Then, hammering home a point which so much appealed to his young friend: " 'Do' is a far finer word than 'Believe,' and 'Action' a far surer watchword than 'Faith.' "

Action! That was it! Arthur, in the early summer of '78, tried to help his family in vacation-time by going out as dispenser and medical apprentice to a doctor in the poorer quarter of Sheffield. Even if he earned nothing at first, he could at least relieve his mother's worries by earning his own board and keep.

But the results were not happy. He was so inexperienced, perhaps so much like a half-tamed bear in the dispensary, that after three weeks he and Dr. Richardson decided to part. Though this first venture later amused him, he held very different views at the time.

"These Sheffielders," he wrote hotly, "would rather be poisoned by a man with a beard than be saved by a man without one."

Three weeks; and there were months before the autumn term at Edinburgh! Hurrying to London, he put another offer of his services in the medical papers. Aunt Jane, Uncle Henry, and Uncle James welcomed him at their home in Clifton Gardens, though he now seemed disturbingly alien and Bohemian. While waiting for a reply to his advertisement, he studied in the mornings and roamed the streets afterwards. By night the gas-lamps showed sights less academic.

"They have invented," he reported, "an atrocity called the 'Lady Teazer Torpedo.' This is a leaden bottle, like an artist's moist-colour bottle, full of water. If you squeeze it a jet of water flies out, and the great joke at night is to go along the streets squirting at everybody's face, male or female. Everyone is armed with these things, and nobody escapes them. I saw ladies, stepping out of their carriages to parties, drenched and seeming to enjoy it highly."

This popularity of the humble squirt-gun, aside from the curious light it throws on Victorian frolics, indicates a truly memorable self-restraint on the part of these ladies.

Arthur was in no mood for such caprices. As week followed week without a reply to his advertisement, he fell into despair and decided he ought to join the Navy as a surgeon. He had outlined all the benefits of this move to his various aunts and uncles when a certain

Dr. Elliot, at a village called Ruyton in Shropshire, wrote to accept his services.

At Ruyton he did well, handling one dangerous case himself, and gaining confidence in the routine work. The one thing which ruffled his temper, he confessed somewhat naïvely, was the extraordinary high-temper of Dr. Elliot himself. Dr. Elliot, "though outwardly a gentleman," had not got one single original idea in his head and flew into a temper if you so much as mentioned one, even in a trite remark.

"I think, Dr. Elliot, it would be well if capital punishment were abolished."

"Sir," said Dr. Elliot, turning purple in the face, "I will not have such a thing said in my house! Do you understand, sir?"

"Sir," instantly retorted his assistant, without troubling to inquire wherein lay the indecency of this remark, "I will express my opinions when and where I like."

At the end of Otober Arthur returned to his studies. He could expect no remuneration from Dr. Elliot, since none had been stipulated. Nevertheless, after four months' work, he secretly hoped for some slight gesture. None was forthcoming. Summoning up all his courage, he asked whether he might be allowed his railway-fare home.

"My dear fellow," said Dr. Elliot, a business-man, "the law stands thus. If an assistant has a salary, he is then a recognized person and can claim expenses. But if he has no salary he becomes, as it were, a gentleman travelling for his own improvement; and he gets nothing."

So Arthur went back to another winter's study, swearing that a medical assistant was the most ill-used, hard-worked, underpaid fellow in the world. In Edinburgh, at least, there was sport to be found. For so heavily built a youth, he was as quick on his feet as a cat. With scant instruction they were turning him into a fast Rugby forward and a first-class boxer. Boxing was the sport he liked best; here, and at rugger, he made friends with a fellow-student named Budd—half genius, half crackpot—whose wild humours amused him as he might have been amused at a play.

But the situation at home was now really desperate. His father's health was breaking. Charles Doyle, frail and old when only middle-aged, had twice been forced to spend a week in bed. The Office of Works raised ominous eyebrows at this slackness after only thirty years' service.

Arthur's worry was for the Ma'am. (Since he went out on his own he never afterwards referred to her or addressed her as 'mother,' or 'mama,' or anything except The Ma'am: a title which this stoutening lady wore gravely, as a badge of honour). For the first time in her life, the Ma'am was frightened. When in the following summer Arthur was offered a real assistant's job— at two pounds a month—he accepted eagerly.

And here he met with pleasure Dr. Reginald Ratcliffe Hoare, of Clifton House, Aston Road, Birmingham. Dr. Hoare was a stout genial red-faced man, all bustle and whipcrack. Though he occupied only a modest brick house, in a street racked by the noise of jarring horse-trams, he had an enormous practice among the poor, and the size of his fees staggered the new assistant. Dr. Hoare drove you hard from nine in the morning until nine at night; but he had such a friendly way that he made you like it. Mrs. Hoare too was a small amiable lady, who enjoyed smoking a cigar in the evenings while Dr. Hoare and Arthur smoked their pipes. But two pounds a month didn't go very far.

Other doubts gnawed at him. What of the future, if he did take his medical degree? He had not quite realized the implications of the religious beliefs he held. And those implications, viewed now, were terrifying.

For centuries his family had been not only Catholics, but Catholics of the most formidably devout kind. Uncle Dick, easygoing as he seemed, had instantly thrown up a job worth eight hundred a year when *Punch* ridiculed the Pope. Arthur could imagine Aunt Annette, stately in her shawl at Cambridge Terrace; and Uncle James, and Uncle Henry. They had more than hinted that, once he had set up in his own practice (in London, of course), Catholic influence would not be lacking to bring him patients.

In God, in the sense of some Controlling Force, he never doubted. But these eternal wranglings and stupidities and throatcuttings about a 'church'! As though a church mattered two brass farthings! If he honestly believed these things, he would have to tell his relatives so.

He was in this state of perplexity, one afternoon in Birmingham as he made up some sixty-odd bottles of physic, when Herr Gleiwitz came into the dispensary and drew him aside. Herr Gleiwitz, an Arabian and Sanskrit scholar of European fame, had been reduced to giving German lessons to support his children; and Mrs. Hoare was his only pupil. Now the tears were running down his face. He had come to the end, he said; his family were starving; could Mr. Conan Doyle help him out with money?

Mr. Conan Doyle had exactly one-and-sixpence in his pocket. But Gleiwitz was crying; the man really needed help; and—well!

"Look here," blurted the assistant, dragging out his

watch and chain; "look here, I'll do what I can. Take this watch and chain, and pop it."

"Pop it?"

"Pawn it! It's a good watch. No, don't argue!" And, embarrassed by the German's protests, he fell to mixing medicines again: half regretting his sudden impulse, but quite convinced it was the only thing any man of decency could have done.

This depressed mood was succeeded by elation. In the spring, to see whether he could do it, he had written a short-story called *The Mystery of Sasassa Valley*. It was based on a Kaffir superstition about a demon with glowing eyes: which eyes, when faced by the hero's, turned out to be diamonds in rock-salt. Word now arrived at Birmingham that *The Mystery of Sasassa Valley* had been accepted by 'Chambers' Journal,' offering payment of three guineas. When later in the same year he read it in 'Chambers' ' for October, 1879, he expressed only one deep regret. They had cut out all his 'damns.'

Meanwhile, amazed and inspired, he dashed off several more stories. One of them, first entitled *The Haunted Grange of Goresthorpe*, showed his mind preoccupied with comedy and horror at the same time, and revelling in both. All these stories except *The American's Tale* were returned with editorial regrets, and the influence of Bret Harte was strong in their style. But in what he referred to as literature, it seemed to him, he had discovered a certainly small but very useful side line.

"I am beginning to think better myself of being a Naval surgeon," he wrote to the Ma'am. "I always said that I would know exactly what I was doing before I put my foot into anything."

Now this, in any matter of business-affairs, was precisely what he never did. In the very next line he expressed a yearning to be ship's surgeon in a South American liner. What he felt was an intolerable restlessness, a longing to burst momentarily this medical bottle in which he felt confined. It therefore seemed a miracle, in the early days of the next year, when a friend named Claude Augustus Currie offered him a berth which Currie was unable to take. How would he like to go, as nominal surgeon, for a seven months' sealing and whaling cruise to the Arctic? The pay, with salary and oil money, should amount to fifty pounds.

Fifty pounds! Fifty pounds for the Ma'am! And merely for doing this?

When the 600-ton steam-whaler *Hope* left Peterhead at the end of February, '80, Arthur was aboard. On the first night he fought the steward, and gained universal respect by blacking the steward's eye. Four days out from the Shetlands, he heard ice grind against the *Hope*'s side; a hundred miles off Greenland they sighted the seal-pack. At the time he wrote one youthfully brutal description of himself—possibly to shock the Ma'am—as a grinning giant covered in snow and blood, a coiled rope round his shoulder, with clotted knife and pole-axe, after a day's seal killing across the ice-floes. Every breath exhilarated him.

"I never knew what it was before to be thoroughly healthy," he wrote. "I just feel as if I could go anywhere, and do anything."

Northwards past Spitzbergen, in endless unnatural daylight, the little ship searched for whales. Arthur, pulling an oar in the whale-boat, heard the boom of the harpoon-gun and the hiss of the uncoiling line that might whisk any man overboard; he tasted danger, and enjoyed it as sport. The voyage seemed scarcely long enough. In early September, taking his fifty pounds in gold pieces to shower on the Ma'am, he returned to Edinburgh fully grown in stature.

His medical degree he took in 1881, though not without fears of the examination, long grinding, and another term as assistant with Dr. Hoare. This was complicated by his inclination, always strong but hitherto controlled, to fall in love with every girl he met.

To be precise, he was in love with five at once. His intentions were honourable, he pointed out; ("And I should think so!" bristled the Ma'am); but it did not seem practical to marry all five, and it left him "in a pitiable condition and perfectly demoralized." There was Miss Jeffers, for instance. "A little darling with an eye like a gimlet," he declared, perhaps not very poetically, "who has stirred up my soul to its lowest depths." Most of this rhapsodizing the Ma'am composedly took for what it was, that of an impressionable young man visiting relatives at Lismore in golden July. But one young lady the Ma'am, her sixth sense aroused, regarded with the darkest suspicion.

"By Jove!" he exclaimed. "Such a beauty! Miss Elmore Welden. We have been flirting hard for a week, so that things are about ripe."

Not all the troubadours of the Courts of Love could have called Miss Welden sylph-like, since she weighed over eleven stone. But her dark-haired Irish good-looks, her melting eye, her languid invalid's manner sometimes combined with violent nerve-storms, completely captivated the large suitor who held her parasol. Their romance (he had her photograph in a plush frame) continued from afar when he took his degree as Bachelor of Medicine and Master of Surgery.

Yet the prospects seemed bleak. His explosive friend Budd—now Dr. Budd—had made a wild marriage in student-days, set up in practice at Bristol, and then gone bankrupt. Arthur, hurrying to Bristol in response to an urgent telegram, found the stocky Dr. Budd, with his yellow hair and his under-slung jaw, first hinting that a friend might back him with money; then scowling blackly when Arthur explained his own position; and finally, in Budd's fashion, laughing uproariously at the whole matter. Yes, the prospects were bleak.

But Arthur's ambition, after passing his final examination, had always been to take another voyage as fully qualified ship's surgeon. It seemed a stroke of good luck when he was offered the post aboard the S.S. *Mayumba*, a cargo-and-passenger liner sailing for the West Coast of Africa. Miss Welden, now 'Elmo,' wept a good deal. The Ma'am encouraged him. A year or two on this African run, she felt, and he might accumulate sufficient funds to set up in practice for himself.

Late in October of '81, when the *Mayumba* was butting a gale beyond Tuskar Light, her ship's surgeon stood on deck half the night, clinging to the rail in admiration as phosphorescent waves boiled round him. It was one of the last times he enjoyed himself on that nightmare voyage to the Gold Coast. By the middle of January, 1882, the *Mayumba* had tied up again at Liverpool. A sickliness of scorched wood and metal still clung to the lounge when Dr. Conan Doyle sat down to scribble a note.

"Just a line," he wrote, "to say that I have turned up safe after having had the African fever, been nearly eaten by a shark, and as a finale the *Mayumba* catching fire between Madeira and England."

With a memory of past fever in his veins, of oil and swamp in his nostrils, he tried to explain. What he wanted was work; not this enervating sluggishness of too many drinks with passengers in a hot glare of day, and by night the native bush-fires glimmering along an unchanging coast. There were excitements in it, as when a ship takes fire carrying a cargo of oil; but still:

"I don't intend to go to Africa again. The pay is less than I could make by my pen in the same time, and the climate is atrocious. I trust you will not be disappointed by my leaving the ship, but this is not good enough. I would do anything rather than cause you pain or disappointment—however, we can talk it over together."

They did talk it over, and the Ma'am agreed. His own suggestion, somewhat consoling her, was that he might get a South American ship. Then came a letter that perhaps both of them had been dreading. It was from Aunt Annette in London, affectionately asking whether he could not come there and discuss his future prospects with his uncles and herself.

Thus he faced the first real crisis of his life. These influential relations could make the fortune of a young doctor. He wrote back to say he was an agnostic, and that under the circumstances it would be unfair to Aunt Annette if he even discussed it further. The Ma'am, who would have given anything on earth to see her son successful, watched him do it and was silent.

In good time came Aunt Annette's reply. They were all deeply perturbed, she said, at the sentiments he expressed. But was he not, if Aunt Annette might suggest it, being a trifle impulsive and headstrong? Such decisions are not lightly to be taken. Would he not, as a favour to those who were fond of him, pay them a visit so that the matter could be talked over? So he went to London.

There are few quarrels more tragic, or more bitter, than when a measure of right can be seen on both sides. *He* wanted no cleavage. He was too much a Doyle. Up there, in the dining-room of the house in Cambridge

Terrace, stood the great table round which had sat Scott, and Disraeli, and Thackeray, and Coleridge, and Wordsworth, and Rossetti, and Lever, and a dozen more: all friends of his Grandfather John, all representing the literary world to which he was so powerfully drawn. The dining-room table became a kind of symbol. Deep in his heart he could not believe his relatives would make so much trouble about this mere matter of religion.

But that, after the fashion of youth, was where he judged wrongly. To this aloof Doyle circle, ageing and childless, all that did matter in life was the Catholic Church. Their ancestors had given up everything for it. Material possessions were ephemeral; the Faith was real. And here was this young man, towards whom they had shown so much kindness, endangering his very soul for a sheer perverse whim!

In the drawing-room at Cambridge Terrace, where the bust of John Doyle stood against one wall, he met Uncle Dick: gaunt-featured now, with a tinge in his face which any medical eye could diagnose. And Uncle James, with his heavy hair and heavy beard. And Aunt Annette, her shawl round her shoulders, in a great chair by the fire.

Aunt Annette he did not mind so much. She was a woman, entitled to certain fads. But in these cold, polite, tight-lipped men it was difficult to recognize the Uncle Dick and the Uncle James of his boyhood; and he raged against it.

"If I practised as a Catholic doctor," he said, "I should be taking money for professing to believe something in which I didn't believe. You could count me the worst scoundrel on earth if I did that! You wouldn't do it yourselves; now would you?"

Uncle Dick corrected him sharply.

"But, my dear boy. *We* were speaking of the Catholic Church."

"Yes. I know."

"And that is an entirely different thing."

"Uncle Dick, how is it different?"

"Because what we believe is true." The cold simplicity of that remark raised between them a barrier at which no fist could batter. "If only you would have faith—"

"Yes," he burst out, "that's what people keep telling me. They talk about having faith, as though it could be done by an act of the will. They might as well tell me to have black hair instead of brown. Reason is the highest gift we've got; we *must* use it."

"And what does reason tell you?" asked another voice.

"Uncle James, that the evils of religion, a dozen religions slaughtering each other, have all come from accepting things that can't be proved. It tells me this Christianity of yours contains a number of fine and noble things mixed up with a lot of arrant rubbish. It tells me. . . ."

Once before, when he was serving as assistant to Dr. Elliot, he had said to the Ma'am that he could never talk freely unless he was excited. And he was excited now. More of this he poured out, much more. Then, catching sight of their faces, he assumed the same air of bursting politeness and said no more.

Always excluding Aunt Annette, he felt towards these people a bitterness almost past description. Let them take their favours and go to the devil. He wanted nothing from them. If they refused to understand so elementary a proposition as that a man might have a conscience, then they might have great artistic gifts but they were nothing better than dignified fools. All he envied them was a certain dining-room table, a certain symbol, from a life he could not now share. Uncle James's voice roused him:

"What do you intend to do?"

"I don't know. I'd thought of going to sea again. Or, better still, applying for a house-surgeoncy."

"Yes. Perhaps that would be best."

Someone rang for tea. The intense pride on both sides would not permit further speech. Each side believed itself wronged past repair. When he left that house, he knew a door had closed forever. To Aunt Annette he might turn; to these uncles he would not turn if the heavens fell. He ceased to be the nephew whom they had entertained so often; he became a stranger. Going back moodily to Edinburgh, recognizing that any outsider would have called *him* a fool with no eye to the main-chance, he reaffirmed his religious views and took a great vow that never, never, so help him! would he accept anything which could not be proved.

And the future? Steamship posts there were none. Applications for a house-surgeoncy brought no reply. What did arrive was a telegram from his formerly bankrupt friend Dr. Budd, shouting of a colossal success at Plymouth—where Budd had evidently moved from Bristol—and urging Arthur to come by the next train. When the latter wrote with questions, Budd's telegram thundered back.

YOUR LETTER TO HAND. WHY NOT CALL ME A LIAR AT ONCE? I TELL YOU I HAVE SEEN THIRTY THOUSAND PATIENTS IN THE LAST YEAR. MY ACTUAL TAKINGS HAVE BEEN MORE THAN FOUR THOUSAND POUNDS. ALL PATIENTS COME TO ME. WOULD NOT CROSS THE STREET TO SEE QUEEN VICTORIA. YOU CAN HAVE ALL VISITING, ALL SURGERY, ALL MIDWIFERY. WILL GUARANTEE THREE HUNDRED POUNDS THE FIRST YEAR.

Unless Budd had gone out of his mind, this seemed too good an opportunity to miss. Arthur packed hastily. The Ma'am, who had always disliked and distrusted Budd, was furious. And yet, when Budd met him at Plymouth station with great teeth exposed in a triumphant grin, the new 'partner' could have no doubt that most of his friend's statements were true.

By a combination of showmanship, quackery, and genuine medical skill, Budd had indeed built up a true Barnum's practice. He lorded it over patients cramming the waiting-rooms, the stairs, the courtyard, the coach-house. He bawled at them; broke windows; prescribed drugs in a way which would have raised any ordinary doctor's hair. At the end of the day he would march slowly through the principal sreets, his day's takings of gold and silver in a bag held at arm's length before him; while his wife and his partner walked on either side of him like acolytes supporting a priest.

"I always make a point of walking through the doctors' quarter," Budd explained. "We are passing through it now. They all come to their windows and gnash their teeth and dance until I am out of sight."

Now it is no part of this biography to detail the extravaganza of the next few months. That has been done by Conan Doyle himself, in *The Stark Munro Letters*, a book which in all but a few incidents is auto-biographical; and to draw on it would be merely to repeat page after page of some of the best comic scenes in our language. But the ending (drawn not only from *Stark Munro*, but from letters written at the time) was not funny in the least.

Budd, for all his entertaining qualities, had a dark streak through the mind almost as visible as a black patch across the eye. Arthur, never very critical of his friends, was sometimes startled by it. The so-called 'partner,' sitting in a cubicle and gratefully earning a pound or two a week by treating a small number of cases with which Budd could not be troubled, had already begun a heated correspondence with the Ma'am.

Dr. and Mrs. Budd were now very prosperous. Had they, demanded the Ma'am, paid off their creditors in Bristol? Arthur, admitting they hadn't, nevertheless hotly defended the Budds and their hundred good qualities. The Ma'am, shivering up to her lace collar and white cap, said that these were no fit associates for her son, and expressed decided views touching Dr. Budd's character. Attack followed defence until mother and son reached the verge of a quarrel. No quarrel was necessary. Dr. Budd and his wife found the Ma'am's letters in Arthur's room, and read them.

Budd said nothing. He waited, brooding, until June. Then he announced, in the friendliest way, that his new associate had been ruining the practice from the first. These thick-witted country people, Budd explained, saw one door with two doctors' names; they *wanted* Dr. Budd, but they feared they might be fobbed off with Dr. Conan Doyle; so they grew nervous and turned away.

The staggered Dr. Conan Doyle, knowing nothing of what was behind this, walked out into the yard, picked up a hammer, and approached the front door. He wedged the forked end of the hammer between wood and brass plate, and ripped his plate off the door. "That won't interfere with you any more," he said.

Urging him not to be hasty and quick-tempered, Budd suggested ways and means. Why not set up in practice for himself? No capital? Well, Budd handsomely offered to lend him a pound a week until he was making as much on his own; then it could be repaid. Let

him open the atlas and choose any town in England!
Each week that generous genie, the postman, should
deposit twenty shillings in his hand. Not without humiliation, Arthur finally accepted, and chose Portsmouth.

It was a risky plunge. He would have to rent a house
with only references in place of a deposit on rent, and
buy a consignment of drugs on credit. The mere details
of house-furnishing could be considered later. In one
of the last letters he wrote from Budd's house, in June
of 1882, he alternated between gloom and a sort of
defiant optimism.

"Write something cheery, like a good little woman,"
he urged the Ma'am, "and don't be always in the dole-
fuls or we shall set you to revise the Hebrew text of the
burial service." Then again: "If I can only get the right
sort of house I'll make a thousand a year within three
years or I'm very much mistaken!" And finally: "I
have made it up with Elmore Welden. I think she is
really fond of me. I shall marry her if I succeed in
Portsmouth."

Portsmouth, and the sense of being free there, buoyed
him up to the skies. There was a fine house, in the
suburb of Southsea, to be had for forty pounds a year.
Giving as one of his references the name of Henry
Doyle, C.B., Director of the National Art Gallery of
Ireland, he received the keys without any palaver about
a deposit. Some odds and ends of furniture he bought
at an auction. It was necessary, at first, to furnish only
the consulting-room: with, of course, a bed for some
upstairs room, and an umbrella stand to decorate the
hall.

It was a proud moment when he closed the door of his
own house, even though the noise of he door went
echoing up through empty rooms. With the carefulness

of an experienced householder he had remembered to buy a bed, but forgotten mattress and bedclothes. On the other hand, the consulting-room on the ground-floor front—with its red drugget of carpet, its oak table bearing stethoscope and dresser's case, its three chairs and three pictures—swam in a mysterious twilight created by drawing brown curtains rather closely together, which made corners of the room appear to be furnished; and, outside, his brass plate glittered in the sunshine.

"No patents yet," he reported enthusiastically, "but the number of people who stop and read my plate is enormous. On Wednesday evening in 25 minutes 28 people stopped in front of it, and yesterday I counted 24 in 15 minutes, which is better still."

The editor of 'London Society,' to whom he had already sold Bret-Harte-inspired stories called *Bones* and *The Gully of Bluemansdyke*, contributed seven pounds fifteen as an advance on future work. This, with additions, made the quarter's rent secure. In default of a servant, he could get the Ma'am to send his ten-year-old brother Innes; and Innes, dressed up as a smart page-boy in buttons, should open his door. By eating bread, potted meat, and bacon cooked over a gas-ring in the back room, they could live famously on a shilling a day. Dr. Budd's pound, arriving each week, would make them safe until the patients came.

But the amiable Dr. Budd had other ideas. Seeing his friend irrevocably committed, with a lease signed and a consignment of drugs in the scullery, Dr. Budd did what he intended to do from the first. He wrote in a tone of outrage to say that, after his friend's departure from Plymouth, torn fragments of a letter had been found in the latter's room. These fragments, when gummed together by Budd and his wife, had proved to be a letter from Conan Doyle's mother in which he, Dr. Budd, was referred to in the vilest terms as 'unscrupulous' and a 'bankrupt swindler.'

(The actual letter, in fact, was in Conan Doyle's pocket at Portsmouth.)

"I can only say," concluded Budd, "we are astonished that you could have been a party to any such correspondence, and we refuse to have anything more to do with you in any shape or form."

So now, on this pleasant September night in 1882, Dr. Conan Doyle—of number 1 Bush Villas, Elm Grove, Southsea—crept out under cover of darkness to polish the brass plate affixed to his area-railings. Two doors away on his right, as he attacked that plate, one or two still lights glimmered against the curved façade of the Bush Hotel. Otherwise Elm Grove was deserted under dim street-lamps. To the left of his fine brick house, where Innes lay asleep upstairs, loomed the cavernous porch of a church.

During the two months since receiving Budd's letter, he reflected, he had not done too badly. He could still swear about it. But more often that picture of Budd and his wife, solemnly gumming together the fragments of a letter they hadn't got, tickled some rib of mirth which set him whooping. After all, as he told the Ma'am at the time, it was not a disaster: he still had several days' provisions in the house, and half a crown in his pocket. He liked Budd; he couldn't help liking the fellow.

Now, slowly, a few patients were coming in. He had learned the virtue of respectability; all his front windows were curtained, so that occupants of the villas across the street should not see the unfurnished state of the upstairs rooms. The virtue of tidiness, no doubt, would come later. Yes; he could hold on. But if only more patients could be lured inside! Or if only—a dazzling hope as yet unrealized—if only he could get a story accepted by the 'Cornhill Magazine'!

IV

MEDICAL:

The Respectable Top-Hat. With Manuscripts

"Messrs. Smith, Elder & Co.," ran the engraved lettering, exactly like a formal invitation, "present their compliments to A. C. Doyle, Esq., and have pleasure in enclosing a cheque for twenty-nine guineas in payment for Mr. Doyle's contribution to the 'Cornhill Magazine' entitled *Habakuk Jephson's Statement*, not yet published." It was dated July 15th, 1883.

To the author of *Habakuk*, smoking a Dublin-clay pipe, behind his desk in the consulting-room, it was the accolade. The 'Cornhill,' formerly edited by Thackeray, now glorified by Robert Louis Stevenson, wore editorial ermine and published only work of literary merit. Its editor, the eminent Mr. James Payn, combined a keen judgment with the most illegible handwriting ever put on paper.

This achievement did not mean that the young doctor need stop writing stories for cheaper magazines like 'London Society,' or 'All the Year Round,' or 'The Boy's Own Paper.' Finances were too straitened, sometimes too desperately serious, for that. But when *Habakuk* (unsigned) appeared in the following year, and one critic attributed it to Stevenson while comparing it with Poe, the author needed all his modesty not to tell everybody he met that the story was his own.

In those first two years of practice, '82 to '84, there seemed little outward change in the household. Ten-year-old Innes, face scrubbed and hair cut by his elder brother, made a smart page in buttons. But, when he saw a patient approaching what his brother called the spider's web, Innes's excitement was often too much for him. On one occasion he threw open the front door, took one critical look at the woman outside, and then his voice went shrilling up the stairs:

"Arthur! Hooray! It's another baby!" And the doctor, settling the shoulders of his frock-coat as he hurried downstairs, had time to give the boy only one glare of awful malignancy before adjusting his features to the suavity of, "Pray step in, madam."

Innes's own version of a typical day in their lives can be found in a Log he prepared at his brother's direction. "This morning after Breakfast," runs the Log, "Arthur went downstairs and began to write a story about a man with three eyes, while I was up stairs enventing a new water-works that will send rokets over the moon in two minutes and they will send small shot at the same distance then it was a quarter past one, so, I had to go and put on the last potatoes the only six we had in the world."

It was not quite so tragic as this. From the beginning their friend Lloyd, in Sussex, sent them a winter stock of potatoes. A neighbouring grocer, who suffered from fits, exchanged butter and tea for medical treatment; and Dr. Conan Doyle seldom passed that shop without a hopeful glance for symptoms of fits in the man behind the scales. A servant for the house seemed out of the question, until he offered board and lodgings in a commodious basement to anyone who would exchange it for domestic service.

This advertisement brought two elderly females, designated in the correspondence as Mrs. S. and Mrs. G. After some short interval of peace and order, a tumult of quarrelling arose from underneath the floor-boards: wailings and lamentations as of souls in a domestic purgatory, and mutual recriminations about stealing bacon. Mrs. S. departed, her handkerchief at her eyes. Mrs. G. followed, after being detected in too close attention to a beer-barrel in the cellar. The doctor, correctly deciding that Mrs. S. (Smith) was the injured one, pursued her and brought her back. Innes was sent to a day school; Mrs. Smith reigned as paid housekeeper. Thenceforward the meals were well-cooked, the knick-knacks dusted, the furniture kept glossy.

In this matter of furniture, at least, he had no cause for complaint. The Ma'am and Aunt Annette, struggling in rivalry, supplied him with everything from a vanload of books to a musical clock. In the hall, where brass stair rods glimmered against a new carpet, the bust of Grandfather John Doyle stood on the table. There were engravings hung on marbly brown-papered walls, and African mats on the floor. "I have had those glazed panes knocked out of the door at the end of the hall," he reported; "and red ones substituted: which gives the whole hall a lurid and artistic sort of look."

By night a red globe glared over the gas-jet, giving the hall that same lurid and artistic (not to say ghastly) appearance. His consulting-room, always his pride, came to have twenty-one pictures and eleven vases. In the room behind it, fitted up as a waiting room, the amount of furniture became an embarrassment. When the Ma'am offered still another book-case for it, he had to remonstrate that there would be no room for the patients. But one gift from the Doyles in London he could not accept.

Since that interview at Cambridge Terrace, which lingered and rankled in bitterness, he had never made it up with his uncles. Once or twice he saw Uncle Dick

—in fact, he saved his uncle's life when the latter was taken with a fit of apoplexy—but the gap remained unbridged. Uncle Dick, whether with subtlety or generosity, sent him a letter of introduction to the Catholic Bishop of Portsmouth, and added that there was no Catholic doctor in the town.

No 'Catholic' doctor. He had his own angry interpretation of this. Come into the fold, they were saying; accept the Faith, and you won't starve. He threw the letter of introduction into the fire.

In the same way, stiff-necked as well as bull-necked, he kept his pride in the bad times. His professional note paper, as suggested and supplied by the Ma'am, bore his family crest. The Ma'am, in fact, asked with spirit why he didn't include the Foley crest as well; but, "Don't you think," he suggested, "that two family crests on one sheet of paper would be a trifle ostentatious?" It was not only that the crest would help his practice with what they called the carriage-trade. It was a beacon of defiance as well. Even when he must delay a letter to the Ma'am for want of postage, it would contain the grim request: "Send more crested paper!"

Through these days flitted Elmo Welden, whom he had sworn to marry when he was making two pounds a week. The dark-eyed Elmo, who seemed recovered from illness, came to stay at Ventnor conveniently near him in the Isle of Wight.

"She is a dashing girl," he cried, "and I am more fond of her than ever!" He took her to London, where they saw Gilbert and Sullivan's *Patience*; he introduced her to Aunt Annette, who was charmed. Once, in a mood of depression, he had a wild idea of going doctoring into the malaria-misted swamp and jungle of northern India. Fortunately he did not get the post. "But

Elmo," he declared, "would be heart-broken if I left her behind; she is a real tropical plant."

The tropical plant, or clinging-vine quality, was what he liked in women. He was not really in love with Elmo; or she, perhaps, with him. But both were romantic-minded; both thought it an excellent thing to be in love with somebody. What kept them incessantly quarrelling is not clear; when this happens, who can ever remember? Elmo was convinced she was right. He, always and invariably convinced *he* was right, would fold his arms with that lofty attitude permissible to males in 1882. Elmo departed in a temper for Switzerland.

Yet the medical practice did pick up. He discovered this when he learned to go out and mix among his acquaintances. His prowess at cricket and football, where he could take off his frock-coat and cut loose with every ounce of suppressed energy, noised abroad the name of Dr. Conan Doyle. He joined the Literary and Scientific Society. He won a cigar-case for his skill at bowls. Pianos banged at smoking concerts. Sometimes, to enliven his life and Innes's, there would be a visit from one of his sisters.

Of the ten children born to Mary and Charles Doyle, seven now survived. Five were the girls: Annette, Constance, Caroline, Ida, and 'Dodo.' Annette, the eldest, had long ago gone out as governess to a family in Portugal. Ida and Dodo—younger than Innes—were still children. The two middle sisters, Connie and Lottie, he saw more frequently.

With his strong sense of family ties, he doted on them all; but he could never quite keep the grin off his face. Hear his description of Constance.

"Connie," he said, "wears her hair down her back in a thick plait, like the cable of a man-o'-war. Her dress comes down to her ankles. She is extremely pretty, with a high, cold, keep-your-hands-off sort of expression." He was delighted to show off such a decorative sister among his friends; to escort her to dances, white-gloved, and watch the young swains crowd round.

But his favourite was Lottie: Lottie, with the Doyle features and the hair so luxuriant that he thought it ought to be photographed as advertisement for somebody's lotion. Too soon, in those Southsea days, Lottie went out to Portugal with Annette, and herself took a position as governess in a romantic house situated across the road from a dynamite-factory. With Lottie her brother exchanged confidences.

"I went to a ball the other night," he wrote, "and by some mischance got as drunk as an owl. I have a dim recollection that I proposed to half the women in the room—married and single. I got one letter next day signed, 'Ruby,' and saying the writer had said 'yes' when she meant 'no'; but who the deuce she was or what she had said 'yes' about I can't conceive."

Despite his bantering tone he suffered agonies of remorse over this. To touch drink in public was the one thing a medical man must not do; it must never be repeated, now that the doctor's bell rang so much more frequently at number 1 Bush Villas.

A commission to perform medical examinations for the Gresham Life Insurance Company helped his income. Dr. Pike, a friendly neighbour, threw many cases in his way. In the homes of the poor or the shabby-genteel, where he hurried with his stethoscope in his top-hat, he saw death and suffering through the eyes of a man grown up: standing on his own feet, groping for his own philosophy. The more he saw of medical practice, the more he turned for recreation to his writing.

After the appearance of *Habakuk Jephson's State-*

ment in January, 1884, he did not attain the heights of
the 'Cornhill' for some time. But *Habakuk,* a highly
fanciful tale based on the derelict mystery-ship *Mary
Celeste*, had repercussions beyond mere critical praise.
Far away in Gibraltar, a certain Mr. Solly Flood read
it and was galvanized. Through the medium of the
Central News Agency, a telegram was thrown back
widespread over England.

> MR. SOLLY FLOOD, HER MAJESTY'S ADVOCATE-
> GENERAL AT GIBRALTAR, PRONOUNCES DR. J. HA-
> BAKUK JEPHSON'S STATEMENT A FABRICATION
> FROM BEGINNING TO END.

Mr. Flood also wrote a long report to his Government
and to the newspapers, pointing out the menace to international relations when people like this Dr. Jephson
professed to reveal facts which on many points could
officially be disproved. Before Mr. Flood was enlight-
ened, the newspapers had good sport. To Dr. Conan
Doyle it came as more than a compliment; it was the
beginning of a revelation.

He could write fiction which many people took for
absolute truth. That was what Edgar Allan Poe had
done in the *New York Sun*, when every reader of the
newspaper believed that Harrison Ainsworth and seven
others had flown across the Atlantic in a steering-bal-
loon. Poe's had been a conscious hoax, wickedly gleeful.
The Southsea doctor was only trying to entertain. But
it did seem to indicate that the spinner of fancies could
beat the realist all hollow at his own game if only (if
only!) he had the knack of inventing just the right
detail.

Thus he had begun the year '84 in a fever of writing.
Unfortunately, "I keep sending things to 'Cornhill' and
they keep sending them back." But he did not rail

against the magazine, as once he had done when James Payn complained that his short, sharp sentences were crude. He was overjoyed when he received an invitation to London for a fish-dinner to 'Cornhill' contributors at the Ship at Greenwich. There he met the shrewd, mercantile-looking Payn, and Du Maurier the artist, and 'a peaky young man with spectacles,' named Anstey, who had scored a great hit with *Vice Versa*. Glasses clinked under the old smoky rafters; and the later members of the party, returning to London, left Anstey in an advanced state of intoxication under the Adelphi Arches.

That was life! That was literary company indeed!

But all his hackles rose, after he had entered a prize-contest in 'Tit-Bits,' when the editor of 'Tit-Bits' awarded the big prize to what was obviously an inferior article. This was what maddened him, because it wasn't a fair call. By George, he would *make* it a sporting event!

"I have written to the editor," he told the Ma'am, "offering to post £25 if he will do the same. The two mss. (mine and the winner's) are then to be submitted to an impartial judge (such as the editor of 'Cornhill'); his decision to be final, and the stakes to go to the winner." But there was no reply.

Also he had commenced work on a novel, at present entitled *Girdlestone & Co.* Satisfactorily? No. Even his enthusiasm glimmered only at odd times. In his heart he knew he was sewing together a fustian of other men's styles, mainly Dickens's and Meredith's. He worked by fits and starts, or not at all. It was not his own self who wrote; it was sensationalism without distinction. Besides, having taken his M.B. degree, he was determined to take his M.D. at Edinburgh as well. By concentrated study at odd hours, between the calls of the practice and his writing, he felt he could pass his M.D. without even going to Edinburgh except for the examinations.

That he did take his M.D. in the following year, despite all these other irons clattering in and out of the fire, can only be stated as a fact. Meanwhile, he still lacked real self-confidence. We see him at the Literary and Scientific Society, longing to join in a debate but uncertain whether he could ever speak well in public: the whole bench shivering as *he* shivered, threatening to dislodge all who sat near him, before his first throaty gurgle of, "M-Mr. Chairman!"

Then he met Miss Louise Hawkins.

It began in one of those pointless tragedies so difficult to reconcile with any idea of a Merciful Providence. His friendly neighbour, Dr. Pike, called on him one day in March of 1885. One of Dr. Pike's patients, it appeared, was a young Mr. Jack Hawkins, son of a widow who had come to stay at Southsea. The boy's symptoms were disquieting: Would Dr. Conan Doyle oblige with a consultation?

In a sedate lodging-house near the sea-front, behind the tallest of lace curtains, they found the patient sallow and dazed of face, with his mother on one side of him and his sister on the other. The younger doctor realized he had been consulted only as a gesture. Jack Hawkins's illness arose from cerebral meningitis. Both physicians knew it was hopeless. It might be a long time, it might be a very brief time; but still hopeless.

Mrs. Emily Hawkins, a tall middle-aged lady, not strong willed like the Ma'am, tried to explain their position. They had nowhere to go. Not because of money, but because no hotel or lodging-house would keep them when—well! (she hesitated) when Jack had one of his violent attacks. His sister, Louise, a gentle and very feminine girl, stood by without speaking, but with tears in her eyes.

After the consultation, at Dr. Pike's encouragement, Dr. Conan Doyle offered to furnish a spare bedroom for Jack in his own house, and to look after Jack as a resident patient. A 'private establishment,' he thought to himself fiercely, was out of the question. But, when they brought Jack to the new bedroom at number 1 Bush Villas, the patient's condition had grown worse. He was flushed and muttering, with a very high temperature, yet a disposition to fall into a doze. The doctor, in the room next door so that he could hear the slightest noise, listened long after Jack had gone to sleep.

Towards daybreak the boy climbed out of his bed, and flung over the wash-stand that held bowl and pitcher. The doctor, hurrying in, found him standing there in his trailing night-shirt, amid smashed crockery and water, with pathetic crazed eyes. He was quietened and put back to bed, not without difficulty. Conan Doyle sat beside him in an armchair, shivering in raw March air, until daylight brought Mrs. Smith with the patient's cup of arrowroot.

A few days later, Jack Hawkins died.

Fortunately, Dr. Pike had seen the patient on the evening before the latter's death. Everything had been done that could have been done. Otherwise malicious gossip might have blown his rising practice to dust. Even as matters stood it was bad enough. Conan Doyle, when he saw that black coffin coming out of his own front door, put his head in his hands. His first duty, he felt, was to console the mother and the sister; instead, he found himself being consoled.

Of Louise, twenty-seven years old—'Touie,' her nickname was—he saw a great deal. Though not beautiful, she was of a type which appealed to him: the round

face, the wide mouth, the brown hair, the wide-spaced
blue eyes, shading to sea-green, which were her finest
feature. Her gentleness, her complete unselfishness,
roused all his protective instincts. Louise, or Touie,
was what they then called a home-girl, loving needlework and an armchair by the fire. He met her in sorrow;
and ended by falling deeply in love. Towards the end
of April they were engaged.

In decency, there could be no marriage so soon after
Jack's death. But he begged and urged forward the date.
By hard study through May and June (a thesis had to
be written), he took his M.D. degree in July. And on
August 6th, 1885, with the strong approval of the
Ma'am, Louise Hawkins and Arthur Conan Doyle were
married.

Young Innes was sent to a public-school in Yorkshire. Mother Hawkins, with her gold-rimmed spectacles
and her elaborate cap with two lace ends trailing down
across her chest, came to live with the newlyweds at
Bush Villas: where, in the snug upstairs sitting-room,
he had red-plush furniture, and a piano on the hire-
purchase system, and Touie smiling at him from under
the lamp. He was full of plans.

"Shall we read aloud together, my dear," he would
suggest, "and improve our minds? Say Gordon's Taci-
tus? Or perhaps, in a lighter vein, Boswell's *Johnson*
or Pepys's Diary?"

"Oh, do!" cried Touie, who would have been just as
eager to hear him read in Sanskrit if he had possessed
that accomplishment.

Marriage, in fact, acted on him with acute exhilaration. His step grew more springy. Geniality radiated
from him like the Spirit of Christmas Present. Though
he admitted to the Ma'am that he was putting on weight,
fifteen stone seven, he presently became the terror of

the bowlers by scoring 111 not-out against the Artillery, and at football the local newspaper called him "one of the safest Association backs in Hampshire."

The medical practice, rising from £154 in the first year to £300 in the third, never passed that figure. Yet it permitted them the necessities, and one or two small luxuries when it developed that Touie had a hundred a year of her own. Most of all, in this inspiration of married life, he found his mental powers stimulated and his brain aglow with story-ideas. He could even understand (or, at least, very nearly understand) the Ma'am's horror at dust under a bookcase and a room left untidy, now that he had attained the dignity of A Married Man.

The newlyweds bought an immense leather-bound scrap-book, inscribed 'L. and A. Conan Doyle, August 6th, 1885,' for press-cuttings and notes of the hopeful future. Today you may turn over the pages of that battered volume; you may breathe the reality, sometimes the pathos, of their lives in a stuffier but pleasanter age. Or there are his own notebooks, exercise-books bound in thick cardboard, of which for years he kept a series in his neat, precise handwriting. In those notebooks you may follow the extent of his reading—not only in every period of history, which he devoured with atlas at elbow and pen ready—but in science and literature, quotations and wit-points boiling together with originalia and story-ideas of his own.

Sometimes he would write a comment about a subject over which he still brooded. "A religion to be true must include everything from the amoeba to the milky way." Or an epigram in the style of Meredith. "A strong mind is as disagreeable in a domestic circle as a very powerful singer in a small room." Or from the mass of books an anecdote which made his eye twinkle:

"The dying Talleyrand remarked that he suffered like the damned. Louis Phillippe by his bedside politely remarked, 'Already?' "

Both before his marriage and after it he had done some good work: the tragic comedy of *A Physiologist's Wife, The Captain of the Polestar* with its icy hinterland of horror, the reversed identities of *The Great Keinplatz Experiment*, in which Herr Baumgarten of Stonyhurst became Professor von Baumgarten of Keinplatz. Towards the end of November he gathered together eighteen tales, which he hoped would make a volume to be called *Light and Shade*. But what he must do, if ever he were to achieve literary success, was a novel. A novel, unquestionably a novel!

Girdlestone & Co. dragged out its heavy length. Begun early in 1884, it was not finished and recopied until the end of January, 1886. He had no great faith in it. If he were to exploit the fancies that seethed in his head, it must be something sharp and striking and new.

"I have read Gaboriau's *Lecoq the Detective*," he wrote; the first reference to Gaboriau in all his papers, "*The Gilded Clique*, and a story concerning the murder of an old woman, the name of which I forget." Looking this up, he inserted *The Lerouge Case*. "All very good. Wilkie Collins, but more so."

And we find, scrawled quickly across the inside cover of the notebook:

"The coat-sleeve, the trouser-knee, the callosities of the forefinger and thumb, the boot—any one of these might tell us, but that all united should fail to enlighten the trained observation is incredible."

Why not a novel about a detective?

Upstairs Touie's piano tinkled; the musical clock

played a fragment of an Irish jig each time it struck. In the consulting-room, as he sat and smoked reflectively, there hung on the wall behind his chair a number of his father's water-colour paintings, 'The Saving Cross,' 'The Coast-Coach,' 'The Haunted House,' all of figures weird or terrible. Charles Doyle, his health broken, had long ago retired to a Convalescent Home. But that was not on the son's mind now. Even the Ma'am, who lived in Yorkshire and would insist on driving a pony-and-trap without wearing spectacles, hardly troubled him.

If he needed a model for his detective, he need look no further than a lean figure in Edinburgh, with long white dexterous hands and a humorous eye, whose deductions startled patients as they would startle a reader in print. Yes; but Joe Bell himself sometimes blundered. Could he, Joe Bell's pupil, shut his eyes and throw himself into an artificial state of mind so that *he* could deduce too?

And there was more than that. It was of no value confidently to pronounce somebody a cobbler or a cork-cutter with asthma, if this could not be developed as a matter of detection. His detective must be a man who had reduced the pursuit of criminals to an exact science.

An exact science! By a study of minutiae, footprints, mud, dust, the use of chemistry and anatomy and geology, he must reconstruct the scene of a murder as though he had been there; and casually fling out information into astounded faces. Unfortunately, no system of scientific criminology existed. In 1864 Lombroso had published a work on the criminal type; M. Alphonse Bertillon, of the Paris police, was now photographing criminals and trying to identify them by a rather heavy-handed method called anthropometric measurement. But no scientific system, in print at least, had appeared to help him. Very well! The Southsea doctor must simply imagine what he would do if he were a detective, and invent a system.*

As he turned over the idea in the first two months of 1886, with the white face of Joe Bell peering down through his imagination, he thought much of London. What he saw was not the London he knew now. It was the vast eerie city he had glimpsed as a boy, with its lamps glimmering through brown fog and its curtained mystery-haunted streets, where he had looked with apprehension into the glass eyes of the murderers at Madame Tussaud's. This should form a background for his stoop-shouldered wizard of lens and microscope. In his notebook he jotted down one false start:

"The terrified woman rushing up to the cabman. The two going in search of a policeman. John Reeves had been 7 years in the force; John Reeves went back with them."

This he discarded. But the cabman-idea, he noted down, was not bad; if a cabman were the murderer, he could go where he liked without rousing suspicion. In his heart, when Conan Doyle thought of a merely sen-

* It must be remembered that the only great text-book on criminology, Hans Gross's *Criminal Investigation,* which forms the basis of every present-day police system, was not published until 1891. Two Holmes novels had appeared before that date; and it is a little startling to see Holmes, on several occasions, anticipating Gross. To take one example: No reader of the second novel will have forgotten the reference to "my monograph upon the tracing of footsteps, with some remarks upon the use of plaster of Paris as a preserver of impresses." Gross, after listing and discarding six currently popular ways of preserving footprints, states he has discovered only one good method: plaster of Paris. In our own time Dr. Edmond Locard, head of the police laboratory at Lyons, has been very emphatic: "I hold that a police expert, or an examining magistrate, would not find it a waste of his time to read Doyle's novels. . . . If, in the police laboratory at Lyons, we are interested in any unusual way in this problem of dust, it is because of having absorbed ideas found in Gross and Conan Doyle."

sational story, he still longed for adventure on the western plains of the United States. His liking for America and Americans, such as Chicago Bill in his own *Gully of Bluemansdyke*, existed long before he ever met one. Such fancies as these suggested revenge. If the motive for the murder were revenge, he could import one of these likeable demons into the prosaic Brixton Road.

The title of this mystery? *A Tangled Skein* would do, and he wrote it down above the passage about the terrified woman and the cabman. But he did not really like *A Tangled Skein*, and he changed it in his notebook. On a different piece of paper he tried to work out the names and background of his chief characters.

'Ormond Sacker' as the teller of the story? No! That suggested Bond Street and dandyism. But there was a real name he might use; it suggested the burly and the commonplace. A friend of his at Southsea, also a leading member of the Portsmouth Literary and Scientific Society, was a young doctor named Watson: Dr. James Watson. Surely Watson wouldn't mind the use of his surname if the first name were changed to John? Down it went as John H. Watson. (But can we wonder if, in later years, the author's pen slipped and Watson's wife called him James? For the signature of the real James Watson, in the minute-book of the Portsmouth Scientific Society, you may find at the Portsmouth Library to this day.)

'Sherrinford Holmes,' as the name of the detective, was not quite right. It was near, but not close enough. It had no clean crack of the bat; it slurred; it lacked the bell-note as from tingling glass. He studied it, toyed with it, and then—entirely at random—he hit on the Irish name of Sherlock.

Sherlock Holmes! This time it had the click of an opening key. There might be far worse names to set up against the stolidity of the commonplace doctor. An empty house, up a yellow-clay path amid a dripping garden. A dead man lying under the flicker of a red wax-candle, with the word 'revenge' scrawled in blood on the wall. And the whole story boiled over.

A Tangled Skein had long been discarded. At the top of his manuscript he put, *A Study in Scarlet*. Writing between breakfast and supper, writing between peals of the doctor's bell and calls from Touie upstairs, he had no idea that he was creating the most famous character in the English language.

V

DISILLUSIONMENT:

The Thinning of the Dreams

"Arthur," wrote Touie to her husband's sister Lottie in Portugal, "has written another book, a little novel about 200 pages long, called *A Study in Scarlet*. It went off last night. We have had no news of *Girdlestone* yet, but we hope that no news is good news. We rather fancy that *A Study in Scarlet* may find its way into print before its elder brother."

It was one of those rollicking happy letters in which husband and wife write alternate paragraphs, pushing each other out of the way to say something, and joyously retiring again. They wrote it on a Sunday late in April, when the chimneys smoked in flighty weather; they were "alone in our glory," as Touie put it, because everybody else had gone to church.

Poor Lottie needed cheering up. It was all very well to live in a Portuguese manor-house near a dynamite-factory; but part of the dynamite-factory blew up, and nearly wrecked the house as well. Lottie had gone on to another position. Her brother described the state of the medical practice: how a certain General Drayson had called him in the other day; as well as a lady who had ruined her constitution in youth, and now, at the age of 102, was bitterly repenting it.

He began *A Study in Scarlet* in March and finished it in April, 1886. It was despatched straight to James Payn, to see whether it might do as a serial before book-publication. Though *Girdlestone* had been rejected twice, and sent out again for the third time, its author did not much care. His highest hopes accompanied the *Study*, because he knew he had written it as well as he could. He had encountered a curious faculty (which, after all, he should have suspected from student days) of being able to drop a mental curtain between himself and the world; and, by inducing an artificial state of mind, becoming himself the character he wrote about. James Payn replied early in May, and he bent over that all-but-illegible scrawl.

"I have kept your story an unconscionably long time," Payn wrote, "but it so interested me that I wanted to finish it. It's capital." Then a short sentence completely indecipherable except for the ominous words 'shilling dreadful.' "I wish they wouldn't publish books at that price. It's too long—and too short—for the 'Cornhill Magazine.'"

Here was a sick taste of disappointment; though this, after all, meant only that the *Study* was too long for a single issue and too short for a serial. It had received high praise, for James Payn. There should be no difficulty about a book-publisher. His spirits grew buoyant again as he posted the manuscript to Arrowsmith of Bristol. On his birthday, when Mother Hawkins gave him cricket-gloves and Touie embroidered a noble pair of slippers, he whiled away the time of waiting at a story called *The Surgeon of Gaster Fell*.

Meanwhile, great political events rumbled in the outside world. Mr. Gladstone, elected Prime Minister for the third time, brought forward his bill to establish Home Rule in Ireland. Mr. Gladstone was defeated. Faced with a general election for the second time in seven months, tempers throughout the country grew frayed. And tempers had not been soothed, at any time during the eighties, by the Bold Fenian Men of Ireland. If Lottie in Portugal knew the sound of exploding dynamite, Londoners had come to know it far better at the hands of the Fenian Men.

They put dynamite in a lavatory at Scotland Yard, and blew out the side of the building. Not a soul was injured, since there seems to have been nobody on duty. But, aside from a fiasco when the police found sixteen cakes of dynamite under the Nelson Monument, there were minor explosions at the office of the 'Times,' the Tower of London, Victoria Station, and even the House of Commons.

In politics Conan Doyle was a Liberal-Unionist: that is, one of Mr. Gladstone's 'dissentient Liberals' who disapproved of Home Rule for Ireland. Does it seem a paradox that this man, Irish on both sides, should have become a burly symbol of everything traditionally English? It was no paradox. He simply regarded Ireland as a part of England (or Britain, if you will) in the same sense that Scotland now was. To hear of Irishmen drilling with pikes for freedom seemed as nonsensical as though you were to imagine Scottish rebels whetting their claymores in Edinburgh's Grassmarket.

"Ireland," he wrote in his notebook, "is a huge suppuration which will go on suppurating until it bursts." At Portsmouth, on the hectic eve of election, he was drawn into it. Major-General Sir William Crossman, the head of the party, had been scheduled to address a big Liberal-Union meeting at the Amphitheatre; and Sir William was delayed. At a moment's notice they substituted Dr. Conan Doyle.

To say that he was petrified would not be putting it too strongly. Some of his earlier nervousness at the Literary and Scientific Society had been shaken off when he read a paper about the Arctic Seas. But this was different. To wabble out to the speaker's table, alone in what seemed an acre of stage, and face three thousand people without anything written or so much as a note, turned his hot face even hotter against the glare of footlights. Nevertheless, without any clear idea of what he was saying, he got excited, and for twenty-five minutes poured out a flood of rhetoric which raised the audience to its feet with cheers.

"England and Ireland," he was later astounded to read he had said, "are wedded together with the sapphire wedding-ring of the sea, and what God has placed together let no man pluck asunder." But his faith in public men was seldom very strong. When long afterwards he had lunch with that same Sir William Crossman, he confessed that a very regrettable parody took shape in his mind:

> "You are old, Boozy William," the young man said,
>   "And you drink something stronger than tea;
> But I cannot help thinking: If you are our head,
>   Pray what can our other end be?"

Mr. Gladstone's Liberals were again defeated at the general election; tumult somewhat subsided. In July there was a great naval review: be-flagged ironclads at manoeuvres off Spithead, and a mimic torpedo-attack. He and Touie went out to see the display in Major Colwell's yacht; but it poured with rain all day, and Touie wept. In July, too, *A Study in Scarlet* was returned from Arrowsmith unread.

This time it did dishearten him. He sent off the manuscript to Fred Warne & Co., and received the same rejection. "My poor *Study*," he complained to the Ma'am, "has never even been read by anyone except Payn. Verily literature is a difficult oyster to open. All will come well in time, however." And he sent the book to Messrs. Ward, Lock & Co.

At Ward, Lock & Co. the chief editor, Professor G. T. Bettany, gave the book to his wife for judgment. Mrs. Bettany, herself a writer, read the *Study* and grew enthusiastic: "This man is a born novelist! It will be a great success!" But the business-heads of the firm, whether or not they shared Mrs. Bettany's opinion, did not err on the side of recklessness when they communicated with the author.

They could not publish *A Study in Scarlet* this year, they said, because the market was flooded with cheap fiction. If he did not object to its being held over for another year, they would give him £25 for the copyright: that is, complete sale of all rights in the book henceforward.

Even to the Southsea doctor these terms seemed pretty hard, and he wrote to suggest a royalty-basis. The answer was incisive.

"In reply to your letter of yesterday's date," they informed him on November 2nd, "we regret to say that we shall be unable to allow you to retain a percentage on the sale of your work, as it might give rise to some confusion. The tale may have to be inserted, together with some other, in one of our annuals. Therefore we must adhere to our offer of £25 for the complete copyright."

The author accepted. There seemed nothing else to be done. At least the book would be published, though that word 'annual' had a disquieting look. And a novel, with any luck, would get his name before the public even if he received not another penny for it. In the new year, 1887, he was toying with an entirely new subject: the study of the psychic.

Now these years at Southsea were the years of mental

development, the years of a powerful intellect setting itself against far deeper problems than the problem of literary style. Superficially it may be followed in his books; but more personally, more deeply, it speaks in the notebooks meant for no eye except his own. It is a truism to say that every man of intelligence must have a guide: whether it be a religion, or merely a philosophy of life. It is less a truism that so few, if they would speak the truth about it, ever find one.

He had discarded Catholicism. Like the historian Gibbon, whom he so much admired, he remained a materialist. It was true, as he wrote, that you must imply a Creator if you saw the universe only as a vast clock-work phenomenon swinging in a vacuum; even clock-work must have a designer. But this remained a toy—stupendous, but still a toy—unless it also implied some purpose, some definition of good and evil, some meaning in the pattern. What he could not find was any evidence for the existence of a human soul.

Early in 1887 a patient of his, General Drayson, spoke to him of the subject called Spiritualism. General Drayson, a distinguished astronomer and mathematician, to whom he later dedicated *The Captain of the Polestar*, spoke of his own conversion to Spiritualism through conversations with a dead brother. The existence of life after death, General Drayson said, was not only a fact; it could be proved as such.

Conan Doyle made a non-committal reply. Neverthe-less, merely a possibility of proof was enough to set every corner of his mind tingling. In his notebook he listed, 'Books to be Read,' a list of psychic works which came to include seventy-four volumes in the year. He not only read them at that time; he pondered over their contents until he had mastered the most abstruse specu-lation. Once he breaks out, in a kind of fury, with a quotation from the Koran: "The heavens and the earth and what is between them: think ye that we created them in jest?" Or again, from Hellenbach: "There is a scepticism which surpasses in imbecility the obtuseness of a clodhopper."

He wrote these comments as he jotted down quotations from books so widely different as Wallace's *On Miracles and Modern Spiritualism* and Binet and Féré's *Animal Magnetism.* "There is a scepticism which surpasses in imbecility the obtuseness of a clodhopper." Was he a sceptic like that? He must not be. With his friend Mr. Ball, a Portsmouth architect, he determined to hold psychic sittings of his own.

The sittings began on January 24th, 1887, and went on at intervals until the beginning of July. He kept a detailed record of them. Those records show how deep his interest was, and his sympathy as well. Six times they sat with an experienced medium named Horstead, "a small bald grey man with a pleasant expression." Before the beginning of the sitting, "Mr. Horstead said he saw the spirit of an old man, grey hair, high forehead, thin lips, with a very strong will, looking fixedly at me."

And again, when during the sitting each member of the circle received a message:

"Mine was, 'This gentleman is a healer. Tell him not to read Leigh Hunt's book.' I had been debating in my mind whether I should get the *Comic Dramatists of the Restoration*, being rather deterred by their lewdness. I had never mentioned the subject to anyone, nor was I thinking about it at the time, so it was no case of thought-reading."

But wasn't it? Pondering over the matter after the surprise of that night, he came to a different conclusion. And he remained unconvinced. Flashes of doubt, inde-

cision, restiveness, will be found all through that journal
in which he is earnestly trying to make progress in
psychic matters. After all his investigation and reading,
he had seen nothing conclusive. He would continue to
study it, because it seemed to him quite possible that
he had not investigated deeply enough.

In the meantime, while he waited for *A Study in
Scarlet* to be published, he would show himself as something better than a writer of glorified shilling dreadfuls.
He had long wanted to try a historical novel. With his
thoughts preoccupied with history, philosophy, and
religion, it is not surprising to see the direction they took.

His favourite fiction-writers, at the moment, were
Meredith and Stevenson. Stevenson he had admired
since he found *The Pavilion on the Links*, unsigned, in
an old back number of 'Cornhill.' Stevenson's genius
lay in compressing, with a sort of literary agony, half
a dozen short words into an image more stabbingly
vivid than a whole passage of description. And Stevenson had been deeply influenced by George Meredith,
who, for all his gymnastic obscurity, could bring out
of a froth of words some such all-descriptive sentence
as: "The farmer laughed his fat sides into a chair."

Yes! And Sir Walter Scott, whose old green volumes
still held place of honour beside Charles Reade's *The
Cloister and the Hearth*, Sir Walter had that same quality too. Always he had it when he discarded intolerable
verbosity for the joy of character or the cut-and-slash
of action. You did not forget, in *Old Mortality*, the
Royalist Bothwell facing the Roundhead Burley: on
horseback, panting, with the price of a thousand Scottish
merks on Burley's head, and their separate defiances
hurled above the clang of the meeting blades:

"Then a bed of heather or a thousand merks!"

"The sword of the Lord and of Gideon!"

But Scott had drawn Burley as demented, inhuman, never making a reader understand the Puritans' religious fervour. Only Macaulay had done that. There returned to the young writer his old vision out of Macaulay, of the Roundhead soldiers putting aside their buff-coats for the arts of peace. Let these men, or their sons, be the heroes of a historical romance towards the end of the seventeenth century, under Catholic King James; and let them rise with sword and psalm-tune to the Protestant banner of 'King' Monmouth. It was the origin of *Micah Clarke*.

He began planning *Micah* in July, '87. Again, with that ever-growing power of memory which (like Macaulay's) could reach back and reproduce everything he had previously studied, he brought together his knowledge of the seventeenth century and supplemented it with months of research on detail. Then, at intervals of tramping medical rounds or studying optics at the Portsmouth Eye Hospital, he wrote the book in three months.

Now the power of *Micah Clarke*, aside from its best action scenes—the bloodhounds on Salisbury Plain, the brush with the King's Dragoons, the fight in Wells Cathedral, the blinding battlepiece at Sedgemoor—still lies in its characterization: that other imagination, the use of homely detail, by which each character grows into life before ever a shot is fired in war. The figure of the moody old father, Ironside Joe Clarke, darkens the opening chapters as they are lightened by the bustling Church-of-England mother and their broad-backed son Micah.

But the author, however he admired the Puritans and disliked the ungratefulness of the Stuart kings, could never keep a straight face before Puritan solemnity. His only real streak of Puritanism was a streak of

Victorian Puritanism. And this implies, a factor often overlooked nowadays, the lusty Victorian sense of humour. At anything holier-than-thou, no matter how sincere, Conan Doyle could never resist a gleeful dig. Thus he describes the feelings of the stern father when Micah, still a small boy, is lured into taking a second glass of Canary and brought home speechless in a cart.

"My father was less shocked at the incident than I should have expected," declares Micah, as solemn as an owl, "and reminded my mother that Noah had been overtaken in a similar manner. He also narrated how a certain field-chaplain Grant, of Desborough's regiment, having after a hot and dusty day drunk several flagons of mum, had thereafter sung certain ungodly songs, and danced in a manner unbecoming to his sacred profession."

Thus he animated Havant, the little town outside Portsmouth. Solomon Sprent, the tattooed sailorman, rolls across a real street, under real elms, to Lockarby's tavern. Out of the sea climbs the artful Decimus Saxon: stringy, drooping of eyelid, whining through his nose with the Puritans or rattling dice with the Horse Guards Blue, a man who would either befriend you or knife your back for a guinea, and tell droll stories while he was doing either; all quicksilver, at once sinister and funny. The author was deep in these adventures when *A Study in Scarlet* appeared as the main item in 'Beeton's Christmas Annual' for 1887.

And nothing happened. It was unlikely that any critic would trouble, at Christmas-time, to review an annual; and none did. At the same time, the edition was sold out. Early in '88 Ward, Lock proposed a new edition in which the novel should appear by itself. Though the author could gain no penny out of it, it was suggested that the new edition should be illustrated by his father,

Charles Doyle. Ill and aged as he was, Charles Doyle produced six black-and-white drawings; and it must have brought tears to the old man's eyes when he learned his work was still wanted in London.

His son finished and recopied *Micah Clarke* by the end of February, 1888. And again, for all the extolling of Puritan virtue, he showed where his deepest sympathy lay. Big-boned Micah, likeable and good-natured, he saw as a man and a brother. But, in modern parlance, the story is almost stolen by Sir Gervas Jerome: the ruined aristocrat, the lounging court-fop, who joins Monmouth's rebellion because he cares not a curse on which side he fights. When Monmouth's thin hopes are blotted out in the night-battle on Sedgemoor, sensible men see the necessity for retreat. Sir Gervas contemptuously refuses to retreat, as his Cavalier grandfather would have refused, and dies as improvidently as he has lived.

Conan Doyle, aware that he had done a very tolerable piece of work, unconsciously indicated the status of young authors when he wrote to the Ma'am about it.

"We must try," he said, "to retain the copyright of *Micah!* I believe it would be an income in itself." He confessed to being used up, but his notion of relaxation was curious. "I shall have a few days' rest," he added in another letter, "though I must really disburden myself of the story, *The Sign of the Sixteen Oyster-Shells*, which is lurking at present somewhere at the back of my cerebellum."

What was this story? He had already made reference to it in his notebook with:

> Idea of writing: *The Sixteen Oyster-Shells*.
> Idea of writing: *The St. Andrews Story*.
> Idea of writing: *His Last Five Minutes*.

THE LIFE OF *Sir Arthur Conan Doyle*   83

Its title remains as tantalizing, as much sandpaper to the curiosity, as those unrecorded cases of Sherlock Holmes which he was later to fling about so prodigally: more tantalizing, in fact, since he meant to write this one; and, though the exasperated biographer searches in vain through his papers, it is possible he did write it. If he did so, it was while he was engaged with a short novel called *The Mystery of Cloomber*.

About the current best-seller, Fergus Hume's *The Mystery of a Hansom Cab*, he expressed decided views. "What a swindle *The Mystery of a Hansom Cab* is!" he wrote to the Ma'am in March, 1888. "One of the weakest tales I have read, and simply sold by puffing." But he was not now concerned with mysteries. Everything centred in *Micah Clarke*. He now believed that his medical talents lay in the direction of becoming an eye-surgeon. And he confided new plans to Lottie.

"If it (*Micah*) comes off," he wrote, "we may then, I think, take it as proved that I can live by my pen. We should have a few hundreds in hand to start us. I should go to London and study the eye. I should then go to Berlin and study the eye." His half-serious dreams grew wilder. "I should then go to Paris and study the eye. Having learned *all* there is to know about the eye, I should come back to London and start as an eye-surgeon, still of course keeping literature as my milk-cow."

It is significant that at this time he began a study of the Middle Ages which was to last for more than two years. Unfortunately nobody would accept *Micah Clarke*.

James Payn asked in a shrill voice how could he, could he, waste his time on historical novels? 'Blackwood's' shook their heads. The 'Globe' newspaper syndicate pointed out that the book lacked love-interest;

Bentley's said comprehensively that it lacked any interest at all. This time the big doctor was really sunk into the depths. For nearly a year the manuscript went its rounds: until, in November of '88, he sent it to Longmans, where it was read by Andrew Lang.

And Longmans accepted it, though they warned him the book might have to be pruned for the somewhat curious reason that it was 170 pages longer than Mr. Rider Haggard's *She*. Jubilant again, he went to London and had lunch with Andrew Lang at the Savile Club.

"Decimus Saxon," chuckled the lean Scots critic, "is a grand character! A bonny character! I warn you, though: They'll say you got him from Scott's Dugald Dalgetty in *A Legend of Montrose*. Tush! I know you didn't. But the dear, good critics, damn 'em!"

Returning to Southsea, he waltzed round the room with Touie; but gently, because Touie was expecting a child, their first child, early in the new year; and he no longer felt any wish (for the moment, at least) to leave Southsea. Since Longmans seemed inclined to hasten the publication of *Micah*, he now speculated as to which would first make its debut: *Micah* or the new baby.

He was not long left in doubt. The howls of Mary Louise Conan Doyle, named after the Ma'am and Touie, were heard at the end of January, 1889. Her father, who attended Touie as he had dealt with hundreds of other confinements, confessed himself awestruck and bewildered when the child was his own. To the Ma'am (he had given her no final bulletins about Touie's condition, causing fury in Yorkshire) he sent a description of the two noses, Mary Louise's and Touie's, over the horizon of the coverlet, and of Mary Louise's red head in a red hood.

"She is fat and plump, blue eyes, bandy legs, and a fat body. Any other points will be answered on inquiry.

I have had no great practice in describing babies. But her manners are painfully free. When she doesn't like a thing she says so, and they know it all down the street."

Micah Clarke, with its dedication to the Ma'am, was published late in February. The author was apprehensive. Deep inside him he distrusted these 'dear, good critics.' But he need not have worried. The critical reception of *Micah Clarke* was so enthusiastic as to have turned the head of anyone less simply convinced that he could do good work. Notice after triumphant notice, including that one dissenting voice from the 'Athenaeum,' he pasted into the big leather-bound scrap-book. And he knew what he wanted to write, now.

Observe how his tone changes, after uncertainty.

"I have been thinking," he had said, before *Micah's* publication, "of trying a Rider Haggardy kind of book called *The Inca's Eye*, dedicated to all the bad boys of the Empire, by one who sympathizes with them. I think I could write a book of that sort con amore. The notable experiences of John H. Calder, Ivan Boscovitch, Jim Horscroft, and Major General Pengelly Jones in their search after the Inca's Eye. How's that for an appetite-whetter?"

But this was only froth, one of a hundred darting ideas. True, it was a very real side of his nature. He could have sat down and turned out the book with enormous zest. But it was only one side of him. It was akin to the popular doctor who had now become captain of the Portsmouth Cricket Club, Vice-President of the Liberal Unionists, Secretary of the Literary and Scientific Society, and at football what the local newspaper called "one of the safest Association backs in Hampshire."

Yet still another man, the inmost one, sat upstairs in the little study which Touie and Mother Hawkins had prepared for him at the top of the house. It was the man who, as a slight intellectual exercise over the week-end, would set down a complete précis of Thiers on the French Revolution or Prescott on the history of Peru. For over a year, now, he had been deeply immersed in a study of the Middle Ages. And then, with sudden clarity, he made a great discovery.

If he might not believe in any religion, he could believe in a creed, a code, a pattern of behaviour. He found it here, among the broken arches and buried swords of the Middle Ages. It could be expressed in two words: knightly honour.

Every instinct, every filament stretching back to his boyhood and beyond to his ancestry, led him towards it. "Fearless to the strong; humble to the weak." "Chivalry towards all women, of high or low degree." "Help to the helpless, whosoever shall ask for it." "And to this I pledge my knightly word."

About the full-flowering of chivalry, in the age of Edward the Third, he had no illusions. He saw its brutality, its grime, its pain. But, stripped of the brutality, the code remained. Its root was honour; and each of its laws became an article of faith which might strengthen and sustain as powerfully as any religion. It was a perfectly practicable code even in this age of Birmingham factories and billycock hats. "And to this," he might himself have added, "I pledge my knightly word."

This is what we must understand if we are to see the inner character of Arthur Conan Doyle. Of this code he seldom spoke or wrote except in the abstract sense. It was too sacred. But it affected all who met him. They felt it, even when they could not express it. Many could and did express it, as we shall see; and each applied to it the same word. When he went out into the great world, and towered up against meanness or injustice,

millions who never met him could hear the fervour of
that code just as they felt it in his books. It explains why
the book he loved best was the one he now prepared to
write—*The White Company*.

It explains, too, the vast labour of research which went
into this story. At Easter, in '89, he paid a visit to the
New Forest, not far from his home, and stayed at a
house on Emory Down. His companions were General
Drayson, Mr. Boulnois, and Dr. Vernon Ford of the
Portsmouth Eye Hospital. It was only a brief holiday, for
walks by day and a rubber of whist at night. But he returned there alone, with a carrier's cart of more books
on the Middle Ages, and shut himself up until autumn.
While he studied, the plan of the story took shape in his
mind.

In addition to setting forth his creed, he had certain
theories to express about these knights and these bow-
men who fought under the golden leopards of the
Plantagenets. Scott, it was true, had depicted the archer.
But Scott, using the same artistic license with which he
clad his knights in armour of a century later than the
date of *Ivanhoe*, had also depicted his mighty archers a
century before the English longbow became a national
institution. It was only in the fourteenth century, when
every boy was taught the use of the bow by the time he
could walk, that the *universality* of this skill triumphed.
It produced the terrible bowman-army which ranged
unconquerable across Europe under the Black Prince.

Nor were the knights, these great paladins out of
Froissart, always the young athletic heroes who rattled
their shields in fiction. More than youth, more than
strength, counted craft in the skill of arms. When the
first lances of all Christendom were Chandos of England
and Du Guesclin of France, John Chandos was over
seventy and blind in one eye. Very retiring, these fel-

lows. Very soft-spoken. And yet, when the earth stirred to a slow thunder of armies moving towards each other, the most dreaded device on a shield was still the double-eagle of Du Guesclin or the red pile of Chandos.

While Conan Doyle studied there, at the cottage on Emory Down, his own characters might have risen living in the sun-dusted summer glades of the New Forest, and walked real paths to real places just as he saw them. Each character, he decided, should truly represent some aspect of life in the year 1366. In autumn he returned to Southsea, carrying those voluminous notebooks on *The White Company* which form a bibliography in themselves, and his dream had a short interruption.

The American editor of 'Lippincott's Magazine,' which was published simultaneously by J. B. Lippincott in Philadelphia and Ward, Lock in London, had read *A Study in Scarlet* and wanted another Sherlock Holmes novel to publish complete in one issue. Could Dr. Conan Doyle dine with him in London and discuss the matter? It was too good an opportunity to miss. At dinner, where he met a genial Oscar Wilde not yet crazed by stage-success, Conan Doyle promised to write the novel. And *The Sign of the Four* later appeared in both the English and the American 'Lippincott's' for February, 1890.

He himself preferred to call it *The Sign of Four*. But let us take the liberty of calling it by its stealthier, more euphonious title. We note, without surprise, that he made not a single contemporary reference to *The Sign of the Four* in letter, notebook, or diary. He was too engrossed in *The White Company*. He did make casual mention of it to a reporter from the London 'Echo,' who interviewed him at Southsea at the end of September, '89, but only as an afterthought.

"Dr. Conan Doyle," wrote the 'Echo,' "is hard at

work on a new historical novel, which he believes will break fresh ground in fiction. He is enthusiastic over this new task, and when he does lay it aside it is only to revise the proofs of *The Firm of Girdlestone*,"—which was at last to achieve publication—"or to write a tale for 'Lippincott's Magazine,' whose editor, Mr. Stoddart, has just returned to the States."

In *The Sign of the Four*, we notice, Watson's memory begins to play tricks. But, whatever this book may prove about Holmes and Watson, it throws a very clear light on the thoughts of the man who created them.

"Let me recommend this book," rather startlingly observes Sherlock Holmes, "one of the most remarkable ever penned. It is Winwood Reade's *The Martyrdom of Man*."

That was Conan Doyle speaking through the mouth of Holmes. He could not help himself. *The Martyrdom of Man*, which he had read during the previous spring, so deeply impressed him that he set down two closely written pages of comments. "Winwood Reade," he summed up, "considers that the true tendency is more and more away from a personal God—a god of reflected human ideas—and towards an unthinkable, impersonal force. Let us concentrate our attention more on serving our poor-devil neighbour and improving our own hearts!"

Such sentiments, perhaps, might have sounded not incongruous from Sherlock Holmes himself. And don't you hear in them, very clearly, the trumpets of *The White Company*?

It might be remarked, in passing, that *The Sign of the Four* (in England at least) had no success. When it was published in book-form by Spencer Blackett, in the spring of 1890, it faded away with scarcely more critical attention than had attended *A Study in Scarlet*. Two full years were to elapse before anyone issued a second edition. More than this, the author had already written the better part of a three act-play in which Dr. Watson . . . but we shall come to that presently.

In the little study upstairs, with its light-blue wallpaper and the bear's skull on the desk, he laboured at the writing of *The White Company*. First of all he had exalted an ideal. Then he was caught by the compelling power of the story. It was as though he were again in the New Forest at midsummer, where all the people of his imagination took life.

Along the road to Christchurch swaggered Samkin Aylward, true type of the archer who at a hundred and fifty yards' distance could split the wooden peg which fastened the centre of the target. Out of Beaulieu Abbey the horrified monks expelled big John of Hordle, all fist and grin. From Beaulieu, into a turbulent world he had never before seen, came young Alleyne Edricson, the student, of the old Saxon line. And these three, along a road of adventure, met and swore friendship before they went to the wars under the five roses of Sir Nigel Loring.

Now this, of course, is the pattern of all the great romantic sagas from the adventures of Tyl Eulenspiegel to *The Cloister and the Hearth*. It is unnecessary to comment on the stirring qualities of *The White Company*; its sweep from Hampshire to France and Spain, its humour, its sword-fights and battle-dust. Where Conan Doyle rises above everyone except Scott is this: that he meant every word he wrote. What his characters would have done, *he* would have done. And did do, until the end of his life.

That is why it has the true ring, the blade that weighs in the hand and is not dead metal. Little Sir Nigel—ageing, bald, gentle-voiced, with his squire Alleyne Edricson —would have ridden on any venture, however mad, to right a wrong or to gain honour. Nor must we confuse this quality with the quality known as sportsmanship or fair play, though one is derived from the other. Sportsmanship is passive: it takes no advantage and does not cheat. Chivalry is active: it attacks; it lashes out. If we seek for fair play, with no idealism about it, we must look among the steel caps of the archers, to Hordle John and Samkin Aylward, tramping a French road and no whit ashamed of feeling proud of their country.

"We are free Englishmen," shouts Aylward. That word 'free' echoes back with sad nostalgia in this year 1948. Yet it was true of Sam Aylward. It was true of those other eternal English types, Sam Johnson and Sam Weller. It was true of Conan Doyle, who gloried in his patriotism and all the things that made England great. Indeed, it is the second force which drives and burns through *The White Company* and its author.

For him the early months of 1890 were darkened by the death of his sister Annette, who had been named for Aunt Annette. On the other hand, there was warmth at home. The baby, Mary Louise, was christened according to the rites of the Church of England. The Ma'am, herself now a convert to the Church of England, had hurried down from Yorkshire to supervise the christening. Touie, sighing, admired the cleverness with which she attended to every detail.

Her husband worked through spring and into summer. A sense of exultation, a feeling that some destiny had been fulfilled, rose in him when he wrote the last page early in July. "That's done it!" he said, and threw his pen across the room at the blue wall-paper, where it splashed ink and fell. A few days later he was writing to Lottie:

"You will be pleased, I am sure, to know that I have finished my great labour, and that *The White Com-*

pany has come to an end. The first half is very good, the second quarter pretty good, and the last quarter very good again. So rejoice with me, dear, for I am as fond of Hordle John and Samkin Aylward and Sir Nigel Loring as though I knew them in the flesh, and I feel that the whole English-speaking race will come in time to be fond of them also."

He sent the manuscript to James Payn. Payn, chary of praise and still more chary of historical novels, immediately accepted *The White Company* as a serial for 'Cornhill,' and pronounced it the best historical novel since *Ivanhoe*. As for the author, black reaction and restlessness set in.

The public picture of Dr. Conan Doyle of Southsea, with his broadening face and bushier moustache, was that of a casual stalwart without a nerve in his body. In point of fact, he was all nerves. But he would have died rather than let this show in public, or say one outward word of praise for his own novels. At the same time, what of the future?

What was he doing? Where was he going? Eight years in Southsea! Aside from the publication of *Girdlestone*, *Cloomber*, and two books of short-stories, he had written *A Study in Scarlet*, *Micah Clarke*, *The Sign of the Four*, and *The White Company*. And what, so far, had it got him? A few hundred pounds in savings; no more.

Towards the end of October, when a great splashing of press reports announced that Dr. Koch of Berlin had found a cure for tuberculosis, he packed his bag and hurried away to Berlin to investigate. He had no particular interest in tuberculosis, though it had touched Elmo Welden in the old days. It was merely something to do, an outlet for restlessness.

He did, in fact, utter the first word of warning in the English press against this alleged cure, which brought poor sufferers flocking to Berlin and sometimes dying in the train. He emphasized it still more in an article he wrote for W. T. Stead's 'Review of Reviews'; "It would be an encouraging of false hopes to pretend that the result is in any way assured."

And this stimulus of the outside world, among the medical men who thronged and chattered in the long grey Hygiene Museum in the Kloster Strasse, revived with a rush his old ambition. Why not leave Southsea? Why not go to Vienna, study the eye, and return to practise in London as an eye-surgeon, keeping the writing as his potentially large source of income? In November he put the proposition before a rather startled Touie, sitting at her needlework before the fire.

"But when should we go, Arthur?"

"Immediately!" said her husband, who would have started for Timbuctoo at five minutes' notice. "Now!"

"With winter coming on?"

"Of course, my dear. Why not? Leave everything to me!"

Mary Louise, who could now walk if you held to her sash, was old enough to be left with Grandmother Hawkins. The furniture could be sold or stored. As for the medical practice, so dwindled with much of his time given to writing, that could be left to dissolve. Yet the roots of eight years are not wrenched up without pain.

The bust of his grandfather, the pictures and the vases, he carefully packed up against harm. It gave him a twinge to see that fine red stair-carpet, now far from new, rolled up at the foot of the stairs in the marbly-papered hall. So many old ties had been broken. Young Annette was gone; Aunt Jane, Grand-Uncle Michael Conan were gone too. Uncle Dick, lionized both as artist and socialite, the 'My dear Doyle' of the Prince of Wales, taken with another fit of apoplexy on the steps of the Athenaeum, had passed beyond recall since the end of '83.

Touie was cheerfully ready for the new venture. "Arthur," she had once written, "wants me to be up and off with him, so I must be quick." The Portsmouth Literary and Scientific Society, we learn from the 'Portsmouth Times' of December 13th, gave him a farewell banquet. In the chair was the president, Dr. James Watson. Dr. Watson—it makes topsy-turvy reading across the years—paid tribute to his friend Dr. Conan Doyle; and the company sang, 'Auld Lang Syne.'

In the days before leaving, he was amazed at the number of the friends and patients who crowded into number 1 Bush Villas to shake their hands. One old woman, a patient who remembered how often the doctor had forgotten to send a bill, brought him her most cherished possession. It was a blue-and-white dinner-plate, which her seaman-son had brought from the Khedive's Palace after the bombardment of Alexandria. It was all she had, she explained; but she wanted the doctor to have it. He could not keep his eyes from blinking.

On a day late in December, 1890, a four-wheeler stood at the door. Their trunks were strapped to its roof. In Elm Grove, the snow was falling past curtainless windows. Once or twice he thought, as he handed Touie into the cab, how much he had tried here and how little he had succeeded in the world. But he put the thought aside, his arm round Touie, as the cab moved away into the snow.

VI

SUNRISE:

The Triumph of Detection

Sherlock Holmes!

Hardly a year later, in December of 1891, the name of Dr. A. Conan Doyle was already famous. The sixth of his new short-stories, *The Man with the Twisted Lip*, had appeared in the December number of the 'Strand Magazine.' Some maintained (and still maintain) it was the best adventure, despite that curious business of Dr. Watson's Christian name. Who could resist it?

In the dim light of the lamp I saw him sitting there, an old briar pipe between his lips, his eyes fixed vacantly upon the corner of the ceiling, the blue smoke curling up from him, silent, motionless, with the light shining upon his strong-set aquiline features.

That lean figure drawn by Sidney Paget, became as familiar as the Strand horse-buses, white or green or chocolate-coloured according to their destination, which rumbled through mud by day and under blue sputtering arc-lamps at night. On the tops of these buses, where no lady dared venture because the driver would turn round and address wicked remarks to the passengers, the driver now made quips about Sherlock Holmes. He shared them with Mr. J. M. Barrie's skit in the 'Speaker,' and with the column-writer who called himself (regrettably) Luke Sharp. But what about the author himself?

Friends of Dr. and Mrs. Conan Doyle knew that they had returned from Vienna late in March, '91, after the doctor had attended eye-lectures and visited Landholt at Paris. In London, together with Mrs. Hawkins and the child, they took lodgings at number 23 Montague Place, Russell Square. In Devonshire Place, among the fashionable physicians, Dr. Conan Doyle then set up as an eye-specialist. Not a single patient ever rang his bell.

After a bout of influenza which nearly ended his life, he made the decision, long under doubt and hesitation, to give up medicine and live entirely by his writing. In June he found a large gabled red-brick house at South Norwood, where he could presently support not only his own family but his sisters as well.

For there was good reason to think success possible.

Brown-bearded Mr. George Newnes, who amassed a fortune out of 'Tit-Bits,' had recently started a magazine called the 'Strand.' Mr. Newnes was that same editor of 'Tit-Bits'—"Put up stakes for a bet; I dare you!"—whom Conan Doyle had challenged in '84.

Whether or not Conan Doyle remembered this does not appear. But it is now history how the young doctor, through his very able literary agent, A. P. Watt, sent to the 'Strand' a short-story called *A Scandal in Bohemia*. Henceforward we can study the life of Sherlock Holmes —with new data—through his creator's letters.

It is customary to say that he planned twelve short-stories, the same twelve which later comprised *The Adventures of Sherlock Holmes*. But he had no such lengthy project in mind. Between the beginning of April and the beginning of August, 1891, he sent off six stories. And these six were all he intended to write.

The acting editor of the 'Strand,' under Newnes's watchful eye, was the shrewd, bespectacled, heavily moustached Greenhough Smith. Greenhough Smith paid the new author on an average of £35, less agent's fee, for each story. That money, with his savings and his novels, should mean reasonable security at the bank. When *A Scandal in Bohemia* appeared in the July number of the 'Strand,' and Holmes blazed into popularity before autumn, the editor was quick to ask for more stories; and Conan Doyle refused.

For he had more interesting matters on hand.

To begin with, he rejoiced in his new house at number 12 Tennison Road, South Norwood. With its window-frames painted white against dark-red brick, its balcony over the front door, its walled garden, the house stood in semi-rural country where you might breathe the air of the distant Surrey Hills. Nearer at hand loomed the Crystal Palace. There was a deep garden in which Mary Louise could play. Next year, he decided, he would have a tennis-lawn. Always fascinated by new contraptions, he had bought a tandem tricycle; in a noble vision he saw himself and Touie dashing about the countryside, covering as much as thirty miles in a day.

Now, throwing aside frock coat and suave professional mannerisms, he could inflate his chest deeply. He was a free man.

Most important of all was the question of his serious literary work. *The White Company*, still appearing as a serial in 'Cornhill,' would be published at the end of the year. He knew, he felt in his bones, it would be a success. And for nearly a year he had been planning a new historical novel. This new novel should be based partly on memoirs of the court of Louis the Fourteenth, and partly on the work of the American historian Parkman. From the court of the Grand Monarch it should move across the Atlantic, to black Canadian forests echoing with the war-whoop of the Iroquois. Its heroes were to be the Huguenots, the French Puritans. At such a date, say 1685, he could bring back Micah Clarke and Decimus Saxon. He could. . . .

Meanwhile, the editor of the 'Strand Magazine' was growing frantic.

Most of his six Holmes stories had been used. Something must be done, in this month of October, if the series were to continue into 1892. Even aside from old gentlemen in clubs, the very lady-readers were singing a hymn of Sherlock Holmes.

" 'The Strand,' " Conan Doyle wrote to the Ma'am on October 14th, '91, "are simply imploring me to continue Holmes. I enclose their last letter."

And here he hesitated. After all, he *had* been well paid for those tales. On the other hand, he was almost ready to begin work on his Franco-Canadian book, tentatively called *The Refugees*. To write half-a-dozen Holmes tales would be to put off everything he really wanted to do; and he chafed at such delay. Could he ask the 'Strand' a price so high, in fact so formidably steep, that the matter would be settled one way or the other?

"And so," he continued to the Ma'am," I will write by this post to say that if they offer me £50 each, *irrespective of length*"—the italics are his own—"I may be induced to consider my refusal. Seems rather high-handed, does it not?"

Whether they thought it high-handed does not appear. But a letter darted back by return of post, agreeing to his terms. And when could they have a copy, please, since the matter was urgent?

"I had called upon my friend Sherlock Holmes upon the second morning after Christmas, with the intention of wishing him the compliments of the season. He was lounging on the sofa in a purple dressing gown. . . ."

So began the seventh adventure, while the author shut his eyes and groped for Holmes's state of mind. In South Norwood, autumn gales sent the leaves flying along that secluded road. "Our house was quite shaken, and I thought the windows were coming in." He developed the habit of working in the mornings from eight until noon. At evening, from five until eight, the lamp burned in his study to the left of the front door.

"In the last week," he wrote at the end of October, "I have done two of the new Sherlock Holmes stories— *The Adventure of the Blue Carbuncle* and *The Adventure of the Speckled Band*. The latter is a thriller. I see my way through the ninth, so that I should not have much trouble with the rest."

In all the clamour, Holmes had no more devoted follower than the Ma'am. To her he had sent the proof-sheets of every novel or story since he began to write; her criticism he deeply and sincerely valued. The Ma'am, herself eagerly plot-spinning, now sent him an idea for a Holmes story. It should concern a girl with beautiful golden hair: who, kidnapped and her hair shorn, should be made to impersonate some other girl for a villainous purpose.

"I don't see my way through the golden-hair episode," he confessed. "But if any fresh light dawns on you, you must let me know."

In the worst of wet weather, which for the most part kept the whole family indoors, he continued his task. On the eleventh of November he was able to report to the Ma'am that he had completed the *Noble Bachelor*, the *Engineer's Thumb*, and the *Beryl Coronet*, all but one of the stories he had promised. He expressed his belief that the stories were up to standard, and that the twelve together ought to make a rather good book of its sort.

"I think," he added casually, "of slaying Holmes in the last and winding him up for good and all. He takes my mind from better things."

This suggestion of killing Sherlock Holmes, first propounded before the end of 1891, struck the Ma'am with horror. "You won't!" she raged. "You can't! You *mustn't*!" Troubled and indecisive, he asked what he could do. She replied, as sharply as though he had again been ten years old, that he could use her golden-hair idea.

So the golden hair of the Ma'am's devising became the less spectacular chestnut hair of Miss Violet Hunter; fat Mr. Jephro Rucastle smiled and smiled in his ugly whitewashed house; and Conan Doyle ended the series with *The Adventure of the Copper Beeches*. Holmes's life had been saved by the Ma'am.

To the author this was the smallest of concerns. While he was at work on the Holmes stories, he received his copies of *The White Company* and the earliest reviews from the press. And the press-notices were disappointing enough to disgust anybody with Sherlock Holmes.

It was not, as he explained, that the critics were hostile to *The White Company*. But they praised it for its qualities as a book of adventure, a roaring story, "whereas I have striven to draw the exact types of character of the folk then living." They did not see it as the first book to depict the most important figure in English military history, her bowman-soldier. It fretted him.

In December he commenced *The Refugees*, and wrote a hundred and fifty pages before the Christmas holidays. He discarded his notion of re-introducing Micah Clarke and Decimus Saxon, as being perhaps too much of a good thing. Instead he centred attention on Amory De Catinat, a Huguenot captain of the King's Guard at Versailles; and Amos Green, a stout woodsman from the

English provinces of America. In addition to all this, he undertook to do a 50,000-word short-novel for Arrow-smith.

At *The Refugees*, to begin with, his enthusiasm failed. It was neither very good, he thought, nor very bad. Somehow, he believed, he could not strike a diamond-sparkle from the court of the Grand Monarch. Those notices of *The White Company* weighted his mind. "You see," he explained to the Ma'am, "I have read and pondered over it for a year, and it has got to be done, so I don't know that waiting will help me. It seems to me most critics don't know the difference between good work and bad." At other times his gusto would take fire, his face would light up, and he would hasten to read the latest pages to Touie and Connie.

The decorative sister Connie, less haughty but large-eyed and even prettier, made her home with them now. Suitors had pursued her all over Europe; more than once she thought she wanted to marry, but always backed out. "Not for the world," her brother several times declared, in almost the same words, "would I interfere. If you love him, that's an end of it. But—he has no brains, my dear."

Connie could manipulate the typewriter, another contraption he had bought at Southsea but wouldn't use. Next year he hoped Lottie would come to live there as well; he could support them now. Innes, nineteen years old, was not far away at Woolwich, preparing for the Army. Eventually, with that large Victorian love of being surrounded by his family, he hoped to have them all there: except the Ma'am, who sturdily maintained her cottage-independence on the allowance he gave her.

So, with the latest pages of *The Refugees* in his hand, he would hasten into his handsome new drawing-room with its huge red flowers in the carpet, and its vases of pampas-grass on the white-marble mantelpiece. Over that scene falls the light of a lamp shaded by a ruffled silk canopy, one of those shades which seldom took fire because of the glass globe over the oil-flame.

"My word," he wrote to Lottie, about the affairs of Louis the Fourteenth, Madame de Montespan, and Madame de Maintenon, "my word, I give the reader his six shillings' worth of passion! Connie and Touie simply sit with their mouths open when I read it. Talk about love-scenes! It is volcanic."

Then, too, there was the pleasure and excitement of being introduced to the literary world. He was invited to the 'Idlers' ' dinner, where he met the likeable and spectacled Jerome K. Jerome, author of *Three Men in a Boat* and now editor of the 'Idler'; the explosive Robert Barr, Jerome's assistant; and J. M. Barrie, whose *A Window in Thrums* he already admired. They were large dinners, never remarkable for teetotalism, and above the table in a cloud of fourpenny-shag rose the eternal strains:

"For he's a jolly good fellow. . . ."

because in the Guardsman-like doctor, with his curling moustache, and his huge face now so rounded that the whole head appeared round, they found an ideal companion. When Conan Doyle laughed, it was with no ultra-refined mirth; he laughed infectiously, and people at the other end of the table joined in without knowing why.

With Barrie—"about whom," as he wrote, "there is nothing small except his body"—he struck up a friendship at once. It was the same with Jerome and Robert Barr. Soon afterwards Barrie dined at Norwood and invited him, for the coming spring, to visit Kirriemuir: the 'little red town' in Scotland which was Barrie's Thrums.

Conan Doyle finished *The Refugees* early in 1892. Whatever he may have thought of the first part, the adventure-scenes in the great forests have never been surpassed for sheer vividness and power of action. They have diabolical reality, as though painted Indian-faces really did look through a suburban window. The stalking and slaying of Brown Moose, a scene done entirely in whispers except for the sudden thud and burst of laughter at the end; the Iroquois war-parties flitting across the light as they gather; the final attack on the stockade and then the blockhouse: it is an uneven book, but there are seven chapters which stand alone.

By this time the author expressed himself as 'fairly satisfied.' And, with regard to the American market, he added a significant word:

"If I, a Britisher, can draw their early types so as to win their approval I should indeed be proud," he told the Ma'am. "By such international associations nations are drawn together, and on the drawing together of these two nations depends the future history of the world." He wrote that in January, 1892.

It was Barrie, preoccupied with Toole's production of his own first play, *Walker, London*, who again roused Conan Doyle's fondness for the theatre. From his short-story *A Straggler of '15*, he adapted and intensified the one-act play which came to be known as *Waterloo*.

Out of *Waterloo* leers a single dominating character: the corporal, now aged ninety, who once drove a powder-cart through burning hedges to the Guards at Hougoumont. Nearly deaf, querulous ("It wouldn't ha' done for the Dook!"), Gregory Brewster yet chuckles in all his old bones when he remembers how the Prince Regent once gave him a medal, and rejoices when the young artillery-sergeant calls on him.

"I've called as the spokesman of my mates at the gun-

ners' barracks," says the sergeant, "to say we are proud
to have you in the town, sir."

"That were what the Regent said," cries the delighted
old man. " 'The ridgment is proud of ye,' he says. 'And
I am proud of the ridgment,' says I. 'And a damned
good answer, too,' says he, and he and Lord Hill bust
out a-laughin'."

Anyone connected with the stage could have seen
that this was an actor's ideal of a character-part, from
the first shuffling entrance to the thundering dream-voice
out of the lungs of a dying man: "The Guards need
powder, and by God they shall have it!" Barrie wanted
to use it as a curtain-raiser; but they both decided
against that. Greatly daring, Conan Doyle sent it to his
boyhood theatrical idol, Henry Irving.

There was an immediate reply from Bram Stoker, the
great man's secretary, another athletic Irishman of con-
vivial tastes. (In Bram Stoker's own admirable biography of Irving, by the way, only the theatrical background prevents a reader from being convinced that
Bram Stoker is Dr. Watson writing about Sherlock
Holmes.) In any event, the monarch of the English stage
bought the copyright of *Waterloo*; and its author attained yet another ambition.

During all these months, at his work, nothing disturbed him. No intrusion was noticed. Small Mary
Louise crawled all over his desk and tore the manuscript
of *The Refugees*. When week-end guests wanted to take
indoor photographs of him at work, he did not merely
pose at writing. The flashlight powder glared and
banged like a cannon; dense white smoke drifted
through the room as it continued to bang; his pen travelled on without pause.

This, however, must be amended. One thing did dis-
turb him. It was the first of another series of notes

bearing the letter-head of the 'Strand Magazine'; and his roar of exasperation could be heard throughout the house.

"They have been bothering me for more Sherlock Holmes tales," he told the Ma'am in February, 1892. "Under pressure I offered to do a dozen for a thousand pounds, but I sincerely hope that they won't accept it now."

But they did accept it, immediately. And the author paused to reflect.

However modest this sum may now seem for a series which was to include *Silver Blaze*, *The Reigate Squires*, and *The Naval Treaty*, it was a very large payment in the year 1892. It somewhat dazed him; he could not get used to being a celebrity, because he felt no different.

On careful consideration, he believed he could work up enough material for the new series. He warned the 'Strand,' nevertheless, that they could not expect the stories at once. He had promised Arrowsmith a Napoleonic novel, copy to be delivered by August, and he intended to take a holiday in Norway with his wife. Though a story or two might be done at odd times, most of them must wait until later in the year.

One gusty morning in his study, the same bewilderment in his mind, he rummaged among old papers (which he seldom destroyed) and brought out three exercise-books bound in thick cardboard.

Waterloo, it may be said, was not his first piece of writing for the stage. What he held now was a three-act play called *Angels of Darkness*. He had written the first two acts at Southsea in 1889, the third in 1890, when Sherlock Holmes seemed of no interest to anybody. *Angels of Darkness* is chiefly a reconstruction of the Utah scenes in *A Study in Scarlet*; the whole action takes place in the United States. Holmes does not even appear in it. But Dr. John H. Watson does very much appear.

Angels of Darkness is full of thorns for any kind of commentator. The biographer, in theory at least, should be as relentless as Gradgrind; he should not indulge in those glorious Holmes-Watson speculations which have caused controversy on both sides of the Atlantic. But the devil of temptation prods horribly. Anyone who turns over the pages of *Angels of Darkness*, then, will be electrified to find that Watson has been concealing from us many important episodes in his life.

Watson, in fact, once practised medicine in San Francisco. And his reticence can be understood; he acted discreditably. Those who have suspected Watson of black perfidy in his relations with women will find their worst suspicions justified. Either he had a wife before he married Mary Morstan, or else he heartlessly jilted the poor girl whom he holds in his arms as the curtain falls on *Angels of Darkness*.

The name of the girl? There lies our difficulty. To give her name, a well-known one, would be to betray the author as well as the character. At best it would impeach Watson in matters other than matrimonial; at worst it would upset the whole saga, and pose a problem which the keenest deductive wits of the Baker Street Irregulars could not unravel.

Conan Doyle, leafing through *Angels of Darkness* in his Norwood study in 1892, knew he must put aside that play forever. There were good things in it, notably the comic scenes not present in *A Study in Scarlet*; but a play about Watson without Sherlock Holmes would now leave the public aghast; and it has not been published even yet.

In March, together with Barrie and "an athletic sporting ruddy-haired youth," Arthur Quiller-Couch, he went down to pay a call on George Meredith at Box Hill. The Old Master, afflicted with some nervous complaint which made his gait unsteady, wabbled down the path and in true Meredithian prose sang them a song of welcome at the gate. A courtly, excitable little man with a spike of grey beard, he talked mainly of war; and fired off a number of anecdotes from the reminiscences of General Marbot, then just published in English. Conan Doyle, though listening eagerly on one of his favourite subjects, was not quite sure whether he liked Meredith or not.

But now, released for a brief holiday from Norwood, he set off to Scotland for a stop-over at Edinburgh, a visit to Barrie at Kirriemuir, and a week's fishing at Alford in Aberdeenshire. After Edinburgh:

"I went down and lunched with the redoubtable one-legged Henley, the original of John Silver in *Treasure Island.* He is the editor of the 'National Observer,' the most savage of critics, and to my mind one of our first living poets. Then I came up here to Kirriemuir, where I found the Barrie ménage even more extraordinary than that of Henley; but I have been very jolly indeed."

In the little red town of Kirriemuir there was one mystery. The guidfolk, for the life of them, could not understand how Barrie came to have such a reputation in London; aye, and to make money out of books. It was not only perplexing; it was maddening.

"Some people here," observed Conan Doyle, "think that Barrie's fame is due to the excellence of his handwriting. Others think that he prints the books himself and hawks them round London. When he goes for a walk they stalk him, and watch him from behind trees to find out how he does it."

It is a gravity-removing picture: the very small Scot and the very large Irishman, solemnly marching with their large pipes, engrossed in debate on a fifteen-mile walk, and the whiskered faces in Scotch bonnets poked out from behind trees.*

In April he had returned to Norwood, deep in the Arrowsmith novel, which he intended to call *The Great Shadow*. The great shadow was that of Bonaparte; we hear the first drum-tap of the Napoleonic romances. His visit to the coast of Scotland had given him the background for the opening chapters, and the book culminates in a description of the Battle of Waterloo. But Waterloo, as in the one-act play, was to him more than an event in a school-book. It was a part of his own family history, alive down to every colour of uniform or set of shako. More than once he made reference to his forebears on that field.

"Five of us fought there," he said; "and three of us stayed there."

The result, in *The Great Shadow*, is a battle-piece which rings in the ears and stifles the nostrils with gun smoke, as it did with Jack Calder and Jim Horscroft of the 71st Highlanders. There is the very wince of the infantryman as the charging French cuirassiers suddenly tower up out of smoke, the unreal dream-atmosphere known to anyone whose head has sung from a barrage. And in the earlier part of the book, by the wash of the sea-side, the reader will find one of his most effective characters: the man from the sea, the man with the brush of cat's-whisker moustache, the man calling himself De Lapp, who plays a cat's game with the people of that village as his Emperor darts a cat's paw over Europe.

* Barrie, as is now notorious, did not smoke. But he usually appeared with a pipe in public. When later he formed his cricket team, this caused loud complaints from friends who were asked to nurse an empty pipe while he was batting.

By midsummer, when he had finished *The Great Shadow*, he could lounge in the garden at the end of the new tennis-lawn, in a straw hat and a corduroy jacket, and take some kind of assessment.

The White Company had been selling into edition after edition, confirming his belief in the ultimate good judgment of the public. So had *Micah*. But then (he had almost said 'unfortunately') so was the book called *The Adventures of Sherlock Holmes*, which Mr. Newnes had published. It reminded him that he must buckle to work again at the heartless calculating-machine if the new series, as they urged, were to begin in December of this year. So far he had completed only three, *Silver Blaze*, *The Cardboard Box*, and *The Yellow Face*.* Nevertheless, there was at least one Holmes kit which had not appeared in the 'Strand.' Never did Holmes more astound Watson with the keenness of his deduction than in this lost adventure.

"The fact is, my dear Watson, that you are an excellent subject," said he. "You are never blasé. You respond instantly to any external stimulus. Your mental processes may be slow but they are never obscure, and I found during breakfast that you were easier reading than the leader in the 'Times' in front of me."

So remarks Holmes in the obscure affair called *The Field Bazaar*. Of all the Baker Street parodies, it is the only one written by Conan Doyle himself. He did not

---

* Originally, we find in his diary for 1892, called *The Livid Face*. And *The Cardboard Box* was deleted from the *Memoirs of Sherlock Holmes* when published in book-form by Newnes. Anyone who looks up the 'Strand Magazine' for January, 1893, will find that Holmes's famous thought-reading deductions about Henry Ward Beecher and the Civil War (now in *The Resident Patient*) originally appeared in *The Cardboard Box*. Save for its first paragraph, the original version of *The Resident Patient*, as published in the 'Strand' for August, 1893, has a completely different beginning.

write it until four years later for Edinburgh University's magazine, 'The Student,' in aid of the bazaar to enlarge the University's cricket-ground; but it may be mentioned here among the legends and the lore.

To interviewers, who flocked to South Norwood that summer, he gave all the credit for Holmes to Dr. Joseph Bell, whose photograph now stood on the mantelpiece in his study. Dr. Bell quickly and generously disclaimed this:

"Dr. Conan Doyle has, by his imaginative genius, made a great deal out of very little, and his warm remembrance of one of his old teachers has coloured the picture."

"Not at all!" said his old student. "Not at all!"

Thus, concealing the great joke that he loathed Holmes, Conan Doyle gravely assured one interviewer that he did not write more because he feared to spoil a character of whom he was particularly fond; and, continuing the joke, he decided to slip into future stories an occasional clue as to the real identity of that irritating gentleman. (Doubtless, Watson, you have noticed such clues in this narrative?)

Meanwhile, there was another great cause for satisfaction. After more than fifty years' struggle on the part of authors and reputable publishers, the United States Congress had last year voted approval of the International Copyright Act: which gave an author the legal right to his own works, and prevented them from being pirated. It puzzled many people, as it had once maddened Charles Dickens, to understand why America so long refused to join an agreement which was shared by Great Britain, France, Germany, Italy, Spain, and every other civilized nation. Even now Congress hedged it with restrictions. But the form was solid enough to add a large new source of income, from his worth-while novels as well as from American readers who persisted in *their* wrong-headed fondness for Sherlock Holmes.

Domestic life at Norwood moved serenely. Connie, at last, was really in love. She met a twenty-six-year-old journalist named Ernest William Hornung, irreverently known as Willie, with a dapper manner and a knowing way of speech. It pleased Connie's brother, it pleased Touie, to watch these two on the tennis-lawn: Connie with her long skirts gracefully swaying as she dapped at the tennis-ball, Willie in his straw hat and peg-topped white flannels.

As for Touie—well! He could no longer take Touie on those spinning tricycle rides. She was expecting another child in the autumn; and this time, of course, it would be a son. Even those cycling expeditions in the past, he recognized, had been a mistake. Touie was not strong, yet she was so eager to join in his pursuits that she never objected to perching herself up in front of him while he drove away at the tricycle pedals. Once, after a thirty-mile ride, he berated himself in a letter to Lottie for his thoughtlessness in tiring her out.

In any case, Touie was looking forward to their holiday in Norway. They went to Norway in August; and by September, when he had just settled back at work again at Norwood, he received a telegram from Barrie. It was a telegram of such urgency that he hurried to Aldeburgh, in Suffolk, where Barrie was staying; and he found the author of *Auld Licht Idylls* in despair.

"Could you possibly," asked Barrie, "help me out with the libretto of a light opera?"

Barrie, it appeared, had rashly promised to write this opera for D'Oyly Carte, who was to have it produced at the Savoy in the great Gilbert-and-Sullivan tradition. It was to be in two acts: Barrie had written the first, and roughed out the second. But he was ill, his nerves in rags. Would his friend write the lyrics for the second act, and perhaps some of the dialogue?

Conan Doyle took off his coat. True, he knew nothing whatever about light opera. But Barrie wanted help. Besides, he argued to himself, a writer worth his salt should be able to tackle anything from a scientific treatise to a comic song.

"What's it about?" he asked Barrie. "What's the plot?"

"Well, the background is Oxford or Cambridge; I don't say which. The scene is a girls' school."

"A girls' school?"

"Yes; a seminary. The two heroes, one an officer in the Lancers and the other an Oxford undergraduate, get into the bedroom floor of the seminary. . . ."

"Good God!"

"No, no, there's nothing in the least offensive about it. The undergraduate," continued Barrie, with a chuckle which illuminated his face, "is pursued by the Proctor, with two 'bulldogs.' The Proctor hides in a grandfather clock, and sings a duet with the schoolmistress. Just glance over what I've done."

In that same month, while engaged both with Sherlock Holmes and with *Jane Annie, or The Good-Conduct Prize*, Conan Doyle had occasion to write a very different set of verses from the kind in *Jane Annie*. In the press it was announced that Lord Nelson's old flagship, *Foudroyant*, once pride of the British Navy, had been sold to the Germans to be broken up for scrap. Now this was the sort of thing which really did send Conan Doyle into a white rage.

Once before, in America, the same suggestion had been made about the frigate *Constitution*, 'Old Ironsides.' And, as it had inspired Oliver Wendell Holmes with those bitter verses beginning, 'Ay, tear her tattered ensign down—!" so the same of Nelson's flagship moved Conan Doyle, in the press, to address a 'humble petition' to her Majesty's naval advisers with savage satire:

> Who says the Nation's purse is lean,
>   Who fears for claim or bond or debt,
> When all the glories that have been
>   Are scheduled as a cash asset?
> If times are black and trade is slack,
>   If coal and cotton fail at last,
> We've something left to barter yet—
>   Our glorious past.
>
> There's many a crypt in which lies hid
>   The dust of statesman or of king;
> There's Shakespeare's home to raise a bid,
>   And Milton's house its price would bring.
> What for the sword that Cromwell drew?
>   What for Prince Edward's coat of mail?
> What for our Saxon Alfred's tomb?
>   They're all for sale!

Calm and sensible people might have said that this was pure sentimentalism. A piece of wood was a piece of wood; a rusty cannon worth no more than its weight in scrap-metal. What is the good of Lord Nelson, even, when both those eyes are blind in death and he can save our skins no longer? Conan Doyle's reply would have been the same as he flung out in those verses:

> You hucksters, have you still to learn
>   The things that money will not buy?

And that was a part of his philosophy. It is a small incident, perhaps. But it foreshadowed matters that were to come, matters of human justice; it was a part of the character which many years later made Coulson

Kernahan say that he would rather face a pistol at five paces than the blaze of anger, or the cold contempt, in the eyes of Conan Doyle.

He was certainly in no such mood as the year 1892 drew to its close. In October Lottie, the favourite sister, arrived from Portugal to make her home with them; she was dragged everywhere to see everything. In November Touie's second child was born. As the father had hoped, it was a boy.

After much debate they named the boy Alleyne Kingsley, the Alleyne being for Alleyne Edricson in *The White Company*. Each Christmas they liked to invite the children of the neighbourhood to a party, Dr. Conan Doyle being especially fond of dressing up as Father Christmas. But this Christmas, decided the father of Mary Louise and Alleyne Kingsley, the children should have a special treat.

Consequently he spent much time devising a Jabberwock sort of costume, so horrible in appearance that one witness remembers it yet. This, he sincerely believed, would amuse and delight the children as he stalked imposingly in. The result, for everybody except the baby, was blind panic. Afterwards, the father, conscience-stricken, had to sit up most of the night with sobbing four-year-old Mary, assuring her with many gestures that the wicked thing had been chased far away and wouldn't ever return.

Early in 1893, when the new Holmes stories were appearing in the 'Strand' and he was finishing the later ones, he took Touie for a visit to Switzerland. The falls of Reichenbach roared in their ears. And he needed that brief rest. He was exhausted with plot-spinning, harried by the necessity for making ideas grow: a feeling which will readily be understood by any writer who is cheerfully expected to write to a deadline and produce a new trick each time. What he had now was no longer a puppet; it was an Old Man of the Brain locked round him with a windpipe-grip.

At home they were asking him to go on a lecture-tour, and this had great appeal. Writing plays had an appeal, too; Irving must intend to appear in *Waterloo* before long, and the light opera *Jane Annie* went into rehearsal in spring. He favoured both the lecture-platform and the theatre.

But he had another task before that. At Norwood on April 6th, 1893—sitting by the study fire with a cold in his head, idly reading *Pride and Prejudice* while legions of painters bumped the outside of the house—he put aside the book and wrote a letter to the Ma'am.

"All is very well down here," he said. "I am in the middle of the last Holmes story, after which the gentleman vanishes, never to return! I am weary of his name." So Professor Moriarty waited by the black rock; the falls of Reichenbach opened; and, with a happy sigh of relief, he killed Sherlock Holmes.

VII

TRAGEDY:

"We Must Take What Fate Sends"

While readers of the 'Strand Magazine' still had no idea
of the death overhanging Sherlock Holmes, the light
opera *Jane Annie* was produced at the Savoy Theatre
in May, 1893. It failed.

"The opera," wrote one critic, who devoted some
twenty-six closely printed lines to intimating without libel
that the composer had plagiarized the music, "the opera
is one long treat for the eye. There are pretty girls in
deshabille dresses as charming as themselves; pretty girls
in golf dresses; gallant soldiers resplendent in Lancer
uniforms; boating undergraduates; and everything that
can give variety of colour or make grouping picturesque.
Whatever may be said of the work done by others on
Jane Annie, or, The Good-Conduct Prize, that of the
manager deserves nothing but praise."

This sort of back-handed wallop was phrased more
tactfully by another critic calling himself 'The Stroller':

"At the completion of the work," he wrote, "there
were the usual calls, which, however, were not in every
case responded to, and some dissentient noises heard."

Barrie and Conan Doyle were plunged into gloom, but
they tried to cheer each other up and eventually succeeded.

"What I hate about a failure like this," said the latter,
who remembered taking Elmo Welden to the Savoy to
see *Patience* in the old days, "is that you feel somebody's

backed you, and then you've let him down. However, there it is."

He did not add (except to the Ma'am) that he could not accept much responsibility for the failure, since he had written so little of the piece; if it had succeeded, he pointed out, he would have shared the glory. But *could* he write for the stage? At the moment there seemed little prospect of seeing *Waterloo* produced. Irving's company at the Lyceum, after a brilliant season in *Henry VIII*, *Lear*, and Tennyson's *Becket*, went off on an American tour which was to last until the following spring. Nevertheless, he had a multiplicity of interests even aside from an English lecture-tour which was to begin in the autumn.

With his vastly widening fame, the number of his friends had increased to a host. Polite society, discovering that here was another representative of the Doyle ancestry, wished to lionize him. He hastened to avoid this, because it bored him. For titles, as such, he cared nothing. Few things amused him more, then or in later life, than a scandalized debate as to who should precede whom at dinner, and the solemn Japanese ritual attending it. He accepted invitations when courtesy required it, and declined when it did not. He much preferred to argue life and letters with the violent-minded Robert Barr, associate editor of the 'Idler.'* Barr would sit on a wicker chair on the lawn at Norwood, while his host practised golf-strokes directed at a tub rather too near the house.

"He's a golf inebriate," said Barr. "He lands the ball in that tub when he makes the right sort of hit, and generally breaks a window when he doesn't." Or again:

"It'd be easy to interview you," shouted Barr, with his

---

* Barr himself was to write a series of detective tales about a semi-comic investigator named Eugène Valmont.

beard and his watch-chain shaking. "All I'd have to do would be to remember what I thought about any given subject, and then write the opposite, and that would be you. What's your opinion about Rudyard Kipling?"

"A very great short-story writer."

But that was not the opinion of Kipling held by George Meredith, when for the second time Conan Doyle went to see him at Box Hill. The little old man, so shaky on his legs, again entertained his admirer at lunch. Kipling, Meredith said fastidiously, had no refinement. After firing off a number of slanderous remarks about celebrities, including the late Lord Tennyson and the Prince of Wales, Meredith asked his guest's opinion about the opening chapters of an old unfinished novel, called *The Amazing Marriage*. Would his guest like to hear him read the chapters?

They climbed a steep path to the summerhouse, overlooking the Surrey Downs, where Meredith used to write. Conan Doyle walked ahead, his host following. On that difficult path Meredith slithered and fell. His guest knew the old man's pestiferous pride. He knew that Meredith, who bitterly resented any suggestion of being an invalid, would have been humiliated if anyone helped him up. So he appeared to notice nothing, and walked on until Meredith joined him. It was all the deeper an act of courtesy in that Conan Doyle never realized it as such.

In the summer Miss Constance Doyle and Mr. Ernest William Hornung were married. He was a little dubious as to how the newlyweds would make out, since Willie's income was not very satisfactory. But he soothed the Ma'am when *she* worried. "Connie," he said, "will have her allowance." In August, with Touie accompanying him, he went to Switzerland for a lecture at Lucerne on 'Fiction as a Part of Literature.' Everything appeared serene with Dr. and Mrs. Conan Doyle, with all the family, when he commenced his English lecture-tour in the autumn.

Then, into his life, struck black tragedy.

Whatever powers govern this world, they seldom vent their spite without warning. There is a failure before a failure, a blow before a blow. The first warning was the death of his father, early in October of 1893.

As a boy, it is true, he had never been very fond of Charles Doyle. But in maturer years he came to understand what he had once considered indolence and weakness, and above all to admire the genius of the paintings on the wall in his study. It was his ambition (how often he had mentioned it recently!) to make a collection of all his father's work, one day, and to exhibit it in London. Again, true enough, the end had not been unexpected. But there it was: a finality, stark and irreparable. Charles Doyle lived and died a devout Catholic; and as such the clay was committed to earth.

Shortly afterwards, when his son had returned to Norwood, Touie complained of a pain in her side and a cough. He considered it nothing very serious, and sent for Dr. Dalton, who lived near by. Conan Doyle has himself recorded his sense of shock when, as he waited in the hall at Norwood, the grave-faced doctor came down from the bedroom and told him the verdict.

Touie had tuberculosis. With her background and medical history, there could be little hope of a permanent cure. It was what was then known as galloping consumption, rapid and wasting; the doctor gave her only a few months to live.

"You'll want a second opinion, of course?" asked Dr. Dalton.

"If you don't mind, yes. Sir Douglas Powell?"

"The very man I was about to suggest."

Tuberculosis. First Elmo Welden, a dim image. Now Touie, who had become so much a part of his life that her absence seemed unthinkable. He showed his state of mind best when he wrote to the Ma'am after the specialist's visit.

"I am afraid," he said, "we must reconcile ourselves to the diagnosis. I had Douglas Powell out on Saturday and he confirmed it. On the other hand he thought that there were signs of fibroid growth round the seat of the disease and that the other lung had enlarged somewhat to compensate. He seemed to think that the mischief must have been going on for years unobserved, but if so it must have been very slight."

His own instinct was to fight. He would *not* yield to this intolerable verdict. He and Touie, he wrote in the same letter, must leave as soon as possible for St. Moritz or Davos, where the climate would give her a chance. If she did well in Switzerland during the winter, they might try Egypt in the spring. As for the Norwood house, it could stay as it was or be sold up; he himself would stay with Touie, taking his work with him.

"We must take what Fate sends, but I have hopes that all may yet be well. Touie drives out on fine days and has not lost much flesh." And then, completely confused and at sea: "Goodbye, Ma'am; many thanks for your kind sympathy. What with Connie's wedding, Father's death, and Touie's illness, it's a little overwhelming."

Though Powell and Dalton were at first inclined to favour St. Moritz, they eventually decided on Davos. At Davos, in a valley of the High Alps, sheltered from all wind and full of sunshine, Touie's life might be spared for some time. By the end of November, with Lottie and the two children, they were living at Kurhaus Hotel, Davos. Touie herself was so cheerful and uncomplaining that sometimes it made her husband ashamed of his own depressed mood.

Being out of England, he did not hear the full clamour which greeted the end of Sherlock Holmes in the 'Strand' for December. But we can scarcely wonder that it made him still more disgusted with his most famous character. Here he was with a real tragedy on his hands, while letters of anger or protest or abuse poured in on him; and, in London, sporting young City men went to their offices with crape bands tied round their hats for the death of Sherlock Holmes.

Settling down to work again, under the high white mountains, his thoughts took only one direction. This was when he wrote *The Stark Munro Letters*: no 'story,' as he was known to do a story, but largely autobiographical. It was a study of the thoughts, hopes, feelings, and above all religious doubts, of a young doctor such as he had been at Southsea.

It is no paradox to find that this book contains some of the best scenes of broad comedy he ever wrote. Humour is often a relief from restraint; more than ever he needed, when he could, to laugh. His old partner Dr. Budd, who appears as Cullingworth, ramps and roars through it. Young Dr. Stark Munro sees, or tries hard to see, at least some Purpose working for good in the universe. Yet gloom is woven into the texture of the book; and at the end, which appears in some editions and not in others, Stark Munro and his wife die in a railway accident.

"I cannot imagine what its value is," he wrote. "It will make a religious sensation if not a literary." He sent the manuscript to Jerome K. Jerome, who serialized it in 'The Idler,' just as Jerome had used several of his medical stories which were shortly to appear in a collection called *Round the Red Lamp*.

Yet despite all gloom, just as he had said, "I have hopes that all may yet be well," so his sanguine temperament rose higher still early in the year 1894. Touie was much better. Every doctor acknowledged it. "I think one more winter," he exclaimed, "might really cure her permanently."

He did not really believe this. He said it as much to reassure himself as to reassure Mrs. Hawkins. At the same time, she was in better health and with sufficient precautions they might keep her in better health for years. It was the most that could be expected; and the headiness of that Alpine air, which exhilarated him as much as it helped Touie, helped to improve his spirits. "When *Stark Munro* is finished," he wrote towards the end of January, "I am going to lead the life of a savage —out all day on Norwegian skis."

Conan Doyle, in fact, was the man who introduced skiing as a sport into Switzerland. "You don't appreciate it as yet," he told guests at the hotel, amid polite sceptical smiles, "but the time will come when hundreds of Englishmen will come to Switzerland for a skiing season." And he said the same thing in the 'Strand' later in the year. Meanwhile, having read Nansen's account, he imported several pairs of skis from Norway.

Wondering villagers, as well as guests on the hotel-verandahs, watched him at his tumbles, gyrations, and leg-swings on the hills. Skis, he complained, were the most treacherous and capricious lengths of wood on earth. "On any man suffering from too much dignity, a course of skis would have a fine moral effect." Two sporting villagers named the Branger brothers, who alone in the Grisons division of Switzerland had ever tried any ski-work, assisted and applauded him.

Late in March he determined to show it was possible to cross the mountains from one snow-isolated villlage to another. Nobody except the brothers Branger had ever attempted this before. The three of them would go from Davos to Arosa, something over twelve miles, across the Furka Pass: about nine thousand feet high. All three were novices who might very well have killed themselves, and very nearly did.

They started at half-past four in the morning, under "a great pale moon in a violet sky, with such stars as can be seen only in the tropics or the higher Alps." By half-past seven, when the sun cleared the peaks and partly blinded them with its glare on white, they were trudging zig-zag through powdery snow. At one point they shuffled sideways along the face of a mountain at a sixty-degree slope, where one mis-step would have sent them over the edge of a thousand-foot chasm. That was where the thin air sang in their ears. Then they were skimming in exhilaration, "the nearest thing to flying," down the other side of the valley, with the toy hotels of Arosa to be seen in the fir woods far below.

Even so, the adventure threatened anti-climax or broken necks. The last long stretch to Arosa resembled a precipice, though it was not quite so steep as that. The Branger brothers, tying their skis together like a toboggan, whizzed down the slope and rolled over, while the waiting inhabitants of Arosa cheered and fastened operaglasses on them all. Conan Doyle, whose toboggan shot from under him, was left stranded. But, seeing the others looking up, he threw himself feet forward and completed a long, majestic descent on the seat of his trousers.

"My tailor," he commented, "tells me that Harris tweed cannot wear out. This is a mere theory and will not stand a thorough scientific test. For the remainder of the day I was happiest when I was nearest the wall." But, when they registered at the hotel in Arosa, a beaming Tobias Branger signed for all three. Under 'Name,' he wrote 'D. Conan Doyle,' and under 'Profession,' he wrote 'Sportesmann,' and D. Conan Doyle seldom received a prouder compliment.

During those first months of 1894, too, he did a good deal of writing. First it was a book called *The Parasite*. Then, inspired, he created a character so heart-warming —who, except Professor Challenger later on, shall compare with Brigadier Gerard?—that we must defer discussion of the Brigadier until Conan Doyle afterwards completed the first series of stories.

By April Touie was so well that she begged to be allowed a visit to England. The Norwood house was still in their possession, with Mrs. Hawkins in charge. Dr. Huggard, the European specialist, thought a visit might be permitted if Touie stayed only a few days before returning to Switzerland. With Touie's condition so much improved, her husband could consider an offer made to him long ago. An American impresario, Major Pond, urged him to go on an American tour, reading selections from his own works, the tour to begin early in October and last until just before Christmas. The prospect of visiting the United States delighted him. If he could leave Touie—

"Of course you can," insisted his faithful sister Lottie, while Touie quickly agreed with only the stipulation that he should return for Christmas. "Anyway," Lottie added, "you couldn't possibly take her."

"No, I couldn't. Half my time, I suppose," he remembered, dismally, the travel-conditions of his English tour, "will be spent in draughty stations at the bleakest time of the year."

"But who are you going to take with you? You've got to take *somebody*. What about Innes?"

It was not a bad idea. Innes, now a straight-backed

Royal Artillery subaltern with luxuriant moustaches, should prove an excellent companion. Conan Doyle spent that summer between the Continent and Norwood, with more good news. Henry Irving, after his own American tour, was ending the summer season at the Lyceum with *Faust*; and, in the autumn, he meant to appear as Corporal Gregory Brewster in Conan Doyle's *Waterloo*.

"You see," confided Bram Stoker, "our difficulty has been how to fit in a play lasting exactly one hour. The Guv'nor," meaning Irving, "plans to do your Waterloo Veteran as a double-bill with *The Bells*. I predict he will be magnificent as old Brewster. We intend to try it out, probably in Bristol, about the end of September."

Consequently the author (with his American sailing-date arranged) could not be there for the opening night. Nevertheless, all the fire of his theatrical ambitions blazed up again. At Norwood he immediately began a full-dress four-act play for Irving and Ellen Terry, taking Willie Hornung into partnership over it.

He was steeped in the lore of the Napoleonic era and the English Regency. Since he had been contemplating a novel with a Regency background, that coloured-print age of the bucks and the dandies, of the coaching-road and the prize-ring, he decided this material should go into the play and be used later for the novel. With Henry Irving as a Regency buck—the lifted quizzing-glass, the posture with one knee advanced, the long lean face above a starched neck-cloth—all the actor's famous mannerisms could turn that character into a kind of demoniac Brummell. This Regency buck should be made a patron of the prize-ring. Thus if all went well, and the plot flowed smoothly, they might have some fine bare-knuckle fights on the stage of the Lyceum.

But the American tour would not wait. Only one act

of the play was finished when the Norddeutscher-Lloyd liner *Elbe* left Southampton late in September. Conan Doyle, in a very small cap, his moustache blowing, stood at the rail beside a straight-backed Innes as the liner's whistle hooted out against the emptiness of Southampton Water.

Both he and Innes were conscious of German hostility aboard that ship. At the captain's dinner, when a dining-saloon thick with German and American flags showed not one British flag, their wrath boiled over. They drew a Union Jack on a piece of paper, and stuck it up above all the others. But he made friends with all the passengers, and wrote to Hornung, "on a cod bank in the Gulf Stream," that he despaired of doing any work on his travels.

Then a voice was shouting, "Dr. Conan Doyle, I presume?" amid the bustle at the New York dock. The hectic whirl began.

New York, though not yet a city of skyscrapers, already towered before English eyes: a city hard and yet sybaritic with its plumbing, its telephones, its electric lights. Its colours, of sky and cloud and building-line, were as sharp and clear as images in a stereoscope. From the Jersey City side the Pennsylvania Limited, said to be the most luxurious train on earth, would whisk you to Chicago in twenty-four hours; you could be shaved aboard the train, or enjoy that new luxury the observation-car. Major J. B. Pond, Conan Doyle's impresario, with his huge head, his large spectacles, and his fan-shaped beard, enfolded the newcomer with enthusiasm.

"Doctor," he said with deep solemnity, "this is going to be a big thing. We'll try you out, before we start west, at the Calvary Baptist Church in West Fifty-Seventh Street."

The church, on the night of October tenth, was packed with his admirers. They came not less to hear him lecture than to see what he looked like. Sartorially absent-minded as usual, he lost his front collar-stud at the last moment and almost walked out on the platform with his tie hanging loose and his collar under one ear. Major Pond rectified this. Hamilton Wright Mabie, who introduced him, painted a gruesome picture of Sherlock Holmes lying dead in the Reichenbach Falls. Then the nervous author rose. The reason for the audience's terrific ovation at the end of 'Readings and Reminiscences' may be deduced in the press-reports.

"The moment the man spoke," wrote the New York 'World,' "Sherlock Holmes would have said he was a 'good fellow'; a generous man, for he spoke in a melodious, hearty, welcoming voice; a modest man, too, for he spoke deprecatingly of himself; modest, also, because of jewellery he showed only a tiny stud and the bar which held in place his watch-chain."

One moment. If anyone here asks in surprise whether the critic expected him to wear an emerald horseshoe or a watch-chain dripping with diamonds, we must remember that this was the age of jewelled adornment and that other British lecturers had appeared in costumes verging on the outlandish.

"He used none of the tricks of elocutionists," continued the 'World,' "very, very few gestures; nor had he any stagy tricks, except that every now and then, involuntarily, he made a motion that fitted the mood of the character of which he spoke or read."

"One wondered, for instance," said the New York 'Tribune,' not without naïveté, "whether he would speak the British or another dialect of the English language. Dr. Doyle solved all such speculations at first sight. His pleasing voice and distinct enunciation mingles the manner of the Scot, the Briton, and the American."

And there we have it.

In the United States of the 'nineties, no type was so detested or derided as that known as the Dude. The dude, whether domestic or English, wore a high collar and a single eyeglass. He spoke in what natives considered a deliberately affected jargon. His manner was very superior. And it was all supposed to originate in England, as in fact it did. But here, not realizing that the dude under another name was also a figure of fun in England, Americans found in Conan Doyle an unaffected speaker, of Irish temperament and Irish gregariousness, whom no stretch of the imagination could call stuck-up. Henceforward the United States claimed him as her own.

He, for his own part, saw straight through the grotesqueness of so much that had been written about America. As the American had a popular conception of the Englishman, so the Englishman had a popular conception of the American as a loud-voiced braggart dividing his time equally between talking about his income and spitting tobacco-juice. The spittoon, in fact, was almost as much an obsession with English observers as the monocle was with American. And the spittoon, like the English dude, did very much exist. Therefore followed the odd Q.E.D. that few Americans could be well educated or have decent manners.

Conan Doyle—whirled out on a mid-Western tour to Chicago, Indianapolis, Cincinnati, then Toledo, Detroit, back to Milwaukee and Chicago—saw a very different picture.

"I have found all the good I expected," he wrote to the Ma'am in a letter headed 'on the cars'; "but the evil things which travellers have said are all lies and nonsense. The women are not as attractive as we had been told. The children are bright and pretty, though there is a tendency to spoil them. The race as a whole is not only the most prosperous, but the most even-tempered, tolerant, and hopeful that I have ever known. They have to meet their own problems in their own way, and I fear it is precious little sympathy they ever get from England in doing it."

He was even more emphatic in a letter to his friend Sir John Robinson:

"By Jove! when I see all these folk, with their British names and British tongue, and when I consider how far they have been allowed to drift from us, I feel as if we ought to hang a statesman to every lamp post in Pall Mall. We've got to go into partnership with them or be overshadowed by them. The centre of gravity of the race is over here, and we have got to readjust ourselves."

"Drift from us" was the right term for that moment. The young Republic and the old Empire, in one of their recurring phases of bad feeling, were growling at each other. It was exacerbated, as it always is, by international sport. In the previous year Lord Dunraven's yacht *Valkyrie II*, racing for the America's Cup, had been beaten by the American *Vigilant*. This year *Vigilant*, in English waters, was beaten several times. It roused more than pointed comments on both sides. Conan Doyle felt the snap and snarl of hostility. At a banquet in Detroit, when wine blurred hospitality and one speaker attacked the British Empire, he did cut loose in reply.

"You Americans have lived up to now within your own palings, and know nothing of the real world outside. But now your land is filled up, and you will be compelled to mix more with the other nations. When you do so you will find that there is only one which can at all understand your ways and aspirations, or will have the least sympathy. That is the mother country which you are now so fond of insulting.

"She is an Empire, and you will soon be an Empire also; and only then will you understand each other, and you will realize that you have only one real friend in the world."

Do the words sound quite so far-fetched as they must have sounded under the stained-glass windows and snaky electric chandeliers of the year 1894? At all events, in that same prosaic England, there had already occurred an event of some importance to the traveller. Irving, appearing in *Waterloo* at the Prince's Theatre, Bristol, scored one of his greatest successes.

So many newspapers wanted to send a representative to Bristol that a special train had to be provided for the critics. Today, perhaps, the spectacle of a train full of dramatic critics sets the mind toying happily with thoughts of detonators and gelignite. But it showed the measure of interest in a new part for Irving and a play by Conan Doyle. Bram Stoker, shaking with excitement in the wings, recorded its effect on the audience and the number of curtain-calls at the end.

"To my mind," he wrote, "*Waterloo* as an acting play is perfect, and Irving's playing was the high-water mark of histrionic art. It seemed to touch all hearts always. When the dying veteran sprang from his chair to salute the Colonel of his old regiment, the whole house simultaneously burst into a wild roar of applause."

Cables carried the echo of that applause across the Atlantic. The author, in Chicago, had the added pleasure of hearing *Waterloo*'s reception described by the owner of the 'Times-Herald,' who had been in Bristol to see it. In Chicago, too, he met the poet Eugene Field and formed a lasting friendship.

For many years Eugene Field had waged a campaign against the production of cheaply made, shoddily bound books, issued by publishing pirates at cut prices. As an admirer of Sherlock Holmes, he had written a special protest that Conan Doyle's pirated books should so often suffer in this way. When he met Sherlock Holmes's creator at the Palmer House, the lean, bald, impish-minded Field gravely held out for autograph a very bad copy of *The Sign of the Four*. Conan Doyle took the joke just as gravely and delighted Field when under his signature he wrote:

> *The bloody pirate stole my sloop*
> *And holds her in his wicked ward.*
> *Lord send that, walking on my poop,*
> *I see him kick at my main yard!*

Back in New York again, where his morning readings drew even larger crowds to Daly's Theatre, he was entertained at dinner by the Lotos Club in the middle of a comprehensive Eastern tour. By this time he was a trifle dizzy. The rattle of trains, the overheated hotels, the constant informal morning, noon and evening speeches he gave in addition to those he was scheduled to give, could be as tiring as the exuberant hospitality. "We don't feel we've done the right thing, Doctor, unless we get a guest so drunk he can't tell a silver dollar from a buzz-saw." Or, "I'm sure you wouldn't mind addressing our little society, would you? Just fifteen minutes?"

New England he loved. The wood-smoke of autumn, the scarlet and brown of the dying leaves, the wigwams of the corn, lent alien beauty to fields and streets and houses such as he might have seen at home. It had associations of sentiment as well.

"Yesterday," he wrote, "I visited Oliver Wendell Holmes's grave and I laid a big wreath on it—not as from myself, but as from 'The Authors' Society.' In one beautiful graveyard lie Holmes, Lowell, Longfellow, Channing, Brooks, Agassiz, Parkman, and very many more." They were the men of New England who in spirit might have been the men of Old England. He stood a long time in Mount Auburn Cemetery, as once he had stood by the grave of Macaulay.

In Brattleboro, Vermont, Rudyard Kipling was now living with his American wife. Kipling, who six years previously wrote a description of Chicago unsurpassed for picturesque invective (there were spittoons in it, too), was not so easy-going as Conan Doyle when Americans twisted the lion's tail. He retaliated by yanking a handful of stern-feathers from the eagle; and this, of course, had a very soothing effect. Conan Doyle, who thought the whole dispute was senseless, wrote in protest. Kipling, taking it good-naturedly, invited him for a visit to Vermont.

He had never met Kipling, though he had been acquainted with Kipling's late brother-in-law, Wolcott Balestier, in the Norwood days. On the train he chuckled to recall a remark once made by his sister Connie when they entertained Balestier at dinner.

"Fancy!" Connie had said, with wide-open eyes. "Mr. Balestier and Mr. Kipling are writing a book together, and they are doing it by writing alternate sentences." Her brother refrained from pointing out that somebody had been pulling the fair Connie's leg.

Kipling, short and wiry and hirsute, his neck and moustache thrust forward, his eyes gleaming behind small spectacles, cherished privacy with a passion beyond the understanding of his fellow-villagers. He made an admirable host, and so did his wife. They welcomed their guest to the famous house, shaped like Noah's ark, which Conan Doyle photographed. The latter, seeing an opportunity for exercise, arrived carrying a bag of golf-clubs: to the stupefaction of Brattleboro, who wondered how the doctor's instruments were supposed to be used.

It may safely be deduced that Kipling never liked golf; no true golfer would ever make the character 'I' refer to it as he does in *The House Surgeon*. But his guest, though far from expert, gave him lessons in a frosty pasture, while the villagers stared at them. Kipling recited his newly written *M'Andrew's Hymn:* where, as in so much of this master-craftsman's work, romance is celebrated under the guise as well as in the literary style of finely poised machinery. They parted excellent friends; and Conan Doyle made one remark which he later repeated to Hornung:

"For God's sake," he urged, "let's stop talking about spittoons."

He was due to leave for England on December 8th. Major Pond, with tears of financial emotion behind the large spectacles, implored him to remain. "Had he not promised an invalid wife to spend Christmas at home," Major Pond afterwards lamented in print, "he could have stayed through the season and returned home with a small fortune in dollars." And, though the major considered him not quite flowery enough as an orator: "There was something about him that seemed to charm everyone he met. If he would return for a hundred nights, I would give him more money than any Englishman I know."

The good impresario could have said no more.

In New York just before leaving, Conan Doyle learned of the death of Robert Louis Stevenson in Samoa. Though he had never met Stevenson, that news came with a shock of personal loss. For Stevenson, whose work he had admired so long, was an admirer of his; and the two had been corresponding for several years. Now the gallant invalid was gone; Tusitala would have no more tales to tell. Invalid, yes. Like Touie.

Once more the steamer whistle blew. The Cunarder *Etruria* moved out past the Statue of Liberty. In the reaction after stimulus he was exhausted and depressed. But he learned, first in London and then at Davos, that Touie continued to improve. In the High Alps again, at the turn of the year, he settled down with a new zest to the exploits of one character who is a joy forever.

In short, to the exploits of Brigadier Gerard.

VIII
EXILE:

Boney's Warriors—and the Dervishes

Our hero, in pitch-black night, stands on a balcony over the Danube with the Emperor Napoleon and Marshal Lannes. Across the river, a league wide and swollen with roaring floods, shine the bivouac-fires of the Austrians. Someone, through storm and wind, must cross the river and bring back a captive to discover whether General Hiller's corps is there.

Even our hero (faster with the music, please!) feels a cold sweat break out on him. And even Napoleon does not command; he merely expresses a wish. Yet our hero's bosom swells with noble pride and love of glory. He reflects that, from an army of 150,000 of the bravest warriors, including the 25,000 of the Imperial Guard, he alone has been chosen for an expedition requiring intelligence no less than boldness.

" 'I will go, sire!' I cried without hesitation. 'I will go; and, if I perish, I leave my mother to your Majesty's care.' The Emperor pulled my ear to mark his satisfaction."

Any reader may be forgiven if here he makes a mistake. He may well attribute these sentiments to our debonair friend Etienne Gerard, Colonel of the Hussars of Conflans, idol of the ladies, the best swordsman in the six brigades of light cavalry: gloriously ridiculous, yet at the same time heroic.

But it is not Gerard. It is not fiction at all. The lines and situation quoted are from the real-life memoirs of

General Baron de Marbot, who, at the time of this episode, was a Captain in Napoleon's army. It may be as
well to state that Marbot *did* cross the river; that he
brought back not one captive, but three; and that Napoleon again pinched his ear and made him a Major.
This is one of the mildest adventures in a book which we
should be tempted to regard as one lyric series of lies if
Marbot's contemporaries had not attested his truth. Even
if we still cannot believe Marbot did all he said he did,
his personality is enough.

For so many of Napoleon's followers, once the most
formidable foes of all, really did think, act, and talk in
this high-posturing way. It was, and is, incomprehensible
on the other side of the Channel. Therein lie some of the
finest effects in the tales about Brigadier Gerard. When
Conan Doyle based the character of the Brigadier on
Marbot, altering it to suit his purpose, much of the
comedy arises from the spotlighting by which the Brigadier's volatility is contrasted with the stolid, plodding
English.

In reading soldier reminiscences, the author significantly said, he had been struck by the fact that many of
these swaggers "were men whose actions recall the very
spirit of chivalry. A better knight than Marbot never
rode in the lists."

Now that is true. And, if you look only at what
Brigadier Gerard did, disregarding the manner in which
he tells it, he becomes a paladin in the line of Du Guesclin. But his naïve boasting, his complacence, his firm
conviction that every woman is in love with him, all
blind the reader with mirth. Above everything, his serene
good nature never fails. He curls his side-whiskers, gives
his moustache the Marengo twist, and rides living out of
the page.

"Napoleon said himself, as you doubtless remember,

that he thought I had the stoutest heart in his army. It is true that he disfigured the sentence by saying I had the thickest head. But we will pass that over. It is unkind to dwell upon the weak moments of a great man."

Thus speaks the Brigadier: not in any of the stories, but in Conan Doyle's notebook about him. The notebook flickers with superb glimpses of Napoleonic background: of Murat "with his sword in his scabbard and his cane in his hand," of the old-moustaches carrying two bottles of wine in their bearskin caps and using their muskets for crutches when they were weary, of the "pale face and cold smile" of Bonaparte. There is mention of one unwritten (or at least unpublished) story: "Story of Brigadier getting the blackmail letter for Josephine."

"For three years," the author said in another place, "I lived among Napoleonic literature, with some hope that by soaking and resoaking myself in it I might at last write some worthy book which would reproduce some of the glamour of that extraordinary and fascinating epoch. But my ambition was greater than my power. . . . And so, at last, after long delay, my considerable preparation ended in one little book of soldier stories."

But this will not do. 'One little book' is both deprecating and deceptive. The fact is that *The Exploits of Brigadier Gerard*, and the series he afterwards wrote as the *Adventures of Gerard*, form the finest picture he ever did of the Napoleonic campaigns. And the reason is this: that he saw it through the eyes of a Frenchman.

The Brigadier is truly French; as French as Marbot, as French as Coignet, as French as Gourgaud. Not a word or a gesture is false. The attitudes he strikes, which so annoy his English foes and amuse us who read, are perfectly sincere. He is life and soul in the Grand Army; his own throat nearly bursts with the war-whoop of,

"Vive L'Empereur!" And his own hits at English character are fully as good as anything they ever say about
him. Etienne Gerard makes a fool only of himself; he
never makes a fool of France or the French. That is the
triumph both of the Brigadier and of Conan Doyle.

The first story about him, *The Medal of Brigadier
Gerard*, was written in 1894. The author read it to
highly appreciative audiences in America. When he settled down again with his family at Davos, this time in
the Grand Hotel Belvedere, he had nearly completed
seven more stories by the spring of 1895.

It was bad weather in Davos that spring. The snow
of the ski-running gave way to dismal rains, and everybody had a cold. In May (we can date it by a letter to
the Ma'am) he paid a visit to England which again altered the whole course of events.

He had faced the fact that apparently they must spend
the rest of their lives (or, to put it more grimly, of
Touie's life) at foreign hotels in Switzerland or Egypt.
He did not mind that, if it had to be done. But in England he met Grant Allen, also a sufferer from consumption, who told him a different story.

Grant Allen, whose name is all but forgotten now,
was then a well-known writer who had first attracted
attention with his sensational novel *The Devil's Die*
and created still more of a stir in this year 1895 with his
frank treatment of sexual problems in *The Woman Who
Did*. Conan Doyle knew him best for his scientific works,
of a strongly agnostic tinge. It was not necessary, Grant
Allen said emphatically, for a sufferer from tuberculosis
to live out of England; he himself had kept the disease at
bay by living on Hindhead, in Surrey.

Touie, who longed to return as much as he did,
begged her husband to investigate. He hurried down to
Surrey, and was more than satisfied.

"It is not merely Grant Allen's case which gives us hope that the place will suit Touie," he wrote, "but because its height, its dryness, its sandy soil, its fir-trees, and its shelter from all bitter winds present the conditions which all agree to be best." He had sold the Norwood house. Why buy another? He would build a house at Hindhead, and it should be a house on a considerable scale.

After drawing a plan of the house, with a large billiard-room tenderly included, he left the entire matter in the hands of his old friend Ball, the Southsea architect. The new house, Ball said, should be ready in about a year. At Davos again he finished the seventh new Brigadier story, to the delight of the 'Strand,' and corrected and revised *The Stark Munro Letters*.

So much of himself had been poured into *Stark Munro* that, as he read it again, he thought it might prove to be his most enduring work. There it was: the ambitions, the fears, the agnostic (or, to be strictly accurate about Dr. Stark Munro, the Deistic) views. There was Touie, appearing under the name of Winnie La Force. At the back of his mind he was compelled to admit that he had never been in love with Touie in the sense of a great love which that term implies. In the Southsea days, ten years ago, he had been too much in love with being in love. But he had for her a deep affection, a fondness which, or so he thought, was better than any love.

Besides, the thought seemed disloyal. He put it away.

His most enduring work? Perhaps. Nevertheless, he had long come to the conclusion that what mattered was the *story*. Once, in an excited moment, he had told Robert Barr that rather than be judged by professional critics he would prefer to be judged by fellow-writers or by schoolboys. That, he admitted, was an exaggerated way of putting the matter: you would not give a school-boy *Robert Elsmere* as you would give him *Treasure Island*. And memories of how they had reviewed *The White Company* lurked in his mind. But it was indicative of what he meant.

"The first object of a novelist," he had said to J. W. Dawson, "is to tell a tale. If he has no story to tell, what is he there for? Possibly he has something to say which is worth saying, but he should say it in another form." It was as though, in the middle of a play, the author were to rush out to the footlights and stop the action while he made a speech on the Irish question.

In this matter of plays, it may be asked what had happened to that four-act Regency play, for Irving and Ellen Terry, which he started before the American tour. For the time we hear no more of it; nor, ever again, of Hornung as collaborator. But we need not invoke Sherlock Holmes to solve the problem. Any suggestion of prize-fights on the stage of the Lyceum would have horrified Irving, who in this year received his knighthood: the first knighthood ever accorded to an actor. And so Conan Doyle, longing to let himself go on a boxing story, discarded the play for a novel different in plot. In summer and early autumn he wrote *Rodney Stone*.

When we learn that Smith, Elder & Co., subsequently paid him four thousand pounds in advance royalties on *Rodney Stone*, and the 'Strand' fifteen hundred for serial rights despite George Newnes's own shock at hearing it was a prize-ring novel ("Why that subject of all subjects on earth?"), some measure of his popularity as a writer may be gathered. But the best tribute to *Rodney Stone* was given by an old Australian prize-fighter, to whom the book was read aloud as he lay in illness near to death.

Few of us will forget the scene at the 'Waggon and Horses' when Sir Charles Tregellis, Buck Tregellis, gives a supper for the Fancy, with the seventeen-stone Prince Regent wheezing at his right hand. In a room hung with Union Jacks, all the real names out of Pugilistica are assembled—'Gentleman' Jackson and Jem Belcher; Andrew Gamble, champion of Ireland; Bill Richmond the black; the great Jewish fighters, Dan Mendoza and Dutch Sam, with twenty more—when the blacksmith's adopted son, Boy Jim, sends up a challenge to the best man in the room. Again we hear the shout of laughter, the dry retort that this newcomer must try himself against somebody a little less experienced than Jem Belcher. In the carriage-house, with the light of the stable-lanterns shining down on the ring, and the cropped heads of the spectators thrust forward, Boy Jim fights the half-drunken Joe Berks as the cries of betting rise higher and higher. Berks, blue-faced, is in trouble; but his young opponent lacks the ring-craft to finish him.

"Get your left on his mark, boy! Then go to his head with the right!"

It was at this point in the story, when they read it aloud to the old Australian professional, that the sick man reared up in bed. "That's got him!" he shouted; "by God, that's got him!" They were the last words he ever spoke. He left the world happy, in an imaginary prize-ring.

As the Brigadier Gerard stories show the French in Napoleon's time, *Rodney Stone* shows the English of the same era. It is done in the same ensnaringly real method as *Micah Clarke*, by which a commonplace village comes to life before Buck Tregellis races Sir John Lade from Brighton to London, two-horse tandem against four-in-hand, or old 'Champion' Harrison comes out of retirement against Crab Wilson. Conan Doyle had finished it when he and Touie and Lottie left their summer quarters in Maloja to spend the winter in Egypt.

They stayed for more than a month at Caux before going on by easy stages from Lucerne through Italy to Brindisi. Before the end of November they were established at the Mena House Hotel, seven miles out in the desert from Cairo.

It should have been an idyllic interlude. The long white hotel in the desert, with the Pyramids looming close behind it, provided billiards and tennis and golf. But the brittle air enervated him; he could do no work except to adapt a three-act play, *Halves*, from a novel by James Payn. He was thrown by a bolting horse, and, still holding hard to the bridle, caught a blow from the horse's hoof which cost him five stitches over his right eye. There were other disturbing factors too.

For the British Empire, at the close of this year 1895, was far from quiet. On the Egyptian border there was distant firing as Arab Dervishes circled and melted away. The clamour of the British Uitlanders, against Kruger in the Transvaal, could be heard from South Africa. In British Guiana an old boundary-dispute festered with the Republic of Venezuela; before Christmas, it threatened to bring on war between Great Britain and the United States.

The rights and wrongs of that quarrel must not be debated here. But its immediate result was explosive: General Crespo, Dictator-President of Venezuela, persuaded President Cleveland that the Monroe Doctrine was in danger. In December President Cleveland sent a special message to Congress, more than intimating that if England intervened in Venezuela, without arbitration, the United States should consider it a cause for war. It was a popular message: the Governors of thirty states endorsed it.

In the Turf Club, Cairo, there was wrath and there was wonder too.

"Why in blazes do they seem to hate us so much? It's the Irish-Americans making trouble, I suppose?"

"It's nothing of the kind," retorted Conan Doyle to that universal remark. "After all, the Irish don't control thirty states out of forty-three." And he embodied the real explanation in a letter to the 'Times.'

"To understand the American's view of Great Britain," he wrote, "we must read an American history-book as it is used in the schools, and accept the statements with the same absolute faith and patriotic bias which our own schoolboys would show in a narration of our relations with France.

"American history, as far as its foreign policy is concerned, resolves itself almost entirely into a series of wrangles with Great Britain, in many of which we must now confess that we were absolutely in the wrong. Few Englishmen could be found now to contend that we were justified in those views of taxation which brought on the first American war, or in the question of searching neutral vessels which was the main cause of the second. This war of 1812 would possibly occupy only two pages out of five hundred in an English history, but it bulks very large in an American one."

Now the truth of that can be attested by any middle-aged American who remembers the school histories of his youth. Not only in text-books, but through patriotic plays and recitations, stalked the figure of the arrogant redcoat officer: he was always defeated by a hero in buff and blue. Few Englishmen, who regarded 1776 and 1812 as mere forgotten pin-pricks in a thousand years of battle, ever realized this. But Conan Doyle saw it.

"After the war," he continued, "there was the Florida dispute, the question of the Oregon line, the settlement of the Maine and New Brunswick line, and the hostile attitude of most of our press at the time of the Civil War. Can we wonder if the American has now reached that state of sensitiveness and suspicion which we have not quite outgrown ourselves in the case of the French?"

The Venezuelan quarrel was eventually patched up. But it worried him. He wrote that letter on December 30th, 1895, the day before he and Touie and Lottie went aboard one of Messrs. Cook's small steamers for a journey up the Nile.

The paddle-wheel churned in a milk-coffee river. Besides Touie and Lottie there were many more ladies, in white dresses and straw sun-hats, who went ashore with Kodaks among the ruins of Memphis. Conan Doyle had said he was more interested in modern Egypt than in ancient Egypt. But the Nile threw its glamour as their steamer moved on. "Sunset," he wrote in his diary, "left a long crimson glow over the Libyan Desert. The river ran as smooth as quicksilver, with constant drifts of wild duck passing between ourselves and the crimson sky. On the Arabian side it was blue-black until the edge of the moon shone over low mountains."

Their destination was the outpost of civilization at Wadi Halfa, nearly eight hundred miles from Cairo. It was all very well, he thought, to prowl among the tombs of the kings and the huge dead stones of Thebes. Temples, temples, and still more temples! But, as the stern-wheeler thrashed past Assouan, he realized that this region was more than eerie. It was dangerous.

For they had entered the Madhi's area, the raiding-ground of the Dervishes. Thick heat pressed down like a blanket. Tourist-parties, half of them women, were constantly being herded ashore with so little protection that they could be scooped up in a handful. In the middle of January, 1896, between Korosko and Wadi Halfa, the steamer touched at a mud village, with castor-oil plantations and a belt of palm trees, which had been raided a very short time before. Ninety red-turbaned Dervishes, noiseless on swift-loping camels, swept over the low hills eastward with no warning except the first crack of a Remington rifle. They shot down half the villagers and melted away.

"I saw one poor old man with a Remington bullet through his neck," Conan Doyle noted in his diary. "These people had a watchman on the hills, but I can't see what there is to prevent incursions upon any of these riverside places. If I were a Dervish General I would undertake to carry off a Cook's excursion party with the greatest ease."

And that view was shared by the garrison at Wadi Halfa, a "dreadful little sun trap" of twenty-five hundred Egyptian and Nubian troops, with about twenty British officers sprinkled among them. Beyond that frontier lay the Egyptian Sudan.

In the Sudan, more than ten years before, the British soldier for the last time had worn a red coat on active service; he wore khaki now. Mr. Gladstone's government, in 1885, withdrew all troops from this part of the Sudan. Sinister, stretching away in yellow sand and black rock, it was ruled under the black flag of the Khalifa. The Dervishes, elated by their recent raid, put thumb to nose and said it took five hours to turn out the Egyptian Camel Corps. This had no soothing effect on the British officers at Wadi Halfa.

"We're like dogs on a chain," complained Captain Lane, while a Nubian brass-band played *The Vicar of Bray* with barbaric screams and clashes. "We can't guard the whole line against raids. Of course, we've got a number of little posts scattered about as ground-bait for the Dervish."

"Yes," agreed the visiting author drily, "so I've heard. Tell me: Wouldn't you rather enjoy seeing a useless excursion party kidnapped? As an excuse for action?"

Captain Lane was shocked. "Oh, I shouldn't like to say that. At the same time," he grinned, "we shouldn't exactly hate to go and have a romp with 'em: Oh, no!"

Two months later, when the civilians had returned to Cairo, Captain Lane got his wish on a full-dress scale. Major-General Kitchener received orders to move across the border to Akasha, and re-take the Egyptian Sudan.

Conan Doyle missed the first note of the bugles, because he was out in the Libyan Desert visiting a Coptic Monastery with Colonel Lewis. But this news was not unexpected. All along the Upper Nile he had noted rumours of some move to be made by the Egyptian Government: in reality by the British Government, since Egypt was a 'veiled Protectorate.' Ever since he was a boy of seventeen, when a recruiting-sergeant nearly persuaded him into the Army during a visit to Aunt Jane, he had longed to see fighting at close range. Here was the opportunity.

He could not be away for long. Touie must leave Egypt before the intense heat at the end of April. He cabled the 'Westminster Gazette' for permission to represent them as temporary correspondent-without-pay. He bought a large Italian revolver. Then, travelling by train, river-boat, and camel, he made another eight-hundred-mile journey up the Nile. Profoundly he distrusted the reptilian head and eye of the camel, and with good reason. But it made tolerable travelling once you got used to the brute's motion. At Assouan, with other war-correspondents, he was ordered to join a regiment of Egyptian cavalry going up to the front. This, he thought, was much too tame; and all the correspondents disliked choking in a dust-fog of cavalry. They slipped away by night, on their camels, to reach Wadi Halfa alone.

The wonder is that these lunatics were not caught by the circling Dervishes. One solitary barbaric rider, passing a palm-grove at dawn, did bring them awake with a start. But, when Conan Doyle reached the front, he found nothing except the bustle of men in khaki and red tarbooshes, engaged in collecting camels. Not a shot had been fired. Major-General Kitchener, with whom he was acquainted and who entertained him at dinner, said it might be a month or two (as in fact it was) before any attack could be made. So he returned to Mena by river-boat.

In May, 1896, he and the family were back in England. There he met another disappointment: the new house at Hindhead, remote and lonely under pine-covered height, was still scarcely begun. Such a mansion, the builders assured him, was a considerable job; he must be patient. In the meantine he rented a furnished house close by at Haselmere. 'Greywood Beeches,' to the delight of seven-year-old Mary and three-year-old Kingsley, had a horse, pigs, rabbits, fowls, dogs, and cats.

The Exploits of Brigadier Gerard, published by Newnes, raised his reputation still higher. "It is pleasant to see so many people fond of the Brigadier, for I was a bit fond of him myself." But his next work troubled him.

"I am labouring heavily over that wretched little Napoleonic book," he wrote in July. The book was *Uncle Bernac*, which he had begun in Egypt without being able to get past two chapters. "It has cost me more than any big book. I never seem to be quite in the key, but I must slog through it somehow."

He did not like *Uncle Bernac* then, and always dis-

liked it afterwards. Though he put too low an estimate
on the book, it is now possible to see why he felt as he
did. Perhaps, by this time, he had spent too long at the
Napoleonic-cum-Regency period; he grew tired of it, for
the moment, without admitting the fact even to himself.
Uncle Bernac, with its picture of the Grand Army
massed at Boulogne for the invasion of England, seems
fragmentary: all head and shoulders. It is as though he
had planned a long panorama, and ended by filling in
only a third of it with the figures of Napoleon and his
staff. Of Bonaparte, he confessed in a special preface, "I
was still unable to determine whether I was dealing with
a great hero or with a great scoundrel. Of the adjective
only could I be sure."

Under his supervising eye, work progressed more rap-
idly on the new house in its four-acre grounds, and the
gardens that were to surround it. "We are exercised in
our minds over many questions connected with the
house, especially the electric light." It was to be a
private power-plant, unheard-of in country places. "I
shall have a very fine hall window, and I want to put up
some of the family arms." At the end of '96 he bought
the horse, 'Brigadier,' which was his pride. At the end of
the year, too, he took his Egyptian adventures as the
background for a novel called *The Tragedy of the
Korosko.*

All the atmosphere of the Upper Nile was in that
novel: the heat, the buzzing flies, the gun-black rocks in
the desert, as he imagined a little tourist-party—of various nationalities and various religious faiths—who go
ashore to see the rock of Abousir and are captured by
Dervishes. His purpose in *The Tragedy of the Korosko*
was to study the characters of these people (especially
the Irish Catholic couple, the Anglican Colonel, the

Presbyterian American women, the French agnostic) during days of pain and fear and despair.

With their escort of Negro soldiers shot down, the tourists are carried across the desert towards Khartoum. They find physical suffering alone until the cavalcade is overtaken by a fanatical Emir, who insists that the captives shall become Mohammedans or be put to death.

Then human nature speaks in every line. The Catholics are ready and willing to die for their faith. The American girl, far from willing, is over-ridden by her strong-minded old aunt. The lean English Colonel grunts out that he'd rather end things here than be sold as a slave in Khartoum; what he really feels is that turning Moslem wouldn't be quite respectable. The French agnostic, maddened, is willing to profess anything but won't be made to do so by force. "Je suis Chrétien," he shouts. "J'y reste." That tension heightens, in a race across the desert with the Egyptian Camel Corps in pursuit, until it is no longer possible to temporize; each must make his choice.

The Tragedy of the Korosko is carried through with a swift rattle-bang of action which almost disguises the author's brooding underneath. As in *Stark Munro*, but more strongly, there is a suggestion of some ultimate Purpose working for the sake of good. But the Frenchman will have none of this. And we read between the lines that in their defiance of the Dervishes nearly all these members of the tourist-party, except the Catholics, are sustained less by religious faith than by human pride.

That was Conan Doyle's state of mind when, in January of the new year, their household moved up to Moorlands, a guest-establishment where he could be much closer to watch the building of the new house. In that house, as its very centre and hub, he meant to put a certain dining-room table.

It was the dining-room table which had belonged to his grandfather John Doyle, at Cambridge Terrace, and round which had sat the great writers, painters, and statesmen out of a vanished age. John Doyle bequeathed it to Uncle Dick. From Richard Doyle it passed to Aunt Annette, and, on the death of Aunt Annette, to her favourite nephew. Since his youth that table, as though its polished surface still reflected the faces of Scott and Coleridge and Thackeray, had symbolized greatness. And it is curious that he should have been thinking of the table at just this time.

In the life of Arthur Conan Doyle there were three turning-points. No such word can be applied to his marriage with Touie, or the tragedy of her illness; these were important incidents and no more. The first turning-point was his quarrel with the Doyles about Catholicism, when at the age of twenty-two he closed the door at Cambridge Terrace and set out on his own path. He was approaching the second turning-point now. For he met Miss Jean Leckie.

IX
ROMANCE:

Jean Leckie

It was 1897, the year of Queen Victoria's Diamond Jubilee. Mr. Joseph Chamberlain, the Secretary of State for the Colonies, persuaded his colleagues to celebrate it with a festival of Empire which should ring throughout the world.

Miss Jean Leckie was just twenty-four. Even the not-very-expert photography of the time reveals her extraordinary beauty. But the colouring of that beauty it cannot show: the dark-gold hair, the hazel-green eyes, the delicate white complexion, the changes of the smile.

Her great talent was for music: she had a fine mezzo-soprano voice, which she had cultivated at Dresden and was later to cultivate at Florence. Jean Leckie was descended from a very ancient Scottish family, who traced their descent back to Malis de Leggy in the thirteenth century; and one of her ancestors (it is impossible to get away from romance either in her line or in Conan Doyle's) was Rob Roy MacGregor. Despite her delicacy (slender, with small hands and feet), she was an expert horsewoman who had been trained to ride from childhood. With her mother and her father, the latter a wealthy Scot of stern religious views, she lived at Glebe House, Glebe, Blackheath. We see her across the years as quick of sympathy, impulsive, strongly romantic; the slender neck rises from a lace gown, and the eyes (read their expression, even in a photograph) tell her character.

Under what circumstances they met we do not know; but the date, which neither Jean Leckie nor Conan Doyle ever forgot, was March 15th, 1897. It was just a few months short of his thirty-eighth birthday. They fell in love immediately, desperately, and for all time. His letters to her, in his seventy-first year, read like those of a man who has been married for about a month.

Meanwhile, it seemed helpless and hopeless.

Conan Doyle was no plaster saint. Anyone who has so far followed his life will have seen that. He was violent, he was stubborn, he was often wrong-headed, he did not easily forgive injury. And yet, with his particular background, upbringing, and beliefs, we can foresee exactly what he did. He could not help being in love with Jean, or she with him. But there it must stop.

He was married to a woman for whom he had the deepest affection and respect, and who had all the more claim on him in the fact that she was an invalid. Over and over he repeats that he will not hurt Touie; and he never did hurt her.

He had no self-delusions. Any ordinary man would have argued himself into finding some excuse for Touie to divorce him, or else would have turned the affair into an intrigue. Any ordinary woman (for observe that Jean Leckie was in most ways his feminine counterpart) would have ceased seeing him altogether, or would have joined the intrigue. These two did neither. "I fight the devil," he cried, "and I win." And this went on for ten years.

He raged that it was not fair to her; but she merely shook her head and said she did not mind. For several years after '97 there was only one person who knew of their feelings, and that person was the Ma'am. He told the Ma'am all about it. This little old lady instantly supported him and, when she had met Jean, supported him still more. More than this, the Ma'am on occasion would take Jean away into the country for a short visit, and he and Jean's brother Stewart would visit them there.

This slender girl with the dark-gold hair utterly captivated Lottie and small Mary Louise. "I hope," we find Lottie writing to her at Christmas of '98, "that next time we meet you will remember that all my friends call me Lottie, and that I hate being 'Miss Doyle' to anyone I like. I wanted to say this the other day, but felt shy."

But there was one incident that cut deeply into Conan Doyle's mind and heart. Though it is not well to anticipate matters, it ought to be mentioned here as showing most clearly his state of mind.

The incident occurred in the late summer of the year 1900, when he was under nervous strain from other causes. He had been playing cricket at Lord's, and Jean was there to watch him. Willie Hornung saw them together, and raised his eyebrows very obviously.

That evening, in case Willie or Connie (a devout Catholic) should get the wrong impression, Conan Doyle went out to the Kensington house where they lived with their small son Arthur Oscar. Taking Connie upstairs, he explained the matter fully, putting stress on the fact that his relations with Miss Leckie were platonic and would remain so. Connie seemed understanding; she promised to lunch with Jean at Lord's next day. Hornung, whom he referred to Connie for details, also seemed understanding.

"Arthur," said Hornung, "I'm prepared to back your dealings with any woman at sight and without question."

Then, over night, the situation altered. Whether Willie changed Connie, or Connie changed Willie, is not clear. But next morning Conan Doyle received a telegram from

Connie, excusing herself from the lunch-engagement because she had toothache and must go to a dentist. Realizing this was an excuse and no more, her brother hurried out to Kensington. Connie was not there; her husband said she had gone up to bed. Hornung, pacing the floor with short fussy steps, pitched in after the fashion of a lawyer dissecting a case.

"It seems to me," he said among other things, "you attach too much importance to whether these relations are platonic or not. I can't see that it makes much difference. What *is* the difference?"

His brother-in-law stared at him. "It's all the difference," he roared, "between innocence and guilt."

And he left the house, controlling his wrath as best he could.

Now his attitude, in modern eyes, may have been reasonable or unreasonable. A modern commentator might say that he was wrong and Hornung was right. But Conan Doyle was not a modern man. He had been brought up in a tradition, and moulded his views in a chivalric code, where this mattered very much indeed. As he said, it was sacred. He was not proud of his action throughout, he added; but he was trying to do the best he could in difficult circumstances. What angered him about Hornung's attitude was just this: If you had a friend, Conan Doyle thought, you stood by him right or wrong.

"When have I failed in loyalty to any member of my family?" he exclaimed. "And when before have I appealed to them?" In very truth that was so. There was no member of his family whom he did not support or help to support; and, apart from the question of money, it was he to whom they always turned for help.

But to fight the devil and win, admirable though it may be, does one thing. It tears the nerves to pieces.

From the time of his meeting with Jean Leckie, slowly but inevitably, we see him begin to change. The Guardsman-shoulders are straightened. The eyes grow narrow. The moustache goes out to points of something very like arrogance. For some years the outer surface of his nature was at times as hard and unyielding as basalt, because he was under a strain which only the Ma'am understood.

Nevertheless, let us return to the year 1897 and the fanfare of the Diamond Jubilee. To London, in that dusty summer, swarmed the hosts of Empire: Imperial Service troops from India, turbaned Sikhs, Mounted Rifles from Canada, from New South Wales, from the Cape and Natal, Hausas from the Niger and the Gold Coast, Negroes from the West Indian regiments, Cyprian zaptiehs, the Dyak military police of North Borneo. Seventy-eight-year-old Queen Victoria, wearing sunglasses in an open carriage, watched the procession go by.

On June 25th some two thousand troops, in every colour of skin and uniform, massed at Chelsea Barracks. Led by the quickstep of the Guards' Fife and Drum Band, they marched through streets lined with cheering people to see Conan Doyle's *Waterloo* at the Lyceum Theatre. Bram Stoker, who in this year published his famous novel *Dracula*, nervously escorted Colonial Premiers and Indian Princes into the boxes. *Waterloo* was received, he said, "with an ecstasy of loyal passion."

One June 26th, too, the Prince of Wales reviewed the Grand Fleet at Spithead: four lines of warships extending for a distance of thirty miles. That was what provoked the wildest outburst of enthusiasm. They were monarchs of the sea, unconquerable; a symbol of the British Empire at the very zenith of its power.

"Nothing could harm us—nothing!" ironically observes a man who remembered it. A new zeal animated the empire-building as Cecil Rhodes and Dr. Leander Starr Jameson ('Dr. Jim,' the lounging man with the eternal cigarette) reshaped the fate of South Africa. In England, jingoism was rife. Who the devil did these Boers think they were, when a year earlier they had arrested Dr. Jim for his raid into the Transvaal? True, in a London court Dr. Jim was sentenced to fifteen months' imprisonment. But the man in the street made him a hero. At an evening party the Prime Minister, Lord Salisbury, met Jameson's counsel, the famous Carson, Q.C., and said to him, "I wish you'd brought Dr. Jim with you."

Conan Doyle, preoccupied with thoughts of Jean, saw the nation moving towards war. The Jameson raid, he said, had been a piece of sheer idiocy. But he was as great a lover of the Empire as Cecil Rhodes. The trouble was, he thought, that these jingoes in shouting against Oom Paul Kruger had a perfectly good case but didn't even know what it was; they simply shouted blindly.

For the moment he could not concentrate on work for thinking about Jean. "I am reading a course of Renan to steady myself down," he said. "That, with plenty of golf and cricket, ought to keep me right—body and mind."

Since the previous autumn he had been doing a great deal of public speaking. He threw a spell over the New Vagabonds' Club, at which assembled nearly every literary celebrity from Mrs. Humphry Ward to a spectacular younger novelist named H. G. Wells. He gave readings for fashionable charitable causes, was chosen to 'respond for literature' at the Royal Societies' Club, and, taking the chair at the annual dinner of the Irish Literary Society, he somewhat startled his audience by maintaining the best in Irish literature had been produced less by the Celt than by the Saxon interloper.

"The Celt," he went on, "is the most conservative of mankind. His thoughts turn backwards, and his virtues and his vices are alike those of his prehistoric ancestor. His life in Ireland is one of unremitting toil, and with a soul which is full above all others of fire and sympathy and humour, he has spent himself in dreams upon the hillside or stories round the winter fire. Give him culture, give him that Catholic University of which we hear, and Celtic Ireland may send its Renans and its Pierre Lotis to London as Celtic Brittany sends them to Paris."

And in August, '97, occurred a sharp brush with Mr. Hall Caine.

It was shortly before the publication of Hall Caine's novel *The Christian*. Conan Doyle, turning over newspapers and periodicals at the Authors' Club, found his eye blurring with wrath at a practice which had been going on for some time. He sat down and addressed the following box of dynamite to the 'Daily Chronicle.'

"When Mr. Kipling writes such a poem as his *Recessional*, he does not state in public what he thinks of it, and how it came to be written. When Mr. Barrie produces so fine a work as *Margaret Ogilvie*, there are no long interviews and explanations to advertise it before it appears. The excellence of the literature commends the poem or the tale to the discerning reader, and the ordinary advertising agencies present its merit to the general public. As a literary man, I would beg Mr. Hall Caine to adopt the same methods. . . .

"Mr. Hall Caine's book has not yet appeared—when it does appear I wish it every success—but I do think it unworthy of the dignity of our common profession that one should pick up paper after paper and read Mr. Caine's own comments on the gigantic task and the colossal work which he has just brought to a conclusion, with minute details of its various phases and of the different difficulties which have been overcome. It is for others to say these things, and there is something ludicrous and offensive when they are self-stated. Each successive book of Mr. Hall Caine has been self-heralded in the same fashion."

In he waded, hitting left and right. "In every high profession—be it law, medicine, the army, or literature —there are certain unwritten laws: a gentlemanly etiquette which is binding upon all, and especially on the leaders of the profession. What of its bad effect on young writers?"

Such views, of course, are not in vogue today. We have changed all that. A young writer nowadays, if told it might advance his new book, would paint his nose blue and walk into the Ivy Restaurant with a placard of of the book round his neck. He is not in a profession; he is in a racket. But Conan Doyle's hatred of self-puffing was very real; he considered it, as he said, merely ludicrous and offensive; and, though a still small voice whispers that this view could never have been shared by Mr. George Bernard Shaw, it was shared by most of his contemporaries. He himself threatened to withdraw a serial from the 'Strand' if they published a laudatory pre-publication note.

The ensuing correspondence with Hall Caine, carried out mainly in private, shows the Irishman as hot-headed and the Manxman as unctuously slippery. Regarding self-advertisement, Hall Caine protested in a hurt tone that he had never done any such thing. In the case of *The Christian*, at all events, Hall Caine declared it was certainly untrue. That interview with him in the 'Daily News,' and the article and paragraphs in the 'Bookman,' had been written without his knowledge, and, indeed, in direct opposition to his express wish and stipulation.

All this may have been true enough, though again the small voice suggests that a man seldom grants an interview with the express stipulation that it shall not be printed. Conan Doyle never forgot this. It was still in his mind when at last, towards the end of October, he moved into the new country-house.

The house was called 'Undershaw,' after the hanging grove of trees beneath which lay its red-tiled gables and its long high frontage. From the lodge-gates, up on the high-road behind the house, a gravel drive led down a steep hill. The house, with its tennis lawn in front, looked out across a wild valley like a scene in a German folk tale. He bought another saddle-horse, a chestnut mare, in addition to Brigadier; the two could also be used to draw the landau when Touie went out driving in that country of wood and heath, and for this he engaged an efficient coachman named Holden.

But he did not enter his house without trouble. In the hall at Undershaw, the great window sparkled with panel after panel of coats of arms. Among all those coloured blazonings, in some inexplicable state of absent-mindedness, he forgot to include the coat of arms of the Ma'am.

On the frequent occasions when he did the wrong thing, he did it in no uncertain way. The feelings and remarks of the Ma'am, as she stood in front of that window and both mother and son suddenly realized what was absent, are best left undescribed. Her ruffled plumage was smoothed down only by his promise that the Foley arms should hastily be installed in the window over the main staircase. But at Undershaw, for the first time in exactly four years, he could work in a study of his own. And it was here, long before the date usually ascribed, that he determined to revive Sherlock Holmes.

It is unnecessary to emphasize how, since the end of 1893, he had been pursued, hounded, worried, and encircled by the Baker Street demon. In America the first question they always asked was about Sherlock. In Egypt the Khedive's Government translated the detective's exploits into Arabic and issued them as a text-book for the police-force. The anecdotes about his demise are too well-known for repetition, except perhaps the remark of a certain Lady Blank: "I was heartbroken when Sherlock Holmes died; I did so enjoy his book *The Autocrat of the Breakfast Table.*"

Conan Doyle was older now. He still didn't like the fellow. But he had got over feeling slightly sick every time the name was mentioned. The public wanted Holmes? Very well, he thought grimly: To put Holmes on the stage might score a great hit; his new house had been costing a great deal of money; and he still wanted recognition as author of a full-length play. Towards the end of '97 he wrote the play, called *Sherlock Holmes,* and sent it to Beerbohm Tree.

The spectacular actor-manager of Her Majesty's Theatre, in renown second only to Irving, liked the play but wanted the part of the central character re-written so that it should be Beerbohm Tree rather than Sherlock Holmes. Again the author hesitated.

"I have grave doubts," he wrote early in 1898, "about putting Holmes on the stage at all—it is drawing attention to my weaker work which has unduly obscured my better—but, rather than re-write it on lines which would make a different Holmes from my Holmes, I would without the slightest pang put it back in the drawer. I daresay that will be the end of it, and probably the best one." But it was rescued by his literary agent, who learned that Charles Frohman in New York was anxious to see it, and sent it to Frohman.

His other play, *Halves*, adapted in Egypt from a novel by James Payn, still remained unproduced. James Payn, the editor who gave Conan Doyle his first chance in the 'Cornhill Magazine,' was nearly seventy and mortally ill. His illegible handwriting, which in the old days caused annoyance or amusement, had been due to the beginnings of rheumatic arthritis; it now made his hands scarcely human.

"Death is a horrible thing—horrible!" Payn would cry out to his old pupil; and then, five minutes later, his shrill laughter would cackle out in a joke. Payn never saw *Halves* on the stage. He died in March of 1898, having once described his own imaginary funeral as the greatest joke in the world.

During that winter Conan Doyle had done, for him, comparatively little work. He collected his verses into the ringing ballads of the *Songs of Action*, touching his closest thoughts only evasively in the troubled self-analysis of *The Inner Room*. The image of Jean Leckie, whom he saw only at long intervals, never left him.

As she wanted to share his interests, he wanted to share her interests even in her absence. Jean spent much time in the hunting-field. He, who had never before ridden to hounds, required little encouragement to take up hunting with zeal. But the actions of a man in love are never far away from comedy. Jean, for instance, had great musical talent. Not even his best friends could have credited him with any ability in this line. But, determined to share her interest and doing the best he could, he set about learning to play the banjo.

"A year ago," he wrote, after two hours' wrestling with *On the Road to Mandalay*, "I could never have imagined myself doing this."

In the spring of '98, just before he paid a visit to Italy, he finished three short stories. As the first of a new series for the 'Strand,' called *Round the Fire Stories*, they were *The Story of the Beetle Hunter*, *The Story of the Man with the Watches*, and *The Story of the Lost Special*. Sherlock Holmes, though not named, is heard off-stage in the third. And anthology-compilers never seem to have noticed that *The Lost Special*, in which a railway train vanishes like a soap-bubble between two stations, is by far his finest mystery (as distinguished from detective) story.

It was anything, anything at all, to distract his own mind. Here is a typical week, beginning at Wednesday's date: "Tomorrow I go up to dine at one of Sir Henry Thompson's octave dinners, on Friday I dine with Nugent Robinson, on Monday we entertain the Bishop of London at the Authors' Club, on Thursday I dine with the Royal Society. I will not, at least, die of hunger." At Undershaw the guest-book, a green volume in which visitors wrote their names, was crammed with signatures for every week-end. At the end of August Major Arthur Griffiths, who among other works wrote *Mysteries of Police and Crime,* invited him to follow the Army manoeuvres on Salisbury Plain.

On Salisbury Plain, amid the red coats and gold shoulder-cords of dress uniforms, he watched a mock battle. He was only a civilian, who had been doing a great deal of shooting at Undershaw. But one thing puzzled him.

It seemed to Conan Doyle in 1898 that, over and above artillery-strength, there was one supreme arbiter in war. Each regular battalion had its Maxim gun, or machine-gun, section. But the Maxim gun was heavy, it usually jammed, the water in its cooling-jacket rose to boiling-point after ninety seconds' use; it was as yet "a weapon of opportunity." The supreme arbiter was the ten-cartridge Lee-Metford magazine rifle, which turned every man into a modified machine-gun. At these manoeuvres, he saw lines of infantry taking no cover of any kind. Without rebuke from their officers or from the umpires, they were all standing out in the open and shooting at each other like bottles on a wall.

When the din of firing had died away, he put questions to a staff officer, and was assured that there had been no mistake.

"But suppose, in a real battle, the enemy took cover and we didn't?"

"Sir," retorted his companion, "forgive me for saying that there is altogether too much talk about cover. The purpose of an attacking party is to occupy a given position. In order to do that, we must not be afraid of a certain margin of loss."

Being a civilian, the visitor said no more. To him it sounded disturbingly like the tactics of the middle eighteenth century. But, apparently, what was there to fear? It was a year of resplendent victory. At the manoeuvres he met and made friends with old Field-Marshal Lord Wolesley, the Commander-in-Chief; they were discussing religion when news arrived from the Egyptian Sudan. The Sudan campaign was ended. General Kitchener had shattered the Khalifa's army and opened the way to Khartoum.

At Undershaw in the autumn, Conan Doyle was meditating—and smiling over—an idea which swallowed up every other interest between October and December. The theme of his new book was going to astonish readers; he could not help that, and did not want to help it. He only hoped that they would see it as he did. Even the title might prejudice them against it, though again he hoped not. Its title was *A Duet, with an Occasional Chorus.*

A Duet is the story of a commonplace suburban

couple, Maude Selby and Frank Crosse, who fall in love, marry, and encounter no more adventures than the small domestic events of everyday life. It is not autobiographical in the sense that *Stark Munro* is autobiographical. Most of the incidents might have happened to anybody, and some of them certainly never happened to him. The explanation lies in his state of mind when he wrote it: *A Duet* is a dream-world. Its fine humour comes not, as usual, from the author's mastery of the ridiculous; the young people's speeches are funny because they are profoundly and even painfully true to life.

Take, for instance, the chapter called 'Confessions.' Maude and Frank have determined to have no secrets from each other. Whereupon Maude asks him whether he has ever loved any woman before he met her. Frank is compelled to acknowledge it. Presently, by the usual feminine sleight-of-hand, he is lured on and convicted of having been in love with as many as forty. Taking a lofty line, he preaches her a lecture about the nature of man; but, as the author points out, women are not interested in generalities. "Were they nicer than me?" "Who?" "Those forty women."

Secretly, of course, Frank is pleased that she is jealous, and is feeling no end of a gay dog. He swears that he will never look at another woman. In fact, he has reached a considerable state of complacence when the following occurs.

"And you, Maude—would you be equally frank with me?"

"Yes, dear, I will. I feel that I owe it to you after your confidence in me. I have had my little experiences too."

"You!"

"Perhaps you would rather that I said nothing about

them. What good can there be in raking up these old stories?"

"No, I had rather you told me."

"You won't be hurt?"

"No, no—certainly not."

"You may take it from me, Frank, that if any married woman ever tells her husband that until she saw him she never felt any emotion at the sight of another man, it is simple nonsense."

"Maude, you have loved some one else!"

"I won't deny that I have been interested—deeply interested—in several men."

"Several!"

"It was before I had met you, dear. I owed you no duty."

"You have loved several men."

"The feeling was for the most part quite superficial. There are many different sorts and degrees of love."

"Good God, Maude! How many men inspired this feeling in you?"

No word of description, not even an adverb to indicate the tone of voice, is at all necessary here. The craftsman knew that. Frank, chokingly maintaining that he is calm and not at all angry, presses Maude for details when it appears she has been deeply interested in several young men.

"No, no, go on! The next stage was?"

"Well, when you have been deeply interested some time, then you begin to have experiences."

"Ah!"

"Don't shout, Frank."

"Did I shout? Never mind. Go on! You had experiences."

"Why go into details?"

"You must go on. You have said too much to stop. I insist upon hearing the experiences."

And so on, until it develops that the experiences are not exactly of a sinister kind. That is the tone of *A Duet*, even in its serious or sentimental moments. And its reception at the hands of the public can be anticipated.

Many of his admirers, expecting to find a corpse in the milk-churn or Prince Rupert leading a cavalry-charge at Naseby, were disappointed. This was not what their favourite usually gave them, and they wondered what was wrong. The more austere critics, who preferred love-problems in the style of Henrik Ibsen, scorned the book as sentimental and naïve. Of course it was. That was the whole point: it was human. Can any of us say that he has never once (or considerably more than once) raved and carried on exactly like Frank Crosse?

For *A Duet*, Conan Doyle reserved a special and particular sort of affection he had for no other book: it was his glorification of love in the abstract. Because Grant Richards, the publisher, had recently been married, he decided that Grant Richards should publish it. He refused large offers for the serial rights, because he believed serialization would spoil it. After its publication when anyone, friend or stranger, wrote him in praise of *A Duet*, that letter he carefully treasured. And the book had powerful friends. When he heard it had been liked by Swinburne (of all people), he was delighted. A letter from H. G. Wells, at Sandgate in Kent, pleased him no less.

"My wife, for whose verdict I waited," wrote Wells, "has just finished the *Duet*. And, as I chanced on a sort of 'slate' of the book last week, it occurred to me you'd not be offended if I wrote and told you we both like it extremely. It seems to me you have the shape and the flavour (or the texture or quality or atmosphere or whatever term you like) just as rightly done as it can be. They're a middle-class couple and simple at that; but the ass of a critic seemed to think that this somehow condemned the book.

"I've spent a year out of the last three at a similarly 'commonplace' story," Wells added bitterly, and, in parentheses "Still at it." "So I'm not altogether outside my province in judging your book."

We can understand Conan Doyle's state of mind, therefore, when he found *A Duet* attacked in the press on the grounds of immorality. Exception was taken to one episode: Frank Crosse, in the story, meets a former mistress; and, when he evades getting back to the old relationship in the private room at a restaurant, she threatens to tell his wife. Grotesque as the charge of 'immorality' seems against this book, or in fact any of Conan Doyle's books, it was made—apparently—by five different critics.

The English 'Bookman,' the American 'Bookman,' *Cladius Clear* and *A Man of Kent* in the 'British Weekly,' *O.O.* in the 'Sketch,' united in condemning it on these grounds. Then he discovered that all five critics were the same man: Dr. Robertson Nicholl, who also popped up at intervals as a sixth anonymous critic in the daily press.

Conan Doyle's roar of rage could be heard throughout the Reform Club. He discussed the matter in the 'Daily Chronicle,' wading over the line into libel and not in the least caring. The man-in-the-street, who never dreamed it was the practice for one critic to review books under several names, expressed astonishment. Conan Doyle was prepared to admit that Dr. Nicholl had not acted for any personal or commercial end, though in private he doubted this. "The wire-pulling gang," he called them. Otherwise, the defence of Dr. Robertson Nicholl and his friends seemed to him singularly weak.

"Mr. Bullock," snarled Conan Doyle, "says there are other and worse groups of papers. It is very possible. Let him name them, as I have done, and he will do good service to literature. As to the quality of my own work, however deplorable, that is entirely beside the question."

Meanwhile, before he had finished *A Duet*, the year 1898 drew to its close. Mr. and Mrs. Leckie, Jean's parents, gave him a pearl and diamond pin-stud for a Christmas present. Jean, with two other girls, was now living in a flat in town. Over the outside world, thunder rumbled. On December 18th, in Johannesburg, a Boer policeman in pursuit of an Englishman named Edgar, whom he wished to arrest for an alleged assault on another man, entered Edgar's house and without provocation shot him dead. They were approaching the fateful year 1899: which, small and insignificant as may have been the conflict in which it ended, has left its mark on the world to this day.

X

WARNING:

Bugle on the Veldt

"Look at the plucky little fellow standing up to the giant!" "Hurrah for these South African Dutchmen; *they* won't stand any bullying!" "It'd be a fine thing, wouldn't it, if the big fellow took a licking for once?"

It was a human sentiment, a natural one; it tingled over the cables in those early peace-time days of 1899. In England the pro-Boer party expressed it even more forcibly. The German Emperor, Kaiser Wilhelm the Second, smiled and set in motion a very active press-service. France, smarting under the Fashoda affair in Egypt, made ironic comments. In all Europe Great Britain had no ally; and it may be doubted whether she even had a friend.

If you see in your mind's eye the vast peninsula of South Africa, curving down into the Cape of Good Hope, imagine against it, to the extreme right-centre, a territory about the size of Germany before the First World War. That territory constituted the two Dutch Republics, the Transvaal and the Orange Free State. The Orange Free State already had complete independence. Over the Transvaal Great Britain exercised, or claimed to exercise, a vague so-called 'suzerainty.' The terms of this suzerainty had never been defined. Nobody, Boer or Briton, knew what it was or what it meant. That was a cause for trouble, but far from the only cause for trouble.

Nearly sixty years before, the Boers had trekked northwards in their ox-drawn wagons from the British Cape Colony. They were Bible-reading farmers, rangy and bearded: good-humoured, slow-minded, ignorant of all books except that devouring Bible. Their new homes lay in the shadow of the dreaded Zulus. Yet in two battles their horsemen with muzzle-loading muskets, galloping in to fire and darting back before the volley of spears, routed the Matabele and crushed the Zulu king, Dingaan. A boy of thirteen, Paul Kruger, saw the defeat of Dingaan and presently conceived himself as inspired by God with a divine mission.

During the ensuing half-century the back-veldt Boers settled down on farms remote from each other, each to itself a law: their boast was that one farm could not see the chimney-smoke of another. There was an occasional sharp brush with the English, who drove them back from the Port of Natal and added more hatred. In 1881 a small British expeditionary force was decisively beaten at Majuba; the stiff Boer faces had good reason to smile. But there was little here to tempt anyone. At Pretoria the Volksraad, or Parliament of the Transvaal, drowsed and grew fat in their urban frock coats. Then, in 1886, came the discovery of the Rand gold-mines.

Gold! And these were no ordinary gold-fields. Their value came to be estimated at seven hundred million pounds.

Into the Transvaal, making a centre at Johannesburg, newcomers flocked to buy concessions from the Boer Government. There were knaves and adventurers among them. But even a dubious observer is compelled to admit that the majority were honest: these gold-fields did not tempt the solitary adventurer. It was less mining than quarrying; elaborate machinery was required, with capital to back it. Capital in turn brought the engineers, the technicians, the miners, the tradesmen: who did not want to live in Park Lane, but only in a decent house. And the great majority of these Uitlanders (as the Boers called them) were British.

The twenty-five burghers of the Pretoria Volksraad awoke with a start. The revenue of their Republic, from scarcely more than a hundred and fifty thousand pounds a year in 1886, soared in 1899 to four million a year. The Government was rich. They were rich. With a little judicious grabbing, they could grow richer. But, as early as 1892 and 1893, the Uitlanders were petitioning for rights.

They were met by President Paul Kruger, an old man now, but stocky and firm-jawed as ever. His broad brick-red face, with its fringe of white chin-beard, peered out implacably. We see him standing, dusty-booted, on the steps of the Raad-house with the four-coloured Transvaal flag above his head. He was sincerely devout; to despoil the Egyptians was a pious pleasure. If most of the Uitlanders' grievances could have been compressed into one conversation with him, it would have run like this.

"We want the right to vote. But you've passed a law that no Uitlander can vote until he's lived here for fourteen years!"

"I have." The grim old President always felt satisfied about that.

"Your Honour," which was the Boer term corresponding to Your Excellency, "let us say one thing first. You're taxing Uitlanders so hard that among us we contribute nine-tenths of the revenue of this whole country. What do we get in return?"

"Gold."

"The mine-owners do, yes. But most of us aren't

mine-owners. We want to live here. And what about living conditions?"

"You don't like them?"

"With all respect, Your Honour: most of your Volksraad are corrupt. They can put any kind of official over any kind of interest. Your police laugh at us. We've got children to educate; but you won't allow our money to educate them. We're not allowed to have sanitation in our houses, or even pipes to carry water. Your concessions and monopolies put any price they like even on household articles we have to buy. We can't serve on a jury or hold a public meeting. Aren't we worse off than the Kaffirs?"

"Nobody," the President retorted unanswerably, "asked you to come here. You are always free to go."

"But can't you grant *any* concession? The franchise?"

"You see that flag?" demanded President Kruger, pointing upwards. "If I grant the franchise, I may as well pull it down."

And in this he was undoubtedly right, since (unrestricted) franchise would have given the Uitlanders a majority vote. Kruger's shrewd old eye watched not only these interlopers; he looked southwards to the Cape. There, with Cecil Rhodes as Premier of the Cape Colony, Rhodes's Imperialist policy was stretching up filaments round the Transvaal itself. True, Kruger might have alleviated the burdens of the Uitlanders, as a group of his own people urged. But most of the twenty-five Old Men, isolated and sealed of God, were implacable. "Come on and fight! Come on!" challenged one of them. Kruger, throwing out his words in grunts, was even more implacable when he spoke to W. Y. Campbell.

"You," he pointed out, "have not got the guns; I have."

It was gun-rule. At the end of 1895 the Uitlanders determined to rise with rifles in Johannesburg and occupy the fort at Pretoria. Where they made their mistake was in appealing for armed help to Cecil Rhodes, of the Chartered South Africa Company, and Rhodes's friend Dr. Jameson. That brought the matter actually if not technically under the British flag. Then both Rhodes and the Uitlanders hesitated. Dr. Jameson, against orders, 'invaded' the Transvaal with the drearily inadequate force of five hundred men.

Kruger, his ear to the ground, chuckled. On the second day of 1896 Dr. Jim, a legendary worker of miracles against the black spearmen of Mashonaland, found himself surrounded near Dornkop by three times his number of Boer sharpshooters in an impregnable position. He surrendered; so did the Uitlanders. The cry went up that this venture had been sponsored, or at least winked at, by Joseph Chamberlain and the Machiavellian British Government.

Now the Machiavellian British Government, as so often happens, had in fact been doing nothing at all. The truth of their intentions may be seen in the number of troops they had in South Africa, not only at this time but up to the middle of 1899. Scattered over these huge frontiers—their two main ports, Cape Town and Durban in Natal, being nearly seven hundred miles apart on opposite sides of the peninsula—they had just six thousand men, including cavalry and three light field-batteries. Whereas President Kruger, in secret treaty with the Orange Free State, had other plans.

One thing the President did not lack was money. Well before the Jameson Raid, he had begun buying arms from Germany and France. By 1899 his arsenals could supply five modern magazine-rifles for every male Boer in the country. His imported field-guns were the heaviest yet built. The President of the Orange Free State clamoured for a share of his twenty-five million cartridges.

More, he had many Dutch supporters in the British Cape Colony. When hostilities began, he believed he would have the fighting-support of Germany; the German minister assured him of this, and the Kaiser, at the time of the Jameson Raid, had sent him an open telegram congratulating him on his triumph over Jameson "without appealing to the help of friendly powers." Into that field, when joined with the Orange Free State, President Kruger could throw from forty to fifty thousand mounted riflemen with forty thousand more as reserves, and better artillery than any in England. His purpose, when the time came, was to sweep fanwise across his borders and drive the British out of South Africa.

Now there was no earthly reason why he should not have done this. We are not taking sides; who shall blame President Kruger, or even fail to cheer for him, if he wanted the Dutch Republics to rule South Africa? But the attitude in which the journalists of the world depicted him—as the pious, simple-minded farmer, rifle in one hand and Bible in the other, heroically defying a gigantic aggressor—was, to say the least, a trifle anomalous.

"God is on our side. I do not want war," President Kruger was later to declare, as he signed an order for further ammunition; "but I will not give more away."

In England, during the May of '99 when Sir Alfred Milner in South Africa was urging Her Majesty's Government to intervene on behalf of the Uitlanders, Arthur Conan Doyle had just concluded his newspaper controversy with Dr. Robertson Nicholl of the five names. Also, he was hard at work.

In the larch-shaded study at Undershaw, where he could look out across the dark-green pinewoods which fell away beyond the front terrace and the tennis court, he worked at a sixteen-thousand-word prize-fighting story called *The Croxley Master*. But reverberations of the South African wrangle were close in his ears. Of all the fierce pro-Boers in England, there were few more fierce than the Ma'am.

"To me," wrote the Ma'am, with her old dream of chivalry, "there seems a want of magnanimity in pushing that small band of Boers into an impossible position, and then proceeding to endeavour to thrash them for being there. It is not worthy of our great nation. But no doubt the same money that started the Raid and kept up this agitation is now being used to bring it to a head."

"No, no, no!" protested her son, though about the raid he had ugly misgivings. He urged her to drop the subject in a birthday-letter he sent on May 22nd.

"Well," he said, "I am forty years old; but my life has grown steadily fuller and happier. On the physical side I played cricket today, made 53 out of 106 made by the whole side and bowled out 10 of my opponents, so I'm all sound yet."

Forty years old? He, who felt all of twenty-five or thirty, could laugh at this. He told the Ma'am, with exultation, that *A Duet* was selling well in America. And he concluded with the excellent news that two of his plays, *Sherlock Holmes* and *Halves*, would be produced before the end of the year. An American actor named William Gillette, in fact, had just arrived in England with the manuscript of the former play.

The play of *Sherlock Holmes*, strictly speaking, was no longer his. Charles Frohman in America had accepted it and turned it over to William Gillette: who, eager to play the part, asked for permission to re-write according to his own discretion. The author, by this time bored with the whole matter, agreed. It got itself so thoroughly re-written into another play that nobody now knows what the original play was about. Then, after a long silence, came Gillette's cable.

MAY I MARRY HOLMES?

The answer to this, of course, should have been a quiet and simple, "No"; backed up, if necessary, with a butcher's cleaver. But Conan Doyle merely replied that Gillette could marry Holmes or murder him or do anything he liked with him. The next information was that Gillette, after losing the first draft of the play in a hotel fire, intended to open in New York during the autumn; that it would be a colossal success, making all their fortunes; and that the actor was on his way to England with the new script for Conan Doyle's approval.

Thus, during the week of his fortieth birthday, he invited Gillette down to Undershaw for the week-end.

At the railway station, several miles from Undershaw, he waited in the two-horse landau with Holden in a shiny top-hat on the box. He had never seen William Gillette, even in a photograph. He knew nothing about Gillette except the latter's high reputation as an actor. The London train, its green-painted carriages then numbered for first and second class, clattered to a stop. And out of it, in a long grey cape, stepped the living image of Sherlock Holmes.

Not even Sidney Paget had done it so well in a drawing. The clear-cut features, the deep-set eyes, looked out under a deerstalker cap; even Gillette's age, the middle forties, was right. Conan Doyle, in the landau, contemplated him open-mouthed. The actor, in his turn face to face with the image of an oversized Dr. Watson, stared back. It is not recorded that the horses shied; but this was the general effect. It dissolved in mirth during the hospitality of the week-end.

"Gillette," he exclaimed to the Ma'am, "has turned it into a fine play!" And to Innes: "Two of his acts are simply grand!" Now William Gillette had charm; by birth as well as manners he was a gentleman; and this may partly have influenced his host's verdict. For *Sherlock Holmes* was not a good play, as those of us who have seen it can testify. Nevertheless, the actor infected Conan Doyle with his own enthusiastic forecast of its success in America. Then, only a few weeks after Gillette had gone, *Halves* was produced at the Garrick Theatre in London.

It was mid-June and very hot weather, which asked for theatrical disaster. *Halves* had no star-name, which still further endangered it. The play closely followed James Payn's story, being a simple domestic comedy of two brothers who, as young men, make a vow to meet twenty-one years afterwards and share whatever fortunes they have gained. Yet despite all drawbacks it had a solid if unspectacular success.

"It is refreshing," declared the 'Daily Telegraph,' "to watch such a piece in these brisk and giddy-pacèd times, this age of daring themes, this season of unrest and change."

Whatever we may think of the brisk and giddy-pacèd times, it was a year of change for Conan Doyle's family. His youngest sister, Dodo, who lived with the Ma'am and of whom he saw comparatively little, married a young clergyman named Cyril Angell. Willie Hornung, modestly strutting, scored his first literary hit with

Raffles, The Amateur Cracksman, which he dedicated to his brother-in-law. And Innes, now a Captain in the Royal Artillery, had gone out for service in India.

"Ever so many thanks, old chap," we find Innes writing on more than one occasion, "for the three blank cheques. I will let you know how I fill them up."

For Innes was playing polo, and his pay went little further than the customary allowance. From Umballa, where he commanded a battery, Innes sent glowing accounts of his life. At twenty-six he was a sporting enthusiast, not a literary man. Yet his letters exude the very breath of India. The lean gun-horses streaked across mud hurdles at steeplechase exercise; by night the frogs croaked deafeningly, and one otherwise-useless servant carried a lantern as a guard against snakes when Innes went across to dinner. Even under the hot deluge of the rains, when banjo-strings rotted and golf-links were closed because of wet 'browns' (not greens), Captain Doyle remained cheerful.

"I can't thank you enough, old chap, for the £100 cheque. I had bought a first charger just before it came, and he cost me 1300 rupees. He is a splendid bay, 'Crusader' by name. . . . Where and when am I to look for *The Croxley Master* and the story about the Brigadier's fox-hunt?"

Innes was not the only one who looked forward to this newly written story of Brigadier Gerard, which has been called both *The Crime of the Brigadier* and *How the Brigadier Slew the Fox*. Of all the Brigadier stories, it was Conan Doyle's own favourite. No follower of the debonair Gerard, pride of Napoleon's Army, can forget that he cherished one particular illusion. Having learned to speak English from 'Adjutant Obriant, of the Regiment Irlandais,' and, as he explains, to say, "Be jabers!" as the French might say, "Ma foi!"—he believes himself to be an authority on all things relating to England or the English.

"I have made the fox-chase with the English," proudly announces the Brigadier. "I have also fought the box-fight with the Bustler, of Bristol."

And this story of how Etienne Gerard made the fox-chase, according to his own personal and peculiar notions concerning the purpose of the hunt, is a little classic. Conan Doyle, writing to Innes in July, explained that he meant to go on another lecture-tour in the autumn, and that he would read *The Crime of the Brigadier* to his audiences. "The devil of it is," he said, "that I can't read it for laughing."

They discussed other plans for the autumn, too. When the rains in India were over, and Lahore became the gaiety-centre of the Punjab, he would send Lottie out for a long holiday under Innes's chaperonage. Lottie had been tied to them for seven years. Lottie, who loved dancing, was tiring herself out over Touie and the children. Lottie, in tears, confessed that she would —well, *like* to go, most awfully, if she could be spared.

And yet, "I don't know what I shall do when Lottie is gone as well as you," he wrote to Innes. Meanwhile, in South Africa, the scale-pans dipped now towards peace, now towards war.

The Bloemfontein conference between President Kruger and Sir Alfred Milner, the British Commissioner, had ended in disagreement. Conference followed conference, note followed note, proposal countered proposal, from July to September. Lord Salisbury's Government, far from trying to force war on the President, were attempting to appease him. They had no wish to send, over six thousand ocean-miles, an army whose lines of communication could be cut the moment they lost control of the sea. There were reports of an alliance against them of Germany, France, and Russia. But on the point of British suzerainty over the Transvaal they would not give way. And President Kruger, now openly joined by President Steyn of the Orange Free State, had never any intention of being appeased.

During this time the thin-sprinkled line of British troops, six thousand men to guard a continent, had received no reinforcements. Their officers ceased even to swear. Large packing-cases from Germany and France, labelled 'Agricultural Implements' and 'Mining Machinery' still streamed into Kruger's forts: not only by way of Delagoa Bay, but before the startled eyes of the British at Cape Town and Port Elizabeth.

The Boer leaders were playing for time. A burgher could not go to war without his horse. A horse needed grass. Grass would not grow on the veldt before rain, and the rain would not come until autumn. When that happened. . . .

In September the British Cabinet, realizing that President Kruger really did mean war, hastily despatched troops from India and the Mediterranean. By the end of the month their forces numbered twenty-two thousand. It was not enough. Under the snapping admonitions of Joseph Chamberlain, the Cabinet faced a clear issue. They had been made a laughing-stock over the Jameson Raid, and over their protracted negotiations with Kruger. Either the British Empire had teeth, or it hadn't; if it had, it must bite. They set about preparing to send from England, if necessary, an Army Corps of three divisions under Sir Redvers Buller.

To the military expert, to the man in the pub, such a force seemed ridiculously large. These Boers, the military expert said patronizingly, were a mere disorganized rabble. The man in the pub was gaseous with pride and contempt. "Old Kruger? Garn! 'E won't last a fortnight!"

(The Boer leaders were saying exactly the same thing about the English.) In London the Little Englanders and the pro-Boers protested against war-preparations. There were fights at public meetings, under naphtha-flares. While the Government was drafting an ultimatum to President Kruger, the latter anticipated them by curtly delivering an ultimatum of his own.

All troops on his borders, said the President, must instantly be withdrawn, and all British reinforcements must leave South Africa. Failing a satisfactory reply from Her Majesty's Government within forty-eight hours, he would not be responsible for the consequences.

"Is the beggar off his onion?"

That was how, between wrath and incredulity, the nation greeted his ultimatum. The Government's reply was short. On October 11th, 1899, a state of war existed. And on the following day, contrary to all expectations, the Boers attacked.

Among the few who had never underestimated these adversaries, as their private correspondence shows, were old Lord Wolesley, the Commander in Chief of the Army, and Conan Doyle. The latter, merely from reading history, knew the back-veldt Boers' Calvinistic courage and their strategic skill at hill-fighting.

"I wish we had such good men with us instead of against us," he wrote to Innes. "It's a horrible business. And yet," he burst out hotly, "they are a most stiff-necked race to deal with. They seem to do nothing save under compulsion, and damned little then."

At the end of September he had gone to Tilbury to see Lottie off for India in the S.S. *Egypt*, on a cold day streaming with rain. No sooner was the liner out into the Thames than Lottie hurried to her cabin and wrote to him.

"My heart was too full to say much, but I felt a lot.

I hate leaving you and am already looking forward to Spring when I return. But also I shall try to have a real good time until then because I know you want me to. It is no good trying to thank you for everything, for I simply can't."

"Nonsense!" growled her brother, but he treasured the letter. He had begun his lecture-tour, fourteen readings, when war was declared. In November, when the readings ended, a cable from his American agent informed him that Gillette's *Sherlock Holmes* had been well received at its try-out in Buffalo. A cable about the New York opening came later.

SPLENDID SUCCESS WITH PRESS AND PUBLIC NEW YORK LAST NIGHT. HERALD ACCLAIMS IT AS DRAMATIC TRIUMPH. GILLETTE SCORED SUCCESS OF HIS CAREER.

That was gratifying enough, and so was the offer of a political career. Since the fall of the Liberals several years before, Conan Doyle's old party, the Liberal-Unionists, had become more and more amalgamated with the Tories. It was suggested that he might like to stand for Parliament in the Unionist interest. But most of the gratification quickly lost its savour.

Although every London street-organ ground out *Soldiers of the Queen*, the news from South Africa came with a shock of humiliation and alarm. Let it be repeated that the Boers attacked.

They struck eastwards through the craggy passes into Natal, to sweep the British into the sea. Watchers on house-tops over the border saw six miles of their canvas-covered ox-wagons winding down the passes. Simultaneously, on the western border, they struck south to Kimberley and north to Mafeking. On the Natal side, five sharp skirmishes ended in a British disaster. Columns from the Transvaal on one side, and from the

Free State on the other, were converging against Ladysmith. At Ladysmith Sir George White, British Commander until Sir Redvers Buller's troop-transports
should arrive with the Army Corps, went out to fight
at Lombard's Kop.

The Boer numbers had been far underestimated.
There was a pleasant delusion that their artillery would
be a mere encumbrance to them. But the Boer artillery,
from the heavy Creusot with its ninety-six-pound shell
to the quick-firing one-pounder pom-pom, made British
batteries look obsolete. On a vast semi-circle of boulder-
strewn hills called kopjes, each a small fort in itself, the
Boer riflemen were invisible until they streamed across
in a flank attack supported by machine-guns. Colonel
Knox sent word that the Boers had prepared a rush on
Ladysmith from the other side. The bugles blew retire.

By the beginning of November, nearly eleven thousand British troops were isolated and besieged round
Ladysmith. Far away on the western border, Kimberley
and Mafeking were besieged. And there was much
worse to come.

But, said everybody in England, Sir Redvers Buller
had arrived! Buller would do the trick! His troop-
transports were nearing Cape Town. There was a month
of evil stirring: the Boers, in fighting-units of which
each unit was called a commando, prepared to invade
the Cape Colony. The Army Corps arrived, preventing
invasion; but Lord Methuen, advancing to the relief of
Kimberley, floundered at the Modder River. Then, between December 7th and December 17th, came England's Black Week.

Lord Methuen, in a night-attack at Magersfontein,
marched his Highland Brigade in assembly formation
straight up to Cronje's trenches without knowing how
close the trenches were. General Gatacre, misled by

guides at Stormberg, found himself at dawn among rifle-blazing kopjes which his maddened troops could not climb. General Buller, who had gone to Natal, tried to relieve Ladysmith by making a frontal attack across the Tugela River. Having no idea that Boer trenches lay just across the Tugela instead of in the hills beyond, and sending Hart's Irish Brigade to cross the river by a ford that wasn't there, Buller had his men shot to pieces by Louis Botha's invisible defences on the other bank.

"The loss of three battles in one week," chorused the German press, more gleeful than even the French, Russian, or Austrian press, "has brought Great Britain's military prestige to its lowest ebb in the nineteenth century."

"We read eight or ten newspapers a day, and wait for the next edition," Conan Doyle had said, in his introductory speech at a banquet given by the Authors' Club to a worried Lord Wolesley as the first bad news trickled in. And he was reading them still more closely now in Black Week. He read of concealed first lines of Boer trenches; and, beyond them, of deep trenches guarded by barbed wire, with shelter-pits to hide even the guns.

Evidently the British generals had never thought of this. It was unorthodox.

To Conan Doyle returned a memory of the manoeuvres on Salisbury Plain, and of soldiers set out in the open like bottles on a wall. How he would like to write a history of this war! But this, in Black Week, must be postponed. Already he had talked of enlisting, and this brought the Ma'am to a state of frenzy.

"How dare you!" cried the Ma'am in an explosive letter. "What do you mean by it? Why, your very height and breadth would make you a sure and simple target!"

It was all very well to get into a fight, she admitted, characteristically mentioning the Percys, the Packs, the Conans, and the Doyles; but to support this cause, where 'that awful gold' was really at the root of the matter, would be crime and folly.

"For God's sake listen to me," she went on. "Even at your age I am God's representative in you. Do not go, Arthur! That is my first and last word. If these politicians and journalists who so lightly drift into war had to go to the front themselves they would be a great deal more careful. They pushed the country into this, and you shall not be their victim if I can help it. I am coming down there," she warned darkly, "if you leave me in uncertainty!"

Whether the Ma'am did go down to Undershaw and make a scene is not recorded. But her son remained unresponsive. The whole nation was roused.

Sir Redvers Buller, losing hope for the first and only time in his life, wavered and suggested to Sir George White that Ladysmith ought to be surrendered. "Surrender be damned!" replied White. At home the Government appointed Lord Roberts to the supreme command in South Africa, with General Kitchener (now Lord Kitchener of Khartoum) as his chief-of-staff. A sixth division had been sent to South Africa; a seventh was mobilized. For the first time they called for volunteers, not only from home but from the Empire.

Now at the outbreak of the war Conan Doyle had said at a cricket-club dinner that the nation ought to make use of her sportsmen, the men who could ride and shoot, in a Mounted Infantry against the Boer mobile horse. He wrote to the 'Times,' again urging it, and his letter was printed on the same day that the Government called for just that kind of force as a Volunteer Yeomanry. He felt he had to act.

"So of course," he justified himself to the Ma'am, "I was honour-bound, as I had suggested it, to be the first to volunteer.

"What I feel is that I have perhaps the strongest influence over young men, especially young sporting men, of anyone in England bar Kipling. That being so, it is really important that I should give them a lead.

"As to the merits of the quarrel: from the day they invaded Natal that becomes merely academic. But surely it is obvious that *they* have prepared for years and that we have not. What becomes of our deep and sinister designs then? I had grave doubts before war broke out, but ever since I have been sure that it was a righteous war and well worth sacrifices."

But he had no luck. He applied to the War Office, Lord Chesham, and the Middlesex Yeomanry; all said he was too old for the ranks, but wouldn't give any civilian a commission. "Which is rot!" he said.

His idea was to go out on his own; and, if men were wanted on the spot, he would be there, "It would bore me to remain in England and have folk say, 'Hullo! I thought you were at the front.' That would become annoying"—especially since top-hatted, high-collared young men from the West End were lining up in queues for the orderly-room. But there was another possibility. Why not go as a doctor?

A friend of his, Mr. John Langman, was sending out a hospital at the donor's own expense. This hospital was to go to the front, unlike other civil ones; and that decided Conan Doyle's mind when his offer to go was quickly accepted. The donor's son, young Archie Langman, now a Lieutenant in the Middlesex Yeomanry, explained the matter as they sat before a blazing fire at Undershaw during frosty Christmas week.

"I'm to go along as Treasurer," young Langman said excitedly. "We've chosen the civil surgeon-in-chief and the younger surgeon. But my father wants you to be senior civil physician, and supervise things generally. Will you do that?"

His host, pipe in mouth, nodded.

"The hospital," continued Archie, "is to be a slap-up affair. A hundred beds, with marquees and thirty-five small tents. Extra comforts for the wounded. We've got some first-rate men, too."

"Who's your surgeon-in-chief?"

"Robert O'Callaghan. Know him?"

"I think I've heard the name. Specialist, isn't he?"

"Yes. Gynaecologist. Women's diseases and—er—all that sort of thing, you know."

Conan Doyle blinked. "He'll have comparatively few patients at the front, won't he?"

"Don't joke, sir! O'Callaghan's a good man. All the same, my father says he'd be happier if you came up and chose the personnel."

Thus was formed the Langman Hospital, of forty-five men altogether, whose corporate photograph (in tropical sun-helmets and khaki uniforms with puttees) presently adorned the pages of the 'Graphic' and the 'Sketch.' Conan Doyle went as an unpaid man, and contributed his butler, Cleeve, whose wages he paid himself. Their War Office official proved to be a whisky-drinking doctor named Major M. O'C. Drury, R.A.M.C., about whom the senior physician felt qualms even before their departure.

As the bells prepared to ring in the new year and the new century, Lottie in India was sending breathless accounts of the dances at Lahore, and the coloured whirl of uniforms at the Governor's Ball.

"The 16th Lancers," she wrote, "have just got their marching orders for the Cape. So they had to scratch for the polo tournament at the last moment"—O England! —"and sell all their lovely ponies. Umballa will soon be empty. Everyone is surprised that our guns have not been sent yet, and for the last fortnight I have led a very jumpy existence." Innes, far from jumpy, raved at the delay. "Why don't they send for the guns? Everybody at home has gone; it's just my infernal luck!"

At the new year, which is midsummer in South Africa, General Joubert's heavy shells exploded in besieged Ladysmith above the spatter of shrapnel-shells on corrugated-iron roofs. Joubert, with his usual chivalry, had permitted all non-combatants to leave; but few went. It was not shell-fire that racked Ladysmith: it was disease. Besieged Kimberley had once heard the growl of Lord Methuen's cannon, and seen the glint of his observation-balloon; their heliograph winked and was answered; but no relief came. Small, unimportant Mafeking in the North caught the hearts and fired the imaginations of the Empire. At Mafeking Colonel Baden-Powell not only kept off the besiegers; he laughed at them, held cricket-matches which he dared them to interrupt, and devilled them with bayonet-raids by night.

"Surrender to avoid bloodshed!" was the message he received.

"When is the bloodshed going to begin?" inquired Baden-Powell.

And yet in the field, despite French's brilliant cavalry-tactics at Colesberg, disaster blackened on disaster. Sir Redvers Buller again tried to cross the Tugela. And this time the attempt succeeded. But on the hill called Spion Kop, where four thousand British troops were ordered into a space which might have afforded cover for five hundred, the Boer artillery pounded flesh in a mortar until General Warren (at the foot of the hill) called back the survivors in shattering defeat.

It was incredible. To the man in the pub this Boer, who sang psalms and would not shell a town on Sunday, seemed to ride in a scent of brimstone or black magic.

"Give us one little victory," some people prayed. "Just *one* little victory." The prayer has been heard before; and since.

At Undershaw the ever-smiling Touie, who always supported her husband, had insisted that of course he must accompany the hospital, and had herself gone to Naples with the children. He prowled through the big rooms while he awaited orders. People still kept asking what was wrong with the conduct of the war. To him it seemed obvious what was wrong. He meant, before long, to write it down. But not before he had met and mixed with the men who saw these things happen. True, the men were no longer flung forward against Boer trenches in mass attacks across an open veldt, forbidden for pride's sake to flop down and fire from behind an ant-hill. The officer no longer raced forward waving his sword, to be kicked over by half a dozen Mauser bullets the moment the sun caught that sword-blade. Conan Doyle reflected that the best troops in the world had learned lessons despite their generals. But, he thought, there were other lessons to be learned as well.

The Langman Hospital was to leave for South Africa on February 28th, 1900. When the chartered transport *Oriental* left Tilbury, the Ma'am came down from Yorkshire to take leave of her son. Already there was news of a change of fortune from the front. Lord Roberts, after secret and careful preparation, was moving north. Though the press-reports were fragmentary, perplexed, and censored, it appeared that in some fashion General French's cavalry had raised the siege of Kimberley.

But the Ma'am was inflexible.

She hated this war. Since the relatives and friends of officers were permitted aboard the ship, the Ma'am sat in one corner of the crowded saloon-lounge, her mouth compressed, while a band played on the boat deck. Jean Leckie had said that she herself would not go to see him off, because she could not endure a last-minute parting amid the thronged and thumping cheerfulness of a transport. He did not learn until afterwards that she was standing in the crowd on the dock, to watch the ship go out.

He had brought with him a mass of Blue books and reference-works, to verify his references when he analyzed the causes of the war for the proposed history. The Ma'am's mouth tightened still more when she saw them.

"Arthur, it's *wrong!*"

"I tell you, Ma'am, it's right!"

Under the circumstances there could not be an open quarrel, though it hovered near one. Over and over he assured her that he would take care of himself. As he watched her go down the gangway, among troops in dress-uniform for the occasion, he was preparing his apology as she was preparing hers. On the day he sailed, though nobody aboard ship knew it, the starving and disease-racked town of Ladysmith was at last relieved by Sir Redvers Buller. On the previous day Lord Roberts, Kitchener, and French, who had outgeneralled and surrounded the retreating Cronje at Paardeberg, forced the Boer General to surrender with his four thousand men.

On the decks of the *Oriental*, hobnailed boots clumped and resounded in an endless hollow tick-a-tack. The band music swelled sonorously over the throb of engines.

"I had got into a rather nervous state," wrote Conan Doyle, "and was feeling the effects of my years of hard work. I shall come back five years younger. Pray forgive me, Ma'am, if I have ever seemed petulant or argumentative—it is all nerves, of which I possess more than most people know."

XI

VICTORIAN:

The End of an Era

Well, his work in South Africa was over now.

Nearly five months later, towards sunset of a July evening, and on the summit of a small kopje, Conan Doyle stood where he had so often stood to gulp a breath of clean air during the evil days. Northwards spread the red-brick town of Bloemfontein, formerly capital of the Orange Free State. Below him towards Bloemfontein lay the Langman Hospital, its small tents and big marquee tents occupying the cricket-field, its main ward housed in the large red-brick cricket-pavilion.

That cricket-pavilion had once been used as a hall for amateur theatricals as well. The staff of the Langman Hospital had been amused, when they arrived, to find that at one end of the pavilion was a gilt-framed stage set for a scene in the operetta *H.M.S. Pinafore*. But their amusement did not last.

They reached Bloemfontein on April 2nd, 1900. The transport *Oriental*, after touching at Cape Town for orders, moved on to the Port of East London and disgorged troops with the Langman Hospital struggling among them. The surgeon-in-chief, Mr. Robert O'Callaghan, was fat and looked rather like Alexandre Dumas père; he preferred a sedentary life. The War Office surgeon, Major Drury, rolled out an affable brogue and supervised their supply of whisky. The hospital-group, forty-five of them, set out in a great troop-train for what proved to be a four-day journey up-country.

The way was clear for them now.

Lord Roberts, after the masterly outflanking of Cronje which was the first step in his plan, had pressed on with his invasion of the Orange Free State. His men, marching sometimes forty miles a day, always on half-rations since Christian De Wet cut up their supply-wagons, fought only two light engagements before they entered Bloemfontein in the middle of March. From thirty to forty thousand men, panting, lay encamped in the green veldt round Bloemfontein or northwards towards Karee Siding.

It was the hot, lightning-streaked gloom of the rainy season when the Langman Hospital arrived. British Tommies, with rangy troops from Canada and Australia and New Zealand, paid Boer shopkeepers a shilling for two cigarettes. The town was full of generals and journalists; Conan Doyle, who kept a diary throughout, lost little of their talk at dinner-parties. He was pleased by their new hospital-site, its cricket-field surrounded by a corrugated-iron fence.

"The Pavilion is a magnificent one," he wrote to Touie, "so with the addition of our tents we hope to take 160 instead of 100 patients. The wounded are coming into the town; this morning we went down to get our stores out of the train."

In a pink undershirt, his face burned red and his sun-helmet on the back of his head, he set the pace for unloading fifty tons of packing-cases. It was so furious a pace that "I could not speak when we had finished, for my tongue clung to my lips." Smith-Dorrien's Brigade, regulars and irregulars, foot and horse, tramped past the railway line. It was a fusion of all elements into the

South African soldier, not prettified as in illustrated papers: tangle-bearded, his pipe in his mouth and the veldt-sores on his hands. With them marched the Gordon Highlanders.

"Good old Gordons!" shouted the dirt-covered man in the pink undershirt, as packing cases bumped from railway-truck to bullock-wagon. Round the town flickered a constant movement of cavalry; "I saw the 12th Lancers, Dragoons, and 8th Hussars go out eastwards against a dark background of rain-clouds."

For the Boers were not idle in the hills. One who was to become their great guerilla leader, Christian De Wet in his tinted spectacles, had already ambushed a British column at Sanna's Post. He had also captured the waterworks twenty miles east of Bloemfontein. No three battles of the war did so much damage as the capture of that water-works.

"Why," more than one person was to rave afterwards, "didn't we go out and drive old Boojer off those waterworks as soon as it happened? *Why?*"

Nobody knows to this day. It seems probable that few people guessed the cause of what happened when it first did happen. It is certain the troops had been drinking tainted water at Paardeberg. Then the enteric fever broke out.

It would be a bad simile to say that the troops, for whom inoculation against enteric had not been made compulsory, died like flies. For the flies were always there, always alive, humming in a black cloud of obscenity. Enteric fever, as it turns a man dizzy and sends his temperature over a hundred, ulcerates the lining of his intestines. It causes constant bowel-pollution of the vilest smell and the most deadly kind of contagion. Death from it is not pretty either.

The Langman Hospital, overwhelmed by Army

stretcher-bearers, was in no worse plight than other hospitals; one of them held seventeen hundred patients with beds for a fourth that number. The Langman lacked disinfectants, lacked linens, lacked utensils. New patients, despite protests, were bundled into the pavilion and left ill or dying between the beds. The grotesque gilt stage, with its set for *H.M.S. Pinafore*, became a latrine. And over everything, each a focus of disease, clustering black on glass-rims or trying to force themselves into the workers' mouths, buzzed the glutted flies.

O'Callaghan, the fat and fashionable gynaecologist, could not face such a death. He went home. Major Drury, with the flies round his bald head, changed from an entertaining companion into a drunken martinet. If Conan Doyle had not taken charge, there might have been a breakdown. But the two junior surgeons, Charles Gibbs and H. J. Scharlieb, were the finest men who could have been chosen; so were the orderlies of St. John's Ambulance Brigade, and every other of the forty-five. They fought that epidemic until twelve of them were stricken down by it, and still the epidemic spread.

There could be no question of graves for most of the dead, who were wrapped in khaki blankets and huddled into shallow graves. Five thousand died between April and May. From Bloemfontein rose such a smell as could be caught, when the wind altered, six miles away. At the beginning the doctors of all hospitals collided with the authorities over strict British respect for the exact letter of the military law.

A deputation of doctors, among them the senior physician of the Langman Hospital, went to beg the authorities that empty houses in and round Bloemfontein should be used to accommodate enteric patients. That was impossible, the authorities said, without the consent of the owners: who were Boers now absent on commando with the enemy. This made Conan Doyle's brain reel. He put forward another suggestion.

"Round our cricket-field," he said, "there's a big corrugated-iron fence. We could cut up that fence and turn it into any number of huts that would at least keep the rain off. What do you say?"

"Sorry. That's private property too."

"But these men are dying!"

"Sorry. It's orders. We must show the Dutchmen they can trust us."

They held to the same code by which Tommy Atkins, trudging through a land of fat sheep and fat cattle, was forbidden to touch as much as a couple of fat geese. Only when snipers fired from a farmhouse under a white flag could Tommy throw his helmet at the fowls or bayonet the pigs; if he touched personal property, he risked being shot. The French military attaché swore that any human being who called himself a human being ought to mutiny under such discipline.

No word of the fever-epidemic was yet permitted to appear in the press. In the middle of April, when victims were dying in the street for lack of a place to put them, the distinguished painter Mr. Mortimer Mempes reached Bloemfontein. He had come from the 'Illustrated London News' to draw sketches of Dr. Conan Doyle in the latter's fine clean shining hospital.

"Just look at this inferno!" was the doctor's blast of greeting, as he met Mempes on the veranda of the pavilion. And he pointed to two black-robed Sisters of Mercy who had come to join the Langman Hospital. "They are angels," he said. "They are angels!"

Mortimer Mempes recorded his impressions when censorship had been partly lifted.

"Dr. Conan Doyle worked like a horse, until he had to drag himself up on a kopje to get fresh air, saturated as he was with enteric. He is one of the men who make England great." Mempes, in a campaign hat with its brim turned up at one side, interviewed him on that kopje. Inevitably, the first question was about Sherlock Holmes.

"Which of the stories do you like best?"

"Perhaps the one about the snake," said the harassed author. "But for the life of me I can't remember the name of it. Do you mind excusing me now?"

Mempes followed him through the miasma of the tents in the cricket-field and through the pavilion-ward. There, while the doctor worked, he made sketches. They were bowdlerized drawings, dressed up for public satisfaction; but they do convey, about the senior physician, some sense of why his patients worshipped him. It was not his medical skill. It was his presence, radiating confidence like a furnace; his contempt for danger, his cheerful breaking of rules.

He nursed them, told them stories, wrote their letters, amid the ravings of delirium or the eager gasping speech of the weak. Tropical rains roared on the roof; outside you tramped through six inches of mud. There were frequent rows with Major Drury, but the Major found another Irishman (insubordinate dog) who could make his superior officer shut up with only a peculiar, dangerous kind of look.

"One man," Conan Doyle noted in his diary, "died as I fanned him. I saw the light go out of his eyes. Nothing can exceed the courage or the patience of Tommy."

Yet human nature worked always underneath.

"We have five Boers, decent quiet men, working in the ward. One of them stood looking at a funeral-party when one of the Tommies threw his stick in his face. The Boer walked away. It was a painful incident. It must not happen again."

A little relief was in sight for that inferno. Orders arrived for fifty of their convalescents to be shipped back to the Cape. Another doctor had arrived. On April 24th, a blistering hot day at the end of the rainy season, Conan Doyle heard that the water-works were to be stormed.

With Archie Langman and two journalists, he rode out after the Mounted Infantry—advancing in open order, their horses at a walk—towards the tall red-brick chimney which marked the water-works. Sprays of Boer horsemen could be discerned far ahead. Once or twice there was the distant rap of a rifle-shot. But there was no necessity to storm; no opposition at all. Rumors of a general advance, all along the line, were flying through Bloemfontein when they returned. And on May 1st Lord Roberts began his advance against Johannesburg and Pretoria.

Heliographs twinkled from hill to hill along a thirty-mile front. As the sun-helmets of the central column swung out of Bloemfontein, the brassy music of their bands rolled a paean of relief at leaving that pest-spot. Reined-in cavalry, armed with swords and light carbines, frisked against the green veldt. Convalescents from enteric (there were still three thousand of them) tried to prop shrunken faces on window-sills so that they could raise a cheer. Conan Doyle, awakened at dawn by the swing-step of *The British Grenadiers*, knew this meant that the Guards were moving up and it would be the real thing. Shortly afterwards he was accosted by an excited Archie Langman.

"You look done up," said young Langman. "The Major can handle things now. Let's take a few days' holiday and ride after the main column. We may get under some shell-fire."

They did. The senior physician wrote an account of it

immediately afterwards in *Days with the Army* for the 'Strand.' Archie on his horse Ginger, and Conan Doyle riding a sleepy mount named Fathead, overtook the main column at Karee. Beyond Blandfort, on a kopje-toothed plain in front of the Vat River, he heard the whine of Boer shells before they spurted earth round the 84th Field Battery. Then shrapnel twanged, stinging up the earth like rain on a pond. He sat just behind the gunners, patting a restive horse, and watched.

The British battery, as usual, had unlimbered full in the open, each of its six guns set just the regulation distance apart. They were well ahead of the skirmishers; they fired first at a farmhouse and then at nothingness. Nobody saw a Boer gun. Nobody ever did see a Boer gun, and had only to guess at its position.

He noted down, again with surprise, that he felt far less nervousness under fire than he had expected. "My mind kept turning on other things. I was so annoyed at losing my haversack that for a time I forgot the shells while I bustled about looking for that haversack."

The 84th Battery, finding that the enemy had their range to a yard, trotted off half a mile to the right and again banged away in full view of any Boer field-glass. Up in support of them jolted two heavy naval guns, each drawn by thirty oxen. These improvised guns, first used at the end of the Battle of Lombard's Kop, were as yet Whitehall's only answer to the Boers' Creusots and Krupps. The naval guns opened with their bursting whack; the khaki lines of the Guards pressed ahead; the heat of the sun died; and round everything (inscrutable, favouring the British but taking no sides) circled mounted Kaffirs.

Three days later Archie Langman and Conan Doyle were back at the hospital. In his tent he found letters from home, letters from India, and copies of his new book of short stories, *The Green Flag*, which had been published early in April. There were thirteen stories, ranging from his pirate-tales of Captain Sharkey to a notable piece of diabolism called *The King of the Foxes*. But at the moment he was not interested in short stories.

The press at home were clamouring about Army Reform. He had long held his own notions about Army Reform, now crystallized by observation and by the multitude of those with whom he had talked. And he jotted down notes of an article for the 'Cornhill Magazine.' But he did not write it until the middle of June, when the Boer War seemed all but finished.

President Kruger fled with the state archives one day before Lord Roberts rode into Johannesburg on May 31st. Tiny, isolated Mafeking had been relieved. Pretoria, capital of the Transvaal, ran up British colours early in June. Far away in London, Mr. Burdett-Coutts was making some sensational 'exposures' of the state of the hospitals during the enteric epidemic; the press raged; Conan Doyle wrote a retort to the 'British Medical Journal,' pointing out the simple truth that no hospitals, military or civil, could have done more than was done in Bloemfontein. Also—with no notion of how he was to outrage the best military opinion, or make old gentlemen in clubs turn purple—he wrote his article on Army Reform, called *Some Military Lessons of the War*.

Here, in inverse order, were the shocking reforms he proposed in 1900:

First, the artillery. British guns must be concealed, as the Boers' were, and not exposed in a line set so close together that a single shell might wreck the crews of several. Observation-balloons must go higher than a few hundred feet, which was their limit now, so that hidden enemy guns could be found by aerial reconnaissance. But this was not enough. The wars of the future, he declared, would employ far heavier artillery. Instead of confining your biggest cannon to fortresses and battle-ships, why not turn them out as field-pieces? In a country of good roads and railways, with steam-power available, they could be run up and manoeuvred with deadly effect.

Second, the cavalry. The cavalry must cease to be armed with swords or lances, which belonged only in a museum. What good were swords or lances against Mauser rifles sighted up to two thousand yards? Equip your cavalry with rifles.

(Here the military experts and the old gentlemen in clubs really did have an apoplectic fit.)

Third and most important, the infantry. They must learn to dig trenches, and not leave this work to the Sappers as was now done. Their officers must not wear distinctive dress or carry swords, lest they be singled out as targets. They must take cover, if only in an individual shelter pit. In this war the quick-firing rifle in the hands of a marksman had proved itself supreme arbiter. Teach your infantry to shoot; and for the love of heaven give them some ammunition with which to practise.

"The lesson of the war, as I read it," he said, "is that it is better and cheaper for the country to have fewer soldiers who shall be very highly trained than many of a mixed quality." Teach them shooting, and don't waste so much time on parade-ground drill.

Take the case of invasion, for instance. Defence of Empire was not the business of a special warrior-caste; it was the business of everybody. If every able-bodied youth and man in Great Britain were taught to use a rifle, those riflemen when combined with artillery could beat back an invasion of England with comparatively few regular troops to assist them. It was the new long-bow, the men of Agincourt sprung to life.

Conan Doyle, as he wrote this, decided that Rifle Clubs in England should be formed for just such a purpose; if nobody else would do it, he would do it himself. But his mind burned with pictures he had seen both in Bloemfontein and on the veldt. Profoundly he disliked those young Guards officers, with their single eyeglass and their drawl. They were brave enough; but bravery was the one quality Britain had never lacked; what it wanted was brains. And so:

"Above all," he concluded at white heat, "let us have done with the fuss and feathers, the gold lace, and the frippery! Let us have done also with the tailoring, the too-luxurious habits of the mess, the unnecessary extravagance which makes it so hard for a poor man to accept a commission! If only this good came from all our trials and our efforts, they would be well worth all that they have cost us."

In other words, as the 'Daily News' was to phrase it, 'democratize' the Army. This was the most shocking suggestion of all.

Shortly after he had posted *Some Military Lessons of the War* to 'Cornhill,' the Langman drew towards the end of its service. It wore a badge of honour: in addition to the twelve who had taken enteric, and the three dead, five more collapsed with hearts cooked by a temperature of 103. If the hospital could not carry on, it did not need to carry on. The military hospitals were more than half empty; and, except for cleaning up, the war appeared finished.

Conan Doyle, who set off to visit Pretoria on June 23rd, wrote home that he would probably leave South Africa some time in July. Even his constitution had suffered from the poison. He could eat very little; and his health was not improved when he fractured several ribs by a bad fall in a football match, so that he had to be strapped up in plaster.

In fact, as he told Innes, he felt damned sick. Nevertheless, after a long journey up the railway-line past burned telegraph-posts, it gave him a pleasurable shock to see the station-sign PRETORIA slide past the train windows at dawn. This haunt of Old Kruger had seemed very remote. He smoked his pipe in President Kruger's chair, as a memento of the visit, and had a talk with the small, spare, white-moustached Lord Roberts. He smoked and argued with the Boers, "who are not bad chaps, but very ignorant." At Pretoria, too, a note from Archie Langman informed him that he could take the liner *Briton* at Cape Town on July 11th; the whole hospital would be leaving for England in less than a fortnight; and he, as an unpaid man, could go on ahead by mail-boat.

And so, in the red sunset on this evening of July 6th, his work finished, he lounged at the top of the little *kopje* outside Bloemfontein where he had so often stood to gulp a breath of air during the evil days. The next day he left for Cape Town, after saying goodbye to Archie, and his staunch friends Gibbs and Scharlieb, and all the rest.

Across the plain, once occupied by the tents of an army, purple darkened the red of the sunset. South African winter days were mild enough, but the nights bitter cold. If ever again his nostrils caught the scent of Bloemfontein, that deathly compound of disease and disinfectants, it would revolt his soul as well as his stomach. He would not now write to anybody that they 'hoped to take' more patients. And yet:

"I go south," he had told the Ma'am in a letter that morning, "with a feeling that there is nothing I have left undone. And, thank God, I am the better, not the worse, for my experience.

"I have my history done within four chapters of the end, unless the end of the war is unduly prolonged. I may hope to have it nearly done before I reach England. But there is considerable re-writing to be done, as new light has been thrown on and fuller knowledge gained of the early actions. This, and a thorough correcting of the proofs, should take a month or six weeks during which I must be at or near London."

London! When he reached Cape Town, and boarded the *Briton*, the plumage of London already surrounded him. The liner's electric light dazzled his eyes after months of candles or paraffin lamps. When he saw immaculate ladies in dresses with very high necks and puffed sleeves, he felt momentarily crude and uncivilized from the life of the camp. But this soon faded as Cape Town itself, where staring Kaffirs wore patriotic ribbons round their heads, faded away in a smooth and hazy sea. The *Briton* carried a number of notable or merely notorious passengers, among whom was a foreign officer of loud mouth, who had lived in the Boer camps. This personage stated that the British had habitually used Dum-Dum bullets. Conan Doyle turned beetroot-red and called him a liar. The officer, Major Roger Raoul Duval, tendered a written apology.

This, however, was the only ruffling incident. Luxuriously smoking his new curved pipe, curved pipes being unknown in England until they were imported during the South African War, he alternately wrote and lazed through the days with his journalist friends Nevison and Fletcher Robinson. The latter, subsequently editor of 'Vanity Fair,' was a Devonshire man, born at Ipplepen on the borders of Dartmoor. Fletcher Robinson's head was full of folk-tales from his home country, legends of the devils and bogles said to lurk in hollows of that eerie waste.

They were all too full of the war to speak of much else. But it may be counted as a fortunate thing that he and the again-ex-doctor agreed to meet, one day in the future, for a golfing holiday.

Conan Doyle had asked the Ma'am to meet him at Morley's Hotel, Trafalgar Square, which was the hotel he so often occupied in town. And the Ma'am was there, peering near-sightedly even with her spectacles. But first he faced a horde of newspaper reporters, not only because he always made good copy but because the agitation about 'Army hospital scandals' had reached its height. In particular, the hospital orderlies were attacked. They were accused of negligence and even of theft. Conan Doyle's defence of the orderly, in the 'British Medical Journal,' preceded his arrival.

"When," he had written contemptuously, "when the scouts and the Lancers and the other picturesque people ride in procession through London, have a thought for the sallow orderly, who has also given of his best for his country. He is not a fancy man—you do not find them in enteric wards—but for solid work and quiet courage you will not beat him in all that gallant army."

Much of the agitation had a political motive. A general election was coming on early in autumn. The Conservative-*cum*-Liberal-Unionist Government was threatened by the Liberals and that advanced section of Liberals loosely termed Radicals. The Liberals contended (a) that the war had been mishandled; (b) that Army Reform was necessary; and (c) that Joseph Chamberlain possessed all the less attractive qualities of Charles Peace and Jack the Ripper.

Conan Doyle, as he had hoped, was asked to stand for Parliament by the Unionists. He was not a Tory, he warned everybody; he was a Unionist, as he had always been. All his life he remained politically restless, a sort of Tory democrat with his belief in the Empire. He might have been a Conservative who held to democratic equality, or he might have been a Liberal Imperialist. The one creed for which he had no use was Socialism. Even towards the end of his life, when he wrote without condemnation of a Labour Government being in power, it was with the important qualification of "in power for a time."

In 1900 he had one overriding conviction: that the present Government must be supported. It was not the politicians who had caused mess and muddle in this war; it was the original gold-lace Army Group.

"The settlement of this war," he insisted, "must not be given over to a party of whom so many have opposed and obstructed it."

But, while the question of candidature was being decided, he had before him more than a month's cricketing. In August he played for the M.C.C. at Lord's, and on one occasion Jean Leckie came there to watch him. It was on this occasion that Willie Hornung encountered them and drew the wrong conclusions; and there occurred that flaming quarrel with Connie and Willie which has already been described. He raged; he was still raging when Mr. (later Sir John) Boraston, the Liberal-Unionist Secretary, approached him in this matter of politics.

"What sort of Parliamentary seat," Boraston asked him, "would you like to contest?"

That was easy to answer. He wanted to go bald-headed for the Opposition champion, and contest the seat of Sir Henry Campbell-Bannerman, leader of the Liberal Party.

"There would be much honour in that," he declared,

and pointed out to the Ma'am that to contest an easy seat would be a dreary business.

The vacancy, he was told, had been promised to someone else. But, if he wanted a difficult seat, would he care to stand for the Central Division of Edinburgh?

"There's nothing I'd like better. I was born in Edinburgh!"

"That district is a Radical stronghold, remember. Chiefly the Trade vote. It's been unopposed for years; and, the last time it was opposed, the Radical candidate had a two-thousand majority in what was then a six-thousand electorate. You can't win; but you might pull down that majority."

Couldn't win, eh? He was not altogether convinced of that. Determined to give no sign of nervousness, he went north to plunge into a far dizzier whirl than he had ever known in the United States.

The flinty, smoky streets in this division of Edinburgh were raucous and rowdy with the stimulus of any political fight. In the press reports, we find every remark of a candidate ringed with the fireworks of "Cheers"; "Loud cheers," "Laughter," "Hisses." The heckler, that puncturing voice from the audience, tuned up an eager throat. Conan Doyle had just ten days, from September 25th to October 4th, to make his campaign.

His first speech was delivered in a type-foundry, while the workmen crowded round. During the ensuing tumult he spoke from seven to ten times a day. He spoke from the top of a beer-barrel in the Parkside Brewery. He spoke in the 'cleansing department' of the Corporation Stables. It always ended in a packed evening meeting at hall or theatre, where questions volleyed; nor was it sweetened by his hecklers' persistence in addressing him as Sherlock Holmes.

"This title," observed the correspondent of the Glasgow 'Evening News,' "the doctor acknowledges genially."

Always with a broad beam on his face, left hand in trousers pocket and right hand regularly swinging, he talked to them. "Notwithstanding the rapidity of his speech, every word is clear; and, though not passionate or fiery, he gradually rouses his audience to thunders of applause." From the beginning he dismissed current political topics—taxation of ground-rents, local option, women's suffrage—as being of small importance.

"There is one question," he hammered at them over and over, "which overshadows all others, to such an extent that the election must turn mainly on it. It is the South African war." (Cheers.) "While that question remains unsettled, for a man to give his vote purely on some social matter is like a man wanting to tidy his sitting-room while his house is on fire." (Cheers.)

The Edinburgh 'Scotsman,' first dubious about a literary candidate, was impelled to lyric ecstasy after two speeches. What puzzled the press in general was this novice's unexpected skill at dealing with hecklers.

"Mr. Sherlock Holmes! What d'ye say tae local option?"

"There ought to be some control of the public-houses, I agree. But, if you throw out the public-house, you must pay compensation to the publican for the loss of his business."

The Scots voice reeled. "*Compensation?*"

"Certainly! The owner of a public-house has his living to make too."

"Mr. Sherlock Holmes! *Are ye no' a believer in Temperance?*"

"Temperance is a good thing, yes. But honesty is a better!"

At Laidlaw's brass-foundry, he met the opposing candidate, a wealthy and very colourless publisher Mr. George Mackenzie Brown, from Nelson & Sons. "I cannot tell jokes like my rival," Mr. Brown complained. Author and publisher shook hands, and both harangued the workmen; after which Conan Doyle was hurried off (by his efficient chairman, Robert Cranston) to address a firemen's meeting. The effect of his personality reached out to other divisions of Edinburgh; it had echoes elsewhere in Scotland and over the border. Mr. Asquith pitched into him during a speech in East Fife. In reply to the query, "Who is going to pay for this war?" he had said it could be paid for by taxes on gold-mines, taxes on railways, and taxes on the Boers; and this roused the ire of the 'Leeds Mercury.'

"Dr. Conan Doyle evidently does not know that we are already paying an income-tax of a shilling in the pound in order to meet the cost of this war, and that additional duties have been imposed on tea, tobacco, beer, and spirits for the same purpose."

And yet, to the disquiet of the Radicals, this interloper was winning votes.

He was doing more than that. "You'll ge' all our crosses," shouted more than one group of workmen. They liked him; there it was. More important, they believed he was honest and they felt they could trust him. As polling-day drew near, the campaign-fever grew to frenzy. At the Old Waverley Hotel, where he scribbled notes to the Ma'am, throngs of supporters followed him home every night; Prince's Street was blocked, and they wouldn't go away until a hoarse-voiced candidate croaked good-night.

His earlier doubts as to the outcome ("Fighting furiously, but doubtful if I can gain as much ground as all that,") had changed to blazing certainty. "I'm going to win," he told his audiences; and he meant it. He won over the Irish quarter in Cowgate, though he still refused to vote for Home Rule. During one of his last meetings, at the Literary Institute, out on the platform came white-haired Dr. Joseph Bell, to assure them that his old pupil would be one of the best members of Parliament if he did half so well as he had done at the Edinburgh Royal Infirmary.

On the night before election, he could hardly sleep. And in sober evaluation he had far more than an even chance. But he felt differently next morning.

Over night, political ingenuity had been at work. Round the three polling-places for the Central Division had been plastered three hundred placards in staring black letters, signed as by 'The Dunfermline Protestant Defence Organization.'

Dr. A. Conan Doyle, proclaimed these placards, was a Papist conspirator, a Jesuit emissary, and a Subverter of the Protestant Faith. He had been born a Roman Catholic: Could he deny it? He had been educated by Jesuits: Could he deny *that*? If he could not deny it, what were Scottish Protestants, supporters of Kirk and Covenant, to think of such a man? What more proof could they want?

"In Central Edinburgh," was the 'Daily Telegraph's' noble understatement, "there is considerable excitement."

Press-reports throw out confused glimpses of that day: the carriages full of voters clattering up to the polling-stations; canvassers pouncing; a suffragette who insisted she had a vote and tried to fight her way in; and the two candidates, Mr. G. M. Brown and Dr. Conan Doyle, meeting at the Marshall Street polling-station, where they "enjoyed a seemingly pleasant conversation for several minutes."

The 'seemingly' may well have been true. Those placards, it was discovered in a few hours, were the work of a religious fanatic named Prenimer, backed by somebody's money. Mr. Brown had instantly telegraphed that *he* knew nothing of the matter; and, though his party machine could scarcely have been so innocent, there was no course but to accept his word. Meanwhile, as Scots workmen read the placard and swore blue oaths, what could the Unionist candidate do?

For the statements about Catholic birth and early Jesuit education were quite true. He could not buttonhole the voter and say, "Look here, I severed relations with my family because I couldn't accept Catholicism," especially against the exclamation, "I've done wi' him!" Sandwich-men paraded, carrying words of encouragement to Mr. Brown from Captain Lambton (a war hero) in Newcastle. As darkness drew on with heavier voting, canvassers in dim-lit streets could not tell the foeman voter from the friendly voter they were dragging inside; fights broke out; the placard did its work.

"Doctor," said Cranston, "we're beaten." And they were.

A crowd of his supporters waited in the Oddfellows' Hall to hear the results. The count was: G. M. Brown (L), 3,028, and A. Conan Doyle (L.U.), 2,459. Liberal Majority, 569. The defeated candidate, smiling, made a speech in which he said that at least they had knocked down that two-thousand majority by nearly fifteen hundred votes. He made no reference to the Dunfermline placards until a chorus demanded reference. Then he dismissed the placards with a statement that he believed his opponent personally had known nothing of them, and strolled off to his hotel.

"As usual," commented one newspaper, "the publisher has downed the author."

But, in his private thoughts, it was some time before

he could be amused at the ironic comedy of that election. Without those placards, he would have won; he knew it, and he resented it.

As yet, of course, he knew little about politics. He was not aware that no holds are barred. He could not guess that the voters, if their credulity or ignorance be used, can do more than defeat a man for Parliament: they can turn out of higher office even the greatest statesman to whom they have ever run for protection when they were in danger. On October 25th, after Conan Doyle returned to London, he took the chair at the Pall Mall Club for a speech delivered by a twenty-six-year-old young man who had just been elected to Parliament. This young man had been in the thick of the Boer War as a special correspondent. His name was Winston Churchill.

But there were many matters, both literary and domestic, to take the Edinburgh candidate's mind off elections. The Unionist-Tory Government survived that general election, and remained in office. Touie had returned from Naples and opened Undershaw. The children were there. Though no official surrender had yet come from the Boers, Smith & Elder published his history, called *The Great Boer War* to distinguish this conflict from the lesser one of 1881. The first edition of the history ended with the capture of the Eastern Transvaal in September, and President Kruger's escape to Europe in a Dutch warship.

"I fancy a storm will break over me sooner or later," wrote Conan Doyle, "when you think how freely I have handled some of our own big wigs. And I shall welcome it."

The Great Boer War, as it happened, pleased both friend and enemy. And the reason? Not without effect had he studied Macaulay's style of historical writing.

There was the same absolute clearness, so that the reader is never left confusedly wondering which character is which, or who is doing what, in a tangle of bad construction. This clarity made a framework for the book's fairness.

In any debated question, he stated first the evidence for one side; then the evidence for the other side. His case in favour of the Boer cause was put so strongly that Boers wrote in praise of the book. With regard to the mess and muddle of the early battles, he weighed up the pros and cons of certain commanding officers with such scrupulousness that at first reading you do not see the bitter denunciation underneath.

But his 'Cornhill' article, *Some Military Lessons of the War,* he appended as a final chapter. It had appeared over a month before the book; and this really did cause a storm.

True, nearly all the Army Reforms he foresaw in 1900—artillery, cavalry, and infantry—became a terrible necessity before two decades had elapsed. True, he had most of the press behind him and a few of the military: including, as it proved, Lord Roberts. But orthodox opinion treated him in terms between rage and a sort of heart-broken pity, like that of Lieutenant-Colonel F. N. Maude.

"Surely it is a little hasty," wrote Colonel Maude, "to conclude, because in this campaign local conditions have interfered to prevent a single real cavalry charge being ridden, that therefore the day of sword and lance is over. . . . The advantage of either sword or lance in cavalry work is that a severe wound drops the man at once. A man may be mortally wounded by rifle or revolver bullet and still fight on for a couple of hours."

(They bred real giants in those days.)

The truth was, Colonel Maude explained, that no

infantry armed with magazine-rifles could possibly stand against charging cavalry armed with swords. You might fill a cavalryman full of holes, but he would still ride up and wallop you with his sword. You could not even stop a horse from charging you after its rider fell off. That, he suggested, was why Dum-Dum bullets were invented, though now not used: "and we shall have to go back to them if our infantry are not to be slaughtered like swine by the first European cavalry we meet."

Now it is not suggested here that the gallant Colonel was a lunatic. He was merely a military expert. Indeed, as he pointed out, you might call him a bit of a modern: agreeing with many of Dr. Conan Doyle's views. But he must dissent from these modern notions about taking cover against artillery or rifle fire. That was the importance, the all-importance, of drill. Drill taught infantry to advance and not return a shot until they were within easy range where they could be sure of hits. Without drill they wouldn't move forward at all.

Conan Doyle's reply to this is not among his papers. But, though no doubt he did underestimate the importance of drill, the reply can be guessed.

He founded his Undershaw Rifle Club before Christmas. Despite the experts' denial that civilian riflemen could ever be of value in case of an invasion, club-members flocked in. Wearing their broad-brimmed hats, turned up at one side with the metal initials U.R.C., they aimed for targets set at an equivalent of six hundred yards. In his study, where a secretary now assisted him, Conan Doyle could hear the intermittent spat-spat of the rifles. Having a secretary, despite the labour it saved, seemed an odd change.

Change! Everything, in this unsteady world, was change!

Since autumn it had been known that Queen Victoria's health was failing. To most people, even old people, a world without the Queen would be a world unthinkable. It was as though, in a long and stately hall, the candles were being blown out one by one, leaving gaps of darkness amid the carving. But the press spoke reassuringly: the Queen went at Christmas for her usual visit to the manor of Osborne, in the Isle of Wight.

If there had not been enough doubt and disaster, it became apparent that the war in South Africa was not over. De Wet, Botha, and Delarey slashed back with guerilla raids; Lord Kitchener called for thirty thousand more men. Conan Doyle, who had been getting the manuscript of *A Duet* specially bound for Jean Leckie, wondered how guerillas could be crushed in an immensity of ideal guerilla country.

Reminders were all about him. On a table in his study was an equestrian figure of Lord Roberts, in massive silver, presented to him by John Langman for his service during the fever-epidemic. Keener reminders had come in letters from patients whose lives he saved. Most poignant was a letter from the father of a young Canadian, whose life he could not save. Private W. S. Blight died during the height of the epidemic. But the father understood.

"May God bless and protect you for the noble work you have done for our boys. Words of mine cannot express to you our gratitude. He was my only son, and I gave all I had to my Queen and my country and only regret that I am so situated that I cannot go and take his place."

This, Conan Doyle thought, was no mere personal tribute to him; as such it was of no importance. But in it the loyalty of Empire, at which the German press sneered, had a few simple words to speak. As the year drew to a close, he settled down to write a short essay that is almost startling in its prophecy. Entitled *An Anglo-American Reunion,* it consisted of a plea for a much closer understanding between the two nations, and he coupled that plea with the warning that, unless this essential relationship was brought about by good will, then it might be forced into existence in some future time as a measure of self preservation against an eventual threat from Russia.

Change! His sister Lottie, who went out to India for what she believed to be a few months, had met and married Captain Leslie Oldham, R.E. Captain Oldham's first stammering letter to his prospective brother-in-law was one of the most likeable messages he ever received. Lottie, ecstatic, told the Ma'am in heavily underscored words that the Ma'am must *not* mention the subject of money to Arthur; but, somehow, blank cheques arrived. He himself, when the heat of the Edinburgh contest cooled, had written to his friends in Scotland that he was no Jesuit emissary or subverter of anybody's faith. His views were those of reverent Theism: if he still could not accept the Bible as divinely inspired, he could feel Reverence toward whatever Power might exist.

Change! The calendar marked the month of January, 1901. Kaiser Wilhelm the Second, on horseback at six each morning, rode from Potsdam to Berlin to manoeuvre his troops for six hours a day. In Washington President McKinley toiled with the settlement of Cuban affairs. And at Osborne in the Isle of Wight, very peacefully, her hands folded on her breast, the old queen went to join Prince Albert.

XII

HONOUR:

"I Believe Such Statements to Be Lies"

The letter-head bore the words, 'Rowe's Duchy Hotel, Princetown, Dartmoor, Devon,' and the postmark was April 2nd, 1901.

"Here I am," he wrote, "in the highest town in England. Robinson and I are exploring the Moor over our Sherlock Holmes book. I think it will work out splendidly; indeed, I have already done nearly half of it. Holmes is at his very best, and it is a highly dramatic idea—which I owe to Robinson."

It was the first baying of *The Hound of the Baskervilles*.

But that was not the first mention of the book, or even of the title. It began in March of the same year, at the small watering-place of Cromer in Norfolk. Through the winter Conan Doyle had been seedy and run-down. The backwash of enteric still poisoned his appetite, and he could not sleep. A few days at Cromer, he hoped, might help in the cure. It did; but not in the way he anticipated when he went there for a golfing holiday with his friend Fletcher Robinson.

At the Royal Links Hotel, one raw Sunday afternoon when a wind rushed off the North Sea and a fire burned in their private sitting-room, Fletcher Robinson began talking of the legends of Dartmoor, the atmosphere of Dartmoor. In particular his companion's imagination was kindled by the story of a spectral hound.

Conan Doyle stayed only four days at Cromer. He was giving a dinner at the Athenaeum whose guests included Major Griffiths, Barrie, Winston Churchill, Anthony Hope (Hawkins) of *The Prisoner of Zenda,* and Edmund Gosse; and he had to return to London. But that gusty Sunday afternoon at Cromer he was already so ensnared as to invent, and sketch out with Robinson, the plot of a sensational story about a Devonshire family accursed by a ghost-hound which should prove to be flesh and blood.

There was every reason why this should appeal to him. Whether he remembered it or not, he had already used almost exactly the same idea in his long short-story called *The King of the Foxes.*

The King of the Foxes, first published in the 'Windsor Magazine' in 1898, is the later novel in reverse. It is a hunting story, seen through the eyes of a young sportsman nerve-shattered by drink. His family doctor, trying to throw an effective scare into him, warns him that he may have delusions. Then young Danbury rides with the Ascombe Hunt: on a nightmare run, through nightmare country, after some fox which nobody ever sees. Danbury, far ahead of the field, is alone in a dim fir-wood. Now listen to the climax, as the hounds go in for the kill:

At the same instant, a creature the size of a donkey jumped on to its feet. A huge grey head, with monstrous glistening fangs and tapering fox-jaws, shot out from among the branches; and the hound was thrown several feet into the air, and fell howling among the cover. Then there was a clashing snap like a rat-trap closing, and the howls sharpened into a scream and then were still.

The 'fox' is a grey Siberian wolf, of gigantic size, from a travelling menagerie. What really caught Conan Doyle's imagination, aside from any question of plot, was the atmosphere of Dartmoor. Certain localities cry aloud for their story. He had never visited Dartmoor. But Robinson's accounts were enough. Already, in his mind, it was tinged with Gothic unearthliness: the rocky waste rolling away to a darkened sky, the swift-gathering mist, the thousand-acre bog, the granite buildings of the prison. Before he left Cromer he wrote to the Ma'am that he meant to do a 'little book' called *The Hound of the Baskervilles*.

"A real Creeper!" he added.

Robinson, refusing his offer of collaboration, volunteered to take him on a tour of exploration over the moor. Before the end of the month they were staying at Rowe's Duchy Hotel in the village of Princetown.

Above them, in spring bleakness which might have been the brown of autumn, lay the prison. Dartmoor then housed a thousand men convicted of the most serious offences: ragtag and devil's crew who not seldom turned on their guards with the edge of a spade. Civil Guards, with carbines and fixed bayonets, patrolled the ground round the outer walls and at the quarries, always alert when mist rose. The cat-o'-nine-tails quelled rebellion.

Originally, as he told J. E. Hodder Williams, it had never entered Conan Doyle's head to use Sherlock Holmes when he planned the story at Cromer. But, as he began to solidify details shortly afterwards, it became clear that some master-of-destinies must preside over it. "So I thought to myself," he told Hodder Williams, "why should I invent such a character when I had him already in the form of Holmes?"

From the correspondence it is not clear whether he began writing the story before leaving London, or began it at the Princetown hotel. He was certainly writing hard at it in the latter place, between such times as he and Robinson, in caps and knickerbockers, tramped fourteen miles a day over the moor. They saw the bog which became (was there ever a more evilly suggestive name?) the great Grimpen Mire. Baskerville Hall, with its toe-printed footmarks in the Yew Alley, loomed in imagination against the rain. They explored the stone huts of prehistoric man. And in one of these huts, in semi-darkness and miles away from any road, they heard what sounded like the stealthy chink of a boot approaching the hut.

It was only another tourist, more startled than themselves when their heads suddenly appeared at the entrance. Dr. Watson had a similar experience, you remember. And can we wonder that Sherlock Holmes himself is revitalized?

Holmes's creator really *wanted* to write this story. He could not distil the atmosphere, the half-lights and shadows, without that same gusto entering into his character. Cool enough in earlier chapters, Holmes towards the end becomes more feverish than Sir Henry Baskerville. Selden, the escaped convict, plunges to death among the rocks, with his screams rising above the noise of what pursues him; Holmes laughs and dances like a madman beside the corpse ("The man has a beard!") as the glow of Stapleton's cigar approaches through darkness. It is perhaps the finest scene in the book, glimpsed by match-spurts, a part of the same texture as the book's autumnal bleakness, its lonely figures silhouetted against the sky line, and, above everything, the baying of the hound.

If *The Hound of the Baskervilles* is not the best detective-novel, and the present biographer will maintain under torture that the best detective-novel came later, it stands by itself as a crime-novel. It is the only tale, long or short, in which the story dominates Holmes rather than Holmes dominating the story; what captures its reader is less the Victorian detective than the Gothic romance.

When Sir George Newnes heard of this new story, which Conan Doyle continued to write on a long homeward journey while he stopped at Sherborne, Bath, and Cheltenham for the beginning of cricket, there was rejoicing at the 'Strand Magazine.' *The Hound of the Baskervilles* was scheduled for the 'Strand' in eight instalments, between August 1901 and April 1902.

True, as Sir George Newnes told his Annual Meeting of Shareholders, the detective had not been recalled to life. About Sherlock Holmes's fall over the precipice Newnes used such terms as 'dreadful' and 'unhappy': as, to a meeting of shareholders, well he might. This new adventure, he explained, occurred before Holmes's demise. It was the only disappointing thing to millions of readers as well.

"Couldn't you bring him back?" the author was persistently asked. "*The Hound of the Baskervilles* is Holmes at his best. But I'm not going to feel really happy until I know he's alive and back in the same old rooms."

"He is at the foot of the Reichenbach Falls," retorted Conan Doyle, "and there he stays." But was he so sure? William Gillette, who had now played the part four hundred and fifty times in America, was coming to England and opening at the Lyceum early in September. Was he so sure?

During the summer he was again in first-class cricket. He had already made a century during his first match at Lord's, and his bowling was as effective as his batting. Against Cambridgeshire he took seven wickets for sixty-one runs. But he could never enter the grounds at Lord's without being reminded of that still-smouldering quarrel, a year before, with Willie and Connie Hornung.

For months the Ma'am had been trying to make peace

in this matter, but her son would not have it. What most upset him was its effect on Jean Leckie.

"Jean gets these fits of depression," he had written at the time of the quarrel, "and she writes as though she had done some awful thing. I never love her more than at such moments."

All the Ma'am's efforts to patch up matters between her son on one side, and her daughter and son-in-law on the other, were able to establish only a partial gesture. "I have written a polite note to Connie," he said, "which, between ourselves, is more than she deserves. And I don't feel better," he added libellously, "by contemplating the fact that William is half Mongol, half Slav, or whatever the mixture is."

We get one glimpse of him, in 1901, which astonished his acquaintances during that time of pondering and brooding. It occurred in the vestibule of the Whitehall Rooms, when he was a guest at the annual dinner of the Royal Society. He was chatting with some friends, waiting for his host. Sir William Crookes, the eminent physicist and chemist who for nearly thirty years had believed in the reality of psychic phenomena, stopped to greet the group in the vestibule.

When Crookes moved on into the crowd, a professor of physics told an anecdote of the last meeting: when a motto on the wall of one room, reading *Ubi Crookes, Ibi Lux,* had been altered to *Ubi Crookes, Ibi Spooks.* Wonder was expressed that a man of Crookes's attainments should believe in ghosts.

"I'm not so sure," Conan Doyle said unexpectedly, "there *is* nothing in Crookes's belief."

"Oh, come now!"

The other persisted that he had been giving attention to the investigations of Crookes and Lodge and Myers.

"I believe," he said, "there's a good deal in it that's worth—"

"Credence?"

"If not actual credence, at least thorough consideration."

And, giving that jerk of the head which all his friends knew, he in turn strode off into the crowd. He volunteered no further hint of what was in his mind; nor, for the moment, need we seek it. "Conan Doyle?" was the exclamation that followed him. "Is Saul also among the prophets?"

On September 9th, in the huge Lyceum Theatre with its caverns of gilt and red plush, William Gillette appeared in what was sub-titled, "a hitherto unpublished episode in the career of the great detective, and showing his connection with the STRANGE CASE OF MISS FAULKNER." Sherlock Holmes was shown lounging at Baker Street in embroidered slippers and a flowered-silk dressing-gown. Madge Larrabee (the villainess) depicted modishness in a full-tailed skirt sweeping dust from the stage, and a beige velvet hat "trimmed with a large white bird."

It was not exactly an unpublished episode. In Gillette's version, half a dozen reminiscences of past plots hovered through the action as Holmes recovered the compromising papers, or faced a soft-voiced Professor Moriarty dressed to resemble Mr. Pickwick. There was one disturbing incident: a part of the gallery couldn't hear the actors, and said so loudly. One or two critics complained of Americanisms in the dialogue: "the use of the word 'notify' jarred on me." But it ended in a triumph.

Old shades, too, were present at the Lyceum that night. Henry Irving, ill and ageing, hounded by bad luck, was about to resign control of the theatre. Irving had paid many visits to Undershaw that summer, after his costly and unsuccessful production of *Coriolanus*. Far into the night he talked and drank port with Conan Doyle, forgetting even that a cabman was waiting outside. Now the Lyceum was going, heaping more earth on the grave of the Victorian age.

Conan Doyle, in the previous January, had been among those who watched the old Queen's funeral procession: a silent multitude, except for some who wept openly, as the small body went past on the gun-carriage.

"And England—how stands England?" he had written. He was as much moved by the faces of elderly people, who had been born and grown old under Victoria, as by the little coffin amid the gaudy uniforms. He wrote of a 'dark road,' and 'a black portal,' hating the thought of extinction. And England? Where would England stand, when that great Symbol was gone? It was certain that the foreign press-campaign against Britain's war in South Africa, notably in the German press, had approached a point of European hysteria.

In South Africa Christian De Wet on one side, Lord Kitchener on the other, fought without gloves. The Boer leaders, their field-army distintegrated and gone home, must wreck railways and cut telegraph-wires when they could not attack in heavier numbers. Kitchener ordered the fighting-areas to be stripped of livestock and forage so that the commandos could get no food. Where there was sniping under a white flag, where railways were wrecked, where Boers gathered in numbers and were sheltered, there farm-houses were burned. Male Boers were rounded up as prisoners of war. Women and children, left behind by husbands or fathers, were rounded up as well.

These things were facts: a waste area was to be cre-

ated without loss of human life. Altogether different was
the picture, drawn from the very beginning of the war,
of the Brutal British Officer and the Fiendish British
Tommy. The Brutal British Officer and the Fiendish
British Tommy now leered over Europe like images bob-
bing in a Carnival at Nice.

The Fiendish Tommy, it was alleged, burned farm-
houses because he liked it. He looted indiscriminately,
and was encouraged to do so by his officers; indeed, he
had been doing this from the start. He always used
Dum-Dum bullets. He bayoneted babies and threw their
bodies into the blazing houses. But his particular taste
was for rape, and he raped every Boer woman in sight.

"I have fought against all the savage tribes of Africa,"
shouted President Kruger in exile, "but never any so savage as the British."

The Boer women and children, it was alleged, were
put into places called concentration camps. (So far, true;
the word is not new.) There they were starved, abused
and brutally treated. Such women as had escaped rape
on the veldt were brought to the camps so that rape
could be accomplished with more facility. Horrifying
stories of disease, of children reduced to dying sacks of
bones, were made more vivid by the sketches of artists.
The symbol of these artists was a British officer showing
all his teeth amid smoking ruins, and inciting Kaffirs to
loot.

Nor did these attacks appear in foreign newspapers
alone. If we in our day want to know the meaning of a
really free press, we must turn back to musty pamphlets
and see what English journalists, of the pro-Boer variety,
were permitted to say about their own troops in the
field.

"Night and day," roared W. T. Stead, of the 'Review
of Reviews,' "the whole hellish panorama is unrolled

in South Africa, and we know that before sunset British troops carrying the King's commission will be steadily adding more items of horror to the ghastly total. The cruel work is being ruthlessly carried on."

W. T. Stead, his red hair and red beard a little bleached by time, still bounced aggressively in the forefront of journalism. He was thoroughly honest. There can be little doubt he believed what he wrote. There can be no doubt whatever that, if he had written it in any other country, he would have landed in jail.

Broadsheets and pamphlets, from *Shall I Slay My Brother Boer?* (1899) to *Methods of Barbarism* (1900), flooded from his "Stop-the-War" press. If W. T. Stead was far from being the only journalist who wrote like this, he was the most inflammatory. The foreign press quite naturally quoted him and then said the atrocity-stories were "admitted by the English."

And nobody in England was taking any steps to deny this.

The Government would not condescend to make any reply. The Government lifted a shoulder, polished an eyeglass, and considered it beneath contempt. The vast majority of people, outwardly at least, seemed to support the view.

"Why trouble?" murmured the apathetic. "*We* know it isn't true."

"Why trouble?" said the arrogant, that group who have made England all her enemies. "We stand alone in splendid isolation; and why not? What does it matter what any damned foreigner thinks?"

Meanwhile, the noise of the pro-Boer press reverberated back from the German sounding-board. Mr. Stead was eloquent on the subject of farm-burning and concentration, but most eloquent of all on the subject of rape. "It is absolutely impossible," he wrote in *Methods of Barbarism,* "to attempt any comparative or quantitive estimate of the number of women who have suffered wrong at the hands of our troops."

Conan Doyle, as he read the public prints through that autumn, could not be sure which charge against the British Army most infuriated him. He had seen Tommy Atkins in the field. He had shared mud and fever and bullets. He had watched the military authorities, in their effort to be fair, enforcing an almost intolerable discipline on their own men. Nor was he soothed by the spectacle of a red-haired journalist, sitting with his feet on a desk in London and believing every anonymous letter.

As for the German press. . . .

Most Englishmen could not understand what was happening in Germany. Prussia, in fact, had been regarded as an ally since the time of Napoleon. And sympathy with the German states, a sense of blood-tie, seemed always to have grown stronger since Queen Victoria's marriage with Albert of Saxe-Gotha. The present German Emperor, with his love of sport and his fluent English speech, was a grandson of Queen Victoria. Hadn't the German Emperor come to England less than a year ago, to mourn at his grandmother's death-bed and confer the Order of the Black Eagle on Lord Roberts?

For Germans, in general, Conan Doyle had always kept the cold, polite dislike he inherited from the Ma'am's teaching, just as he inherited his liking for the French. He could not understand, any more than the rest of his countrymen, what prompted Germany's attitude now. But he knew who had prompted the press to clamour as it did.

"The Germans are a well-disciplined people," he was

shortly to write. "Anglophobia couldn't have reached this point of mania without some official encouragement."

The international situation, as a result of this uproar, had grown really serious. At Edinburgh, on October 25th, Joseph Chamberlain made a speech which was interpreted, in Germany, as a slur on Prussia for her conduct of the Franco-Prussian War. Dr. Leyds, envoy from the Transvaal, told lurid stories in Berlin. Six hundred and eighty Rhineland clergymen, in all sincerity, signed a petition against British atrocities.

It was the last straw to an Irishman in Surrey.

On a morning in the middle of November, 1901, he read that petition in the 'Times' as he travelled up by train to London. Finally he crumpled the newspaper into a ball, and threw it up into the luggage-rack.

Why were the British so very slow in defending themselves? No charge was ever answered by silence; it was only confirmed. If your personal honour came into question, you would not hesitate to cram the facts down your enemy's throat. Wasn't it the same, but far more important, in a question of national honour? This hoity-toity, high-and-mighty policy might be apathy; it might be arrogance; it was certainly folly. To the devil with frozen dignity! Hit a lie, and hit it hard!

How could foreign countries be expected to see another side to the question, if they heard only one side? British press-reports they dismissed as of no value. British Blue-books were crushing opiates which nobody ever read. Why didn't somebody, who was well-informed in the matter, wallop out with the facts in a statement which should be clearly worded, beyond refutation, and above all readable?

Well, why don't you do it yourself?

He was the very person to do it. Already he had accumulated so many materials for his complete history of the war that his death-bed, he once exclaimed to Reginald Smith the publisher, would find him still re-writing and correcting it.

He would write a little book, say sixty thousand words long, to be bound in paper covers and sold for sixpence. This book—not hysteria, but fact—should present another side of the question to English-speaking peoples. From the sales of that book, from public subscription, from his own pocket if necessary, he would raise the funds to get the book translated into every foreign language. And these translations, in as many thousands as possible, should be poured out and given away wholesale throughout the civilized world.

Was it feasible? Could he tackle the enemy single-handed?

That night, at Sir Henry Thompson's dinner-table, he outlined his scheme in the hearing of Sir Eric Barrington of the Foreign Office. "Every foreign journalist," he vowed, "ought to get a copy of the facts! Every schoolmaster, every clergyman, every politician in Europe and every priest in Ireland!" And the Foreign Office (though he never realized it) knew very well when they had found a good thing. For this was not 'just any author.' This was the man whose words would be read in countries which hated England or knew nothing of England. This was the creator of Sherlock Holmes.

The Intelligence Department of the War Office put its records at his disposal, to use uncensored anything or everything he liked. The Foreign Office promised funds. On November 20th he wrote of the project to his friend Reginald Smith, of Smith, Elder & Co. Reginald Smith immediately offered to print the book free of charge, and entered into a partnership from which neither derived— or ever intended to derive—a penny of profit.

Then, in the midst of his work, came a happy-hearted letter from W. T. Stead.

This is not said as sarcasm. Nor was W. T. Stead's letter meant as sarcasm: its chirruping note, which rings so strangely in the ear, carolled out in all sincerity.

"My dear Dr. Conan Doyle," wrote the Prince of the Rape-Ravers. "I am delighted to read the announcement in the 'Mail' today that you have been preparing a detailed refutation of all the charges brought against the British troops in South Africa. It was high time someone undertook this task. The persistence with which our own soldiers have borne witness to the charges, in their letters home, has rendered the task of the apologist extremely difficult.

"I suppose you have had all the publications which we have issued, including 'Pen Pictures of the War.' If not I shall be glad to send you copies. Meantime I send you my Annual. It deals with a subject on which I venture to hope we are more in accord than on the S.A. War."

It may or may not be remembered that Conan Doyle, nearly a dozen years before, had written an article for Stead on Dr. Koch's tuberculosis-cure. Having met the 'Review of Reviews' editor, he could acquit Stead of any subtle sense of humour.

"I cannot think that anyone has seen more soldiers' letters than I have," he retorted, "since I have been the only man who has been systematically advertising for them. I believe such statements to be lies; and I do not envy the prominent part you have taken in spreading them."

Long afterwards, remembering the incident in tranquillity, he felt that seldom in his life had he been so conscious of a direct imperative call which drove every other interest from his mind. But he was in no mood of philosophical detachment. Germany he loathed. W. T. Stead he could have murdered. "Publishers report seven distinct libels," he wrote when he had completed the first draft of the book, "so I must get out the blue pencil and delete." But the very heat of rage kept him cool when he presented the finished version.

"There never was a war in history," he wrote, "in which the right was absolutely on one side, or in which no incidents of the campaign were open to criticism, I do not pretend that it was so here. But I do not think that any unprejudiced man can read the facts without acknowledging that the British Government has done its best to avoid war, and the British Army to wage it with humanity."

And he set out to change the opinion of the world.

XIII

DILEMMA:

How a Champion Refused to Be Knighted,
and What Came of It

"Stick to facts and don't lie! Writing penny novelettes is more in your line."

"For God's sake don't drag golf into your defence of the slaughter of 12,000 babies in the camps. Truth is dearer than cash or golf."

"You remind me of the gentleman of whom Sheridan said that he drew his facts from his imagination and his fancies from his memory."

Here were three of the postcards he received amid the piles of letters emptied on his desk, day after day, following the publication of *The War in South Africa: its Cause and Conduct,* in the middle of January, 1902. But such comments, usually anonymous, were about one hundredth of one per cent in the flood of letters whose burden ran, "Thank God, somebody's said a word on our side."

The War: its Cause and Conduct, price sixpence, sold three hundred thousand copies in six weeks. Fifty thousand more went to the United States and Canada. But what mattered most was the question of foreign translation. And those who wrote in gratitude sent donations for the translation, from 'A Loyal Briton' with £500 down to postal orders for half a crown or a shilling.

As regards 'A Loyal Briton,' we find a letter from the manager of the Oxford Street Branch of the Capital and

Counties Bank. (Yes, the Capital and Counties Bank really existed; it was not invented, as so many have imagined, for Sherlock Holmes; it was Conan Doyle's own bank.)

"I beg to advise you," wrote the manager, "that the sum of £500 in notes was paid in yesterday, by a stranger who would not give his name, to the credit of the War Book Fund account."

This brings happy visions of a mysterious masked personage, finger on lip, slipping out of a hansom in the fog and removing his mask only to the bank-manager. It would have delighted Robert Louis Stevenson in the *New Arabian Nights*. It was, in fact, the Foreign Office's way of representing King Edward the Seventh. The only other high contributions in Smith, Elder's long lists were given by Lord Rosebery and A. H. Harman, with fifty pounds each; and a certain A. Conan Doyle, who matched them with fifty. But, large or small, the funds poured in.

For *The War: its Cause and Conduct* was not a book which attempted to whitewash its own side. Therein lay its deadly impact. It can scarcely be called a pamphlet, as everybody including the author did call it: it is sixty thousand words long. Where any fact was capable of a damaging interpretation, the author stated it. Though he agreed with the necessity of making a waste-area, he insisted that any farm-house destroyed for this purpose must be rebuilt and full compensation made to the enemy.

But the charges of brutality, of looting, of rape were flat lies. Here he argued very little. Instead of arguing, he devoted page after page to quoting eye-witness testimony, which included Boer burghers, Boer women, Boer field-commandants, Boer judges, Boer parsons, the

American military attaché, the French military attaché, the Austrian General Hübner, and the head of the Dutch Reformed Church at Pretoria.

"Which are we to believe?" he asked. "Our enemy upon the spot, or the journalist in London?"

What were the facts about these concentration camps? The British authorities, having decided to round up the women and children because nothing else could be done with them, had to feed and take care of them. Were they held as hostages for torture?

"I have the honour," wrote Lord Kitchener, in reply to a frantic protest from Schalk Burger, "to inform you that all women and children at present in our camps who are willing to leave will be sent to the care of Your Honour, and I shall be happy to be informed where you desire that they be handed over to you."

This offer was not accepted. The Boer commandos had no wish to receive these women and children; they were glad to be relieved of the responsibility. The 'starvation' rations in the camps (pro-Boer figures, not British) consisted of a daily allowance to each person of half a pound of meat, three quarters of a pound of flour, half a pound of potatoes, two ounces of sugar, two ounces of coffee; to every child under six, a quart bottle of milk.

Again the author marshalled his witnesses. Nobody could deny the terrifying prevalence of disease, or the high rate of infant mortality. But the disease was not typhus or diphtheria, from bad sanitary conditions: it was measles, chicken-pox, whooping-cough. Mothers clung screaming to their children and would not let them be segregated when doctors or nurses tried to do it; an epidemic swept the tents. In a dozen instances it was the same kind of testimony:

"Many of the women would not open their tents to admit fresh air, and, instead of giving the proper medicines supplied by the military, preferred to give them home remedies. The mothers would not sponge the children. . . . The cause of the high death-rate is that the women let their children out as soon as the measles-rash has subsided. They persist in giving their children meat and other indigestible foods, even when we forbid it." What the Stead-like screamers failed to point out was that English refugees from Johannesburg had been living in exactly the same kind of English camps since the beginning of the war.

Much more Conan Doyle wrote on other charges, his careful piling-up of facts in sharp contrast to the anger he felt in private. Twenty thousand translations of *The War* were sown throughout Germany. Twenty thousand went to France. It reached Holland, Russia, Hungary, Sweden, Portugal, Italy, Spain, Rumania; even at home a special edition of ten thousand was translated into Welsh. For the Norwegian edition a part of the book was flashed to the publishers by heliograph from peak to peak; access to Oslo was impossible because of storms and snow. Abroad a translator or publisher often faced obloquy or worse; sometimes a censorship-clamp must be pried loose; but friends of baneful Britain were there to help.

Well, was he tilting at windmills? "We had no delusions," he afterwards wrote to the 'Times.' "We expected no wholesale conversions. But at least we could be sure that the plea of ignorance could no longer be used."

If he did tilt at foreign windmills, he wrecked the windmills. Many of them, far more of them than he had ever hoped, stopped grinding wheat for President Kruger. Others slowed down. They followed the lead of influential journals like the hitherto anti-British 'Wiener Tageblatt,' the 'Independence Belge' of Brussels, the

'National Zeitung' of Berlin. When H. A. Gwynne said that his work had been equal to that of a successful general, it was less than the truth. Joseph Chamberlain at one dinner table, Lord Rosebery at another, told him much the same thing. Most of the press at home, like his correspondents, were grateful that somebody had spoken up. But there were some who, while praising his patriotic work, wondered uncomfortably whether Great Britain's dignity did not suffer if somebody spoke out in her defence.

You doubt that? Then listen to these lofty strains from 'Country Life':

There are still plenty of Britons who, quite foolishly, do despise "those————foreigners," and do not care a straw what they think. I understand their feelings, and I would not like to swear solemnly that I was out of sympathy with their belief in the theory of splendid isolation. But at the same time comes to my mind the haunting suspicion that, at any rate, we should be none the worse off if foreigners thought better and more justly of us.

You see, the writer has a 'haunting suspicion.' He is uncomfortable. Almost he is persuaded to come off his perch. *That* was the sort of attitude Conan Doyle was fighting, the arrogant priggishness he fought all his life. And, when we count over services rendered to a nation, let us not forget whose voice spoke out forty-seven years ago.

In April, 1902, the translations were completed. Again restless after the end of a task, he decided to go abroad for a short holiday. His second-youngest sister, Ida, was now married to Nelson Foley and living on the Island of Gaiola, Naples. To visit Italy again, to swim in the Mediterranean, and travel back by easy stages in a fortnight or so: that, he thought, was the ideal rest. His dispute with the Hornungs had been patched up, at least outwardly; Connie and Willie visited Undershaw now. All the credit for his war-book he gave to Jean Leckie.

"It is a high and heaven-sent thing, this love of ours. First *A Duet* and then this Pamphlet have come straight from it. It has kept my soul and my emotions alive."

Then:

"It was kind of you, Ma'am, to write Jean such a letter and offer her Aunt Annette's bangle. I always feel that Aunt Annette knows and approves of our love. We often have that sense of a Guardian Spirit."

That last sentence may have been written in a mood. We allow for moods in our own friends' correspondence; we dare not judge by a hasty note written overnight; and still less must we make confident pronouncements here. Yet he had never before written anything like this. He had groped from the fighting agnosticism of his youth to the reverent Deism of what some have called charity towards God. Reverence in itself is an important step. That Jean Leckie influenced him here, in any active sense, is difficult to believe. But his idealization of her? That may well have been a different matter.

On April 10th, 1902, he sailed in R.M.S. *Austral* for Naples. Jean accompanied him aboard ship to say goodbye.

"She decorated my cabin with flowers and kissed my pillow on both sides. I last saw her face in the shadow of the shed as she tried to hide that she was crying. I tell you these things, Ma'am, because you have insight and you know how the little things count in life. We left the very wharf from which the *Oriental* sailed for South Africa on the rainy day when you were here."

And yet, for the first time in his life, he was on the edge of serious trouble with the Ma'am.

The South African War gasped its last; the Boer leaders were suing for peace at Pretoria. Nothing, except the taste of a foe ill-chewed and badly digested, marred appetite for the coronation of King Edward the Seventh. It was an open secret that the Coronation Honours List would contain the name of Dr. Conan Doyle if he cared to accept a knighthood.

He knew this, of course. He had already met King Edward, of whom George Meredith long ago told him: "When the Prince laughs, he laughs from the tip of his beard to his bald head, and he laughs all round his neck." King Edward, very stout and grizzled-grey in his sixtieth year, invited Conan Doyle to a small dinner and had the author of *The War: its Cause and Conduct* seated beside him.

"He is an able, clear-headed, positive man," the guest noted, "rather inclined to be noisy, very alert and energetic. He won't be a dummy king. He will live to be 70, I should say."

The trouble was that Conan Doyle did not want to accept a knighthood, and had made up his mind to refuse one. This came from no sense of democratic principle, but rather the reverse: it was black ancestral pride. If he had done any service for England, it was because he hated the enemies of England. He would not be what he considered patronized, or have cheap crumbs thrown at him from anybody's table.

"Surely," he wrote to the Ma'am, "you don't mean that I should take a knighthood: the badge of the provincial mayor?

"It is a silently understood thing in this world that the big men—outside diplomacy and the army, where it is a sort of professional badge—do not condescend to such things. Not that *I* am a big man, but something inside me revolts at the thought. Fancy Rhodes or Chamberlain or Kipling doing such a thing! And why should my standards be lower than theirs? It is the Al-

fred Austin and Hall Caine type of man who takes re-
wards. All my work for the State would seem tainted if
I took a so called 'reward.' It may be pride and it may
be foolish, but I could not do it."

And:

"The title I value most is that of 'Doctor,' which was
conferred by your self-sacrifice and determination. I
won't descend from it to another."

The Ma'am, who seriously believed that the figurative
spurs of knighthood meant what they had meant five
centuries before, was incredulous and horrified. She
could not understand this. She thought her son must be
losing his mind. All the way to Italy she bombarded him
with letters. At Ida Foley's house on The Island, in a
top-floor room overlooking the Bay of Naples, he immersed himself in plans to revive Brigadier Gerard for a
new series of Napoleonic adventures. By this time the
Ma'am was raging at him.

"I have never approved of titles," he retorted, "and I
have always said so. I could imagine a man at the end
of a long and successful career taking a peerage as a
mark that his work was done and recognized, as Tennyson did; but that a youngish man should saddle himself
with a knighthood, a discredited title"—this was what he
loathed—"I tell you it is unthinkable. Let us drop the
subject."

But the subject could not be dropped. When he returned to England, towards the end of May, his mother
lurked in waiting.

Everybody at Undershaw was accustomed to a cat-
and-dog fight, over something or other, nearly every
time these two met. They would see the wagging white
cap of 'the clever one,' and the son flailing his arms
above her head; and the children would run and hide.
But this was far quieter, far more serious. The Ma'am,

who meant to accomplish her end if she accomplished nothing else in life, left off anger for the coolness of inspiration. She knew her son. She knew how she had brought him up.

"Has it not occurred to you," she inquired, "that to refuse a knighthood would be an insult to the king?"

This checked him in mid-flight.

His common sense told him, as he forcibly explained, that the king had nothing to do with this beyond approving the appointment: beware any recommendation of which martinet King Edward did not approve. The Ma'am said no more. She merely smiled a peculiar smile, looked into the distance, and let him worry about it. The more he worried, the more he wondered. A free-for-all-fight was one thing; discourteous behaviour was another.

"I tell you, Ma'am, I can't do it! As a matter of principle!"

"If you wish to show your principles by an insult to the king, no doubt you can't."

That was how his name appeared in the Honours List. The date of the coronation had originally been fixed for June 26th. In the long-distant future he was to write a story, *The Three Garridebs,* in which he made Sherlock Holmes refuse a knighthood on this date. But, two days before the date, King Edward was taken ill and had to undergo an immediate operation for a new disease called appendicitis. Following the king's speedy recovery, operations for appendicitis became so fashionable that surgeons' incomes soared all over the country. On August 9th, when the bells clanged for Coronation Day, Conan Doyle was herded into a pen at Buckingham Palace with Professor Oliver Lodge, who was to be knighted at the same time. Amid feathered, silken pageantry these two debated psychic matters, almost forgetting the purpose for which they were there; and he emerged into the sunshine, still a little rebelliously, as Sir Arthur Conan Doyle.

"I feel," he growled in a letter to Innes, "like a new-married girl who isn't sure of her own name. They have also made me Deputy-Lieutenant of Surrey, whatever that means."

Human nature being what it is, he directed all his outward complaints at this appointment as Deputy-Lieutenant, and in particular at the uniform. The uniform was in truth an elaborate one, having gold epaulettes and a fore-and-aft hat. He, who never troubled about the expense of anything, complained bitterly of its expense and said it made him look like a monkey on a stick.

Yet again it was not in human nature that he should fail to be pleased, and his great pride was in the messages of congratulations which showered on him.

"I think," wrote H. G. Wells, "the congratulations should go to those who have honoured themselves by honouring you." There was even a message from the crippled, dying Henley, whom he had not seen in years. One letter, which prattled of admiration for his work, came from the grim old hanging judge, Lord Brampton, who during years on the bench had loved horses and dogs but in general hated mankind.

"The pleasure I have in sending you this line," wrote the ancient judge, "is enhanced by my vivid remembrance of a happy walk we took through Cliveden Woods"—they had talked about murders—"as guests of our friend Astor." When Conan Doyle once wrote of Sherlock Holmes in a room ankle-deep with congratulatory telegrams, he only anticipated what happened now.

This accursed Sherlock, to tell the truth, cast still another shadow across what pleasure he felt. It is not a modern joke that Conan Doyle owed his knighthood to the demon, and to the demon's reappearance when *The Hound of the Baskervilles* ran its triumphant course through the 'Strand.' You will find mention of this in the contemporary press, once or twice quite seriously. That is why, when he received a parcel of shirts addressed to Sir Sherlock Holmes, he momentarily lost his sense of humour and a very sticky time ensued until the mistake was explained.

Otherwise it was a golden summer and autumn, with brief visits both from Lottie and from Innes, who had seen the last of the fighting in South Africa. Returning to the Napoleonic era with all his old gusto and more than his old skill, he wrote the second series of Brigadier stories which appeared as the *Adventures of Gerard*. Three of these were published in the 'Strand' before the end of the year; five more, counting the Waterloo episode as two stories, in the spring of 1903. In the spring of 1903, too, the six saddle-horses in the stables at Undershaw kicked out and screamed at a new noise. It was the chugging of his first motor-car.

Motoring was the new sport, the new thrill. At Birmingham he bought a ten-horse-power Wolseley, painted dark blue, with red wheels. It had seats for five persons, or seven at a squeeze-in. "It will give me," he declared, "a new interest in life." His coachman, Holden, he sent to Birmingham for three weeks' driving instruction. But most of the driving he meant to do himself.

"When all is ready," he explained to Innes, who begged him for heaven's sake to be careful, "when all is ready, I propose to go up and drive it down myself the whole way. It would be rather a sporting performance, would it not, to drive 150 miles the first time I had ever been on the road?"

It would. And that is what he did. From all over Hindhead a crowd gathered at news of his approach.

They watched him, sitting high-placed and be-goggled at the vertical column of the steering-wheel, as the blue-and-red car chugged along the road amid barking dogs, and swept magnificently through the gates at Undershaw. It might have symbolized the Edwardian age, that age of motoring-veils and flounced curtains, of palm-rooms and brass beds, which had come to full dawn now.

At the age of forty-three, as yet far from the height of his powers, he was one of the most famous men in the world and perhaps its most popular writer. The strength of that popularity may be judged by an offer he received in that same spring of 1903. The offer, which came from America, was this:

If he would restore Sherlock Holmes to life, in some fashion explaining away that matter of the Reichenbach Falls, they were prepared to pay him at the rate of five thousand dollars a story for six short-stories or as many more as he cared to write. These were only the American rights. George Newnes, if not equalling that sum, would offer more than half as much for the English rights.

On a postcard he wrote just three words to his agent: "Very well. A.C.D."

He was in a mood of calm cynicism. That mood never changed afterwards. If this was what readers wanted, he would henceforward give them a sound, workmanlike job and accept as much money as slightly deranged editors were willing to pay. He might even, in a very mild sort of way, enjoy doing it. But before long, in a year or so perhaps, he meant to write another mediaeval novel, a companion for *The White Company*, and show them their error by demonstration.

What was the fascination of this Holmes-puppet: that he, who dangled the strings and mouthed the dialogue, could never understand it? Surely it must be obvious that Sherlock Holmes was only himself?

The supreme irony was that popular voices who called him by this name—newspapers, hecklers, friends, and countrymen—were perfectly correct. Assuredly he had put enough clues into the stories to show that Holmes was himself. He did not propose to admit the fact publicly; but, sooner or later, he would include a clue so blatantly plain that it could not be missed. Meanwhile, he must somehow get Sherlock out of that chasm. And the Ma'am, to whom he mentioned the new series only when he had written the first story, made a wrong tactical approach.

"I am not conscious of any failing powers," he retorted sharply. "I have not done any Holmes short-stories for seven or eight years"—in fact, it was just ten years to the month—"and I don't see why I should not have another go at them.

"I might add," he went on, "that I have finished the first one, called *The Adventure of the Empty House.* The plot, by the way, was given to me by Jean; and it is a rare good one. You will find that Holmes was never dead, and that he is now very much alive."

The first four stories he wrote, *Empty House, Norwood Builder, Dancing Men,* and *Solitary Cyclist,* he considered crucial. They would show whether he had his hand in; he was anxious about them. His idea for one, the *Dancing Men,* he got on a motoring visit to the Hill House Hotel, at Happisburgh in Norfolk, then kept by a family named Cubitt. The hotel-proprietor's small son had a habit of writing his signature in dancing men. Conan Doyle worked at the story in the Green Room, overlooking the bowling green, and left his room strewn with dancing sketches.

If we wish to see him most clearly during that summer, indeed as he might have seemed during any summer at home since 1897, we can see him through the eyes of his own children. Mary, with her round face and long hair, was now fourteen years old. Kingsley, sturdy and intelligent though with less artistic gifts than his sister, was not yet eleven. During their years at Undershaw they united in at least one feeling about their father: they were terrified of him.

Their mother remained the same. Touie, grey-haired since Mary could remember her, was the benevolent deity who smiled and could not play games except to pose in tableaux. Mary very dimly remembered a roystering father, a man who dressed up as Father Christmas and was boisterous at devising new games. But this man, if he ever existed, had long ago become an unpredictable stranger.

For one thing, he was seldom with them. But always he loomed in the background; as once, when Mary forgot a message and went to bed without delivering it, he suddenly loomed in the lighted doorway of the dark bedroom: cat-footed, radiating wrath, an avenger. They must not make a noise in the house while he was writing, or he would come storming out of his study, in an old rust-coloured dressing-gown, and punishment would ensue.

True, there were flashes of geniality from this remote figure, who would invite them to carry his golf-clubs on Sunday when they should have been in church. They were permitted liberties envied by the children of more starchy parents: they could run wild in the country, or go on holidays by themselves. They gloried in the rifle-shooting (Mary proudly had herself photographed with the Club); they gloried in the cricket-matches, and the first day of the summer holidays when they were allowed to go barefoot.

And yet, despite all his laughing among the grown-ups, this father remained awesome and unpredictable. Even when he said nothing, he had a certain Look. There was one occasion when Mary, with Father in the same room reading the 'Times,' began happily discoursing on the fertility of rabbits. Round the corner of the newspaper appeared one eye, no more; and Mary stopped petrified, mouth open, conscious of some enormity without knowing why.

That Look, of course, had its effect on persons far older than the children. The man who completed the *Adventures of Sherlock Holmes* in 1892, letting Mary crawl all over his desk and writing undisturbed amid the bang of flashlight-powder, was considerably different from the man who laboured at the *Return of Sherlock Holmes* in 1903.

But the first four Holmes stories, in what he called his new manner, reasonably satisfied him. "I have got three bull's-eyes and an outer," he decided, being not quite pleased with *Solitary Cyclist*. "And you can't help me with the writing, Ma'am. The writing is easy. It is the plots which butcher me; I must talk over the plot with somebody. Will they take to Holmes?"

How they took to him, when *The Adventure of the Empty House* appeared in the 'Strand' for October, 1903, is a matter of history.

"The scenes at the railway-bookstalls," writes one lady who vividly remembers it, "were worse than anything I ever saw at a bargain-sale. My husband, when he was drunk, used to recite to me pages from *A Duet;* but I could never see anything in that. Holmes was a different matter."

"It is as we suspected," raved the 'Westminster Gazette.' "That fall over the cliff did not kill Holmes. In

fact, he never fell at all. He climbed up the other side
of the cliff to escape his enemies, and churlishly left poor
Watson in ignorance. We call this mean. All the same,
who can complain?"

"Bah!" scoffed 'The Academy of Literature,' when
Conan Doyle's Collected Works were published at about
the same time by Smith, Elder. "No one really likes his
work because he created that arch-humbug, that Egyp-
tian-Hall man of mystery! Our children's children will
probably argue that Holmes was a solar myth. Give us
The White Company, give us *Rodney Stone*! He is too
big for the other sort of thing."

("Sir," wrote the author in question, "may I say a
word of heartfelt gratitude for your notice?")

But these two were in the minority. Newnes could not
print copies fast enough; the queues in Southampton
Street surpassed any fish-or-theatre queue of today.
Thud went the air-gun in the dark house; glass tinkled;
Colonel Sebastian Moran, who had already killed the
Hon. Ronald Adair, struggled in a police grip; and a
new era was inaugurated when Sherlock Holmes re-
turned to 221b across the street.

The present-day legend—that readers found a slight
decline in Holmes's powers—is not borne out by contemporary press-reviews or by the author's correspondence. Nor can anybody in his senses bear it out today.
We must be careful of these generalities, remembering
that even a master-hand is not always ready. If the
Adventures, for instance, can rise to the height of *The
Man with the Twisted Lip,* they can go in another direction with *The Noble Bachelor.* In the *Memoirs,* anyone
not mummified must admire *Silver Blaze* or *The Mus-
grave Ritual*; but it requires a more ardent Sherlockian
to find high merit in *The 'Gloria Scott'* or *The Yellow
Face.*

As for the author of these stories, he would not have argued. Once sure his touch had not lost its firmness, he could look back with far more satisfaction on other matters.

Between his own efforts and those of Reginald Smith, than whom no publisher ever worked more disinterestedly, they had accumulated a surplus of more than twenty-five hundred pounds on the sale of *The War: its Cause and Conduct*. All this was devoted to charity, from a fifteen-hundred-pound-scholarship for South Africans at Edinburgh University to a gunnery-challenge cup for the Channel Fleet. The first winner of the scholarship astonished them, but they could not deny the justice of the claim.

"I am a full-blooded Zulu," the candidate pointed out unanswerably.

Nelson, too, had published a one-volume edition of Conan Doyle's *The Great Boer War*—and such was his power in the land that he compelled them to alter the whole edition when he received the first bound copy.

His reason? We find it in that single copy, which they sent him in advance and which contained his picture as frontispiece.

"This volume," he wrote across the title-page, "should be unique. When I saw, with horror, that they had put my portrait upon it, I said I would destroy the whole edition rather than pass it. They then put Lord Roberts, as was proper."

No comment need be made on a man who carried knightly ceremony to so fine a point as that. It sums him up at this stage of his life. In his eyes the greatest of his tributes was a huge silver bowl, which was presented to him by popular subscription for his work both during the Boer War and in vindication of his fellow-countrymen afterwards. It stood gleaming on his desk, with an inscription treasured afterwards.

To ARTHUR CONAN DOYLE, WHO, AT A GREAT CRISIS, IN WORD AND DEED SERVED HIS COUNTRY.

XIV

GROPING:

The Doubts of All This World

Through the grounds at Undershaw, skimming down into hollows and flashing out over rises, the miniature railway-carriages hummed on their single rail.

It was the Monorail, driven by electricity and steadied by gyroscope. Many believed it to be the train of the future; H. G. Wells, in fact, wrote a novel of the future which foresaw England veined with Monorails. When Conan Doyle grew interested in the project—as he would interest himself in so many fascinating ventures from sculpturing machines to buried treasure—he had them build a model Monorailway whose carriages were nevertheless big enough for small passengers.

The children loved it, and whooped.

True, in this early summer of 1906, Mary was growing up and a trifle on her dignity. Kingsley, now at Eton, had grown into a rangy and raw-boned fourteen-year-old, athletic like his father.

"Can't the train go faster, Daddy? *Can't* it go faster?"

"No, it can't. Do you want to hurt yourselves?" virtuously thundered his father: who, during those years '03 to '06, had several times escaped breaking his own neck only by the narrowest of margins.

In the stables were two motor-cars, the later one a twenty horse-power, as well as a Roc motor-cycle. When he casually suggested that he meant to get rid of his horses and carriages, he had more trouble with the

Ma'am. The Ma'am's violent objection lay in the removal of the dignified carriage harness stamped with the family crest. She had no objection to motor vehicles as such. On the contrary, she was in the tonneau of the old Wolseley when it collided with two farm-carts full of turnips.

The horses went mad; the carts overturned, and showered the old lady with turnips. Her son, springing out of the car, found that the Ma'am was not in the least disturbed. She continued to ply her knitting-needles among the turnips—aloof, disdainful of vulgar bickering —while her son and the farmer exchanged opinions of each other which could be heard in the next county.

His motoring misadventures do not seem to have been caused by any lack of skill, though there are those who testify that all his life he would reach for the gear-lever like Sandow the Strong Man reaching for a wrestling-hold. Nevertheless, it was just as well he had once taken lessons from that same Sandow, considering what happened in the winter of '04.

He and Innes, who had returned permanently to England and was at the Staff College, were out for a drive in the Wolseley. Nobody, including the newspapers, seemed quite clear about what happened. But the car, shaving in at the gates on its return to Undershaw, bumped against one of the gate-posts. Then it shot down the drive towards the house, slurring gravel under its hard-rubber tyres. It lurched, swerved, climbed straight up the steep bank at one side of the drive, and turned over backwards on top of its two occupants.

Mary, in the house, heard the shaking crash. She ran to a window of the dining-room, just in time to see the overturned car with one red-spoked wheel still turning. Innes was flung clear. But his brother, at the wheel, remained underneath though dislodged from the steering-wheel. As the car crashed over backwards, its full weight was caught and momentarily held by the vertical steering-column. That saved his life. Then the steering-column snapped off. The weight of the car settled down across his back and shoulders just below the neck.

With the weight of more than a ton across his spine, he supported it on his back-and-shoulder muscles until Holden's shouts brought enough help to lever up the car. Then, dishevelled but unhurt, he staggered to his feet and pushed up his motoring-goggles. "All right? Of course I'm all right!" he hooted at Innes. All the same, he had been calculating just how long it would take before his spine snapped.

It was at this time, too, that he bought his motorcycle. To an eager young reporter from a magazine called 'The Motor-Cycle,' who came down to see him three months later, he explained that he found his machine very simple, despite its (also) mysterious tendencies to fly up over a bank and turn a somersault.

"I cannot leave Undershaw," the reporter quotes himself as saying, in an interview published on February 27th, 1905, "without referring to my old friend Sherlock Holmes."

"Ah," murmured his host.

"May I ask," pursued this rather lyrical reporter, "whether we can expect to hear of the famous detective hunting down his quarry, accompanied by the faithful Watson, both mounted on the newest and finest type of motor-cycle?"

"No!" said the host with some vehemence. "In Holmes's early days motor bicycles were unthought-of. Besides," he added more mildly, "Holmes has now retired into private life."

The Return of Sherlock Holmes had recently been published by George Newnes, after the stories' 'Strand' appearance from October, '03, to December, '04. Henceforward Holmes could never die again; he could only retire; he was forever condemned to life. Conan Doyle, who wrote all thirteen stories in one rapid batch, had not been compelled even to think of his detective for well over a year. He had been deep in studies for a literary work closer to his heart. And he was knee-deep, for a time, in politics both national and international.

In August, 1905, the northern squadron of the French battle-fleet—with Vice-Admiral Caillard in its flagship, *Masséna*—lay at anchor off Spithead. It was more than a mission of mere routine courtesy and handshaking. Diplomatically, it emphasized the *entente* with England.

For, in restless Europe, the balance of alliance had begun to change. Germany was at the throat of France over the Moroccan dispute; if France did not submit humbly, Germany threatened war. Before a year had passed, it brought Great Britain—and Russia as well—squarely on the side of the French. As though an iron door had clanged shut, Germany presently found herself with Austria as her sole ally.

Germany steadily increased her war-fleet. The Kaiser, in a speech at Reval, modestly styled himself the Admiral of the Atlantic. England said nothing; but at Portsmouth they were building the first of the great Dreadnought class battleships, carrying an armament of ten twelve-inch guns.

Diplomats could smell trouble. It might amount to nothing; there had been so many crises. But, when the French fleet visited England in August of '05, there was to be a gala reception. The officers were to travel to London in a long procession of motor-cars, and be shown the sights. Was there any person, asked Officialdom, whom they would especially like to meet? The reply of the French officers was prompt and unanimous.

"His Majesty the King! And Sir John Fisher: he is the Grand Admiral Anglais!"

Ah, yes. And anyone else? Officialdom rather expected them to say Mr. Balfour or Mr. Chamberlain. Again the reply was prompt and unanimous. "Sir Conan Doyle!"

"In fact," wrote the 'Daily Chronicle's' naval correspondent, who travelled with them, "they seemed to regard Sir Arthur as the one and only non-official Englishman." Unofficially, a message was sent to him: When the French officers returned to Portsmouth by road, would he entertain them at Hindhead? By George, he would! He regarded the *entente* with France as an ideal long wished-for.

"I'll do it up properly," he promised. "You see if I don't."

The reception began as the motor-cars neared Hindhead. Their host had stationed four brass bands at various points. British ex-service-men, wearing their medals, stood at attention on each side of the road. The prettiest girls of the district threw nose-gays of flowers. The French officers—in their long blue coats and white uniform-caps—stood up in the cars and exclaimed, "Magnifique!" like Frenchmen in an English play.

They were really pleased and touched. They had expected only formal politeness, if not veiled hostility. At the entrance-gate to Undershaw, over whose tall arch of leaves ran a banner inscribed BIENVENUE, stood a burly man with a Napoleonic moustache, informally dressed and wearing a very small straw hat. A big marquee tent, with flags, had been set out on the tennis-lawn. Ladies all in white (white parasols and leg-of-mutton sleeves) thronged among the gratified guests; and above them beamed their host. They were more and more convinced that he was the one and only non-official Englishman.

"During the whole of their visit," wrote the 'Chronicle,' after the fleet had departed, "the French looked keenly for any symptoms of English sentiment towards Germany. They see in the *entente* the promise of peace for France. They regard us as people cheerfully indifferent to the German swaggerer."

That was true enough; some people might have said too cheerfully indifferent, when visitors to Berlin could hear (behind guarded enclosures) the drup-drup-drup of machine-guns at practice. But at home there was distracting political chaos. As for Conan Doyle, he had sworn several years ago that never again would he become entangled with politics.

"If you stood for Parliament again," a reporter asked him at Buxton, "what would be your party?"

"The name of that party," he said, "has not yet been invented."

It was only the appeal of his old friend and leader, Joseph Chamberlain, which made him break that resolve. Mr. Chamberlain, over sixty but with monocle still glittering, had been waging a campaign—and, incidentally, splitting his own party—in favour of a protective tariff on foreign goods. Mr. Chamberlain's argument, summarized, ran like this:

"At the moment, cheap foreign goods are being dumped on us without tax. England is importing more and more, and exporting less and less. Because other countries like Germany and the United States have a high protective tariff, our chief exports are to our own colonies. You grant that?

"Then give the colonies preferential treatment in dealing with us! Put a tariff on imports from foreign countries; let your free trade, without tax, be with the colonies: who will give us advantages in return. Cherish the colonies; draw closer to the colonies; think imperially, or you may have no Empire left!"

That was also the position held by Conan Doyle. In the long series of clashes which ended with the bitter general election of 1906, he again stood for Parliament. Once more it was in Scotland, where he contested the Border Burghs of Hawick, Selkirk, and Galashiels. And once more he was beaten. The Government, Unionists and Conservatives alike, went down to crushing defeat before the Liberals in that general election.

"My dear fellow," complained William Gillette, in a letter written during the campaign, "what singular tastes you have! Why all this energy? Is it not much better— like me—to care for nothing?"

But he could not do that. And, with his idealization of women, it is easy to understand the attitude he took over a political issue growing more and more vexed with each year. As he stood in the Volunteer Hall at Galashiels, facing forty minutes' heckling, let the press tell his opinion on votes for women.

" 'Is the candidate prepared to grant universal female suffrage?' 'No, I am not.' (Cries of, 'Oh, oh,'). 'Will the candidate tell us why not?' (Cheers). 'Certainly I will. When a man comes home from his day's work, I don't think he wants a politician sitting opposite him at the fireside.' (Cheers, hisses, and general uproar.)"

'General uproar' marked most of the press reports. He could not persuade the electors, whose woollen-trade had suffered so much from foreign competition, that a tax on foreign goods would benefit them at home. They said it would increase the working man's cost of living, and one heckler dangled a loaf of bread in his face like a death's-head. But for several years he had persisted in his plea that Britain's economic security lay in encouraging the Empire.

"Take Ireland as an example," he insisted, in a speech at Selkirk. "What has Ireland ever had out of the Empire? Is it any wonder her people are discontented, and that she is the weak spot in our structure?

"Ireland had manufactures, and British laws killed them. Then she had a flourishing agriculture, and again British laws—the law of free trade—let the produce of the whole world in, and swamped her home market. She produces butter, eggs, bacon; but what advantage has the Irishman over the Dane, or the Norman, in sending these to us? He should, as a fellow-citizen, have advantage. He has none; and the result is a chronic discontent which is a deadly danger. Don't you see the advantage if all our dominions, in spite of geography, were welded as closely together as are the states of America?"

Captain Innes Doyle, who came up to visit him at Hawick for the last two days of the campaign, had not heard his brother speak in public since the American tour of 1894. Innes was astonished. "In America," he wrote to Lottie, "old Arthur was not at all bad, but now —by Jove!" He was so deeply impressed that he mentioned the matter on the night of January 17th, in their hotel room at Hawick.

"You know, Arthur," he said, "it'd be strange if your real career should prove to be political and not literary."

His brother, who was writing a letter, did not look up. "It will be neither," he answered. "It will be religious."

"Religious?"

Conan Doyle, roused abruptly, stared back at his brother with such obvious bewilderment that they both burst out laughing.

Why on earth, he wondered, had he made that asinine

remark? He had no intention of saying it, even as a joke. The words slipped out and uttered themselves. Whatever his future career might be, he could have affirmed it might concern anything except religion.

In the matter of religion, even with regard to his psychic studies, he still faced a blank wall. True, as in the old Southsea days, he felt sympathetic towards Spiritualism. He sympathized because it included all religious faiths. It did not hurl perdition right and left, or tell a man his soul was lost over a point of doctrine. Religious intolerance, which his instinct hated as a boy, his intelligence still hated as a man. But sympathy was not enough; it was not proof.

And, as he had informed his surprised friends in 1901, he believed that there had been much truth in the investigations of Crookes and Myers and Lodge, as in those of Alfred Russel Wallace which he read at Southsea. These were all men of science employing scientific tests. You could not accept their arguments merely because of their distinguished names. But they had investigated the subject thoroughly: whereas their opponents, in general, had done nothing of the kind.

"Lord Amberley," he had written in his notebook, "decided against Spiritualism after five séances. Tyndall after only one. Huxley said the subject did not interest him. Let us oppose this if we like, but why hide our faces?"

Frederick Myers's book, *Human Personality and its Survival of Bodily Death,* published after Myers's own death in 1901, took strong hold of him. Like Myers and Lodge, he experimented for himself. He held more table séances, and sat with mediums. And at the end of it. . . .

Well! Certain phenomena existed. He was convinced of that. 'Forces' existed, call them what you like, outside the borders of the normal sphere; and they existed even when you made every provision against trickery and fraud. But where was the evidence that these messages, or these phenomena, came from the other side of the grave?

They need not have come from a discarnate intelligence. They might have some scientific, if extra-normal, explanation which the world did not yet understand. Besides (and this was where he always broke down) in the last analysis these phenomena seemed so small, so puerile. A heaving table, a flying tambourine: Would spiritual powers be likely to concern themselves with such infantile games? And, if the manifestations had no spiritual meaning, then what was the good of them?

He did not know. He could argue no further. But he had reached this point on that night in January, 1906, when Innes spoke of his future career being political rather than literary.

"It will be neither. It will be religious."

Why had he made that inane remark? Probably, he decided, because he was tired. He and Innes went out next morning, a day showering with sleet, to watch the voters go to the polling-stations. Radicalism won again in the Border Burghs. He was depressed, if not surprised, to find that Mr. Thomas Shaw had defeated him by a count of 3133 votes to 2444. But he looked forward to the summer; and the summer seemed long in coming. In the July number of the 'Strand' appeared the first instalment of his new novel, *Sir Nigel*.

Now *Sir Nigel*, to him, was far more than his 'new novel.' It was *the* book. It was *the* dream. It was his bid to crush this nonsense of regarding him primarily as the creator of Sherlock Holmes, and to establish his place as a writer in its true perspective. With *Sir Nigel*, a companion-book to *The White Company*, he returned to the lances and pennons of chivalry.

He had begun a re-study of the background, with ever-accumulating notebooks in the meticulous handwriting, early in 1904. In the summer of 1905 he began to write. When he finished it, in a fury of rapid writing towards the end of '05—it was just before he went north for the Border Burghs election, and Edinburgh University had conferred on him the degree of LL.D.—he showed his state of mind in a post card to the Ma'am.

"Sir Nigel," he wrote briefly, "Dei gratia, finished! 132,000 words. My absolute top!" And you have a true picture of him, exulting, as he posted that card late at night.

The novel, which did not appear in book-form until December, 1906, is a sort of inverted sequel. Chronologically its action takes place before that of *The White Company.* We see Nigel Loring as a boy, of ancient lineage but as poor as Lazarus: burning to do great deeds but lacking even a suit of armour; full of stiff-necked pride, living in a house whose lands have been stolen, his only companion the stately grandmother Dame Ermyntrude.

That is one reason why the book was so close to its author's heart. That is why young Nigel Loring learns his heraldry, his lore of chivalry, his creed and his hopes, from Dame Ermyntrude at the fireside. In symbol if not in actuality, Nigel Loring was himself; and Dame Ermyntrude was the Ma'am.

We, who have seen the Ma'am at close hand, may at first be tempted to smile at this. We have seen the Ma'am's tempers, not to say her tantrums: her essential Irishness. But remove that Irishness, and out of it peers the formidable old lady, compounded of shrewdness and idealism, a terror for genealogy, who really did write to her son, "The Conan arm is strong, and his lance is keen," exactly as Dame Ermyntrude would have done.

Through the exploits of Nigel Loring, who goes out to gain renown, and vows himself three great deeds before he may win his lady, runs that same faint thread of symbolism. It was seventeen years since the author had written of the days of Edward the Third. His hand had gained in craft without the spirit lacking in gusto: the sea-fight in the Channel, the storming of the Butcher's castle, the onrush of the Battle of Poitiers, do not suffer by comparison with *The White Company*.

And yet, when Sir Nigel appeared, it was to him a bitter disappointment.

Here, however, we must understand what the disappointment really was. Some commentators have been misled by the statement, made many years later in his autobiography: "It attracted no particular notice from critics or public." From this have been constructed various babyish theories, including the notion that the public taste had changed and that historical romances were no longer wanted.

The trouble with such speculations is that they are not true. In one of his scrapbooks, labelled SIR NIGEL REVIEWS, you will find sixty-five pages of laudatory press notices. The sales-figures, still available, show it as the best-seller of the Christmas season.

"I spent all yesterday evening," wrote Rudyard Kipling, from Burwash in Sussex, "reading *Sir Nigel* at one gulp. From cover to cover I read it, and I put it down still hungry for more." The misunderstanding, in Conan Doyle's retrospective remark, arises from what he meant rather than what he said.

He had hoped and dreamed that this book, together with *The White Company,* would be regarded as his masterpiece and his best representative work. Passionately he had sought the verdict, "This book is living history; it reproduces the Middle Ages in all their Gothic richness." And in a number of reviews, such as the 'Spectator' and the 'Athenaeum,' this was what they did say. But in so many cases it was the reception of *The White Company* all over again. "What a capital adventure-yarn he tells!" they exclaimed. And, though it may have been ungrateful of him to fret and fume, he knew this already.

Indeed, where any criticism was directed at him in *Sir Nigel,* it was directed at him for doing just what he had set out to do. He had troubled himself too much, some said, with being accurate. He had revelled in colour and atmosphere and background. Occasionally he had intervened in the fighting to explain what the fighting was about.

Now the glory of the historical novel *is* its colour and atmosphere and background. Strip these qualities from (say) *Henry Esmond* or *Notre Dame de Paris,* and you destroy the feeling which created them. The real reason for this odd criticism lay deeper. *The White Company,* first seen as a good yarn alone, could now be recognized as one of the greatest of all historical novels. But that lay in the past. He must not be permitted to do it a second time, even if he had written a book far better than *The White Company.* The popularity of his other work defeated him before he began.

However, the reception of *Sir Nigel* still lay ahead during the spring, while he occupied himself with a series of book-chats, called *Through the Magic Door,* for 'Cassell's Magazine.' It brought back the memory of old Southsea days, of old enthusiasms, of the worn books in the battered old case. With it, in that hot summer of 1906, came tragedy.

Touie was dying.

Though it had been inevitable for fully thirteen years, ever since Dr. Dalton gave her only a few months to

live, they had deferred it for so long that the actual fact
—the full realization—came to them as a shock. Louise
Conan Doyle, the most cheerful and unselfish person her
husband or her family had ever known, seemed a little
more wasted; nothing more. Her husband's first intima-
tion occurred one night in the middle of June, when
Touie was a little delirious. Specialists arrived from London next morning.

The model railway was stilled. The rifle-range was
stilled. In the possession of Innes Doyle, then at the
Staff College at Bedford, there was for a long time a
little bundle of letters and postcards, sent to him by his
brother during that month when Touie's frail life alternately strengthened and faltered. They were only reports,
a line or two at most. At first they were fiercely hopeful.
"T. holds her own well." "Touie better." "Better; sat up
to tea; I hope for the best."

But on June 30th:

"It may be days," he wrote, "or it may be weeks, but
the end now seems inevitable. She is without pain in
body, and easy in mind, taking it all with her usual
sweet and gentle equanimity. Her mind is sluggish but
clears at intervals and she was able to follow with interest the letters I read her about Claire's marriage."

The end was not far off. There were two more postcards on the same day. One, in the morning: "About the
same." The other, in the evening: "Not so well—sinking." Mrs. Hawkins, who lived not far away at 'The
Cottage,' Hindhead, was at her bedside. Touie's husband
was there, holding the frail hand. In the press on July
5th appeared a brief paragraph.

"Lady Conan Doyle, the wife of Sir Arthur Conan
Doyle, the novelist, died at three o'clock yesterday
morning at Undershaw, Hindhead. The deceased lady,
who was forty-nine years of age, had been in delicate

health for some years. She was the youngest daughter of Mr. J. Hawkins, of Minsterworth, Gloucester, and her marriage took place in 1885."

It was, so far, the darkest day in her husband's life. Though he had not been in love with Touie, he was as fond of her as he had ever been of any person; and to say this is to say much. It was as though, in this year, every incident drew his mind back to the old days. Every incident conspired to remind him of struggle and semi-poverty at Southsea; of Touie, as merry and loyal in those times as she had been merry and loyal during thirteen years of illness. In the little batch of letters kept by Innes there is one final message. It is edged with black, written after the funeral, and speaks for itself.

"All thanks, old boy, for your practical sympathy, which upheld me much. I am just going to her with some flowers."

Touie was buried at Hindhead, with a marble cross over her grave. His own state of mind may be described by telling what happened during the ensuing months. He, who had never been troubled with anything beyond a toothache or a fit of indigestion, became seriously ill. "I have no symptoms; only weakness." Charles Gibbs, his medical adviser since South African days, could do little. It was nerves. The insomnia returned, worse than before. "I tried," he wrote to the Ma'am, "never to give Touie a moment's unhappiness; to give her every attention, every comfort she could want. Did I succeed? I think so. God knows I hope so."

Every person in this world, at a time of bereavement, asks himself: "Did I do enough? Was I kind enough?" He, who set himself an almost unattainable ideal, did the same. The shadow passed. It was bound to pass. But summer became autumn, and autumn winter, before he shook off the illness and the lassitude that followed it.

Then, just before Christmas, he was roused.

His correspondence, which averaged sixty letters a day and with most of which he dealt himself, had been handled during the illness by his secretary. But, if Alfred Wood found among the letters anything he believed would be of interest, it was sorted out and left on the study desk.

One evening he picked up, from among the others, an envelope of press-cuttings dealing with a criminal case now three years old. He began to read the cuttings idly. The case was mysterious, it was sensational, it was as complex with bizarre clues as any of his own detective stories. But that was not what caught and held his attention. The cuttings had been sent to him, with a cry for help, by the man most deeply concerned in this business.

If this man's statements were true, and it seemed to him that the ring of truth was in them, then the case needed further investigation. It needed deep investigation, to set right a damnable injustice.

Now follow the details of this three-year-old detective-story, as each detail unfolds. For he went out to investigate a crime puzzle in real life.

XV

DETECTIVE:

The Great Wyrley Mystery

In Staffordshire, from the potteries on the north to the mining districts on the south, they were trooping to work on that smoky August morning. The village of Great Wyrley, less than twenty miles from Birmingham, lay in an area partly agricultural and partly mining. The Great Wyrley Colliery, whose morning shift began at six o'clock, stood some distance away amid fields and slag-heaps and coal-tips.

The night before had been stormy, with heavy rain-squalls which began half an hour before midnight and ended at dawn. The field near the colliery, its yellowish-red soil a mixture of clay and sand, was slimy under-foot. A boy named Henry Garrett, on his way to work at 6:20 A.M., stumbled over what had been done in that field.

In a morass of blood, still alive, lay a pony belonging to the colliery. The pony had been ripped up the belly with some very sharp blade. It had not been disem-bowelled; the cut, though sharp-slit, had not gone deeply enough. The pony moved feebly, and blood still trickled from the wound.

"Blood," young Henry Garrett testified, "was drop-ping pretty freely."

Meanwhile, he yelled for help. That yell brought a horde of other miners hurrying to see the pony. It also brought the police. Twenty constables and plain-clothes men, drawn from all districts, had been patrolling these lanes all night as they had been doing every night for some time. It was the eighth case of animal mutilation in six months.

Between February and August, in that year 1903, horses and cows and sheep died at the hand of some adroit maniac who seemed all but invisible. At the same time, the police received a spate of jeering letters. The letters were signed by various forged or false names. But the most important of them, with which we have to deal here, bore the 'signature' of a lad at Walsall Grammar School, six miles from Great Wyrley; and this boy was proved by all sides concerned to have had nothing whatever to do with them.

The anonymous letters did not make pleasant reading. A sort of jumping-jack mania danced through them. In his first letter the writer made several glowing references to the sea; and he smacked his lips, with unholy relish, over the details of the mutilations. He said he was the member of a gang, wrongly accusing a number of people as accomplices; and how they enjoyed ripping up cattle! Of one of them: *"He has got eagle eyes, and his ears is as sharp as a razor, and he is as fleet of foot as a fox, and as noiseless, and he crawls on all fours up to the poor beasts. . . ."* Or again, chortling: "There will be merry times at Wyrley in November when they start on little girls, for they will do twenty wenches like the horses before next March."

This last threat added horror to wrath in the seething community. Then, on the morning of August 18th, the pony was found dying in the field. Somebody had done it again, although twenty alert policemen had been patrolling the district and three of them were actually watching the field.

It was like Jack the Ripper in the countryside, a Jack

the Ripper with skill in handling animals before he slashed. Inspector Campbell, of the Staffordshire County Constabulary, examined the pony and made up his mind.

Inspector Campbell quite honestly believed, as did all his colleagues up to the Chief Constable, that he knew who was guilty. He believed he had known it all along. Half a mile away from the field—beyond the raised line of the London and North Western Railway—lay the vicarage of Great Wyrley. Inspector Campbell set out for the vicarage with several of his men. If he found any evidence, he meant to arrest the vicar's son.

Now the Rev. Shapurji Edalji, who had been for nearly thirty years vicar of the parish, was a Parsee. That is, he was born of a sect from India; he was, in popular parlance, a Black Man; and therefore alien and sinister. How had a Parsee come to be a Church of England clergyman? Nobody knew. But the Rev. Shapurji Edalji had married an Englishwoman, Miss Charlotte Stoneman, and the eldest of their three children was the twenty-seven-year-old George Edalji.

George Edalji, with his dark skin and his curiously bulging eyes, practised as a solicitor in Birmingham. Each morning he took the seven-twenty train to his office there; each evening he returned to the vicarage at half-past six. George Edalji had grown up small and frail, nervous and reserved, a brilliant student. At Mason College, later the University at Birmingham, he had passed his final examinations with honours; he had taken prizes from the Law Society, and written a well-known handbook on railway law. His very virtues made the young Black Man, with the goblin eyes, seem far more terrible than his father.

" 'E's *funny*," ran the muttered comment. "Don't drink or smoke. 'Ardly seems to notice you, even, when 'e looks straight at you. And what about last time?"

It was 'last time' which had started all the rumour.

Years before, between 1892 and the end of 1895, beginning at a time when George was at Rugeley School, there had been an outburst of anonymous letters and ugly hoaxes. Some of these missives went to outsiders, including one to the headmaster of Walsall Grammar School. But for the most part the persecution was directed at the Rev. Shapurji Edalji. Letters, cursing his wife and his daughter and in particular his elder son, were slipped under door-sills or through windows at the vicarage. The vicar was also devilled with practical jokes.

Bogus advertisements, signed with his name, were inserted in newspapers. Postcards, also signed with his name, were sent to various other clergymen. One clergyman, far away in Essex, was astounded to receive, from 'S. Edalji,' the following:

Unless you apologise at once and by telegram for the outrageous hints you give in your sermons concerning my Chastity, I shall expose your adultery and rape.

Now this sort of thing might have been merely funny. But anonymous malice is seldom funny to the man who experiences it. Under cover of darkness, somebody strewed the Edaljis' lawn with old spoons, old knives, the refuse of dustbins. On one occasion a large key, stolen from Walsall Grammar School, was left on the doorstep. And the malignant amusement went on for more than three years.

But the Chief Constable of Staffordshire, Captain the Hon. George Alexander Anson, kept a stolid face. Captain Anson was one of those people who thought Black Men less than the beasts. Captain Anson believed that the culprit was none other than young George Edalji, hounding his own family. The vicar protested that this was a manifest absurdity, because letters had been pushed under the door of the vicarage at a time when George (as his father's and mother's eyesight bore witness) had been in the house. The Chief Constable remained adamant. About the key left on the doorstep he wrote: "I may say at once that I shall not pretend to believe any protestations of ignorance which your son may make about the key." Later Captain Anson declared that he hoped to get for the offender "a dose of penal servitude." Still the hoaxing antics continued.

Abruptly, at the end of December in 1895, the persecution ceased. There was a last bogus advertisement, signed S. Edalji, in a Blackpool newspaper. Afterwards a great balm of silence descended on Great Wyrley— and it lasted for seven years without a break, until 1903.

Then somebody began ripping horses and cattle. Each animal bore a long, shallow wound which caused a spurting effusion of blood, but did not penetrate far enough to pierce the gut. Who attacked the cattle?

"George Edalji," thought the authorities. Special constables swarmed into the district. Captain Anson's instructions were to watch the vicarage and see whether anybody left it at night. They did this before their receipt of the second outburst of anonymous letters, from which we have quoted with, *"He has got eagle eyes, and his ears is as sharp as a razor—"* These letters, finally, repeatedly accused George Edalji of being a leading member in the cattle-slitting gang.

Mr. Edalji is going to Brum . . . about how it's to be carried on with so many detectives about, and I believe they are going to do some cows in the daytime instead of at night.

Who wrote these letters, according to the Chief Constable?

George Edalji himself. (Presumably he wanted to wreck his own career as a solicitor.)

That was the position, on the morning of August 18th, when Inspector Campbell went to the vicarage after the maiming of the pony. Inspector Campbell arrived there, with several constables, at eight o'clock. George Edalji had already left for his office in Birmingham. But George's mother and sister were downstairs at breakfast. As soon as they saw the policemen's shadows across the coloured-glass panel of the front door, Mrs. Edalji and her daughter knew what to expect.

"I must ask you," said Inspector Campbell, "to show me your son's clothing." (There were bound to be widespread blood-stains.) "Also," he continued, "any weapon that might have been used in this."

The police found nothing more in the nature of a weapon than a case of four razors, belonging to the vicar, which razors were proved chemically to be free of blood-stains. But they did find a pair of George Edalji's boots, wet and stained with black mud. They found a pair of blue serge trousers, stained with black mud round the lower edges. They found an old housecoat, whose sleeve bore whitish and darkish stains which might prove to be saliva and blood from the dying pony.

"This coat," declared Inspector Campbell, "is damp."

The vicar, who by this time had joined the others downstairs in his study, passed a hand over the coat and denied that it was damp. The Inspector further asserted that he saw horse-hairs adhering to the coat. Shapurji Edalji, holding the coat close to the window, hotly denied that there were any horse-hairs, and challenged his companion to produce any. This protest had already been made by Mrs. Edalji and Miss Maud Edalji.

"It's a roving!" insisted the latter, meaning a thread. "I'm sure what you saw is a roving!"

In any event, as Arthur Conan Doyle was later to point out, the police did not secure any specimens of this hair and seal them in an envelope. The house-coat, together with a waistcoat belonging to it, was removed from the vicarage without further comment. Meanwhile, the pony had been killed to put it out of pain. A strip of its hide was cut off, and then—very carelessly, to say the least—packed in the same bundle as George Edalji's clothes. Not until four o'clock did a disinterested witness, Dr. Butter the police-surgeon, examine the clothes. Whether or not there had been horse-hairs on the coat at a previous time, there were certainly horse-hairs on it now. Dr. Butter found twenty-nine of them on the coat, and five on the waistcoat.

It was as well to have this ace of trumps, since the other evidence dwindled badly. Dr. Butter reported that the whitish and darkish stains on the coat were food-stains, with one possible exception. On the right-hand cuff were two spots, "each about the size of a three-penny-bit," which showed traces of mammalian blood. These might have come from a pony, or they might have been splashes from the gravy of underdone meat. In any case, the spots were not fresh.

They arrested George Edalji late in the same day. They found him at his office in Birmingham, looking ill when they arrived. Edalji, conscious of his physical disabilities, felt himself penned in a corner. He was alternately sharp-tongued and sunk in utter despair.

"I'm not surprised at this," he said on his way to the police-station. "I have been expecting it for some time." These words were noted down and used at his trial as evidence of a guilty conscience.

"Will you give an account of your movements on the night of August 17th, when the pony was mutilated?"

George Edalji's testimony, then and at various times afterwards, is easily gathered together in a summary.

"I returned home to the vicarage from my office," he said, "at half-past six in the evening. I transacted some business at home. Then I walked along the main road to the bootmaker's at Bridgtown, and got there a little later than half-past eight. I was then wearing a blue serge coat." This was confirmed by John Hand, the boot-maker. "My supper wouldn't be ready until half-past nine. So I walked round for a while. Several persons must have seen me. It had been raining during the day, though it was not raining then."

(And thus, noted Conan Doyle, accounting for the mud on the trouser-legs and on the wet boots. It was the black mud of the roadway. Surely they could make an elementary distinction between the black mud of a village road and the yellowish-red soil, a mixture of sand and clay, in the fields roundabout?)

Meanwhile:

"I returned to the vicarage," persisted Edalji, "at nine-thirty. I had supper, and went to bed. I sleep in the same bedroom as my father, and I have been sleeping there for seventeen years. I did not leave that bedroom until twenty minutes to seven on the following morning."

That night of August 17th had been wild and wet, blowing with rain from before midnight until dawn. Shapurji Edalji, a light sleeper, racked with worry and lumbago, had been restless all night. "And," he added, "I always keep my bedroom door locked. If my son had left at any time, I should have known it. He did not do so."

When news spread of George Edalji's arrest, after all these months of nocturnal cattle-slitting, popular fury boiled over. The young Black Man was in danger of being lynched. The police carried him in a cab to appear before the magistrates at Cannock; a crowd in the street attacked the cab, and tore the door from its hinges.

"Many and wonderful," said a reporter from the Birmingham 'Express and Star,' "were the theories I heard propounded in the local ale-houses as to why Edalji had gone forth in the night to slay cattle, and a widely accepted idea was that he made nocturnal sacrifices to strange gods."

On October 20th, 1903, Edalji was brought to trial. He was tried at the Court of Quarter Sessions, before a county justice so lacking in legal knowledge that a barrister was hired to advise him. At the trial, too, the prosecution altered its whole line of attack.

The original theory of the police, as presented before the magistrates at Cannock, was that Edalji had committed the crime between eight and nine-thirty in the evening: that is, during the time covered by his visit to the bootmaker's and his walk before supper. But this theory had holes in it. Witnesses had seen him during that walk. The pony, when discovered next morning, was still bleeding; and a veterinary surgeon, who saw it afterwards, testified that this fresh wound could not have been made at any time before two-thirty in the morning.

Thus the case—as actually and finally presented to the jury—did a complete about-turn. Edalji, it was claimed, had acted between two and three o'clock in the morning. He had slipped out of the vicar's bedroom into the rain. Escaping the lurking police, he had walked half a mile, crossed the fenced line of the railway, mutilated the pony, and returned home by a more roundabout way through fields and hedges and ditches.

Well, hadn't the police been watching the vicarage on the night the crime was committed?

The answer of the police, in effect, was 'Yes and no.' On the previous night, stated Sergeant Robinson, there had been six men watching it. But, on the night in question, they could not be sure. There had been no specific order to watch the vicarage; only what might be called a general order. Then a powerful impression was made on the jury by the evidence (not mentioned before the magistrates) of Footprints on the Scene of the Crime.

A constable, it was stated, compared one of George Edalji's boots with footprints going to and coming from the place where the pony had lain. True, the whole ground around had already been trampled in all directions by the footprints of miners and sight-seers. (Here the author of Sherlock Holmes was to utter a groan.) But the constable had found some likely-looking prints. Taking Edalji's boot, he pressed it into the soil *beside* one of these prints—thus making an impression and, incidentally, getting yellow-red mud on that single boot. He measured these impressions, together with other impressions, and judged them to be the same.

"Were these footprints photographed?"

"No, sir."

"Was a cast made of them?"

"No, sir."

"Then where is the evidence? Why didn't you dig up a clod of earth, so as to get a perfect impression?"

"Well, sir, the ground was too soft in one place and too hard in another."

"But how did you measure the footprints?"

"With bits of stick, sir. And a straw."

But it is time to end this tragi-comedy of the trial. A handwriting expert, Mr. Thomas Gurrin, went into the box and gave it as his opinion that Edalji had written the letters accusing himself of cattle-maiming. Mr. Gurrin was the same authority whose expert testimony had helped send an innocent man, Adolf Beck, to prison in 1896. In this case the jury found George Edalji guilty. The layman-judge, emphatically denying that justice would have been served better by transferring the case to London out of a prejudiced area, then sentenced Edalji to seven years' penal servitude.

"Lord have mercy on us!" cried the prisoner's mother.

That was late in October, 1903. It was true that there had been another case of horse-maiming while Edalji remained locked up awaiting trial, but counsel for the prosecution explained it as being more work of the 'Wyrley gang' to confuse the issue over Edalji's guilt. In November arrived a further anonymous letter, and another horse was killed. Edalji had disappeared into prison, serving his time first at Lewes and then at Portland. As a last unconscious stroke which would have pleased M. Anatole France, his prison-work at Lewes was that of making parts for feed-bags for horses.

Late in 1906, when he had served three years of his sentence, there was an occurrence as mysterious to him as any in the case. He was released from prison.

He was not pardoned. Nobody told him why he was released. He remained under police supervision, as a discharged convict. His friends, headed by Mr. R. D. Yelverton, formerly Chief Justice of the Bahamas, had never ceased to urge the weakness of the evidence against him; at the time of his conviction, a petition to the Home Office for reconsideration was signed by ten thousand people, including several hundred lawyers. The petition had no effect. Recently Mr. Yelverton had taken it up again, strongly aided by the magazine 'Truth.' But the Home Office, whatever the reason for the action they took, offered no explanation. The gates of Portland clanged open; that was all.

"And what," asked the convict, "am I to do now?"

It was a bleak prospect. "I have been struck off the roll of solicitors, naturally. In any case, I could hardly practise my profession while still under the supervision of the police. But am I innocent, or am I guilty? They won't tell me."

"They won't, eh?" said Conan Doyle.

That was the situation when he had finished reading the bundle of press-cuttings and the appeal George Edalji sent him. To this case he devoted eight months' intensive work, between December of 1906 and August of 1907: doing no work of his own during that time; paying all the expenses involved; and, incidentally, solving the mystery of who was guilty. To fight the case, he considered, was a matter of simple justice.

"Either this man is guilty," he wrote, "or he is not. If he is, he deserves every day of his seven years. If he is not, then we must have apology, pardon, and restitution."

Sending for all available evidence, and writing to everyone who could testify in the matter, he studied the results over many ounces of tobacco before arranging an interview with George Edalji. Early in January, 1907, he met the young man in the foyer of the Grand Hotel, Charing Cross.

"The first sight which I ever had of Mr. George Edalji," wrote Conan Doyle, in the bombshell he exploded a week later, "the first sight which I ever had of Mr. George Edalji was enough to convince me of the extreme improbability of his being guilty, and to suggest some of the reasons why he had been suspected.

"He had come to my hotel by appointment; but I had been delayed, and he was passing the time by reading the paper. I recognized my man by his dark face, so I stood and observed him. He held the paper close to his eyes and rather sideways, proving. . . ."

At this point, still watching, the newcomer crossed the foyer and extended his hand.

"You're Mr. Edalji," he said, and introduced himself. "Don't you suffer from astigmatic myopia?"

We have no indication of the young lawyer's feelings on being greeted in this way; but we know his replies as the newcomer went on:

"It's only that I once studied to be an eye-surgeon. The astigmatism is marked, and I think there's a very high degree of myopia. Don't you wear glasses?"

"I never have, Sir Arthur. I've gone to two ophthalmic surgeons, and they can't fit me with glasses that are any use. They say——"

"But surely this point was raised at your trial?"

"Sir Arthur," replied the other with desperate sincerity, "I wanted to call an optician as a witness. You can verify that. But my legal advisers said the evidence against me was so palpably ridiculous that they wouldn't trouble."

Edalji, Conan Doyle reflected, would be more than half-blind in full daylight, would have to grope his way at dusk through any locality with which he was not perfectly familiar, and at night-fall would be helpless. The idea of such a man constantly scouring the countryside at night—to say nothing, of the fatal night, in pouring rain, when Edalji makes a circular tour of a mile without *any* of his clothes being sopping wet—this idea, he decided, lacked elementary good-sense.

Could Edalji be shamming blindness? He did not believe so. But every step must be made secure. He sent Edalji to a well-known eye-specialist, Kenneth Scott, who reported eight diopters of myopia: a worse case than the investigator had thought. He was already in correspondence with Edalji's father. He went down to Great Wyrley so that he could investigate and question witnesses on the spot. The details he now had in his hands.

On January 11th, 1907, the first instalment of his eighteen-thousand-word statement, *The Case of Mr. George Edalji,* appeared in 'The Daily Telegraph.'

First he held up the evidence against Edalji, and carefully tore it into small pieces along lines which have been indicated. Then, hating colour prejudice as much as he hated racial or religious prejudice, he cut loose. It was easy, he said, to excuse the feelings of uneducated countrymen towards the strange-looking Edalji. It was not so easy to excuse that English gentleman, the Chief Constable, who had cherished his dislike since 1892 and infected the whole police-force.

This, said Conan Doyle, was a kind of squalid Dreyfus case. In each affair you had a rising young professional man ruined by authority over a matter of forged handwriting. Captain Dreyfus, in France, had been made scapegoat because he was a Jew. Edalji, in England, had been made scapegoat because he was a Parsee. England, the home of liberty, had cried out in horror when such things happened in France. What did we have to say when it happened in our own country?

And what had been the attitude of the Home Office, under two administrations, when a legal authority like Mr. Yelverton presented evidence that Edalji had been wrongly sent to prison?

"Evidently," he wrote bitterly, "the authorities were shaken, and compromised with their consciences." After three years they turned the victim loose; but without pardon. Serenely they cried, "Go free," while adding, "You're still guilty." But the matter could not rest there. Who had made this illogical decision? And on what grounds? He, Conan Doyle, deprecated a public outcry:

"But the door is shut in our faces," he concluded.

"Now we turn to the last tribunal of all, a tribunal which never errs when the facts are laid before them, and we ask the public of Great Britain whether this thing is to go on."

It would be unnecessary to write, 'Sensation.'

George Edalji, over night, became the talk of the country. The columns of the 'Daily Telegraph' bulged with controversial letters. Another legal authority, Sir George Lewis—students of criminology will remember him in the Bravo poisoning case and the Hatton Garden diamond robbery—agitated for Edalji's innocence. "Who," the query rose to a roar, "was responsible for making the decision of free-but-guilty?"

The Home Office did not explain this; or, indeed, explain anything. The Home Secretary, Mr. Herbert Gladstone, son of the late Grand Old Man, courteously said that Edalji's case would receive full investigation. Unfortunately, there were difficulties. There was as yet no such thing as a Court of Criminal Appeal, though the need for such a court had been under consideration since the affair of Adolf Beck. The question, therefore, was how to get the case re-opened.

"Do you mean," demanded the man in the pub, "that Edalji's sentence has got to stand because there's no legal machinery for dealing with it?"

As regarded a re-trial, yes. But this (the Home Office quite agreed) was an exceptional set of circumstances. They were prepared to appoint a Committee of three unbiased men: this Committee to meet in secret session, to examine all data which should be presented, and to recommend what course should be taken by the authorities.

"Excellent!" said Conan Doyle. He did not mind delay, because he believed he could name the guilty person. Occupied with heavy correspondence, and with secret visits to the Wyrley neighbourhood, he was gathering proof which he could put before the Committee.

"The case I have against my quarry," he wrote to the Ma'am as early as January 29th, "is already very strong. But I have five separate lines of inquiry on foot by which I hope to make it overwhelming. It will be a great stroke if I can lay him by the heels!"

Then *he* began to receive wild letters from the merry joker-cum-cattle-slasher of the Wyrley district. They dropped into his letter-box like feebly-venomed snakes.

I know from a detective of Scotland Yard that if you write to Gladstone and say you find Edalji is guilty after all they will make you a lord next year. Is it not better to be a lord than to run the risk of losing kidneys and liver. Think of all the ghoolish (*sic*) murders that are committed why then should you escape?

There could be no doubt these letters were from the joker. Aside from any question of handwriting, there were too many intimate local references, too much harping on exactly the same themes which had obsessed and tortured the joker for years. As an example:

There was no education to be got at Walsall when that bloody swine (name given) was high school boss. He got the bloody bullet after the governors were sent letters about him. Ha ha.

Always the joker screamed that Edalji, Edalji, Edalji had written all abusive letters.

The proof of what I tell you is in the writing he put in the papers when they loosed him out of prison where he ought to have been kept along with his dad and all black and yellow faced Jews. . . . Nobody could copy his writing like that, you blind fool.

More than malice breathed out of it. This man, Conan Doyle had long ago decided, belonged in an asylum. But he was eager to get each scrawl, so that he could compare them with specimens of all the other letters dating back to the beginning of the whole affair. He said:

On the evidence of handwriting, I have come to one conclusion. I contend that the anonymous letters of 1892 to 1895 were the work of two persons: one a decently educated man, the other a foul-mouthed semi-literate boy. I contend that the anonymous letters of 1903 were nearly all written by that same foul-mouthed boy, then grown into a man in his twenties. On further evidence I contend that Foul-mouth not only wrote the letters, but did the mutilations.

But to say this is to put the end at the beginning. Let us go back. Let us take the facts in the Wyrley mystery as they are presented to us, and see what inferences we can draw from them.

At the beginning, one point is so obvious that I wonder it has escaped notice. This is the extraordinarily long gap between the two sets of letters. Letters, childish hoaxes, abound up to late December of '95. Then, for nearly seven years, *nobody* gets an abusive letter. To me this did not suggest that the culprit had changed his whole character and habits overnight, reverting to them with equal malice in 1903. It suggested absence; that someone had been away during that time.

Away—where? Look at the very first letter in the outburst of 1903. In it the writer makes no less than three glowing allusions to the sea. He recommends an apprentice's life at sea; his mind is full of it. Taken in conjunction with the long absence, may we suppose that he has gone to sea and recently returned?

Note, too, that the final hoax against the Edaljis in '95 is a bogus advertisement in a Blackpool paper. This is perhaps coincidence; anyone may go to Blackpool for a holiday; but it is also the pleasure-resort of Liverpool—a seaport.

Suppose, for the sake of argument, we take this line as a working hypothesis. Where are we to look first for traces of this hypothetical person? Surely in the records of Walsall Grammar School!

Walsall Grammar School, clearly, is the connecting link between the two sets of letters. In Group A, a scurrilous message is sent to the headmaster of that time. A large key, stolen from Walsall Grammar School, is left on the Edaljis door-step. In Group B, the false signature on the letters is actually that of a pupil at Walsall. I myself, in 1907, receive a letter which breaks out into irrelevant ravings against the headmaster of fifteen years ago.

My first step in the enquiry lay at Walsall. I must inquire whether there had been at the school, during the early nineties, a boy who (a) had a particular grudge against the headmaster, (b) was innately vicious, and (c) subsequently went to sea? I took this obvious step. And I got on the track of my man at once.

Such was his own explanation to the Home Office; the above deductions, omitting the final paragraph, he later published in the 'Daily Telegraph.'

Meanwhile, between February and April, his five lines of inquiry tightened. He was able to give the Home Office Committee, with the testimony of each witness appended, the following dossier:

At Walsall, from 1890 to 1892, there had been a boy named Peter Hudson.* Hudson, expelled at the age of thirteen because nobody could handle him, showed peculiar tastes even then. He forged letters, very clumsily. His particular taste was for using a knife. In a railway-carriage, on the way to school, he would turn over the

---

* This, of course, is a compound name derived from two sea-faring characters in the stories. The real name of 'Peter Hudson,' who may still be alive, will be found in a copy of Conan Doyle's Home Office dossier, pasted into the scrap-book labelled *The Edalji Case, 1907.*

cushions and rip up the underside, so that horsehair should emerge.

More than once Peter Hudson's father had to pay compensation when his son cut the straps on railway-carriage windows. At Walsall there was one boy, Fred Brookes, with whom Peter Hudson had a bitter feud; and this boy's family were deluged with anonymous letters during 1892-1895. After expulsion from school, Hudson was apprenticed to a butcher, thus learning to use a knife on animals.

At the end of December, '95, he was sent to sea as an apprentice. His ship (name of ship, captain, and owner given) sailed from Liverpool. Early in 1903 he returned from the sea permanently, and was living in the neighbourhood of Great Wyrley during all the time of the attacks on animals.

Furthermore, for ten months of the year 1902 he had served aboard a cattle-ship. He knew how to handle animals: a vital necessity, Conan Doyle pointed out, for the approach of the deft, nimble horse-slasher. "Compare this man," he wrote, "with the studious and purblind Edalji." But from Hudson's service in the cattle-ship emerged clinching evidence.

In July, 1903, a certain Mrs. Emily Smallking visited the house, its back to the open fields, where Peter Hudson lived. Both Mrs. Smallking and her husband had long been friends of the family's. On this occasion the fever over the cattle-maiming had grown high. Mrs. Smallking spoke of it to Peter Hudson, who grew gleefully confidential. He went to a cupboard, took out a horse lancet of unusually large size, and held it up.

"Look," he said. "This is what they kill the cattle with."

Mrs. Smallking felt a trifle sick. "Put it away!" she

THE LIFE OF *Sir Arthur Conan Doyle*

said. And then, hastily: "You don't want me to think you're the man, do you?"

Peter Hudson put away the horse-lancet. Conan Doyle later obtained possession of it. How he managed this we had better not inquire; but here is the continuation of his dossier to the Home Office.

"Now the wounds in all the outrages up to August 18th," he wrote, "were of a very peculiar character. In every case there was a shallow incision; it had cut through skin and muscles, but had not penetrated the gut. Had any ordinary cutting-weapon been used, it must certainly in *some* instance have penetrated far enough to pierce the gut with its point or edge. Note that the blade of the horse-lancet is like this:

"It is very sharp. Yet it could never penetrate more than superficially. I submit this very large horse-lancet, obtained by Peter Hudson from the cattle-ship, as being the only kind of instrument which could have committed all the crimes."

Up and up he built his case, demonstrating that John Hudson, Peter's elder brother, had collaborated in the letters of 1892-1895; and that the Edalji family had long been the butt of both Hudsons' dislike. In fact, some of his strongest and most damning points cannot be quoted here, because they would too closely identify 'Peter Hudson.' But officialdom read them.

While he waited for the report of the Committee-to-examine-evidence—consisting of Sir Arthur Wilson, Sir Alfred De Rutzen, and Mr. John L. Wharton—Conan Doyle's confidence grew. Justice *would* be done. He felt certain of it. Besides, this was to be his miraculous year, his year of fulfilment: in September, he would be married to Jean Leckie.

"And," he wrote, "we will ask Edalji to the wedding."

Late in May the recommendation of the Committee, and the decision of the Home Secretary, were made public. A Government publication, 'Presented to both Houses by Command of His Majesty,' set forth their findings. Mr. Yelverton, Edalji's first defender, read it thunderstruck.

George Edalji, said the Committee, had been wrongly convicted of horsemaiming; they could not agree with the verdict of the jury. On the other hand, they saw no reason to doubt that Edalji had written the anonymous letters. "Assuming him to be an innocent man, he has to some extent brought his troubles on himself." Therefore he would be granted a pardon, but denied any compensation for three years in prison because he had brought his troubles on himself.

In other words, they compromised again.

This was too much. In the House of Commons, questions flew at the Home Secretary like poisoned darts. The Law Society, demonstrating the opinion of the legal profession, immediately re-admitted Edalji to the roll of solicitors with leave to practise. The 'Daily Telegraph' raised a subscription of three hundred pounds for him. And Conan Doyle, with murder in his eye, stalked into the Home Office.

"Do you maintain," he demanded, "that George Edalji is raving mad?"

"There is no indication to that effect."

"Has there ever been any suggestion that he is mad?"

"No, there has not."

"Then do you seriously suggest that he sent *me* seven violent letters threatening my life?"

"We can do no more than refer you to the Committee's report, page six. 'These letters,' they state, 'can have only a very remote bearing on whether Edalji was rightly convicted in 1903.' We regret that this must be final."

It was not final. Again Conan Doyle charged into battle, first with 'Daily Telegraph' articles called *Who Wrote the Letters?* and then with letters of his own through June to August. "I won't leave the job half finished!" he wrote. He secured, by means best known to himself, specimens of Peter Hudson's and John Hudson's handwriting. These, with the anonymous letters, he submitted to Dr. Lindsay Johnson, Europe's foremost authority on handwriting, who had been called by Maître Labori in the Dreyfus trial. By means of internal evidence, backed up by Dr. Lindsay Johnson's verdict, he demonstrated that Peter Hudson was the principal author and John Hudson the secondary author.

Officially, this did not matter. The authorities, sticking together, announced blandly that there was no case against Peter Hudson either as writer or cattle-maimer; and there could be no further investigation. It is only necessary to add that the merry joker, when Edalji had long been forgotten, was still writing an occasional mad threat in the Midlands in the year 1913.

But church-music, the organ-roll and the babble of excited voices, drown out that ugly story now. On September 18th, 1907, like a red carpet in the Hotel Métropole, the press unrolled its headlines:

MARRIAGE OF SIR A. CONAN DOYLE ('London Morning Post'). SIR ARTHUR CONAN DOYLE WEDS MISS JEAN LECKIE ('New York Herald'). SIR A. CONAN DOYLE'S WEDDING ('Manchester Guardian'). And, as we turn over the pages of two scrap-books of press-cuttings, we catch reverberations from far places. DETECTIVE-MASTER AND HIS BRIDE ('Berliner Zeitung'). SHERLOCK

HOLMES QUIETLY MARRIED ('Buenos Aires Standard').
LADY DETECTIVES ('La Chronique, Bruxelles'). This last
headline seems mysterious until we translate the even
more startling explanation of the Belgian reporter.

"Conan Doyle, the English writer who invented the
genial type of detective, Sherlock Holmes, has just been
married. A French journalist tells us that the young lady
was enthralled into marriage by the extraordinary adventures of the king of detectives."

They were married at St. Margaret's, Westminster.
To avoid crowds of sight-seers, a prospect Conan Doyle
loathed, the name of the church had not been disclosed.
Only near relatives and one or two close friends had
been invited there. When the striped awning was put up
outside St. Margaret's, in the drowsy sun-dusted corner
beside the Abbey, no more than a few passers-by
stopped to watch.

First arrived the bridegroom, marching massively in
orthodox frock-coat and white waistcoat, a large white
gardenia in his button-hole, and looking, said one reporter, 'supremely happy.' He was attended by a much-
flustered Innes as best man. Next followed the guests,
led by the white hair and grey brocade of the Ma'am.
At two o'clock Jean Leckie, in a gown of white silk
Spanish lace embroidered with pearls over silver tissue,
and a long court-train, got out of the four-wheeler on
the arm of her father.

The officiating clergyman was Cyril Angell, the bridegroom's brother-in-law. Cyril and Dodo's five-year-old
son, dressed as a page, carried the bride's train as Jean
went down the aisle with her bridesmaids, Lily Loder-
Symonds and Leslie Rose. The church, cool and scented
with banked flowers, was charged with emotion. A witness notes that the bridegroom sang out his responses

"in a clear, fervent voice; but the bride's replies were hardly audible."

If that service seemed solemn, the voices of the choir echoing in a church almost empty, it was a different matter afterwards at the wedding reception in the Whitehall Rooms of the Hotel Métropole. He carried Jean up the red-carpeted stairs so that she should not become entangled in her train. There, against a background of tall palms and more white flowers, two hundred and fifty guests were waiting.

He greeted Dr. and Mrs. Hoare, with whom he had served as medical apprentice more than twenty-five years ago, and Boulnois of the Southsea days. Barrie was there, and Jerome K. Jerome, and Bram Stoker, and Robert Barr still growling like a bear over the champagne. There were other friends: Sir Gilbert Parker, Max Pemberton, Frank Bullen. Sir John Langman, to say nothing of Archie Langman, who brought back memories of the Boer War; and Sir Robert Cranston, who had been his chairman at the Edinburgh election. To Conan Doyle, as the orchestra played and they opened three baskets of telegrams and cables, it was like an album of auld lang syne.

And there was one guest whom everybody welcomed. That was George Edalji. Edalji, whose wedding-gift had been one-volume editions of the works of Shakespeare and Tennyson, stammered out his thanks and his congratulations. He tried to do so once more, at five o'clock, when the bride and groom drove away for a continental honeymoon which was to carry them as far as Constantinople. But the bridegroom would admit he deserved congratulations only on the grounds of his marriage.

"I am very lucky. I am very happy. God bless you."

In that same year, largely due to the case of Adolf Beck and the case of George Edalji, a Court of Criminal Appeal was at last established. It mingled with other modern portents: Signor Marconi bridging the ocean with wireless, and Mr. Farman staying for nearly an hour in the air with a biplane flying-machine. But, as we look back on Conan Doyle's detective-work in the case of George Edalji, we can ask a question to which the answer will be self-evident.

Who *was* Sherlock Holmes?

XVI

ARCADIAN:

Windlesham, With Interludes of the Theater

"As the sole surviving witness of the burial of Edgar Allan Poe," wrote Mr. Alden in February, 1909, "and one of the few remaining who have seen him in life, I regret exceedingly that my advanced age and impaired health will prevent me from joining the centenary dinner at which you are to preside.

"As a then resident of Baltimore, my native city, I often saw Mr. Poe; and as a young man with some sentiment I had a great fancy for him apart from his literary genius.

"On a cold dismal October day, so different from ordinary weather of that clime, I had just left my home when my attention was attracted by an approaching hearse, followed by two hackney carriages, all of the plainest type. As I passed the little cortege, some impulse made me ask the driver of the hearse, 'Whose funeral is this?' To my great surprise he said, 'Mr. Poe, the poet.' "

So the letter continued, with its glimpses of the lean, hungry genius in life and in death. Conan Doyle, as he read it, had moving memories of one of his earliest literary idols. Edgar Allan Poe, he had already declared, was the supreme original short-story writer of all time. And he stressed it again, with his tribute to the inventor of the detective-story among other things, when he took the chair at the Hotel Métropole dinner to honour the centenary year of Poe's birth.

He was just on fifty years of age. There were faint streaks of grey in his hair and moustache. But his enormous vitality, the happiness of his domestic life, chuckled out against any suggestion of middle-age. The wheel had turned full circle to his old-time geniality. Those seven years, from the time of his marriage in 1907, stretched out as perhaps the happiest period of his life. They centred round his wife, and round his new home: 'Windlesham,' at Crowborough in Sussex.

Windlesham, set in the lonely open country which stretched from Crowborough Beacon to the Sussex Downs, had been greatly changed and enlarged from the modest country-house he bought before his marriage. Jean's parents had long kept a summer place at Crowborough; and near them, he decided, she should live. That lonely nook of Sussex, a hundred years before inhabited only by gypsies, smugglers, charcoal-burners—gypsy-cast features lingered even yet—stirred his imagination like the breeze from Beachy Head.

From far away you could see Windlesham, with its five gables, its grey-painted shingles and white window-frames, its red roof-tiles and red chimney-stacks. The main façade, in front of which lay Jean's rose-garden, looked south-west. Two of the gables (on the right-hand end as you faced the main façade) contained his study.

In the outer study sat his secretary, Alfred Wood, a burly military-looking man some half a dozen years younger than himself. It was divided by crimson curtains from the other room. In this inner study, at the corner of the house, two lines of windows and a balcony looked out over what had once been Ashdown Forest, the red flags of the golf-course, then the purple and yellow of gorse merging into the blue haze of the Sussex Downs toward the Channel.

"Look there!" he would exclaim, pointing out of the window. "You see that clump of trees, about a quarter of a mile down and to the left?"

"What is it?"

"It's called Slaughter Glen. In smuggling days there was a notable fight with the revenuers there." And he would look round at the leather chairs, the book-shelves, the old familiar desk with its magnifying glass on the blotter and its derringer pistol in the drawer. "A man ought to be able to work here, oughtn't he?"

In those early days, however, he did little work. Mainly to please Jean, he wrote two more Sherlock Holmes stories: *Wisteria Lodge,* in two parts, and *The Bruce-Partington Plans.* Also to please Jean he pitched into gardening with a vigour which made her plead with him to remember he was gardening and not excavating. The house overflowed with guests; two days of the week they spent entertaining or being entertained in London.

He was so proud of her charm as a hostess—she liked wearing blue, setting off the hazel eyes and dark-gold hair—that the largest entertainments no longer bored him. As for Jean, aside from her fondness for music and animals and gardening, she had only one interest in life: her husband, who could do no wrong. Whatever Arthur said or did, that was right. Once, after a dinner at which Lord Kitchener seemed to have put some slight on her husband, she sat down in super-feminine rage and wrote Kitchener a letter instructing him in the manners of a gentleman. Her husband, smiling secretly but happily, affected not to notice and let her do it.

Above all in their minds at Windlesham, then as afterwards, was the great billiard-room which came to be filled with so many memories.

This billiard-room ran the full breadth of the house, east to west, with a wall of windows at each end. A hundred and fifty couples could dance there when the rugs were cleared away. Conan Doyle had it built into the house as their living-room, the centre of their lives.

At one end, amid palms, stood Jean's grand piano and the harp. At the other end was his billiard-table, under the muffled green canopy of the table-lights. Both piano and billiard-table, in that room, seemed almost as small as the brocaded chairs and animal-skin rugs. Over one fireplace hung the Van Dyck painting, of Black Tom Stafford, which had belonged to his Grandfather John. Over the other fireplace, in an alcove as big as a room, was a stag's head draped with the cartridge-bandolier he had brought back from the Boer War. Round the walls, blue-papered, ran a frieze of Napoleonic weapons. His own portrait, by Sidney Paget, hung among them.

After nightfall, with the light of gas-mantles in pink silk and glass wall-shades reflected back from a polished floor, he and Jean listened to many voices which come back to us out of that billiard-room from a time before 1914.

There is Sir Edward Marshall Hall, the Great Defender, showing how Dr. Crippen *could* have been acquitted. At the billiard-table, drawing sketch-maps, is Stefansson the Arctic explorer. In the alcove sits Rudyard Kipling, smoking a Havana and telling the story of a murder 'by suggestion' in India. There is William J. Burns, the American detective, explaining the working of the Detectaphone and plying his host with questions about Sherlock Holmes. There by the piano is Lewis Waller, the romantic actor, unmatched in *Henry V*; as he recites from it, his fine voice catches the bell-note of the silk-draped glass wall-shades and sets them tingling like wine-glasses.

But these scenes, in 1909, were scenes from the future. When Conan Doyle presided at the Poe centenary dinner in March of that year, he was looking forward during the same month to the birth of Jean's first child. And, though no novice as a father, he was "more racked with anguish than I care to confess." The child, a boy, was born on St. Patrick's Day. The Ma'am, in Yorkshire, knew rapture.

"And now," wrote the Ma'am, briskly getting down to business, "what of the name? Considering the day, the grandfather, and my people, I am inspired with Patrick Percy Conan Doyle."

The parents were not enthusiastic about this, and said so. Her next letter, three days later, shows the Ma'am at her haughtiest.

"You must please yourselves," she declared, lifting an epistolary shoulder. "That is certainly your *right*." The Ma'am now believed that all her own children should have borne "the grand old name," Percy of Ballintemple, which she would now like to see "coupled with Conan, as they are in the Salle de Chevaliers at Mt. St. Michel. Nigel, too, has much to recommend it," she added. But their own suggestion, Denis Pack—after Sir Denis Pack, also in the Foley line—at first mollified her; finally, they compromised.

Hardly had Denis Percy Stewart Conan Doyle been christened when his father, with renewed fire, was again fighting in public for the oppressed, the helpless, the men who could not hit back. His subject, both for campaigning and for a booklet he wrote late in the year, was *The Crime of the Congo*. His quarry was Leopold the Second, King of the Belgians.

In the Dark Continent lay nine hundred thousand square miles of country, much of it literally dark with jungle. Officially, it was called the Congo Free State. In

1885 it had been recognized by a treaty of nations. It was to be benevolently administered by the King of the Belgians: his purpose being "the moral and material improvement of the native races."

"The moral and material improvement of the native races" may originally have been the intention of King Leopold, a toughened old satyr mingling geniality with cynicism. But His Majesty knew a good thing. The Upper Congo hid a Solomon's wealth in rubber and ivory, if black labour could be flogged or maimed or murdered into working hard enough. For years this wealth went into his own pocket. He published no accounts. Aside from his close advisers, few people in Belgium knew how the Congo was being administered. But occasionally, in consular reports and missionaries' protests, Europe caught a whiff of the jungle; and it was the smell of torture and death.

In 1903 Great Britain protested. It was not altogether disinterested: they wanted free trade as well as humanity and fair wages. Belgian humanitarianism rose as well. Nevertheless, in a three-day-debate at Brussels, King Leopold's policy had clear utterance.

"Pay the natives?" exclaimed the Comte de Smet de Naeyer. "They are not entitled to anything. What is given them is a pure gratuity."

A year later the report of the British Consul at Boma, an idealistic Irishman named Roger Casement, really roused humanitarianism in Europe. King Leopold then appointed a Commission to investigate. This Commission smothered the facts, but promised reforms which were never made. The new British Liberal administration, with Sir Edward Grey as its Foreign Minister, threatened trouble. President Theodore Roosevelt turned his famous teeth and eyeglasses towards the Congo.

Again King Leopold temporized, promising true

beauty of government. Still the chicote, a whip of hippo-potamus-hide, cut flesh into wire patterns along the Upper Congo. At a village called Boendo, rebellious natives had seen their women murdered—with long sharpened stakes—in a curious manner not used even in our own unsqueamish age. Towards the end of 1908, the Congo Free State ceased to exist; it was formally annexed to Belgium.

Conan Doyle, when he first read the evidence, refused to believe it. But it compelled belief; there were too many eyewitnesses from America, France, Sweden, and especially Belgium. Then he stormed into the fight beside E. D. Morel and the Congo Reform Association. For two years afterwards, amid all his other activities, he worked and lectured with Mr. Morel for Congo reform.

"I am convinced," he wrote in his introduction to *The Crime of the Congo,* first published in October, '09, "that the reason why public opinion has not been more sensitive upon the question of the Congo Free State is that the terrible story has not been brought home to the public."

This was his purpose in *The Crime of the Congo,* an-other sixty-thousand-word booklet from which he would accept no penny of profit. Like *The War in South Africa: its Cause and Conduct,* each statement was care-fully documented with facts and figures; the grisly record carried added shock in translation, and had just as wide-spread an effect.

"I am very glad," wrote Winston Churchill, then Pres-ident of the Board of Trade in the Liberal administra-tion, "that you have turned your attention to the Congo. I will certainly do all I can to help." From Redding, Connecticut, the dying Mark Twain sent word through Albert Bigelow Paine that *he* would help if he could.

But: "Careful!" warned the Foreign Office.

Sir Edward Grey, the Foreign Minister, had already declared in a speech that this Congo affair might endanger European peace. The Admiralty, uneasy about a German crisis, wanted six more Dreadnought battleships. However, in this matter of the Congo Germany remained aloof, uninterested; if anything, sympathetic. Conan Doyle's campaign was well launched when, in December of '09, he found himself in a serio-comic interlude provided by two messages from America.

At Reno, on the following Fourth of July, Jim Jeffries was to fight the Negro challenger, Jack Johnson, for the heavyweight championship of the world. Due to the colour question, they could not yet agree on a referee who would be acceptable to both managers. Would Sir Arthur Conan Doyle consider acting as referee? Both sides would accept him.

"By George," he said, "this is the most sporting proposition I ever heard!"

He had never given up his boxing; a sparring-partner came down to Windlesham each week. Jean, who knew him, was far less shocked at the American offer than some of his friends.

"Then you'll go?"

"Go? Of course I'll go! This is a real honour!"

Willie Hornung, even Innes, tried to dissuade him. They pointed out that an Englishman, refereeing an American prize fight strongly tinged with the colour question, might be lucky to escape alive. Here they made a tactical error. This was the very thing to make him accept at once, which he tentatively did. When after a week's consideration he swallowed the cold water of having to refuse, it was because his conscience had been pursuing him as relentlessly as the Ma'am.

"This Congo campaign," said conscience, "has only

begun. You can't desert Morel and his work; now can you? Besides—what about the play?"

He had one shadowy compensation. Long before July 4th, 1910, when Johnson stopped Jeffries in the fifteenth round, the man who had wanted to referee was standing at the back of the Adelphi Theatre, in the Strand, listening to the thud of fists in his own prize-fighting play, *The House of Temperley*.

That year 1910 was the play-year, of fretted nerves and near-disaster. To be strictly accurate, it began six months before when *The Fires of Fate*, his dramatization of *The Tragedy of the Korosko* with many variations in plot, had a considerable success at the Lyric.

Lewis Waller, of whom mention has been made, played the lead in *The Fires of Fate* as a rather-too-young Colonel of the Bengal Lancers. Waller required a dashing rôle, his most popular parts being D'Artagnan and Monsieur Beaucaire. He was a matinée-idol of the virile sort; his personality animated the stage like a humming-top; he could even play (what actor dares it?) against a leading lady taller than himself. As far back as 1906, when for some time he had been actor-manager of the Imperial Theatre and co-starred with Mrs. Lillie Langtry, he appeared in Conan Doyle's *Brigadier Gerard*.

We have not dealt with the play of *Brigadier Gerard* because, to judge by the script at least, Gerard was not at his best. The Brigadier requires monologue, requires to be his own narrator, requires to paint his own background and clank the sabre of imagination: he would be supreme in a modern radio-play. Besides, although the author had worked hard to achieve broad comedy with his swashbuckler, Lewis Waller's female worshippers were mystified and resentful. Where was the heart-throbbing solemnity? Where was the misty-eyed Beaucaire?

"Do you know"—Conan Doyle overheard one girl say it in the foyer—"do you know, there are times when I can hardly keep from laughing?" And the author smote his forehead, as well he might.

But Waller, as Colonel Egerton in *The Fires of Fate,* was supported both by the melodrama and by the force of the 'morality play' which was its sub-title. Its success in the summer and autumn of '09, when he shared the expenses with Waller, confirmed Conan Doyle's long-cherished belief that he could conquer the theatre— every manager said he couldn't—if he took a gamble and backed *The House of Temperley* out of his own pocket.

The House of Temperley, originally titled *In the Days of the Regent,* called for seven sets and forty-three speaking parts, to say nothing of supers. No manager would touch such an expensive show. But it was an old dream of his: a spectacle, a panorama of sporting England in 1812. It should come to life with every detail accurate. It should show that there was nothing degrading about professional boxing if the blacklegs were kept out. And, as for the fights on the stage. . . !

Taking the gamble, a very risky one, he signed a six months' lease on the Adelphi Theatre. His expenses would work out at six hundred pounds a week, on top of a production-cost of two thousand. He was in a box at the Adelphi, hidden well back behind its drapery, with Jean's hand in his, when the curtain went up on the night of December 27th, 1909.

Word of something sensational had already rippled through the press. The 'Weekly Dispatch' sent Freddie Welsh, the British lightweight champion, as its dramatic critic; causing the 'Westminster Gazette' acidly to remark that henceforward plays of the Raffles type should be reviewed by professional burglars. In the front stalls could be seen Eugene Corri, referee of the National Sporting Club, and Lord Esher, chairman of the County of London Territorial Force Association. The Adelphi, traditional home of melodrama, was packed to the top of the gods.

They discovered that *The House of Temperley* was not a dramatization of *Rodney Stone,* though it had many similar incidents. The first act, against a background of stately Temperley Manor, was slow and stilted; it had a perfunctory love-interest in which nobody, including the author, could be much interested. Conan Doyle, writhing in the box, scribbled, "Too anaemic!" on his programme. But from the first finger-snap of the second act, in Tom Cribb's snuggery outside the Sparring Saloon, the whole play burst into life.

Ginger Stubbs, Captain Temperley's soldier-servant (played by Mr. Edmund Gwenn) had spoken the keynote during that slow first act.

" 'E's got the straightest, quickest left of any man in the country," whispers Ginger, speaking of Captain Temperley. "I'm not saying anything against his right, mind you! It's a good right. But his left—well, there! Just get 'im to 'it you. It's a real treat, I tell you!"

Every sporting character, from the swaggering Corinthian to the crooked bookie, had that same authentic speech. The dinner to the Fancy at Tom Cribb's was (and remains) a fine bit of effective theatre, culminating in the glove-fight between Ginger Stubbs and Joe Berks. By this time the stalls were applauding and the galleries were cheering.

For the realism of the fighting nearly jolted them out of their seats. And not all of it was faked. The actors' tutor had been Frank Binnison, boxing-instructor to the First Surrey Rifles; aided by the author, who had joined in rehearsals and was a stickler for reality. There was the same Regency exactitude, in the third act, for the bare-knuckle fight in a twenty-four-foot ring on Crawley Down.

It was a crowd-scene expertly handled by Herbert Jarman, the producer. The beaters-out, in their tall white hats of the Pugilistic Club, used horse-whips to clear the ring. The villain's champion, Gloucester Dick, played by Reginald Davis, threw his hat over the ropes. ("Who buys the Yellow man? Gloucester Dick's colours! The Yellow man for 'alf a guinea!") But Sir Charles Temperley's champion, Ginger Stubbs, had been kidnapped. ("Ten to one on Gloucester Dick! Ten to one!") Real suspense was built up until Captain Temperley, Sir Charles's younger brother, himself went into the mill with Gloucester Dick for a ten-thousand-pound wager.

Nothing like that fight, the press conceded next day, had ever been seen on the stage. More followed the fight: a scene at Watier's Club, and a Peninsular War battle-piece erupting bangs and powder-smoke. This was overdoing it, as the author later confessed. But it added to the patriotic appeal. When the final curtain fell at eleven o'clock, the stalls were cheering and the galleries delirious.

"Sir Arthur," wrote the 'Evening News' next day, "had a great reception when he came to make his bow."

He had done it. He had staged his fights. The public liked it. He was happy. And yet, after playing for four months to slowly dwindling audiences, *The House of Temperley* had to come off.

Clement Scott, in 'John Bull,' seems to have been the only critic who warned him this would happen. Other reviews predicted it would run until Doomsday. It was a man's play. But men seldom go alone to the theatre. They take a woman, or the women go on their own.

And, though women did not really dislike prize-fights in 1910—'London Opinion' found "the latest fashion in frills and foamy frocks cheering in the half-guinea seats" —still women will not support a play in which there is no feminine interest.

You may have a strong love-affair or you may use the never-failing theme of girl-in-danger; but you cannot discard both. A general slump affected even *The Dollar Princess* at Daly's. Conan Doyle, losing money every week and with a ruinously expensive theatre on his hands, tried every expedient to save *Temperley*. When the Ma'am berated him for neglecting his correspondence, especially since Innes had just been made a Major, he hadn't the courage to tell her things were going very badly.

"My one-act play, *A Pot of Caviare*"—it was adapted from one of his best short-stories—"went on as a curtain-raiser to *Temperley,* and did very well. Things have been shocking in London," he wrote on April 21st, 1910, "but we hope to increase continually."

On May 6th King Edward died. It was a sudden death; few people knew he was even seriously ill. Momentarily it put a crape band round the West End. We know now, from a letter whose existence he did not acknowledge, that Conan Doyle could long previously have sub-let the Adelphi to a musical comedy and saved some of his losses. But he was too stubborn; he would not admit defeat. Even before his letter to the Ma'am in April, he had been driving away at another play, which he wrote in a week and immediately set about casting.

To the devil with 'em! He'd show 'em!

Temperley closed its doors shortly before King Edward's funeral. On June 4th, less than a month later, the Adelphi's lights kindled again for the first night of a new play. It was *The Speckled Band.*

The Speckled Band recovered far more than he had lost; and, in addition to its own long run, had two touring-companies on the road before September. It was Holmes and Watson: and the old gods made their medicine again. They were even overshadowed by a potent juju in the burly Dr. Grimesby Rylott (instead of Roylott), with his little tuft of chin-beard and his twitching eyelid. He kept the snake in a wicker basket, petting it while his Indian servant Ali piped weird music on a reed.

Nevertheless—in our own days when exact dates in Holmes's adventures seem to have become so important —any adherent is cautioned against reading the play-script of *The Speckled Band*. He will find Holmes and Watson at the top of their form. But he will go mad trying to straighten out the chronology.

Against the familiar Baker Street background, there emerges an effulgent Watson who has just become engaged to Mary Morstan from *The Sign of the Four*. Holmes, in dressing-gown, has startled him by appearing in another disguise.

"Good heavens, Holmes! I should never have recognized you."

"My dear Watson, when you begin to recognize me it will indeed be the beginning of the end. I shall retire to an eligible poultry farm." Whereupon the great man, looking at him keenly, deduces that he has recently become engaged, and to whom.

"But, Holmes, this is marvellous! The lady is Miss Morstan, whom you have indeed met and admired. But how could you tell—?"

"By the same observation, my dear Watson, which assures me that you have seen the lady this morning." He picks a long hair off Watson's shoulder, wraps it round his finger and examines it with his lens. "Charming, my dear fellow! There is no mistaking the Titian tint."

(Red hair, we perceive. But Mary Morstan had fair hair, and would never have stooped to dye it. With whose affections has Watson been trifling this time?)

What is more, we are angered to find that Sherlock Holmes himself has stooped to the indignity of having a waiting-room full of clients, like a dentist. In that waiting-room sits none other than Charles Augustus Milverton, the blackmailer, with whom he has a skirmish about the Duchess of Ferrers's letters. Billy the page-boy, whom Gillette introduced into the play *Sherlock Holmes,* now presides over this waiting-room. And Billy ought to be kicked down the whole seventeen steps to the front door. Not only does he smash the cocaine-bottle when Holmes wants it, but he assumes insufferably arrogant airs in speaking to Watson.

"The Pope's been bothering us again," he pipes up. "Wants us to go to Rome over the cameo robbery. We are very overworked."

Never mind! Such matters the creator of them hurled about the stage as carelessly as he left Holmes's violin with only one string. The main thing is that Watson—a friend of the Stonor family—engages his interest in the horrible and mysterious death at Stoke Place, Stoke Moran, of Miss Violet (*sic*) Stonor, over which there has been an inquest.

"My dear fellow!" says Holmes, taking the pipe out of his mouth. "It all comes back to me. An inquest, was it not, with a string of most stupid and ineffectual witnesses?"

"I was one of them."

"Er—of course. So you were, so you were. I docketed the evidence." The game's afoot, gentlemen! Up goes his hand to that treasure-house of scrapbooks. "Let's see: it's R. Ranter, Romanez, Rylott. . . ."

At the Adelphi Theatre, amid evil and moving shadows, the part of Dr. Rylott was played by Lyn Harding, who once told a young protégé that any actor who knew his job could recite the multiplication-table and still hold an audience spellbound. Miss Christine Silver played Enid (not Helen) Stonor, the girl in danger. H. A. Saintsbury was Sherlock Holmes, Claude King was Dr. Watson.

Every effect led up to that third-act climax, in the dim bedroom, when the ray of the dark-lantern fell on the snake at the top of the bell-rope. For the snake, originally a real one, they had substituted a dummy so ingeniously jointed, and worked on invisible packthreads, that it could move with hideous realism even away from the bell-rope.

When Holmes struck at the bell-rope, the audience heard the cry from the next room as the snake turned on Dr. Rylott. The reed-flute music, which had been rising higher and higher, stopped dead. They heard running footsteps in the passage. Holmes flung open the door, sending a yellow path of light across the dark stage. In that light stood Dr. Rylott: huge, distorted, silhouetted, the snake coiled round his head and neck.

Crying out hoarsely, he took two steps forward and fell. Then—with as crashing a piece of theatre as was ever invented—the snake slowly uncoiled from his head and writhed across the stage, until Watson lashed down with a cane again and again. Now listen to the curtain:

WATSON: (looking at snake) The brute is dead.
HOLMES: (looking at Rylott) So is the other.
         (They both run to support the fainting
         lady.)

HOLMES: Miss Stonor, there is no more danger for
you under this roof.

Late in September, when *The Speckled Band* had
transferred to the Globe Theatre and settled down to its
run, Conan Doyle packed his bag at the Hotel Métropole to return to Windlesham for a rest. Throughout that
year, amid the frets and anxieties, he had never ceased
to agitate and seek supporters for the Congo Reform
Association. One he sought was Theodore Roosevelt,
now ex-President Roosevelt. His sympathies had always
gone out to T.R., both as statesman and sportsman. Nor
was there any more eager reader of detective-stories
than T.R. As early as 1903 we find a letter, dated at
Oyster Bay in July: "The President has heard that Sir
Arthur Conan Doyle will soon be in this country"—it
was a mistaken report—"and wishes to know when he
will be here and where he can be reached on his arrival."

But they did not meet until May, 1910, when Roosevelt was in London on his way back from African game-
trails. It was at a lunch shortly after King Edward's
funeral.

"I *liked* being President," said T.R., showing his teeth
in a grin and whacking the table by way of emphasis. He
talked twenty to the dozen, including the statement that
the American fleet was in fine condition and could beat
Japan any day. He also asked after the health of Sherlock Holmes, being gleeful to hear *The Speckled Band*
was in rehearsal.

Conan Doyle, as he packed his bag at the Hotel
Métropole, wanted to hear no more of *The Speckled
Band* or any other play. His play-writing days were over.
He swore as much to a reporter from the 'Referee' who
interviewed him on September 18th.

"I am not leaving stage-work because it doesn't interest me," he said. "It interests me too much. It's so absorbing that it draws your mind away from the deeper things of life.

"Don't misunderstand me! For those who can treat the deep matters of life dramatically it's different. But I recognize my own limitations." He was thinking, as he added a moment later, of *The Fires of Fate,* the 'morality play' in which, it was bitter to recall, audiences had missed or ignored the meaning. "So I make an absolute pledge that I will not write again for the stage."

"What are your plans?"

"Oh, I mean to spend the winter in a course of reading."

At Windlesham, where a page in buttons opened the door just as in *The Speckled Band,* they had been doing little entertaining that autumn. Jean's second child, another boy, was born on November 19th. They named him Adrian Malcolm: the second name for Dr. Malcolm Leckie, Jean's favourite brother, but the first name simply because she liked it. During that winter Conan Doyle had been dipping again into Roman history, and writing the Roman stories that later formed a part of *The Last Galley*.

Roman history was only one of a number of studies which filled his accumulating notebooks through the years at Windlesham. His mind, always restless, must work at something; it must stretch out; it must occupy itself or stagnate. Coins, archaeology, botany, geology, ancient languages: each in turn became a hobby, and, when he had spoken of a course of reading, he did not mean idle browsing.

Last year, for instance, it was philology. While on holiday in Cornwall, he studied the ancient Cornish language and became convinced that it was akin to the Chaldean. The Cornish holiday provided him with the background for another story published in this year: *The Devil's Foot,* where a death-lamp burned in a poisoned room. Then, too, there was his correspondence.

In the Windlesham days, one recurring item in that correspondence would always be appeals for help in the detection of crime. Once upon a time they had been addressed to Sherlock Holmes. Since the Edalji case, significantly, they were sent to him under his own name.

When a murder was committed in Poland, for instance, and a Polish nobleman under strong suspicion, the latter's relatives told Conan Doyle he could name his own fee—offering to send a blank cheque—if he would come to Warsaw and clear up the case. He refused. It was very different with a girl named Joan Paynter, a nurse at the North-Western Hospital, Hampstead, whose distracted letter might have come out of one of his own stories.

"I am writing to you," she appealed, "as I can think of no one else who could help me. I cannot afford to employ a detective myself as I have not the money, neither can my people for the same reason. About 5 weeks ago I met a man, a Dane. We became engaged & although I did not wish him to say anything about it for a little while he insisted on going down to Torquay to see my people. . . ."

In a few details it resembled *A Case of Identity,* though there were different features of interest. The young Dane loaded her with gifts, persuaded her to give up her position at the hospital, and then, when all preparations for the wedding had been made, disappeared like a soap-bubble.

But the girl had no money, and he had always known it. There was no question of seduction or attempted seduction. Miss Paynter, frantic, had gone to Scotland Yard, who believed her fiancé had got into the hands of

sharpers and failed to trace him. The Danish police had
failed as well. If he had disappeared voluntarily, if he
had not been kidnapped or murdered, then what was
his game? And where was he?

"*Please* don't think it awful cheek on my part," Miss
Paynter's letter concluded. "I feel so *awfully* miserable &
it was only this morning that I thought of you, please,
please do all you can for me and I shall be eternally
grateful."

Could chivalry resist such an appeal? The answer will
be obvious.

Well, he traced the man. "I was able," he afterwards
wrote, "by a . . . process of deduction, to show her very
clearly both whither he had gone and how unworthy he
was of her affections." Of this we have ample testimony
in the last of a series of Miss Paynter's letters.

"I don't know how to thank you sufficiently for all
your kindness. As you say, I have had an extraordinary
escape & I hate to think of what might have happened
if he hadn't gone away when he did. I am returning the
letter & will certainly let you know at once if ever I hear
of him again."

But how did the investigator manage this? We have
only her side of the correspondence. Where, in those letters, was the clue which seemed so plain to him? It is as
exasperating as that case in which Holmes sees the truth
by the depth to which the parsley has sunk into the butter. The biographer, who risks justified abuse for telling
so incomplete a story, can only report that there appears
to be no sign of a clue anywhere.

His interest in crime had never been keener. In
October, 1910, he went to London for the trial of Dr.
Crippen. Early in that same year there had been published, as one of the "Notable Scottish Trials" series, a
book dealing with a murder mystery in which he was

presently to become so deeply involved. The book was admirably edited by Mr. William Roughead, one of our finest criminological writers. It was called *The Trial of Oscar Slater*.

At the moment, in the red-curtained study at Windlesham, he wrote his Roman stories and made jottings in a new commonplace-book. Among his first jottings he noted down some opinions of Theodore Roosevelt.

In King Edward's funeral procession, Roosevelt had snorted, the German Emperor was jealous of the king's little white dog which "shared the chief attention at the funeral." Conan Doyle, always moved by any act of courtesy, had strongly praised the Kaiser for his presence there despite the friction between Britain and Germany.

As yet he could not see the reality of a German menace. There might, or might not, be the iron of Chancellor Bethmann-Hollweg behind the uneasy posturing of the Kaiser. It was common knowledge that in German Army messes there were toasts drunk to *Der Tag*. But, with France as an enemy on her western boarder, and Russia as an enemy on her eastern border, would Germany dare provoke war with the British Empire? What could she hope to gain from it? Where was the practical sense?

Seven months later, in the midst of another adventure, he changed his mind.

XVII

FANTASIA:

Sport, Beards, and Murder

They lined up the motor-cars at Homburg in Hesse-Nassau, fifty British entries against fifty German, for a grand parade before the start of the race called Prince Henry's tour. It was the first week of July, 1911. Among the cars could be seen Sir A. Conan Doyle's twenty h.p. Dietrich-Lorraine, with a horseshoe stuck on the front as mascot.

Prince Henry of Prussia, affable and bearded, claimed he had organized this tour as a gesture of sporting good-will, in honour of King George the Fifth's coronation. Each entrant must drive his own car. Each car must carry, as observer, an Army or Navy officer of the opposite country. Starting at Homburg, they would go by way of Cologne and Münster to Bremerhaven; beginning again at Southampton, they would make a circular tour of England and Scotland for the finish at London.

"It is the reliability of car and man which counts, not speed," wrote Conan Doyle on May 5th, when he informed the Ma'am he had joined. "The team which drives best, and loses fewest marks for contretemps, will be the winner. I take Jean as passenger. It should be a fine rush."

"The prize," Prince Henry was quoted as saying, "will be a young lady carved in ivory, with the word PEACE engraved below. Whether it be won by the Kaiserlicher Automobil-Klub or the Royal Automobile

Club, decidedly it will be a token of friendship and good cheer."

Decidedly it was not: though the English press, from diplomatic necessity, told almost as many lies as Prince Henry. The starting-signal was given on July 5th. The long procession of cars, smothered in a dust-cloud all the way, rattled out of Homburg with Prince Henry's white Benz marked Number 1.

Four days earlier, the German Government suddenly made a characteristic move. The French were in Morocco, and the Germans also had designs there. A German financial firm claimed large interests in a harbour, called Agadir, on the Atlantic seaboard of the Moroccan coast. Until July, the Wilhelmstrasse played delicately. Then they sent the gunboat *Panther,* followed by the cruiser *Berlin,* to 'maintain and protect German interests' at Agadir. And, as Mr. Churchill afterwards wrote, "all the alarm-bells in Europe began immediately to quiver."

The motorists of Prince Henry's tour heard this as they clattered through a dust-fog in pursuit of the ivory lady called Peace. Tempers were already on edge. As an honour to Prince Henry, the British had sent high-ranking Army officers for observers; and these discovered that their companion-officers were German captains or lieutenants. The effect on a British general, as he lived on terms of equality with a foreign junior officer, can be imagined. But there was far more than this.

Conan Doyle, at the wheel of the landaulette, with Jean in the open tonneau and a cavalry-officer named Count Carmer beside him, felt disquiet growing to alarm. He spoke German, but his own efforts towards goodwill were lost. These young Prussians not only envisaged the possibility of war: they accepted it as a fact. Also they showed that heavy-handed German humour, a blend of archness and arrogance, which on a Briton acts like itching-powder; it is an atmosphere; it can almost be smelt.

"Wouldn't you like one of these little islands?" asked little Captain Türck of the Navy, as the steamer *Grosser Kurfurst*, carrying cars and personnel, moved out into the North Sea past the Frisians. It was the German secret-guffaw.

Temperamental differences, sharpened by heat and engine-breakdowns, grew worse after the continuation of the tour at Southampton. Leamington, Harrogate, Newcastle, Edinburgh: the visitors were getting some fine views of the country, and all carried cameras. At Windermere, on the return journey, a Germany observer forgot his camera and caused an hour's delay while he went back for it, which so incensed the English driver that *he* smashed into a motor-bus coming up Ambleside.

"In general," Conan Doyle insisted, "these Germans are very good fellows." He could have forgiven almost anything to the man who, each morning, put flowers in Jean's corner of the car. "But—!" He could not help adding the 'but.' He did not like them either.

At London, late in July, all competitors drank the Kaiser's health in the Long Gallery at the Royal Automobile Club. The British team had won, and Prince Henry presented them with the ivory lady.

"We have seen a beautiful country," he cried in his presentation-speech; "we have seen a lovable country and a lovable people. The whole tour from beginning to end has been a great 'thank you.'" And they arranged a final display of cars at Brooklands autodrome for the following day.

Meanwhile, behind the closed doors of governments, tension grew steadily more acute in England and France. Germany refused to say what she meant by sending warships to the Moroccan coast. The British administration,

Liberal Imperialists and Radicals, seemed hopelessly split. But Mr. David Lloyd George, Chancellor of the Exchequer, unexpectedly united both wings; in a soft-voiced speech at Guildhall he intimated that if Germany insisted on war with France she could have war with Britain too.

"I have just received a communication from the German Ambassador," said Sir Edward Grey, "so stiff that the fleet may be attacked at any moment."

Outwardly, England felt only sunlight and serenity over that final race-meeting at Brooklands. The cars, with their tall windscreens, sparkled in every colour from green to crimson. Prince Henry himself, head of the German Navy whose *Panther* and *Berlin* had gone to Agadir, professed to know nothing of international dilemmas. German officers, of course, had come here only for sporting purposes. In 'The Car' for July 26th we find a large photograph, and no doubt sporting, with the caption: LIEUTENANT BIER, ON HIS ETRICH MONOPLANE, PASSING OVER THE CARS AT BROOKLANDS.

Conan Doyle, who earlier that year had taken his own first flight in a heavier-than-air machine—it was one of Mr. Graham-White's two-guinea flights at Hendon—could not guess at the gravity of the Whitehall situation. But he had grave doubts about the future. On his return to Windlesham, after driving more than two thousand miles, he dropped a note to Innes.

"Billy, our car, has made no mistakes and come through with much credit. Otherwise I don't like the look of things. But I won't trouble you at such a time."

For Innes, in August, was to be married to a Danish girl, Miss Clara Schwensen, at the Holmens Kirke in Copenhagen. His brother, with a whole family-party, went to Denmark for the ceremony. At the wedding-reception Innes made a memorable speech. It convinced his Danish friends, whooping and doubled up with mirth, that at last they had met a true Englishman. Propelled to his feet behind the banquet-table, deeply embarrassed by all the complimentary things said about him, Innes uttered the following words:

"Well . . . I say, don't you know! By Jove! What?"

And he sat down.

His brother, in fact, could never repeat Innes's words without tears of joy. Altogether, despite a German menace about which he might have been mistaken, he was a very happy man that autumn as he considered the materials for his new novel.

He had written no novel since *Sir Nigel* six years ago. And no more of *Nigel's* disappointments, for the moment! This should be something to suit his mood, something adventurous, something which should charm the public with his old spell and, at the same time, cast its spell over him. The first suggestion had drifted into his mind from the shape of the iguanodon, a prehistoric monster twenty feet high, whose fossilized footprints were found on the Sussex Downs beyond his study-windows. He kept those fossil-feet in the billiard-room now.

This, in the autumn of 1911, sent him to Professor Ray Lankester's book on extinct animals. Its illustrations showed nightmare-shapes of sabre-teeth and witless eye. Suppose, one misty evening, a stegosaurus came looming up over the misty downs? Better still: Suppose in some remote corner of the earth—a high plateau in the jungle, say, untouched and untouchable in primitive life—such creatures still existed?

What game for a sportsman! What wonders for a zoologist!

The leader of an adventure-party, undoubtedly, must be a zoologist. His memory moved back to Edinburgh University and Sir Charles Wyville Thomson, the zoologist who had gone exploring in the corvette H.M.S. *Challenger*. In Thomson himself there was little pictureesqueness. But it suggested Professor Rutherford: a stunted Hercules, with barrel-chest and black Assyrian beard, marching in stateliness along the corridors while his booming voice rolled ahead with. . . .

Professor Challenger. And *The Lost World*.

If any chronicler can even write that name without a glow of pleasure, he must have the soul of a dried grape. Challenger! Edward Malone! Lord John Roxton! Professor Summerlee! Let the exclamation-points stand; those names are linked together, like the Musketeers; and, like the Musketeers, they all capture our affections. They are immortal in our boyhood, nor any whit undimmed to middle-age.

Professor Challenger grew on his creator, as Porthos did on Dumas, but far more quickly. Conan Doyle came to enjoy G.E.C. more than any other character he ever created. He would imitate Challenger. He would, as we shall see in a moment, dress up in a beard and beetling eyebrows like Challenger. And the reason is not far to seek. Barring the colossal vanity, he made Challenger a completely uninhibited version of himself.

As Challenger, in *The Lost World* and subsequent stories, he could say or do all those things which ordinary social usage forbids. If so inclined, he could bite the housekeeper to see if anything would upset her composure. He could take a reporter by the slack of the trousers and run him half a mile along the road. He could talk in those sonorous rolling sentences, of bland and elaborate insult, which he so often longed to use in speaking to the fatuous.

And, pushed to the limit, he was quite capable of doing these things in real life. That is why we like both characters.

As for *The Lost World,* the author was so engrossed that his dreams were peopled with brontosauri and ape-men and the vegetation of that wild plateau. He would make the story so realistic, within its own premises, that many people might be inclined to believe it. How lifelike was his prehistoric jungle may be judged by a letter from Professor Lankester, the zoologist in whose book he had found the animals.

"You are perfectly splendid in your story of the 'lost world' mountain-top," wrote Dr. Lankester. "I feel proud to have had a certain small share in its inception. It is just sufficiently conceivable to make it 'go' smoothly. I notice that you rightly withhold any intelligence from the big dinosaurs, and also acute smell from the ape-men."

Whereupon Dr. Lankester burst out with suggestions.

"What about," he went on enthusiastically, "introducing a gigantic snake sixty feet long? Or a rabbit-like beast as big as an ox (Toxodon)? Or a herd of pigmy elephants two feet high? Can four men escape by training a vegetarian pterodactyl to fly with them one at a time? Will some ape-woman fall in love with Challenger and murder the leaders of her tribe to save him?"

The last might have been wondered by Jean, and by Jean's closest friend, Lily Loder-Symonds, who had come to live at Windlesham. Each evening through October and November he would read them what he had written during the day. He would sit in the big white-painted alcove off the billiard-room, filling the Viking chair that was a present from Denmark, with a great fire burning under the mantelpiece and the stag's head. Through the jungle, in imagination, crashed the dauntless four: Lord John Roxton like a ginger-haired Don Quixote, the acid Summerlee, the eternally likeable Malone; and, at the head of them, Challenger in a very small straw hat and pointing his toes when he walked—both hat and gait, by the way, being a picture of Challenger's creator.

"I think," he wrote to Greenhough Smith, editor of the 'Strand,' when the story was finished in December, '11, "I think it will make the very best serial (bar special S. Holmes values) that I have ever done, especially when it has its trimming of faked photos, maps, and plans."

Then came the real joy of the matter.

"My ambition," he added, "is to do for the boys' book what Sherlock Holmes did for the detective tale. I don't suppose I could bring off two such coups. And yet I hope it may."

It did. For this adventure-with-dinosaurs, in the last analysis, is not the true secret of *The Lost World*'s charm. Some of the best scenes—Malone's evening with Gladys at the beginning, the first interview with Challenger, the rowdy proceedings at the Zoological Society, reported rather like one of Conan Doyle's political meetings in Scotland—occur apart from Maple White Land; the zoologists are as interesting as the zoo. Note, too, the comic-skill with which grave-bearded men of science, where some abstruse theory is concerned, behave exactly like temperamental prima donnas and are fully as jealous of each other.

That is the touchstone. When Challenger threatens an injunction against the telephone-company for letting his 'phone ring when he wants to be undisturbed, as he does in a later story, he is fully as good as when he struts among the ape-women. Challenger and his friends carry everything before them with their creator's vitality. They would fascinate us even if they only went for a day's excursion to Margate. Admittedly, of course, something would happen at Margate. Challenger would see to that.

But our very recognition of this fact, our anticipatory grin as we imagine him doing it, show that he is flesh and blood: an ageless flesh and blood, side by side with Micawber and Tony Weller.

At Windlesham, on Christmas Eve, a centuries-old custom was seen for the last time in Sussex. The Christmas Mummers, with their dragon and their silver-scale armour, performed a miracle-play in the billiard-room. The pink-shaded lamps shone on hopping, mouthing figures; Jean and her husband held up the young children so that they could see. Meanwhile, he occupied himself with the faked photographs he had promised Greenhough Smith.

"What do you think of this?" he proudly asked.

In an immense black beard, with adhesive eyebrows and a wig, he glared out at the camera as Professor Challenger. There was another picture, showing him seated among three friends who represented Roxton, Summerlee, and Malone. But the full-face close-up, decorated with a silk hat, was to represent Challenger as an illustration in the 'Strand.'

"The frown is characteristic," he wrote to Greenhough Smith on February 9th, 1912. " 'The scowl of the Conans,' Sir Walter Scott calls it at the end of one of his novels."

Greenhough Smith was alarmed. He said that the disguise, though sufficiently hideous, was not undetectable and might get the magazine into trouble for hoaxing. "Very well," agreed Conan Doyle three days later. "Not a word about the photo of Prof. C. I begin to realize my own audacity. After all, it is *not* me. I am only a block on which an imaginary figure has been built up. But don't give it away."

At the same time, he was so pleased with his Challenger disguise that he had to try it on somebody. Some thirty-odd miles away, the Hornungs and their son Oscar were living at West Grinstead Park, the estate of Willie's brother Sir Pitt Hornung. The obvious move, he thought, was to try it on Willie.

This caused trouble. Announcing that he was der Herr Doktor von Somebody, this hirsute apparition towered in the doorway. He said he was a friendt of Herr Doktor Conan Doyle, who was from home, und would Herr Hornung receive him?

Hornung, fortunately or unfortunately, was short-sighted. Moreover, he was used to the fact that a friend of his brother-in-law might be anybody from some broken-down tramp to the Prime Minister. His welcome was effusive. The visitor, rattling off long strings of German, really did get away with it for several minutes. Then Hornung was furious. Showing his guest to the door, he swore he would never forgive this. The silk-hatted Herr Doktor, his shoulders heaving with chuckles, departed in disgrace.

That was one side of his life. Now, for the forthcoming year 1912, spin round the shield and look at the other side.

It was a rush of work, controversy, and activity. The Congo Reform Association had gained its victory under King Leopold's successor, the young and very different King Albert. Already Conan Doyle had altered his opinions and declared himself in favour of Home Rule for Ireland. "I said in 1905," he wrote, "that Home Rule could only come with time, that it would only be safe with altered economic conditions and above all after the local representative institutions had been adequately tested. It seems to me that these conditions have now been fairly well complied with."

In 1912 he allied himself with the Divorce Reform Union, fighting against the Church and the House of

Commons for some moderation in England's primitive divorce-laws. In the same year, he extended his hospitality to the Council of the British Medical Association, who held their annual conference at Windlesham. He took on himself—at Lord Northcliffe's suggestion that he was the only sporting-leader who could do it— the burden of uniting two discordant factions and raising funds so that British athletes might be better trained for the Olympic Games of 1916. It was diplomacy, it was complexity, it was vexation; it lasted a year, and might have been abandoned in disgust by anyone less tenacious. Above all, he set out to solve a murder mystery and again set free an innocent man. There, most clearly, we see what Robert Louis Stevenson once called "the white plume of Conan Doyle."

Here were the circumstances of the murder case, flavoured as though by a dream-reek out of De Quincey. It had happened more than three years before.

Take a quiet side-street in Glasgow; seven o'clock on a December evening; the gas-lamps dimmed to sparks in a mist of rain. A little way down on your right, as you turn in from Queen's Crescent, is number 15 Queen's Terrace.

Miss Marion Gilchrist, a wealthy old lady of eighty-three, had been living there for a very long time in the year 1908. Anyone who visited Miss Gilchrist first opened the 'close' or street door, and went up a flight of steps to the door of her flat, which she kept double-locked. Lying loose in the spare bedroom of the flat, or hidden at odd places among clothes in the spare-bedroom wardrobe, Miss Gilchrist kept three thousand pounds' worth of jewellery. She had arranged with Mr. Arthur Adams—who lived in the house next door, and whose dining-room was under hers—to knock on the ceiling if she felt nervous or needed assistance.

"She was never afraid of anyone doing a personal injury to her," testified a former servant. "But she had a great fear of the house being broken into."

On the evening of December 21st, 1908, the old lady was in the flat with her one servant, a twenty-one-year-old girl named Helen Lambie. Now mark what happens.

The grandfather clock in the hall of the flat strikes seven. Helen Lambie goes out for a brief errand. There are two patent locks on the flat-door.* Helen Lambie locks the door behind her, taking both keys. She leaves the old lady alone in the dining-room, a stuffy room hung with big gilt-framed pictures. Miss Gilchrist, her spectacles on, is reading at the dining-room table with her back to the fire. Another gas-jet, in a blue-glass shade, burns in the hall. With a pounce, inside ten minutes, there is murder done.

In the house next door Mr. Arthur Adams, with his sisters Laura and Rowena, sat in his dining-room just below Miss Gilchrist's. They heard a thud on the ceiling, and then three distinct knocks. Laura Adams called her brother's attention to it.

"Did she suggest that you should go up and see if anything was wrong?" he was afterwards asked.

"She sent me up immediately."

Mr. Adams, a musician, went out in such haste that he forgot his eyeglasses. It was cold in the street, with rain still falling. The outer door of Miss Gilchrist's house stood ajar. He ran up the flight of steps to the door of the flat, and three times pulled hard at the door-bell. No reply: it was as still as death.

But, through a long glass panel on each side of the door, Mr. Adams could see the blue gas-lamp burning

---

* The patent lock was the predecessor of the spring-lock. It could be opened from inside.

in the hall. And after a few moments he could hear, from what he imagined to be the kitchen, a series of faint noises which made him assume the servant-girl was at home.

"It seemed," he said, "as if it was someone chopping sticks—not heavy blows."

Chop, and chop again! Doubtless the girl, Helen Lambie, cutting wood for the kitchen fire, and not troubling to answer that jangling doorbell. Mr. Adams went downstairs again.

"I told my sisters the house was all lit up, and I did not think there was anything wrong; I thought it was the girl. My sister Laura thought otherwise. She made me go back again."

Again the doorbell jangled through that flat. There was no other noise this time, none at all. Hesitant, on a dim-lit landing smelling of old stone, Arthur Adams still had his hand on the bell when he heard footsteps on the stairs below. It was Helen Lambie, returning from her errand of buying a newspaper. He told her there must be something seriously wrong, and that "the ceiling was like to crack."

"Oh," says the girl lightly, "that wud be the pulleys." She meant the pulleys of the clothes-lines in the kitchen; they sometimes fell down. Then she unlocked the door which guarded Miss Gilchrist. What happened next, to Mr. Adams, had at once that brightness and blur of half a dozen impressions flashing past in a few moments' time.

As Helen Lambie went through the hall towards the kitchen, a man appeared in the hall from the direction of the spare bedroom. Mr. Adams, without his glasses, saw the man's face very indistinctly; but he appeared "gentlemanly and well-dressed." This man walked calmly to the door, after which he went downstairs "like

greased lightning." Helen Lambie, apparently unsur-
prised, looked into the kitchen and then went to the
spare bedroom, where a light was now burning. Much
jewellery still lay on the dressing-table, though a box
containing Miss Gilchrist's private papers had been
overturned on the floor amid its scattered contents.

Only then did Mr. Adams find his tongue.

"Where is your mistress?"

Helen Lambie went over to the dining-room, and
opened the door. Across the years we cannot hear the
tone of her voice, but her words were: *"Oh, come here."*

The old lady who so feared burglars lay by the fireplace, with her head towards the fender and her false
teeth nearby. Though an animal-skin rug had been
thrown across her body, anyone could see the blood on
fireplace and fire-irons and coal-scuttle. Her head and
face had been battered shapeless with injuries which
it is not necessary to describe.

Such was the murder of Marion Gilchrist on the evening of December 21st, 1908. The real evidence, including much that was said and done the very same
night, did not appear until many years later. When
Conan Doyle first studied the case, we follow only outwardly the conduct of the Glasgow police.

The only article which appeared to have been stolen
from Miss Gilchrist's flat (according to Helen Lambie,
sole witness) was a diamond crescent brooch about the
size of a half-crown. Much distressed, she indicated this
to Detective-Inspector Pyper on the night of the murder.

On Christmas Day the police learned that a pawn-
ticket for a diamond brooch had been offered for sale
in the Sloper Club by a dubious character whose (most-
often-used) name proved to be Oscar Slater. On Christmas Night, as though to add whipcrack, Slater departed
for Liverpool with several trunks and a fancy-woman

called Madame Junio. On Boxing Day Slater and Madame Junio sailed for New York in the Cunarder *Lusitania*.

The pawned diamond brooch seemed sound evidence. But, as the police immediately discovered, it wasn't the same brooch as Miss Gilchrist's. Oscar Slater had pawned a brooch, his own property, more than a month before the murder.

Whereupon the police lost their heads. They offered a reward of £200 and cabled New York to arrest Slater on arrival. In the meantime, a fourteen-year-old girl named Mary Barrowman—she had been passing Miss Gilchrist's house on the night of the murder—came forward with evidence of a man who rushed out of the house, knocked against her, and ran away at a time coincident with the murderer's escape.

Though she had only one glance on a black rainy night in a street indifferently lighted, fourteen-year-old Mary described every detail of the man's face and clothing. Her description did not agree with the more vague testimony of Mr. Adams and Helen Lambie. And neither fitted the real Oscar Slater. But, after some days' questioning, Helen changed her mind and agreed with Mary about the man's clothes.

Hustled aboard ship, where they shared a cabin and swore they never exchanged a word about the case, Mary and Helen were sent to New York to identify Slater. They had seen photographs of him. When Slater, handcuffed, was marched down the corridor to the courtroom between two United States deputy marshals, a Glasgow deputation conveniently arranged for Mary and Helen to be in the corridor.

Then, in the American courtroom:

"Yes, I can identify him," was the decision of both girls after much shuffling.

Subsequently, they both swore fervently they had never had any doubt of his identity.

In vain Slater cried, with emotion, that he had never heard of Miss Marion Gilchrist or her jewellery; that he was new to Glasgow; and that (as he later proved) he had arranged for his trip to New York weeks before the tragedy. Against the advice of his American lawyer, he waived extradition proceedings and returned to Scotland for trial.

Now Oscar Slater was no hero of fiction: on the contrary. That he was German and Jewish may or may not have helped cause the intense prejudice against him. But he had run gambling clubs in London and New York; he lived by his wits; he kept a mistress who was also (perhaps) a prostitute. This made prejudice boil to the top when Slater appeared for trial on May 3rd, 1909, in the High Court of Justiciary at Edinburgh.

Slater—thick-chested, broad-faced, with dark hair and moustache, pleasant-looking but a Sinister Foreigner —writhed in the small dock between two police-constables. The full evidence at the trial, since its ugly under-the-surface story had not yet emerged, need not detain us. The prosecution claimed Slater had committed the murder with a small tin-tack hammer from a card of tools, though both their medical witnesses were doubtful. Slater had an alibi; but this was invalidated because it rested on the word of his mistress and a servant-girl. Mary Barrowman and Helen Lambie positively identified him. Our old friend Mr. Adams, who had also gone to New York, would not swear to Slater as the murderer-in-the-flat.

Cross-examined by Mr. M'Clure for the defence:

"And, even after all you have heard, you do not give an absolutely confident opinion that that was the man?"

"No," answered the witness. "It is too serious a charge for me to say from a passing glance."

Counsel for the Crown, Mr. Ure the Lord Advocate, made a terrific speech. How had the murderer got into a double-locked flat with undisturbed windows? He did not mention the subject. How did Slater know Miss Gilchrist had any jewellery? He promised to explain this, but never did. In addition Mr. Ure made several flat misstatements of fact, damning to Slater, which the judge did not see fit to correct.

The jury, by the majority verdict which is permissible in Scotland—nine for Guilty, five for Not Proven, one for Not Guilty—found Oscar Slater guilty of murder.

Some thought it a pity that Slater, in his babbling and broken English, made such a painful scene by interrupting the proceedings when the judge was about to sentence him to death. People who won't live respectable lives, it seems, can't feel sick with bewilderment and fright. Slater's outburst stumbled over and over the same words.

"I know nothing about the affair, absolutely nothing! I never heard the name! I know nothing about the affair! I do not know how I could be connected with the affair! I know nothing about it! I came from America on my own account!" and then: "I can say no more."

They were to hang him at Glasgow prison on May 27th. But Scots conscience, sobered after this morality spree, roused twenty thousand petitioners for a reprieve. Slater had just one more day to live when he heard that the Secretary for Scotland, Lord Pentland, had commuted his sentence to one of penal servitude for life. The prisoner disappeared into Peterhead: there he was likely to remain.

Conan Doyle, as he wrote to the Ma'am, had been

approached by 'the lawyers,' presumably Slater's. He went into the case with reluctance. This was different from Edalji's affair; he thought Slater a blackguard, and said so in the booklet he wrote. But never mind a man's character! If he is not guilty of murder, then all hell must be moved to secure his release. And:

"That paladin of lost causes," writes Mr. William Roughead, so that again we hear the word 'paladin,' "found in the dubious circumstances of the case matter after his own heart."

He had already launched his press-campaign. In August, 1912, Hodder & Stoughton published his booklet *The Case of Oscar Slater*. He was not yet in that white fury which caught him when he learned of some moves behind the scenes.

"It is impossible," he wrote, "to read and weigh the facts . . . without feeling deeply dissatisfied with the proceedings, and morally certain that justice was not done." And step by step he tore the evidence to pieces. But an alternative theory?

Those who supported Slater had noted some significant points from the start. Why had the girl Helen Lambie expressed no surprise when she suddenly found a stranger in that locked flat? Was it because the man was not a stranger? Because the girl recognized him? The same applied to the victim herself. Had Miss Gilchrist been expecting the man, and admitted him to the flat?

Conan Doyle, in *The Case of Oscar Slater,* advanced a new line of suggestion.

"One question which has to be asked," he wrote, "is whether the assassin was after the jewels at all."

Consider the murderer's behaviour! After battering in the victim's head with some unknown instrument, the author pointed out, this murderer went straight to the right bedroom and lit the gas. But he did not touch the valuable rings and watch lying openly on the dressing-table. Instead he broke open and rifled a wooden box which contained Miss Gilchrist's private papers, leaving the papers strewn over the floor.

"Were the papers his object," asked *The Case of Oscar Slater*, "and the final abstraction of one diamond brooch a blind?" It might have been a document: a will, perhaps. This would bring the matter much closer home.

There was still another theory, based on interrupted jewel-robbery. Yet all theorizing returned to the problem of a double-locked flat with undisturbed windows. Either Miss Gilchrist admitted the murderer, or he had two duplicate keys. Even if he had keys to patent locks, he could only have got moulds for them with the conscious or unconscious connivance of someone who lived there.

As to the outcome of Oscar Slater's plight. . . .

But we are now in the present, in the year 1912. The riddle of what happened during those fatal ten minutes, of who showed his face to Marion Gilchrist in the blood-stained dining-room, passes momentarily out of Conan Doyle's life. For two encounters during that year, we breathe better air. We see the pleasing, the classic countenance of Mr. George Bernard Shaw.

XVIII

SHADOWS:

Now Came Danger!

At the Memorial Hall in Farringdon Street, that night in December, Mr. Shaw and Conan Doyle were speakers at a gathering so large that its overflow into other streets had to be controlled by the police.

Though they had been friends for many years, ever since Conan Doyle was writing the early Holmes short-stories and Mr. Shaw's greenish face and red beard were such a painful sight to Henry Irving, these two met infrequently. But they had two encounters in 1912: the first, at the beginning of the year, being acrimonious and on paper.

It was occasioned by a famous sea-disaster. The *Titanic*, largest and most luxurious passenger-ship afloat, left Southampton for her maiden voyage on April 10th. The *Titanic*'s watertight compartments were said to be an engineering wonder. She carried more than the regulation number of lifeboats required by the Board of Trade. What did not appear until afterwards was the fact that these Board of Trade Regulations, unchanged since 1894, applied to ships of ten thousand tons: nearly five times less than the *Titanic*'s size.

Late on the night of April 14th the *Titanic*, moving at twenty-one and a half knots, failed to swing her helm in time. Captain E. J. Smith, following the practice of other commanders, had posted lookouts and run the risk of ice. This iceberg ripped open the *Titanic*'s side like a biscuit-tin, though she remained afloat for two and a half hours. There were 2206 persons on board. The capacity of the lifeboats, including four collapsibles and two emergency sea-boats, was 1178 persons. Even if the coolest and best judgment had been preserved (which it was not), those boats had capacity for little more than half the liner's human cargo.

W. T. Stead, Conan Doyle's old friendly-enemy, went down with the *Titanic*. So did many another human being, including the stokers who worked waist-deep in water until two o'clock in the morning to keep the lights burning and the pumps going. "We've lived for forty years together," said Mrs. Isidor Straus, refusing to enter a lifeboat without her husband; "we won't part now." Only 711 persons were saved.

Reports of the disaster—the wireless calling, the distress-signal rockets flaring up against a moonless night —came back to England in confused and fragmentary rumours. The British press were rash enough to say that aboard the *Titanic* there had been bravery and even heroism.

And this roused the scorn and disgust of Mr. George Bernard Shaw.

Any suggestion of the 'romantic' or the 'sentimental' was always anathema to Mr. Shaw. He wrote a letter to the 'Daily News and Leader,' upbraiding the British press for an orgy of romantic lying. Satirically he outlined the British "romantic demands" for heroism in time of shipwreck, and compared them with what he called "authentic evidence" to show that the behaviour of officers, crew, and passengers had been anything but heroic.

This infuriated Conan Doyle, who wrote a reply pointing out that Mr. Shaw's authentic evidence did not agree with all the facts; and that this was not a time playfully to spray vitriol on the *Titanic*'s victims, living or dead.

In counter-retort Mr. Shaw was brisk and poised, like a ballet dancer.

He hoped his friend Sir Arthur Conan Doyle, after this romantic and warm-hearted protest, would read his letter again three or four times. He, Mr. Shaw, had been misunderstood. If journalists uttered words of praise before knowing the particulars, they were guilty of lying. It was of no importance—Mr. Shaw waved aside the detail—that authentic evidence arrived later to confirm some of the journalists' notions of people in the *Titanic* who had done their duty. He, Mr. Shaw, had been quoting only the *first* evidence—thereby ballet-dancing over the fact that he himself had used both first and later evidence to ridicule his quarry in the original letter.

"All right," a detached observer might have said. "It's been good fun. Now stop."

But he, Mr. Shaw, could permit no sympathy for Captain Smith. Captain Smith had lost his ship, which was unpardonably inefficient of him. No excuse, however good, could turn failure into success. Captain Smith had gone down with the ship and was dead; he, Mr. Shaw, would not have whispered a syllable to upset Captain Smith's family if journalists had not praised the fellow; in the Royal Navy, of course, such a man would have been court-martialled. For "sentimental idiots, with a break in the voice" he, Mr. Shaw, had only impatient contempt. He was always logical.

Therefore it is interesting to study the behaviour of Mr. Shaw and Conan Doyle, at the end of the same year, when both made a speech on Ireland.

For the great meeting in the Memorial Hall, Farringdon Street, the music of Irish pipes ushered speakers to the platform. The platform was festooned with both green and orange bunting to represent the Catholic and Protestant sides of Ireland. It was a meeting of English and Irish Protestants. They objected to the attitude taken by Protestant Northern Ireland: the attitude that Home Rule would mean persecution of the Protestant minority by the Catholic majority.

And this was no tragedy like that of the *Titanic*; we can applaud every word they said.

Though there were other speakers besides Mr. Shaw and Conan Doyle, these were the two on whom the press concentrated. Both were on the same side, maintaining that there would be no persecution by Catholics. Out strode Mr. Shaw amid the orange and green bunting, to face his audience with deep earnestness.

"I am an Irishman," he said. "My father was an Irishman. My mother was an Irishwoman. My father and my mother were Protestants, who would have been described, owing to the intensity of their faith, as sanguinary Protestants." Then Mr. Shaw attempted to touch his listeners' hearts.

"But many of the duties of my mother were shared by an Irish nurse, who was a Catholic," he cried. "And she never put me to bed without sprinkling me with holy water."

Here, it is regrettable to state, his Irish audience could not keep a straight face. The picture of Mr. Shaw being sprinkled with holy water, somehow, lacked an element of pathos both to Protestants and to Catholics. The speaker, furious and in a logical frenzy, demanded to know why they laughed at such a touching scene. Perhaps it lent wings to his eloquence later.

"I have now arrived at a time when I can look back on my life," he declared. "And it is a curious and un-

reasonable position that none of my achievements due
to my talents, industry or sobriety have ever caused me
any pride of any kind. But the fact that I am an Irishman . . . has always filled me with a wild and inextin-
guishable pride.

"As regards the local Irish feeling," he continued,
with or without a break in the voice, "I cannot describe
what I feel. People tell me I am in danger of being per-
secuted by your Roman Catholic countrymen, and
England will protect you. I had rather be burned alive
at the stake by Roman Catholics—"

He ended his sentence "—than protected by the
English." But it was almost drowned by a whoop of
mirth from the audience. We, of course, can see that it
was not fair to Mr. Shaw. It was not just. Such patriotic
sentiments ought to have been funny only if he had put
them into the mouth of some Englishman or American
on the stage. Poor fellow, they should not have laughed
at him.

Conan Doyle, one of the sentimental idiots, had
spoken in a different vein.

"I seldom attend political meetings," he said. "But I
would go a long way anywhere to protest against religious persecution. We have good reason for our belief
that Irish Catholics will give fair play; the Church of
Rome in Ireland has never been a persecuting church.
This same problem has been solved in Bavaria, in Sax-
ony, where a Protestant minority is never molested.

"The thing that matters is a prosperous and happy
country. We people of Irish blood are always running
to the past to take sides. One person's ancestors have
lined Derry Wall; another person's have fought at the
Boyne, or been evicted in the year of the famine. If the
Irish can only let their grand-dads alone, they can get

a much clearer view of what they need now, and a better chance of obtaining it."

This subject of religion had been much in Conan Doyle's mind, not only at this gathering but all through the autumn. He jotted down many speculations in his common-place book. It was reflected, too, in a short novel called *The Poison Belt*, another adventure of Professor Challenger, which he wrote before Christmas.

"Bring oxygen—*Challenger*." The end of the world! A belt of deadly gas slowly drifting across the earth, annihilating all life. Conceive of some lonely group of five persons, shut up in an airtight room (in imagination it was his own study at Windlesham, with its windows overlooking golf course and downs), while they watch life die and listen to the hissing of the oxygen tube.

They are like passengers of the *Titanic*, grinding into ice amid cushioned safety. What do they think, during the dark hours? What do they feel, when the last dawn comes up and the last cylinder of oxygen is turned on?

Such was the theme of *The Poison Belt*, though most readers are apt to remember best its sensational qualities. The trickle of alarming reports into the newspaper office, the erratic behaviour of Londoners, the humorous beginning slowly turning grey; then the final morning when to Challenger and his wife, to Malone and Roxton and Summerlee, the tide of death seems at its height.

"Into the hands of the power that made us we render ourselves again!" thunders Challenger, and throws the field-glasses to break the window.

"If I live after death," Conan Doyle was writing in his common-place book at about the same time, "I shall feel no surprise whatever may confront me as I pierce the shadows. Only one thing would amaze me. That would be to find that orthodox Christianity was literally correct."

In *The Poison Belt*, after the smashing of the window, there is that long silence while five wait for their end. Then comes the brush of clean air, the noise of birds bickering, the realization that the poison belt has cleared and that they alone (apparently) have survived. It is not anti-climax; the most powerful part of the book follows; but the psychological interest is here.

The Lost World, published by Hodder and Stoughton in October, had been sheer rollicking adventure. Challenger, in the sequel, is no less full of bristle and bounce. Yet in *The Poison Belt* Challenger is given the lead in a fundamentally serious story. The author knew Challenger, and loved him; he could trust the old boy.

It is certainly not suggested that he had any vision of world catastrophe like the dead cities and sprawled dummies in *The Poison Belt*. But several curious lines of thought were converging at this time. In the same period as this novel, he was writing an article called "Great Britain and the Next War," which appeared in the 'Fortnightly Review' for February, 1913.

That Imperial Germany meant war—and what she meant to do, and how she meant to do it—became plain to him when he read General von Bernhardi's book, *Germany and the Next War*. He saw it as a sketch-plan printed with memories of faces from Prince Henry's tour. General von Bernhardi, one of the most knowing of the Junkers, spoke with remarkable candour. Listen to the General's philosophy:

Strong, healthy, flourishing nations increase in numbers. From a given moment . . . they require new territory for the accommodation of their surplus population. Since almost every part of the globe is inhabited, new territory must be obtained by conquests, which thus becomes a law of necessity.

France, said von Bernhardi, must be annihilated. Great Britain, perfidious towards Germany since 1761 and marked as a foe to be struck down since the time of the Boer War, must follow.

Conan Doyle, visualizing the course of such a war, later said he was not conscious of any process of reasoning. It jumped into his mind fully outlined, another sketch-plan, but vivid with new and unsuspected dangers. Great Britain considered herself isolated, wound round with the iron chains of her Navy. And so, in a sense, she was. But Great Britain had to import food. If Germany attacked France, which seemed the more likely supposition, Britain must also transport an army to the continent and keep up a line of supplies.

"The element of danger," he wrote in his article "Great Britain and the Next War," "is the existence of new forms of naval warfare which have never been tested in the hands of competent men, and which may completely revolutionize the conditions. These new factors are the submarine and the airship."

The aeroplane or the dirigible balloon, he considered, was not yet "sufficiently formidable to alter the whole conditions of a campaign." But the submarine was a different matter. No blockade could hold these water-snakes in harbour, no skill avoid them when they struck at merchant-shipping. Then:

"What effect a swarm of submarines, lying off the mouth of the Channel and the Irish Sea, would produce upon the victualing of these islands is a problem which is beyond my conjecture," he wrote. "Other ships besides the British would be likely to be destroyed, and international complications would probably follow."

It was as though the word DANGER wrote itself in very large red letters. His views, though expressed in the small scope of the 'Fortnightly Review,' were heard —if not listened to—throughout the country. How was this danger to be met?

Well, he could think of three solutions. The first was to grow food at home, compelling the measure by a high tariff on imported food; but politics would never permit this. The second solution was to construct submarine food-carriers, ships as invisible as the attackers; but this appeared nautically impossible.

The third solution, which he strongly urged, was the construction of a Channel Tunnel: two hundred feet underground, twenty-six miles long, connecting England with France. England and France must stand together.

"I presume," he wrote drily, "I need not argue the point that it is our vital interest that France be not dismembered and sterilized. Such a tragedy would turn the western half of Europe into a gigantic Germany with a few insignificant states crouching about her feet."

Such a Channel Tunnel, an Underground Railway of its own, would be a pipe-line, a life-line, valuable both in commerce or in war. The project had been suggested before; it had been entirely feasible thirty years before. In 1913, with modern engineering methods, the Channel Tunnel could be made within three years—if three years were not already too late—and at a cost of five million pounds.

"We tap (*via* Marseilles and the tunnel) the whole food supply of the Mediterranean and the Black Sea." In the unlikely event of England being invaded, reinforcements could be hurried back from France. In any event, my lords and gentlemen, the submarine is your real menace. How are you going to meet it?

Though he had many strong supporters, including

General Sir Reginald Talbot and General Sir Alfred Turner, most people in high official places were not inclined to take him very seriously. A large meeting in the Cannon Street Hotel, where he was chief speaker, produced adverse comment.

Said Mr. Asquith, the Prime Minister: "The question of our power of feeding our people, or of preserving our communications across the Channel, is a question of whether or not we have got an Invincible Navy and command of the sea."

Commented 'The Times' with polite derision: "We leave it to Sir Arthur Conan Doyle to square this dictum of Mr. Asquith's with the fancy picture of twenty-five hostile submarines off the Kent coast and twenty-five in the Irish Channel."

Said Admiral von Capelle, the German Naval Secretary, speaking exultantly in the Reichstag three years later:

"The only prophet of the present form of economic warfare is Sir Arthur Conan Doyle."

At the moment he was not popular among military authorities in his own country. Since he did not believe in an invasion, he wanted the Territorials (in the event of this possible war) to support the Army abroad as a fighting-force.

Compulsory military service he detested. He believed in the volunteer soldier, and doubted the worth of the conscript: a mistaken view, but twined into his boyhood and an essential part of his character. Compulsory service, of course, might become necessary in war-time. In peace-time, he correctly judged, no such measure would ever pass Parliament.

"Train the Territorials better," he kept insisting, "and you'll have reserves to draw on!"

This in particular occasioned a heated argument when

that picturesque Irishman General Wilson, the Director of Military Operations, invited him to a conference about *Great Britain and the Next War*. After lunch at the house of Colonel Sackville-West, General Wilson pitched in to question the bristling civilian, and fists pounded the table on both sides. They could not convince him of the necessity for conscription; he could not make them see any danger from submarines.

There was also danger from the floating mine, which had proved so deadly in the Russo-Japanese War. He pondered over this, wondering if he could think of some defence both against the submarine and the mine. Somehow, he felt, he must wake up the public. All outward affairs seemed to run so smoothly, so silkily, in that spring of 1913, except when they were pierced by the cry of the militant suffragettes.

"*Votes for women!*" shouted the militants.

They smashed windows, assaulted Cabinet Ministers, padlocked themselves to iron railings. They went on hunger-strikes and had to be forcibly fed. They made demonstrations at theatres and public meetings, until dragged out screaming and clawing in a cascade of dishevelled hair. To the dull-witted it seemed funny. Most people were merely bewildered. It was as though a vicarage tea-party had been suddenly changed into a Witches' Sabbath, or staid dowagers sang *Alexander's Ragtime Band*.

Conan Doyle, never well disposed towards suffragism, bitterly opposed it when the witch screams began. It was not a matter of political principle. What he disliked was their behaviour. He considered it grotesque, a reversal of roles, like men dressing up as women and doing needlework. Jean, like most women at that time, had no wish to vote and said so without any prompting from him.

"Why should I? I'm perfectly happy."

Their third child, a girl whom they named Lena Jean Annette, had been born on December 21st, 1912. The following summer found Windlesham in its richest bloom of happiness. This new family did not in the least alienate his elder children, Mary and Kingsley; on the contrary, it bound them closer to him.

Mary, in the billiard-room, had always been surprised to see Denis and Adrian playing on the floor under his feet while he practised billiard-shots. (He reached the third stage for the Amateur Championship in 1913.) Instead of flaring out with nerves—as he would have done in the old days—he stepped absent-mindedly over the children, or let them run according to their fancy, as he moved round the table.

Real understanding had been achieved with Mary and Kingsley. Kingsley—tall, strongly built, very reserved and gentle-handed—was preparing to take his medical degree at St. Mary's Hospital after studying at Lausanne and Hanover.

"I sometimes feel," Conan Doyle had confided in a letter to Innes, "I can't penetrate the boy's reserve; that I don't understand him." Such awkwardness dissolved. Kingsley's specialty was throwing the hammer; his father competed with him on the lawn of Windlesham.

"Kingsley," he told Jean, "must be the only non-talkative Doyle who ever lived. But he can be really eloquent when he writes to all his girls."

" 'All' his girls?"

"I can't open a desk-blotter in this house without finding a half-finished letter beginning 'Darling Susan,' or 'Darling Jane.' " Here he could imitate himself, puffing out his cheeks and giving a huge start. " 'Kingsley! Great Scott! What's this?'—The boy's a terror. Excellent!"

He made many speeches in that year for the Divorce Reform Union. "The foundation of national life," he would say, "is not the family. It is the happy family. And that, with our obsolete divorce laws, is what we haven't got."

In addition to his interest in the auto-wheel—a motor wheel attached to the rear wheel of a bicycle, on which they all went chugging round the grounds—every sort of interest involved him. Mr. Stoll wanted Sherlock Holmes in what Mrs. Humphrey Ward called "these new schemes for the cinematograph reproductions of novels," when she wrote to him for advice about her own film-rights, but his first story to be filmed was *Rodney Stone*.

The Lost World still had its repercussions. In the press for April 1st (it cannot be helped; that really was the date) he saw the following item:

Sir Arthur Conan Doyle's stirring romance *The Lost World* has aroused the adventurous spirit of a party of Americans. A few days ago the yacht *Delaware* left Philadelphia and sailed away for the broad waters of the Amazon. The yacht is the property of the University of Pennsylvania, and is bound for Brazil with a daring party of explorers, who propose penetrating to the far reaches of the Amazon and to the headwaters of many of its tributaries in the interest of science and humanity. They seek Conan Doyle's 'lost world,' or some scientific evidence of it.

We may suspect, here, that some American reporter was adding spice to an authentic story. Real names were mentioned: Captain Rowen, who commanded the yacht, and Dr. Farrable of the University. Jean was horrified.

"You don't think they took it seriously?"

"No, of course not. In any case, let 'em go! If they don't find the plateau, they'll certainly find *something* of interest."

In April, too, the man who was then known as America's greatest detective came down to Windlesham for a week-end. William J. Burns, with his reddish moustache and genial eye, had "the easy and polished manners of a diplomat over something else that can be polished—granite."

"He told me," Conan Doyle wrote in his commonplace book, "that when he conducted the San Francisco prosecutions he was told he would be shot in court. Upon which he gave instructions that in that case his men should kill all the lawyers and witnesses on the other side. 'I would be dead, Sir Arthur; so it would be all the same to me.' "

Burns wanted to talk about Sherlock Holmes. He said Holmes's methods were practical, and exhibited the 'detectaphone' by which you could listen to conversations in another room. But his host, parrying questions with chuckles behind the pipe, persuaded him instead to tell stories of the Burns Detective Agency and from the long history of Pinkerton's. One story—it was that of the Molly Maguires in the anthracite coal-fields of Pennsylvania, 1876—excited his imagination long after Burns had gone.

Will the great recognition-line be remembered here, if quoted without comment? "*I am Birdy Edwards!*"

Thus two separate lines of thought, the process of calling attention to submarine-danger and the hazy outline of a detective-story, worked together through the summer into the autumn.

In the past five years just five Sherlock Holmes stories, from *The Adventure of Wisteria Lodge* to *The Disappearance of Lady Frances Carfax*, had been scattered through the 'Strand.' How, he asked, would they like a full-length detective novel? And, at the same time, would they cooperate with a scheme of his for demanding comment from naval authorities on a proposed short-story?

In the interval, the common-place book ran more and more on the subject of religion. He wrote also of Spiritualism: a subject he could never discuss with Jean, because she disliked it and was frightened of it. To read that common-place book is to watch his approach.

"Even granting that Spiritualism is true," he wrote, "it advances us but a little way. And yet that little way does solve the most important problem of immediate question—does death end all?

"Fancy a London which went mad on Spiritualism as it recently did on glove-fighting, and which flocked round a successful medium as round Georges Carpentier!"

(They flocked round young Carpentier when he knocked out Bombardier Wells in the first round on December 8th, 1913.)

"What a nightmare it would be!" wrote Conan Doyle. "What an orgy of fraud and lunacy would be cooked! We should all regard such an outbreak with horror. And yet it would still not be incompatible with a belief that all the Spiritualists claim is true."

Between the winter of 1913 and the spring of 1914, at the very peak of his inventive powers, he wrote his last and best detective-novel, *The Valley of Fear*. And he wrote a long short-story called *Danger! Being the Log of Captain John Sirius*, which must remain forever a landmark in prophecy.

XIX

ROYAL TOUR:

The Peak of Success

The submarine, mounting on her deck a twelve-pounder collapsible gun as well as the torpedoes inside, slipped out of Blankenburg harbour at sunset. She was the *Iota*, commanded by Captain John Sirius.

Blankenburg was the fictitious capital of a very small fictitious country called Norland. *Iota* also was imaginary. But she was the first submarine to be fitted with a gun, so that she might come to the surface against harmless ships and reserve her torpedoes for the dangerous ones. Nobody, with the possible exception of Imperial Germany, had thought of such an idea.

Conan Doyle, in *Danger!,* imagined this small, apparently weak nation at war with Great Britain. With a flotilla of only eight submarines, Captain Sirius promises he will bring the enemy to terms even while Britain's great fleet is blockading Norland's harbours. Captain Sirius will touch no war-vessels. He will sink only grain-ships, cattle-ships, food-ships of any kind or any nationality.

"It was all the same to me," he explains airily, "what flag she flew so long as she was engaged in conveying contraband of war to the British Isles." The first neutral ship he sinks, with gun-fire, is an American.

A port to hide in? What does he want with ports, where he may be spotted by aeroplanes or hydroplanes? All he needs is an isolated fuelling-base along the coast.

Out go his marauders, in touch by wireless; they play starvation-murder from the mouth of the Thames to Land's End, where Sirius torpedoes the mighty liner *Olympic*.

The English newspapers, plastering their front pages with headlines of victory when Blankenburg is captured, relegate a small item to an obscure page.

"Several of the enemy's submarines are at sea, and have inflicted some appreciable damage on our merchant-ships," it begins characteristically. Then it dismisses this as of no importance. "Since a submarine cannot keep the sea for more than ten days without refitting, and since the port (Blankenburg) has been captured, there must come a speedy end to these depredations."

England is brought to terms in an impossibly short time, it is true, and with too few submarines. But anyone who reads *Danger!* nowadays, after two wars, begins to have an eerie sensation that this is where he came in. Merchant-ships, to avoid torpedoes, steer a zig-zag track. Some are armed as auxiliary cruisers; Captain Stephan's *Zetta,* seeing no guns through the periscope, has her conning-tower blown off by return-fire when she surfaces. Captain Sirius finds his greatest danger from the bombs of swooping aircraft. Every casual detail is so realistic that we turn back, with relief, to February of 1914—when it was all a dream, and Conan Doyle wrote it.

There it was, a whole blue-print of exactly what happened in the future. He asked Greenough Smith to get the opinions of, say, a dozen leading naval experts. Could this happen? they were to be asked. Then print the opinions in the 'Strand,' after his story.

"The naval opinions," he wrote, "should not be more than 100 words or so each, or they will overbalance the story. We must also keep out of politics as far as possible."

This must be done. It was vital, vital, vital!

At the same time he was working hard at his novel, about which Greenhough Smith pressed him for information.

"The 'Strand,' " he replied on February 6th, 1914, "are paying so high a price for this story that I should be churlish indeed if I refused any possible information.

"The name, I think, will be *The Valley of Fear.* Speaking from what seem the present probabilities it should run to not less than 50,000 words. I have done nearly 25,000, I reckon roughly. With luck I should finish before the end of March.

"As in *A Study in Scarlet* the plot goes to America for at least half the book while it recounts the events which led up to the crime in England. . . . This part of the story will contain one surprise which I hope will be a real staggerer to the most confirmed reader. But in the long stretch we abandon Holmes. That is necessary."

Across the top of this letter he wrote in afterthought: "I fancy this is my swan-song in fiction."

This was disturbing news for Greenhough Smith, who begged him to explain.

He replied in amusement that by his swan-song—"or goose-cackle, I should say,"—he only meant he was far from being a poor man; he had sound commercial interests; he could devote himself to the historical work he loved. For the present:

"As my procedure has been to write two opening Sherlock chapters and then branch off into the American part (which will not be the published order) it is difficult to send you anything which will not give a false impression."

Some critics have been inclined to play down *The*

Valley of Fear. They dislike what they think is the 'political' aspect of the second part, the Scowrers in the coal fields, and then profess to wince at the technique. It is often the complaint of those Left Wing writers who themselves can't construct a plot for beans. But the easily-upset feelings of these gentlemen must not blind them to the fact that the first part, a separate unit called *The Tragedy of Birlstone,* is a very nearly perfect piece of detective-story writing.

From the opening chapter, with its noble Holmes-Watson dialogue, to the solution of the crime in the study, the reader is told every vital clue. These clues are emphasized, flourished, underlined. More than this, it is our clearest example of Conan Doyle's contribution to the detective story.

At moated Birlstone Manor, a man is messily murdered with a shotgun amid curious clues involving a candle and a blood-mark. Holmes notices that one of a pair of dumb-bells, kept in the study for exercise, is not there. Later Holmes debates the case with Watson.

"I don't say that we have fathomed it—far from it—but when we have traced the missing dumb-bell—"

"The dumb-bell!"

"Dear me, Watson, is it possible that you have not penetrated the fact that the case hangs upon the missing dumb-bell?"

Holmes goes on and on about it until both Watson and the reader become desperate. What is the meaning of the dumb-bell? What enormous significance is attached to Watson's umbrella? At first mention of the dumb-bell's importance, Holmes sits there "with his mouth full of toast and his eyes sparkling with mischief, watching my intellectual entanglement." Yet the truth stares us in the face.

It is customary to say that Conan Doyle derived one

device from Poe, or another device from Gaboriau, or a third device from somebody else. This obscures what he really did do: he invented the enigmatic clue. We find it running far back through the stories, notably illustrated by a passage which has been repeated over and over:

"Is there any point to which you would wish to draw my attention?"

"To the curious incident of the dog in the night-time."

"The dog did nothing in the night-time."

"That was the curious incident."

Call this 'Sherlockismus'; call it any fancy name; the fact remains that it is a clue, and a thundering good clue at that. It is the trick by which the detective—while giving you perfectly fair opportunity to guess—nevertheless makes you wonder what in sanity's name he is talking about. The creator of Sherlock Holmes invented it; and nobody except the great G. K. Chesterton, whose Father Brown stories were so deeply influenced by the device, has ever done it half so well.

Now the missing dumb-bell, if anything, is better than the dog in the night-time; or (if we include any device from *The Hound of the Baskervilles*) both dogs in the night-time. Holmes as a character, whether solving Porlock's cipher or lecturing on architecture to a mystified Inspector MacDonald, has lost no stature in 1914. Let aesthetic critics devote themselves to *A Study in Scarlet* or *The Sign of the Four,* which really did have uncertain handling. But let them refrain from talking nonsense about *The Valley of Fear.*

He finished it in April, having been, as he wrote to Greenough Smith, "much distracted by many other things." Some came close to home.

For the militant suffragettes were at it again. They burned the Nevill Cricket Pavilion at Tunbridge Wells, causing a meeting of suffrage-opponents at which Conan spoke strongly. In London, when he was to make an address for divorce reform at the Ethical Church, they tried to get into the church. Public feeling against the militants grew steadily more wrathful at the mutilation of art-gallery pictures and a few cases of arson. It explains a number of his remarks later.

A year before, when he regretted he had been too busy to accept, the Canadian Government invited him to inspect the National Reserve at Jasper Park in the northern Rocky Mountains, and make a tour of Canada as their guest. They repeated the invitation for 1914.

"The Grand Trunk Railway System," wrote Colonel Rogers, "will have a private railway car to meet you at Quebec or Montreal, will send you wherever you want to go in Eastern Canada, furnish you with the best of their steamers on the Great Lakes, have another car waiting for you at Fort William, and send you all over the Western portion of the trip on their lines."

It was an honour he had no wish to decline; it would lead him through Parkman-land, the Iroquois forests of *The Refugees*. His progress through Canada, which has a habit of doing honour handsomely, became almost a royal tour. First, however, he and Jean spent an uproarious week in New York, where America again claimed him as one of her own. In 1894 he had been a well-known writer. Now he was a great man. But still he had absolutely no sense of false dignity, as the sequel showed.

Messages of welcome had already appeared in the press when on May 27th, 1914, the liner *Olympic* moved up past the skyline of lower Manhattan. He and Jean posed for a motion-picture machine, for press-cameras, and, it appeared, for all the reporters in creation.

How that skyline, now dominated by the Goliath of the Woolworth building, had changed!

"Why, when I was last here the highest of them was the Tower building! What's that? Women's suffrage?"

The thermometer stood at ninety-two degrees. Sweltering in black coat, white waistcoat and bowler hat, he fired off replies. A fellow-passenger in the liner was a Mr. R. H. Baskerville, which roused great curiosity and some confusion.

"Colonel Roosevelt, did you say? He's a great man. If he says he's discovered a river in Brazil, you can depend on it he has. Women's suffrage? In my opinion—"

They stayed at the Plaza. More newspaper men cornered him in the lobby; while Jean, upstairs in the rose-coloured sitting-room of their suite, watched a thunderstorm over Central Park and answered questions from the female contingent. He was especially pleased when they wrote unanimously that he looked about forty years old and would have made a fine traffic policeman. But some of the headlines, that evening and next day, jolted his eyes like a bright light flashed into a dark room.

New York 'World,' May 28th:
> SHERLOCK'S HERE; EXPECTS LYNCHING OF 'WILD WOMEN.'

New York 'Mail':
> LYNCHING IS CONAN DOYLE'S SUFF REMEDY.

New York 'American':
> CONAN DOYLE SAYS: LET THE MILITANTS DIE OF STARVATION.

"I never said that!" he thundered a horrified protest to Jean.

"But, darling. It did seem to me you said something very like it."

"I said I was 'afraid' they would be lynched. The 'Journal' has me saying I would lead a lynching party and hang them with my own hands!"

He was deeply worried. He, with so punctilious a code that he would not even say damn in the presence of a woman, pictured as stringing up suffragettes to lamp-posts in Regent Street? And it could not now be corrected.

But it was corrected. The same newspapermen, camping on his trail for every moment except when Warden Clancy shut him up in a cell at Sing Sing, printed what he said in reply; and that was that. Only one formal invitation, received by Marconi message in mid-Atlantic, would he accept: a luncheon of the Pilgrims' Society, of which he had been one of the original members in London. Joseph H. Choate, former Ambassador to Great Britain introduced him as the best-known living Englishman and he spoke on Anglo-American relations.

Otherwise—"Everybody in this city seems determined to show us about!"—the week whirled past dizzily. The new dance was the tango; Broadway already prided itself on its lights; they saw John Drew and Miss Ethel Barrymore in *A Scrap of Paper*. In the seventh tier of the old Tombs he was introduced to an English prisoner calling himself Sir John Grey, better known to the police as Paper-Collar Joe.

"Sir Arthur," wrote the 'Evening Sun,' "was interested in Charles Becker. He knew all about Gyp the Blood, Lefty Louie, and the other gunmen."

Crack went the clean noise of a base-hit, in the greatest game of all. Baseball fascinated him as he watched Shawkey pitch for Connie Mack's unrivalled Athletics: unrivalled, though that same year they lost four straight to the Boston Braves in the World Series. The spectacular side of it caught the visitor from the first.

In Canada, a little later, he seized a chance to step up to the plate himself. The pitcher, thinking he would hold out his bat for a kind of unintentional bunt, let him have one in the groove. He, in turn, imagined he was hitting a full-toss at cricket. Opening his shoulders, he connected solidly and slammed a drive between first and second, nearly murdering a photographer who had crept out towards pitcher's box.

In New York, at the last of their week:

DOYLES IN FROLIC AT CONEY ISLAND: New York 'Sun,' June 1st.

'Evening World': LADY DOYLE FINDS CONEY ISLAND FASCINATING, BUT SHERLOCK FAILS TO SOLVE HOT DOG MYSTERY.

The fantasia of coloured light against a night-sky, the side-show barkers, the roar of a diving roller-coaster, seemed to these two the most enjoyable part of the week. Their party (about twenty in all) went out across the moonlit sea to Steeplechase Park at the end of the pier. At Luna Park, where the crowd shrieked its loudest, he hastened to try the shoot-the-chutes, and the Whip, and the Crazy Village.

"It was lovely!" said Jean, removing her motoring-veil and dust-coat at the Plaza when (with more reporters) they returned early in the morning. But there was one incident nearly lost in all that newsprint. As he stepped through the gate of Luna Park, the manager had a band stationed nearby and gave the signal to strike up a certain tune. This need not interest us; it was good showmanship. But the spontaneous behaviour of the crowd is a different thing.

They knew the creator of Sherlock Holmes was to be there. They knew the tune had words different from the familiar ones. And everyone within earshot stood silent, at attention, to hear *God Save the King*. There they remained at attention until the various guests had taken their seats at their own table.

Before the visitors left for Montreal, the press made him intimate ("he did not actually *say* it," admitted the conscientious 'Sun' on June 2nd) that he would bring Holmes to New York and let the detective live in Washington Square. "He certainly does like this town," observed the 'Journal'; and he certainly did.

Then began the fascination of the Canadian tour. In their private Pullman car, a self-contained unit of living-room, bedroom, and dining-room, they travelled nearly three thousand miles between Montreal and Jasper Park on the border of British Columbia. From Lake George to the Richeliu River, where the Iroquois scalping-parties used to creep, he kept remembering the stealth of Stevenson's eerie lines:

> There fell a war in a woody place,
>   Lay far beyond the sea,
> A war of the march in the mirk midnight,
>   And the shot from behind the tree . . .

Old visions out of *The Refugees* faded in the long journey from Ottawa to Winnipeg and Edmonton.

"I've done nothing else but talk ever since I landed in Canada," he told his audience in a speech at Edmonton, "and there's little I can tell you about England that you don't already know. The real danger is impending war; and, when we see Germany levying a huge tax without giving any reasons, we have to levy a tax on ourselves. The difference is that they are borrowing their money, and we're not."

Beyond Edmonton, towards the far edge of Alberta, rose the blue line of the Rocky Mountains. Once upon a time, in imagination, he had shot many a grizzly there with Captain Mayne Reid. There was no question of shooting, now, in the game-preserve of Jasper Park, where they were guests of Colonel Maynard Rogers.

But they went riding—Jean was in her element on horseback—amid endless fir trees below the snow-line. They camped in wigwam-tents and fished in ice-cold lakes. And each and every day, a horseman would come galloping with a cable from Lily Loder-Symonds to assure Jean that all was well with the children.

"We just wandered about," he explained on their way back, "and began to think we were all alone in the world until we met a cinnamon bear. Then our dreams vanished and so did we."

The whole Canadian tour took just under a month. He mulled over the idea of another Canadian novel, and mentioned the matter to the press at Winnipeg. "No, no, it will not be about either Sherlock Holmes or the Northwest Mounted Police, or both together." They were back in England early in July—the fateful July of 1914.

When the boat-train from the *Megantic* reached Waterloo, he could see on the bookstalls copies of the 'Strand's' July number, containing the story *Danger!* To this the editor appended twelve opinions from naval authorities, which the author had seen in proof-sheets, regarding whether or not the situation in *Danger!* might come true.

Seven of the commentators were admirals, mainly retired. Most of these regarded the danger very lightly, pointing out that the British Isles could not be hurt by so few submarines and envisaging any such attempt as a raid by a few daring men.

"I am compelled to say," wrote Admiral Sir Compton Domville, K.C.B., "that I think it most improbable, and more like one of Jules Verne's stories than any other author I know."

"The British public," said Admiral C. C. Penrose Fitzgerald, "will not recognize the extreme improbability of the technicalities with which he deals. I do not myself think that any civilized nation will torpedo unarmed and defenceless merchant ships."

"No nation would permit it," agreed Admiral William Hannam Henderson, going on to declare that any submarine-commander who tried this would be court-martialed and shot by his own people.

Commander Jane, while agreeing that super-submarines like those in the story might exist in a few years' time, thought that the best way to stop submarine-attack would be to hang any captain and crew who fell into British hands.

"Terror must be met by Terror," he wrote in an imaginary Admiralty Order. We can retaliate! Hang a few of them, *pour encourager les autres,* and they'll be intimidated; they won't try it again!

So ran the arguments.

But we who read such arguments must not, for our soul's sake, think we can criticize these gentlemen for being wrong. Who could have foreseen the German mind? How, at the outset of the war, could the Admiralty have prevented it? Weren't we saying and thinking far less sensible things just twenty-five years later? The obvious is obvious only when it has happened, as Dr. Watson so often discovered. Nothing is disturbed, not even an ornament on a mantelpiece, until the house is rocked; and in July, all unperceived, from what seemed only a little affair in the Balkans, the great tempest began to blow.

Immediately after his return, Conan Doyle again fought for the innocence of Oscar Slater—the case of the old lady battered to death in the Glasgow flat—because of partial new revelations in a Government White Paper published on June 27th, very shortly before his return.

Detective-Lieutenant John Thomson Trench, of the Glasgow police, had been one of the officers who investigated Miss Gilchrist's murder. For more than five years he had been badly worried about the Slater case. Yet he could not, without violating his official duty, speak publicly of the reasons for his belief in Slater's innocence.

In March, 1914, Lieutenant Trench took his worries to Mr. David Cook, a Glasgow solicitor. Speaking under what he believed was a promise of immunity from the Secretary for Scotland, Lieutenant Trench made some explosive revelations.

He testified that, for whatever reason, there had been a suppression of evidence which might well have caused Slater's acquittal at the trial. Part of his evidence related to Helen Lambie, the servant-girl.

If we recall the scene of the murder—Helen Lambie hurrying back from her errand, Arthur Adams pulling at the jangling doorbell—we shall recall how these two came face to face with the murderer in the lighted hall. *Helen,* said Lieutenant Trench, *had recognized the man in the flat, and had admitted it that same night to one of Miss Gilchrist's female relatives.*

The female relative in question was Miss Margaret Birrell, then living in Blythswood Drive. Lieutenant Trench begged to submit Miss Birrell's statement. Part of the document:

I can never forget the night of the murder. Miss Gilchrist's servant, Helen Lambie, came to my door about 7:15. . . . On the door being opened, she rushed into the house and exclaimed:

"Oh, Miss Birrell, Miss Birrell, Miss Gilchrist has been murdered; she is lying dead in the dining room; and, oh, Miss Birrell, I saw who did it."

I replied, "My God, Nellie, this is awful. Who was it; do you know him?"

She replied, "Oh, Miss Birrell, I think it was A.B. I am sure that it was A.B."

I said to her, "My God, Nellie, don't say that."

'A.B.' like A.N. Other or John Doe, covered a real name in the subsequent report. This and four other questions raised by Lieutenant Trench were so serious a matter that an inquiry had to be ordered. Though Helen Lambie and Miss Birrell denied having made such remarks, Trench was able to prove suppression of evidence vital to Oscar Slater.

But they held the inquiry in secret; the prisoner was not represented or the witnesses on oath; asterisks appeared at interesting places.

"I am satisfied," said the Secretary for Scotland, "that no case is established that would justify me in advising any interference with the sentence." That was on June 17th, 1914. Ten days later, as though to underline his judgment, appeared the Government White Paper with the results of the secret inquiry.

Conan Doyle, already believing in Slater's innocence, from that moment on became a never-ceasing attacker. For sixteen years, beginning with his booklet in 1912, he continued his fight for the convict in Peterhead prison. Both men's hair had grown grey before they stood in the same court-room to hear the sentence revoked at last. It was the old question and reply:

"What do you want?"

"Justice, that's all! Justice!"

At the moment he was fifty-five years old: a little heavier in bulk, his hair and moustache not much tinged with grey, the blue-grey eyes ever more kindly in the big good-humoured face. That Herculean strength remained unimpaired; he could still raise a service rifle by the muzzle in each hand to shoulder height. And still he had found no religious philosophy.

"Even granting that Spiritualism is true," he had written a year before, "it advances us but a little way. And yet that little way does solve the problem of immediate question—does death end all?"

At some time between 1905 and 1913 (the exact date we do not know, because he never confided it to his son) he had broken through one of the strongest barriers of doubt. This was his feeling against the smallness, the trifling quality, of so much psychic phenomena. Would discarnate intelligences trouble themselves with such footling things as tables or moving lights?

But this, it suddenly occurred to him, was a purely romantic demand. It was the demand of dignity, which had nothing to do with religious thought. It was the demand for great manifestations, required by savage tribes. Most people, from childhood, have an inborn notion that true portents must write in lightnings from Sinai, or smite Sennacherib's army, or do other things which if persisted in would only upset the order of the universe.

"Am I judging this matter by its possible meaning," you might ask, "or am I judging it by its size?" You did not judge the importance of the message by the ring of the telephone, or the identity of the visitor by the tap at the door. If something tapped, if something plucked at the sleeve—very faintly and weakly—it might be calling attention. It might need to be heard.

But proof of this? He had found none; none at all!

At Windlesham, that summer, there was much rejoicing and entertaining.

"We hope to be able to visit you, old boy," wrote Innes, now the father of a two-year-old son named John. Innes remained very chirpy in what he called his stolid, steady-going way. "And *was* America the same as we left it twenty years ago? How do you like the fine weather?"

The children at Windlesham, five-year-old Denis and four-year-old Adrian with their smaller sister Jean, pounced on the toy trains brought back from abroad. Kingsley, tall and smiling, set up a network of toy tracks. Connie and Willie Hornung, with their son Oscar—he was a little younger than Kingsley—drove over from West Grinstead Park.

To Conan Doyle's children, afterwards, some of their most vivid fragmentary memories remained in images from days before the cataclysm. There would be a formal dinner at Windlesham, with a murmur of voices rising from the long dining-room off the billiard-room. The two boys, after they were supposed to be in bed and asleep, would get up and creep part way down the staircase on whose wall hung illustrations from *Sherlock Holmes* and *The Lost World*. They would look over the banisters through the open door of the dining-room, remembering best the pink-shaded lamps on white shirt-fronts and shimmering gowns.

Lord This or Sir Somebody That conveyed little; but there would be soldiers, explorers, not to mention the less interesting statesmen and writers, whose talk would be wildly fascinating if only it could be understood.

There was the familiar table, in which their father took such pride. Opposite the fireplace, between two basket-hilt swords, hung the painting of Sir Nigel's marriage, which was said to be their father and their mother. A laugh over the buzz of conversation, the flash of a jewel, a sense of something exciting and tremendous; memory held no more.

On July 23rd, 1914, the Austro-Hungarian Empire delivered its sudden ultimatum to Serbia.

"It would be a good thing," Count Berchtold had said to the Austrian Commander-in-Chief a fortnight earlier, "if you and the War Minister would go on leave for a time, in order to preserve the appearance that nothing is happening."

All that had been built and polished was now ready. Small Serbia was the excuse. Though Serbia had made humble reply to the Austrian ultimatum, Count Berchtold said it was not satisfactory. On July 28th the aged Emperor Franz-Josef was persuaded to sign a declaration of war; one day later, Austrian monitors on the Danube opened fire against Belgrade.

Germany stood behind Austria. Russia must stand behind Serbia or back down to Germany. If Russia backed down altogether, well and good. For Russia was bound by treaty to join France if either were attacked by Germany; and France was the German warlords' true objective. If Russia showed fight, the Austrian Army and a few German divisions could hold Russia helpless in the East.

Meanwhile—westwards—irresistible Germany would fling two million men through Belgium and crush France within six weeks.

Russia showed no disposition to back down. Russia was mobilizing against Austria. Germany expressed indignation at this unfriendliness. Nicholas the Second, Czar of all the Russias, genuinely sought for peace. The Kaiser as usual blew hot, blew cold; the ornaments were rocking on the mantelpiece; he was not so sure, now, he wanted a real war with blood in it. Czar and Kaiser exchanged friendly telegrams, in English, signed Nicky and Willy. But the men in the spiked helmets had gained control.

As the clamour grew louder and louder in England:

"What's happening?" asked the bewildered man in the pub, who had been concentrating on Irish troubles. "It's no concern of ours, is it?"

On August 1st Germany declared war on Russia. To

France, allied with Russia by treaty, the German Ambassador addressed a keep-out demand so barbed with humiliation that all of it did not need to be communicated. France must not be allowed to negotiate: the Teuton Invincibles, after a night declaration of war on August 3rd, crashed into Luxemburg and Belgium next morning.

Ms. Asquith and Sir Edward Grey, who during this turmoil had done their best for peace, knew what stand had to be taken. Great Britain's ultimatum to Germany was to expire at eleven o'clock on the night of August 4th.

Conan Doyle, at Windlesham, had watched the past week with the feeling of one who stands in the middle of a railway track and watches the hypnotic eye of the locomotive. On August 4th, a hot day when the ultimatum had hours to expire, he received a note from the plumber in the village of Crowborough.

"There is a feeling in Crowborough," Mr. Goldsmith solemnly informed him, "that something should be done."

He laughed; it was a relief to laugh. And yet, after all, Mr. Goldsmith was quite right. Crowborough represented a thousand villages whose concerted effort could mean much. Suppose there were to be organized a body of Civilian Reserves, men up to sixty who could handle a rifle, to free the Territorials for active service and to defend the nation in case of invasion? That evening, when summer dusk had deepened into night, he was organizing the first Volunteer Reserve company in England.

In London, at the same time, a holiday crowd waited. Some were joyous; all were uplifted. Outside Buckingham Palace, along the Mall under the tall pale lamps, they gathered in their multitudes and sang "God Save the King." Over that song rose the first quivering gong-note of Big Ben striking eleven.

They were a great people. A quarter of a century afterwards they were to be greater still. But they were young in heart for the last time.

XX

CHAOS:

But the Groping Ended

When he wrote about those four years afterwards, or even at the time, he wanted to set down any possible pleasant memory. It offset, if only a little, the memory of the long days and the pain.

He liked to think of Private Sir Arthur Conan Doyle, number 184343, 4th Volunteer Battalion Royal Sussex. His Crowborough company was the first of two hundred thousand men, the prototype of the modern Home Guard. In the initial week of the war he showered the country with leaflets, and other villages mustered their companies.

At the end of a fortnight the War Office ordered him to abandon his project. But a committee under Lord Desborough, of which he became a member, recreated it and gave Crowborough company the certificate of being first. He liked to remember sleeping in a bell-tent on the Downs, with nothing to worry about except polished buttons and a clean rifle. "Old Bill," he later called himself; and, "the very last line of defence."

He liked to remember the one brief outing he had, in the summer of 1915, when he took Jean and the children for a day's drive. But all this time, at the back of his mind, horror dwelt with him. As he walked in the rose-garden before breakfast, he heard a certain sound.

"It is very faint and very far, and yet with a deep

throb in it," he wrote. "There it is again, rising and falling."

It was a hundred and twenty miles away, perceptible in the early-morning hush of sun and clear sky, the grass still wet from dew. "For a week now, ever since the wind has been in that quarter, we have heard it." It was the sound of the guns in Flanders.

Since the early months of the war, nearly a year ago, the first hollow feeling of disaster had scarcely faded. From August 8th to the middle of September, '14, the best troops of seven warring nations had shocked together in the open like a murderous football match. Joffre of France, with a million and three hundred thousand men, attacked the invaders along every border instead of standing at defence.

French masses, crazy with patriotism and hate, in blue coats and red breeches, charged shouting with the bayonet against the drup-drup-drup of machine-guns. (Had there never been a Boer War?) Artillery-power deadened the mind. More men were killed or wounded in that one month than in any whole year of the war.

In England patriotic fervour remained undimmed. No newspaper-correspondents were permitted for the first six months. But there was sensing, feeling, all topsy-turvydom, as the communiqués trickled in.

"I chafe at not having anything definite to do," Conan Doyle wrote to the Ma'am, who felt the frailty of her seventy-six years. "I live only for the newspapers. Malcolm"—Captain Malcolm Leckie of the Royal Army Medical Corps, Jean's favourite brother,—"Malcolm is in the firing-line. I expect they will want Kingsley soon. I have thoughts of trying for a commission in the New Army, though Innes and others are against it. It is very hard to do nothing."

Then:

"Londoners," he afterwards wrote in the 'British Weekly,' "will never forget that terrible week, August 24th-30th, which began with the news that Namur had fallen and that the British Army was heavily engaged."

It was Mons, with the grey German masses coming on like Dervishes at Omdurman. We have another picture: giant Kitchener, not yet wearing his famous uniform, clutching in one hand a bowler hat and a telegram, his face as though it had been punched with a fist, as he told of the retreat from Mons.

A fortnight before this, Conan Doyle wrote to the War Office and tried to get to the front. He was too long out of practice as a doctor, he admitted; he was not a young man; but couldn't he help with the wounded on the battlefield? The War Office courteously refused, in a letter dated August 21st; and he searched for something else.

Malcolm Leckie was the first of the family to be killed.

He was mortally wounded at Mons, but insisted on continuing his doctor's duties until he died four days later. Jean and her husband heard nothing of him— only that he was missing—until late in December they learned of his posthumous D.S.O.

Meanwhile, there was the Marne. The Ma'am afterwards cried when she heard how her beloved French had turned in their retreat and fought the Teuton Invincibles to a standstill. It was not quite as simple as that; but the French kept their heads, the Germans lost theirs. They lost their gamble to crush the French Army; they hesitated, retreated, and then Von Kluck drove for the Channel Ports.

Kingsley joined the Royal Army Medical Corps at the beginning of September.

"One of his pals at St. Mary's," wrote 'London Opinion' on October 3rd, "received a letter from him the other day, which made highly entertaining reading."

Kingsley loathed the idea of war. Long ago, in a letter to his father, he had said that his first experience in a dissecting-room turned him up. But, when he thought it over, he felt he could not in decency keep out.

"I'd rather not have a commission," said Kingsley. "A ranker will be good enough." And he went away, like the other young men; and into October the endless grey Dervishes, reinforced with fourteen fresh divisions, advanced under their paralyzing artillery fire to take Dunkirk, Calais, and Boulogne.

Kingsley's father, refused active service, found that the Government had plans for him in the way of lecturing and writing. But this was not enough. The real extent of his labours he created for himself.

At daybreak on September 22nd, in a calmer sea after gales, the submarine U-9 sighted three British cruisers on patrol in the Broad Fourteens. The cruisers were *Aboukir, Hogue,* and *Cressy,* old ships whose destroyer-escort had been kept back by bad weather. At the impact of U-9's first torpedo, *Aboukir* heeled over to starboard like a tin kettle. *Hogue* and *Cressy,* steaming up to rescue, made dead-flat targets; all three sank, with a loss of fourteen hundred men.

"If," cried a bewildered and angry public, "submarines can do that—?"

But this, to the author of *Danger!* was not the point. He had already some idea of what submarines might do. But what about the poor devils who choked and drowned when a warship went down?

A modern warship carried few boats because boats were inflammable and smashed to matchwood when you went into action. But you did not go into action against a torpedo or a floating mine: you only drowned. From stricken *Aboukir* the seamen threw overboard anything, even empty petrol-tins, to which they could cling and keep afloat.

"Is it really impossible," Conan Doyle wrote to the 'Daily Mail,' beginning a campaign in several other papers as well, "to devise something—if it were only an inflatable rubber belt—that they may have a chance in the water? Now that their consorts are forbidden to stand by," i.e., rescue-ships as marks for torpedoes, "the question becomes an even more pressing one."

Within a week there was a rush order for a quarter of a million inflatable rubber collars, each weighing three ounces, which the seaman could carry in his pocket and blow up for himself. And these were supplied to the fleet.

But this was not enough. In cold weather or heavy seas, such a life-saving device might only prolong agony. To Conan Doyle this necessity grew urgent when in bright moonlight, with wind and sea rising on the last night of December, the battleship *Formidable* was torpedoed in the Channel.

His solution to the problem?

It was the use of inflatable rubber boats. The full value of the inflatable rubber boat for saving lives has been demonstrated only in World War II. You will find his letter suggesting them in the 'Daily Chronicle' for January 2nd, 1915.

To him it was the lives of the men which counted. "We can spare and replace the ships. We cannot spare the men." "Ah, but can't we?" might have been the reply. "We propose to spare them until somebody is exhausted."

For, with 1915, began the long butchery in trenches. The All-Highest's drive for the Channel Ports had been stopped and held, leaving Britain in a mood of shaky optimism. Now nobody could move. Across France, in a crooked semi-circle from the North Sea to the Alps, ran a line of trenches whose flank could not be turned at either end. How could either side pierce it, except by frontal attack? Follow the names, down the length of that crooked curve: Ypres, Arras, the Somme, Soissons, Verdun: for nearly four years the line swayed only a matter of miles, even yards.

And, from the beginning, Death reserved no favours for the Western Front. In the East the armies of Czarist Russia thrust so deeply into East Prussia that the alarmed Germans withdrew two Army Corps from France and Belgium; it may well, as Conan Doyle wrote, have decided the battle of the Marne. The names of Tannenberg and the Masurian Lakes were smeared in Russian blood. Before the end of '14, Turkey had joined the Central Powers against the Allies.

Thus, early in '15, Great Britain tried to break a Western Front deadlock by turning the only possible flank. If the Straits of the Dardanelles could be forced by a combined sea-land operation, they might strike up through the underside of Europe and aid Russia by attacking the enemy from the other side. Warships butted into narrow waters against the fire of the Turkish forts.

Or look again—so it seemed to the man at Windlesham—only at the British on the other side of the Channel.

"And so, after midnight, to bed," he wrote in early summer. "The window of my bedroom is open. As I take a last look at the sky I hear far off the same dull throbbing roar with which the day began."

It was the second battle of Ypres, long-drawn-out, spattered with the agony of poison-gas.

Poison-gas added sickness to the newly disclosed shortage of British munitions, which was said to be critical. There were Whitehall rumblings and a Coalition

Government. But Ypres had worse lessons, if not new ones.

"Such attacks as that on May 9th," Conan Doye wrote in July, "where several brigades lost nearly half their numbers in attempting to rush over the 300 yards which separated us from the German trenches, makes it clear that unprotected troops cannot pass over a zone swept by machine-guns. You must either abandon such attacks or you must find artificial protection for the men."

To the War Office he urged some form of body-armour which would give the troops at least some protection for two vital spots: the head and the heart.

"The head," he wrote in the 'Times' on July 27th, "should be protected by a helmet such as the French have now evolved. The heart could be covered by a curved plate of highly tempered steel."

It was only the beginning of his experiments; the idea had come from stories of Ned Kelly the bushranger, moving about ghostlike in armour while the law fired in vain. The Ministry of Munitions agreed in principle, saying that there might be a secret they would confide in him presently.

At the moment he was working on a history of the British campaign in France and Flanders, in addition to the speeches and articles which the Government asked of him. His sources of information for that history were the actual commanding generals, who supplied him with every detail he wanted.

As the mass of detail accumulated in his study (his secretary was now Major Wood at the front, not many miles from Lieutenant-Colonel Innes Doyle), even that nook of the country turned khaki-brown with troops. In Crowborough, where they billeted a regiment of Terri-torials, Jean had opened a home for Belgian refugees. He was shortly to open a wing of Windlesham as a club for Canadians; and, in addition, a hundred Canadian officers dined with him every Saturday night.

By night the east coast lay dark, a blackness spreading inland. Over England, in a shape so slow-moving as to seem motionless, had appeared the six-hundred-foot zeppelin with its *whirr* like a gas-bag rattlesnake.

"Half a dozen able-bodied suffragettes," he snarled, "would do more damage." And, more seriously, in *A Policy of Murder:* "The policy is idiotic from a military point of view; one could conceive nothing which would stimulate and harden national resistance more surely."

If he hated the enemy for the cool, reasoned, smiling use of terror methods, he still would not see the enemy out of perspective. His most characteristic word was in *The Great German Plot,* where he addressed those who had been his friends in Prince Henry's motor-car race in 1911:

"Good luck to you, Count Carmer, and bad luck to your regiment! To you also, little Captain Türck, *Fregattenkapitän am Dienst,* the best of luck, and ill betide your cruiser!"

The outburst of spy-mania he refused to join. He championed a group of elderly foreign waiters, without money and in trouble, and was accused of being pro-German for doing it. At one of his war lectures in London, where Lord Haldane introduced him, it enraged him when Haldane was greeted with a few cries of "Traitor!" because of supposed German sympathies; and he never ceased paying tribute to the builder of the Territorial Army. "Fair play!" he kept insisting, though nobody knew better than Conan Doyle what a maker of German war policy would think of this.

"War is not a big game, my British friends," he had made Captain Sirius say in *Danger!* "It is a desperate business to gain the upper hand, and one must use one's brain in order to find the weak spot of one's enemy. Do not blame me if I have found yours."

No, you did not blame it. You only wanted to smash its sneering face. And yet:

"Consider," he wrote in the third chapter of his history, "that wonderful panorama of victory which is known all over the Fatherland as *'Die Grosse Zeit.'* " And dispassionately he narrated the German triumphs of 1914. "I do not know where in history such a succession of victories is to be found."

He wrote this in the summer of '15, and continued his history while the Allies met reverse after reverse. Late in September the first of Kitchener's New Army were thrown into the Battle of Loos. Papa Joffre directed it. Thirty British and French divisions at Loos, forty French divisions in Champagne, surged forward against the grey spike-helmets; in the first week of the battle they lost three hundred thousand men.

"This can't be true," muttered even those who knew.

It was not real. It was not their world. They had no vision of men blown into quite so many pieces, no feeling of loss which became quite so shocking in the throat. "Where are our dead?" they began to ask. "Where are our dead?"

One mother who had lost a son tried to express it. "He was there," she wrote, "and then a shell exploded. And there was nothing left of him, nothing even that they could bury."

At the end of August the 'International Psychic Gazette' had addressed to a number of eminent men and women the question, "What would you say in consolation to those in grief? How would you help?" There were more than fifty responses. Conan Doyle's reply was the briefest of all.

"I fear I can say nothing worth saying. Time only is the healer."

Italy had entered the war. Heavy firing swept the Balkans. At the black end of the year the whole British expedition failed in the Dardanelles. It failed only through lack of support, but it failed amid disease and slaughter. When the last evacuation-ship glided away, it left only the flames of burning stores lighting up a deserted beach at Gallipoli.

"I fear I can say nothing worth saying. Time only is the healer."

When that curt remark was published in the 'Psychic Gazette' for October, 1915, it was not because he lacked in sympathy for the bereaved. It was because he had too much sympathy, and would not utter words of false hope. We must look at another line of thought which, concurrently with all his other activities, had occupied him since the beginning of the war.

As one who had been expecting it, he found no surprise in the tactics by which it was waged. The immense artillery quickly moved and manoeuvered by railway, the guns concealed against balloon reconnaissance, the necessity for cover, he had predicted at the time of the Boer War. Aircraft, he correctly saw in 1913, were formidable "as a means of acquiring information," but not yet "sufficiently formidable to alter the whole conditions of a campaign." On the submarine we need not dwell.

But the immensity of the struggle? Half the world in arms, and the other half joining in to destroy? Carried a few steps further, now or in the future, and it would mean the extinction of the human race.

Was there, or wasn't there, a portent in this?

Their own group at Windlesham formed a microcosm of what was happening everywhere. First Malcolm

Leckie went away; and Jean, who loved him so much, was left for nearly five months without news before they heard of his death. "God be with you," Kingsley had written during that time; "the suspense must be terrible."

Lily Loder-Symonds, who lived at Windlesham and was Jean's closest friend, had three brothers killed in the Ypres Salient. A fourth brother had been wounded and taken prisoner. Oscar Hornung, Connie and Willie's only son, was killed there not long afterwards. So was Alec Forbes, Conan Doyle's nephew by marriage.

And Lottie, Lottie the favourite sister, who had gone out to India for a brief visit sixteen years ago?

Lottie, with her daughter Claire, was now staying with the Ma'am in Yorkshire. She hoped to go out soon with the French Red Cross. A brief, restrained note informed her brother that her husband, Major Leslie Oldham of the Royal Engineers, had been killed during his first day in the trenches.

These things, during 1915, turned Conan Doyle's heart sick. All those deaths had taken place when he wrote, "Time only is the healer"; but he could say nothing else. Those of whom he was proudest, Kingsley and Innes, remained as yet unscathed. Kingsley, back from Egypt, had won a commission and was doing a bombing-course—grenade-bombing—at Lyndhurst before leaving for the Western Front.

"It is a ripping place," Kingsley wrote on February 5th, 1916, "and wonderful conditions."

And Colonel Innes Doyle, at the front where his organizing talents were being recognized, was always Innes. If you look for the original of Lord John Roxton, you will not have to look far.

"The unusual sequence of fine days," Innes wrote on February 11th, after heavy bombardment, "has livened things up a good bit in these parts. It made me think a bit." Then, apologetically: "If anything were to happen to me. . . ."

He explained his arrangements for his wife and small son, who were then living at Windlesham in his brother's care. Then, hastily, he dismissed the matter to tell how interesting were conditions out there. Only a short time before Innes wrote that letter, Jean Conan Doyle had suffered another heavy blow. Lily Loder-Symonds died after a short illness.

The nightmare spread wider wings; the guns opened against Verdun. Conan Doyle, weighing up the matter, had already come to certain conclusions.

For a very long time before her death, Lily Loder-Symonds had developed the power of automatic writing. "That is to say," he explained in a subsequent speech, "some power seemed to take possession of her arm and write things which purported to come from the dead."

This he distrusted, watching it for weeks. "Automatic writing," he wrote, "should always be regarded with suspicion, for it is so easy to deceive oneself. How can you tell that she is not unconsciously dramatizing strands of her own personality?"

Lily Loder-Symonds, a tall fair-haired woman of sensitive temperament, had lost three brothers, and a friend in Malcolm Leckie. These messages purported to come from one or the other of these four young men. Some proved to be accurate. "The communications were full of military details which the girl did not know. One of the brothers said he had met a Belgian, giving the name, and we found that he had done so." On the other hand, many of the messages were inaccurate. He was impressed; not yet impelled further.

Then something else happened. He himself received a message. "I felt at last no doubt at all."

Now we have noted his intense distaste for speaking

or writing in public of anything too intimate or personal. What the message was he did not say in his books, or in the speech from which we have quoted. He told it only at home, and even there not completely.

It was a message from Malcolm Leckie. It was a reminiscence or reminder so intimately personal that it could have been known to no person in the world except to Malcolm Leckie and himself. In it he found the objective proof which he had been seeking for nearly thirty years.

In *The New Revelation*, written two years later, he said of this and of past phenomena:

"In the presence of an agonized world, hearing every day of the deaths of the flower of our race in the first promise of their unfulfilled youth, seeing around one the wives and mothers who had no clear conception whither their loved one had gone to, I seemed suddenly to see that this subject with which I had so long dallied was not merely a study of force outside the rules of science, but that it was something tremendous, a breaking down of the walls between two worlds, a direct undeniable message from beyond, a call of hope and of guidance to the human race at the time of its deepest affliction. . . .

"The telephone bell is in itself a very childish affair, but it may be the signal for a very vital message. It seemed that all these phenomena, large and small, had been the telephone bells which, senseless in themselves, had signalled to the human race: 'Rouse yourselves! Stand by! Be at attention! Here are signs for you. They will lead up to the message which God wishes to send.' "

His conversion to a belief in communication with the dead may be placed between early September, 1915 (reply to 'Psychic Gazette') and late January, 1916 (death of Lily Loder-Symonds). Thenceforward he set out to discover the religious significance of this revelation.

"The objective side ceased to interest; for having made up one's mind, there was an end of the matter. The religious side was clearly of infinitely greater importance." The religious side! The long seeking and now (God grant) the finding!

In his study at Windlesham, towards the left-hand side in the wall facing his desk, was the mantelpiece whose ledge had been turned into a kind of family shrine. There were the photographs, the decorations, of those who had died in battle. On many a night, with curtains drawn lest any chink of light show to zeppelin or aeroplane, he had sat at the desk and made occasional notes in his common-place book.

Here, in the spring of 1916, is one of them.

"The breath of the Spirit can blow through this room tonight as easily as it once did through the upper Chamber in Jerusalem. God did not die two thousand years ago. He is here and now. . . . The only thing that is solid and eternal is the memory of what we have discussed tonight, the bridge of death, the assured continued journey in the world beyond."

He had come to the third great turning-point of his life.

XXI

CRUSADE:

The Last Battle

Now the doors of controversy are opened. And, before the full thunder of the First World War rises and dies away, a word must be said about the latter stage of Conan Doyle's life.

The writer of this biography is not a Spiritualist. Spiritualism is not a subject on which he yet feels qualified to pass an opinion. But the religious views of the biographer, it may be suggested, should not make a farthing's worth of difference to his task. He must try to present, however imperfectly, a living image of the only man in question: what *he* said, what *he* thought, what *he* believed.

Under these circumstances a biographer is barred from making comments about a future life, beyond stating what his protagonist thought about it. But he is not barred from making comments about this life. And it is necessary to consider some of the misconceptions about Arthur Conan Doyle.

Often, even today, we hear Conan Doyle described as a good man gone wrong. He is pictured to us as a man who suffered cruel bereavement, who thereupon lost his emotional balance or his mental grip, and at a moment's notice 'took up' Spiritualism as an elderly spinster might take up a patent-medicine.

"What would Sherlock Holmes have said?" some exclaim.

Well, let us see. Let us study him between the outbreak of the war in 1914 and his public announcement of belief in 1916.

Anybody who has read this record will not need to be convinced that he did not go blindfolded into Spiritualism. He had studied the subject for nearly thirty years before coming to a judgment. Cruel bereavement he certainly had suffered, though not the greatest bereavement; and deeply he felt the agony of a world in chaos. The question, therefore, is: Did the war affect his judgment? Did it turn him into a moonstruck visionary, credulous and incapable of seeing clearly?

Let us apply the test of practical life. This same war (in which the men died) made passions boil, warped eyesight, blinded judgment, brought the country face to face with new perils and weapons untried by experience. So we can examine Conan Doyle's record as we might examine the record of a Cabinet Minister, and note what he said then.

Of the German Army, at a time when his kinsmen were being slaughtered: "Consider that wonderful panorama of victory which is known all over the Fatherland as *'Die Grosse Zeit.'* " Of soldiers: "The head should be protected by a helmet such as the French have now evolved." Of sailors: "Is it really impossible to devise something—if it were only an inflatible rubber belt— that they may have a chance in the water?" Of air-raids: "One could conceive nothing which would stimulate and harden national resistance more surely."

Do you detect any sign of emotional instability? Is this Tam o' Bedlam chasing wish-fulfilments through a fog? Was the man who had foreseen the weapons knocked endways by their effect?

This is what we must remember when somebody bursts out with, "Oh, he was credulous." Was he? By all the wordly evidence in that year 1916, his judgment had never been keener or his faculties more alert. The psychic experience was an intimate personal reminder of whose authenticity only its recipient could judge. He may have been right about Spiritualism. He may have been wrong about Spiritualism. But nobody can say he was far wrong about anything else.

Therefore, regarding the psychic, let us agree or disagree; but keep a sense of proportion. In this man there was something a little larger than life: some quality beyond chivalry, some flash that escapes analysis. You can sense it. You can almost touch it. Yet it cannot be spun into words by one who (like the biographer) is so much of the earth earthy.

In any event, the story goes on. Before any statement of what he believed and why he believed it, we find him recently returned from a visit to the war-fronts. At Windlesham, in July of 1916, it needed no special hush or eddying air-currents to hear the rumble of the bombardment heralding the Battle of the Somme.

He had already seen something of what lay beyond the Channel, where the Foreign Office sent him on a tour of inspection. Wearing one of the soup-plate shrapnel-helmets, under a fiery sun, he stumbled and slipped through the clay of communication-trenches to the British front-line. It was during a lull, except for a racket of guns. He found little in the front-line except a smell of corpses inside the rusty wire, once or twice a sniper's bullet. Waiting, watchfulness, kept taut a whole area marked by the sausage-shaped balloons.

"Arthur," Innes wrote to Jean on May 28th, "went off this morning to lunch with Sir Douglas Haig. We kept him very busy during his visit, but I think he was interested and he said he slept well here."

Haig, who had succeeded Sir John French as Com-

mander-in-Chief, proved impressive if not very exhilar-
ating. What the visitor remembered best were small
details: crows wheeling over a waste of shell-holes, or
the moment on the Sharpenburg—how it would have
surprised him twenty years ago!—where he lowered his
head to pray. At instructions from the Commander-in-
Chief, Kingsley was allowed to come up the line and
meet him. They walked and talked casually, Kingsley
grinning and brown-faced.

"Going to be a big push soon," Kingsley said; and
explained. The Boer War seemed very distant.

On the Italian front—the Foreign Office wanted him
to write up the Italians, and give them a boost—Italy
was locked against Austria in the same problem of
getting past the machine-guns and the wire. He saw
TRIESTE O MORTO! chalked on the walls all over North
Italy. There were sharp air-attacks. Once a shell-burst
nearly ended him: "Don't tell me Austrian gunners
can't shoot." Much of the time he felt refreshed and
light-hearted, partly because he was in action again and
partly because he felt conscious of a great truth to be
told in the world.

But the old trouble of insomnia devilled him. In a
hotel-room, sunk in half-doze, he seemed to hear the
word, *Piave, Piave, Piave* ringing through his head.
Why Piave? He knew the name only vaguely as a river
far behind the Italian lines. Nevertheless he wrote it
down and showed it to his friends; it was in his mind
when, on his return to Paris, a red-capped military
policeman growled out bad news as he left the train.

"Lord Kitchener, sir. Drowned." And: "Too much
talking in this war."

The red-cap was wrong; no betrayal of secrets killed
the old Field-Marshal on his secret mission to Russia.
The light cruiser *Hampshire*, butting a gale off Mar-

wick Head in the Orkneys, struck a mine and sank within twenty minutes.

But nobody yet knew what had happened. In Paris Conan Doyle, oppressed in heart, met the editor for whom he had been doing his war-sketches: sketches later collected in *A Visit to Three Fronts* and reproduced (though not entirely) in his autobiography. Mr. Robert Donald, editor of the 'Daily Chronicle,' had arranged for both of them to visit the French lines.

"Where are we going?"

"The Argonne Forest. That's as close to Verdun as they'll let us go."

For the French Conan Doyle had even more sympathy than the Ma'am. He did not admire their strategy. But for over four months the enemy had been hurling everything at Verdun, including liquid fire; and they did not pass; and, better than those words about not passing, the French loved Pétain's snap of, "On les aura!" "We'll have 'em!"

The nation was bleeding to death. After seeing Soissons, Conan Doyle wrote perhaps the most savage remark he ever made:

"May God's curse rest upon the arrogant men and the unholy ambitions which let loose this horror upon humanity!"

What he did not write was the tremendous welcome the French gave him. He regarded himself, apologetically, as a comic civilian entitled to wear uniform only because he was a Deputy-Lieutenant of Surrey. The French took a different view.

In the dim Argonne—where shellbursts splintered beeches and oaks like a nightmare of the New Forest or the Adirondacks—they polished up the band instruments. Many persons have heard of the French general's barking question about Sherlock Holmes. The editor of the 'Daily Chronicle' was the only one who has described what led up to it. At St. Menehould, on June 11th, there was an elaborate dinner and a special menu-card whose crest bore a drawing of pipe, revolver, and violin to represent Sherlock Holmes. If such honours were paid to the absent Englishman, General Humbert wanted to be sure about his patriotism. That was why he drew his eyebrows together and shot out the question:

"Sherlock Holmes, est ce qu'il un soldat dans l'armée anglaise?"

"Mais, mon général," stammered the embarrassed visitor, "il est trop vieux pour service." And the general, grunting but still vaguely suspicious, returned to the dinner.

It was among the French that Conan Doyle noticed the wound-badges, later to be called wound-stripes; on his return to England he recommended them to General Sir William Robertson, to whom he had dedicated his first volume of the war-history, and this measure was adopted by the British War Office.

Life had taken its grey grip on England. In the spring of '16, before he left for his visit to the three fronts, his youngest son Adrian nearly died of pneumonia; and he had brought the boy through it not by words of formal encouragement, but by telling him the story and showing him a picture of the knights at Agincourt. In July, to relieve the hammering at Verdun, came the British big push of which he had heard.

It was the Somme, where the British had sixty thousand casualties in the first day. Such football-match-murder deadened the mind, paralyzed the senses. One speck in that multitude was Captain Kingsley Conan Doyle.

Kingsley, though badly wounded with two bullets in

the neck, was expected to recover. In his battalion, the 1st Hampshires, every officer had been killed or wounded on that same first day. Kingsley's father learned that, on ten successive nights before the attack, his son had crawled out into No Man's Land and fixed white crosses to the wire so that gunners would pulverize it where it remained uncut.

It could be argued, and it has been well argued, that this apparently useless Somme battle—in which nearly half a million of the best young men were lost before the November mud-freezing—was a heart-punch to Germany. The Imperial German Army, great as it was, never fought quite so well afterwards. But the consolation?

From the beginning of the Somme Conan Doyle continued his plea for body-armour.

"We have recognized the facts," he wrote, "to the extent of giving the men helmets. It was done slowly, but it was done."

Some form of breastplate or body-shield, he added on August 5th, 1916, would help to stop flying bits of metal. He experimented with his own rifle on various kinds of shields ordered from half a dozen firms. Denis and Adrian, forbidden to come close, would hear the *whing* of the deflected bullet or the thud as it went through.

Meanwhile he had tried to save the life of Roger Casement. Casement, now Sir Roger Casement with a knighthood won for his faithful service to Britain in the tropics, he had met in the old days of the Congo agitation. The erstwhile patriot, his shrunken features ivory-white under the beard, stood in the dock on a self-confessed charge of treason.

It is difficult to sympathize with Casement in anything except his idealism. But he was honest, thoroughly honest, even when he took the pay of Germany and landed in Ireland to stir up rebellion there. Conan Doyle believed—not without reason—that the man was mentally as well as physically ill from his years in the tropics.

"Don't hang him!" urged the champion of lost causes, who hated to see any under-dog strung up. "Sentence him to any form of imprisonment you like. Spare his life. He is not fit to plead."

But to acknowledge the validity of Casement's plea would have been to acknowledge Ireland as a free state at war with Britain. They hanged him at Pentonville; they could do nothing else; and the din of the Somme bombardment grew ever louder.

The autumn of '16 and the beginning of '17 saw not only slaughter, but national peril. If a fictitious character called Captain John Sirius could have seen the country he described in *Danger!* he would have laughed. At long last it was unrestricted submarine warfare, with two hundred U-boats set loose.

Conan Doyle's family drew still more closely together. The Ma'am, at long last feeling lonely and frightened and very old, left Yorkshire to be nearer her son. But she still would not accept his hospitality. Taking a house almost opposite West Grinstead Park, she called it Bowshot Cottage. Kingsley, though weak, was convalescent and talked cheerfully of returning to the front. Mary was voluntarily assisting at Peel House, where troops bound for the front were served with comforts before their departure. Dated October 21st, 1916, there appeared in the psychic magazine 'Light' Conan Doyle's article announcing his belief in communication with the dead.

Pondering his words carefully, he said that in the

face of the evidence for survival there were two courses of thought.

"It is absolute lunacy, or it is a revolution in religious thought," he wrote; "a revolution which gives us an immense consolation when those who are dear to us pass behind the veil."

Religious consolation! A religion! Therein centered his whole approach to the psychic question. Sir William Barrett, a believer in Spiritualism but not one who believed in it as a religion, disagreed with him here; though the scientist endorsed his conclusions as to the reality of the phenomena.

"I am glad of the opportunity which the editor of 'Light' has given me," wrote Sir William Barrett, "of expressing my thanks to Sir Arthur Conan Doyle for the brave and timely article which he has contributed. . . .

"Nearly a quarter of a century ago (to be exact on January 4th, 1893) Sir Arthur—then Dr.—Conan Doyle took the chair at a lecture on 'Psychical Research' delivered by me at the Upper Norwood Literary Society, of which he was president. In the full report of my lecture, which appeared in the local paper, and is before me, Dr. Conan Doyle, in moving a vote of thanks, referred to the deep interest he had maintained for many years in the subject of the lecture, and also to some past experiences of his own."

At Windlesham Jean no longer regarded his psychic studies as uncanny and dangerous. Her brother, her relations, her closest friend had all been swept away. She was sharing his experiences. She believed. And, if he believed:

"I must proclaim it," he said.

So, in 1917, began those psychic lectures which were

to last for the rest of his life. On this subject he had a talk with Jean to which we shall revert presently. His voice as a lecturer, under the bellow of guns, could not as yet reach far. He knew it. And there was so much else to be done.

There were his war-lectures, and above all the history. Each day some officer would come down by car to Windlesham, remain shut up with him in his study while he took notes, and slip away back to London after lunch. Even after the change in Government at the end of '16, with David Lloyd George as Prime Minister, a Germany victorious over Rumania loomed more formidable than ever.

At the Admiralty the terrible graph of merchant-ship sinkings, a red line on blue paper, crept up and up and up. The press discovered a story called *Danger!* There was a shock and shout. One or two writers declared Sir Arthur Conan Doyle must have put the whole thing into the Germans' heads; as though, from German statements, it needed to be put into their heads.

In March of '17 mighty Russia fell. Somebody could laugh again; at a time when her Army weaknesses had been overcome, when she was stronger than at the outbreak of the war, they split Russia from within and presently handed her over to jackals. As a counterbalance—but too late?—the United States entered the war in April.

"God helping her," President Wilson said to Congress, "she can do no other."

In April Conan Doyle had breakfast with the Prime Minister at Downing Street. They were alone, helping themselves to bacon and eggs; the Welshman grey-haired and smiling, tirelessly capable, the Irishman engrossed in explaining the necessity for body-shields.

"They've got to be used!" he insisted.

True, they had the lumbering monster called a tank. The Ministry of Munitions had let him into this closely guarded secret at the time of the Somme battle. But the tanks had not been used as General Swinton intended them to be used. A handful of them, not even enough deeply to impress the Germans, had roamed about in September of '16.

A genius named Winston Churchill—who invented, among other things, the smoke-screen by sea and land —had long ago been developing the tank independently of the Army group who completed it. Mr. Churchill's idea was to use tanks in great numbers, supported by shield-bearing infantry, in a surprise attack all along the line.

"Don't betray your attack by a bombardment," ran the substance of his argument, first in a memorandum of December 3rd, 1915. "Tanks can crush wire. Use great numbers and the element of surprise; you will break through and end the deadlock."

We find Mr. Churchill saying the same thing in a private letter to Conan Doyle, dated October 2nd, 1916, and adding that their two aims should be the torpedo-proof ship and the bullet-proof man. At Downing Street, on that April morning in '17, Mr. Lloyd George showed most excitement about the Russian Revolution.

"The Czarina's general character," he said, "isn't unlike Marie Antoinette's. She'll probably have the same fate as Marie Antoinette. It's like the French Revolution."

"Then," answered Conan Doyle, "it will go on for some years and end in a Napoleon."

Well, both those remarks came true. Few things did Conan Doyle loathe more than those Communist elements who took control of Russia by the end of the year. "He is no Socialist," was one of holy Lenin's sayings, "who will not sacrifice his Fatherland for the triumph of the Social Revolution." The thought is still with us in England.

During 1917 Conan Doyle wrote for the 'Strand' only two articles and one short-story. The articles were, 'Is Sir Oliver Lodge Right? Yes!' and, 'Some Personalia about Mr. Sherlock Holmes,' nearly all of which he later reproduced in his autobiography. But the story—a memorable one—was *His Last Bow*.

We need little jogging of memory to recall how Von Bork, cleverest of the German secret agents, stands with Baron von Herling "beside the stone parapet of the garden walk, with the long, low, heavily gabled house behind them," looking down at the lights of the shipping in the bay. In the story it is nine o'clock on the night of August 2, 1914.

Then, after the departure of Von Herling, comes the Irish-American, with his long limbs and his spitting hatred of Britain, who is Von Bork's own cleverest spy.

He was a tall, gaunt man of sixty, with clear-cut features and a small goatee beard which gave him a general resemblance to the caricatures of Uncle Sam. A half-smoked, sodden cigar hung from the corner of his mouth, and as he sat down he struck a match and relit it.

We know, or guess from the beginning, that he is Sherlock Holmes come out of retirement. It increases the reader's thrill of expectancy as we watch the old master outwit the upstart Von Bork. But the interest of the story, from a biographical point of view, lies elsewhere.

Even without our private knowledge of the author's state of mind, we can feel in the texture of *His Last Bow* that it is more than another adventure of Sherlock Holmes. It was, as the author sub-titled it, an 'epilogue.'

It was to be, really and finally, *His Last Bow*. There is foreboding in it; and true emotion, and, towards Holmes, even a strong touch of affection. In it Conan Doyle at last identified Holmes with himself.

Now it need not be stated, even with a suppressed grin, that he himself did not take cocaine, did not fire revolvers indoors, did not keep cigars in the coal-scuttle. After all, comparatively few people do. He had no brother who 'was' the British Government; and, barring his brief try at the banjo, he scarcely knew one note of music from another.

But there are more personal characteristics than these. His fondness for working in old dressing-gowns, for clay pipes—a relic of the Southsea days when Dublin clays cost only a penny—for compiling scrap-books, for amassing documents, for keeping a magnifying glass on his desk and a pistol in the drawer, form a more presentable domestic picture. Wound among them we find the Holmesian phraseology of his letters, the insistence on an Anglo-American partnership, the religious views of Winwood Reade.

Many of the identifications, of course, were unconscious. Does he insist, like Holmes and Watson, that Holmes is an emotionless calculating-machine? But this is precisely what Holmes is not; there lies the joy.

"If the young lady has a brother or a friend," exclaims Holmes to Mr. James Windibank, "he ought to lay a whip across your shoulders. By Jove! it is not part of my duties to my client, but here's a hunting-crop handy, and I think I shall just treat myself to—"

Down the stairs clatters the panic-stricken Windibank, out of *A Case of Identity*; and Conan Doyle, in real life, would have followed him. We can scarcely dip into the stories anywhere without finding Holmes telling us how unemotional he is, and in the next moment behaving more chivalrously—especially towards women— than Watson himself.

The deliberate identifications with Holmes, at the time of all the endless queries at the top-tide of success in 1892, Conan Doyle slipped into the *Memoirs*. Who could resist some reference to Holmes's early struggling days on his arrival in London? Holmes took rooms in Montague Street; his creator, equally "filling up my too abundant leisure time," took rooms in Montague Place. And the family background?

"My ancestors," says Holmes in *The Greek Interpreter*, "were country squires." So were his creator's. But Holmes had a French grandmother; Conan Doyle's grandmother, Marianna Conan, was of direct French descent. Holmes tells us his grandmother was a sister of Vernet, the French artist; and a large landscape by Vernet, which remains among his collection of paintings today, was given to Conan Doyle in his youth by his uncle Henry Doyle. Thus two sides of his own ancestry met and mingled.

"Art in the blood," observes Sherlock Holmes dryly, "is liable to take the strangest forms." John Doyle and his four sons would have bowed agreement.

There are seven other identifications, but the Sherlockian will have found these for himself. If a full account of the Edalji case could have been published at the time it happened, inquirers need have gone no further. What concerns us here is that emotional story called *His Last Bow*, written at a time of harassment and danger.

Sherlock Holmes, disguised as the Irish-American spy, takes off the mask when he hands Von Bork his little book, *Practical Handbook of Bee-Culture*, and then grips and chloroforms the Prussian. Holmes and Watson, no longer young, sip Imperial Tokay in the book-lined room. Then follows the magnificent scene when Von Bork, bound and writhing, glares at his captor from the sofa.

Von Bork is speaking:

"Then who are you?"

"It is really immaterial who I am, but since the matter seems to interest you, Mr. Von Bork, I may say that this is not my first acquaintance with the members of your family. I have done a good deal of business in Germany in the past, and my name is probably familiar to you."

"I would wish to know it," said the Prussian grimly.

"It was I who brought about the separation between Irene Adler and the late King of Bohemia when your cousin Heinrich was the Imperial Envoy. It was I also who saved from murder, by the Nihilist Klopman, Count von und zu Grafenstein, who was your mother's elder brother. It was I—"

Von Bork sat up in amazement.

"There is only one man," he cried.

And so speaks the world. It is the last thrill, the final drum-beat, the apotheosis of Sherlock Holmes. The whole series should have ended with *His Last Bow,* as the author formally and finally meant it to end. It was identification too. To Sherlock Holmes in disguise he gave the name of 'Altamont'; and the full name of his father, we remember, was Charles Altamont Doyle.

But *His Last Bow*, given in the 'Strand' as 'The War Service of Sherlock Holmes'—had it been inspired by that remark of General Humbert?—was swept out of his mind by the crisis at the end of the black year '17. The long slaughter in the mud at Passchendaele was only partly offset by what happened at Cambrai, when the General Staff of the Tank Corps were at last permitted to have their way.

Nearly five hundred tanks rumbled forward in a surprise attack, supported by infantry and over ground unploughed by shells. They cracked the German trench-system on a front of six miles, blinding the defenders with death or panic, and taking ten thousand prisoners before dusk.

"It is a turning-point in the history of war," Conan Doyle wrote to Innes, now an Adjutant-General. He also wrote a note of congratulation to Major Albert Stern, who first let him into the secret of the tanks, acknowledging that whatever doubts he may have felt were now gone.

But on November 20th, the same day as Cambrai, the Soviet Government ordered their High Command to make peace proposals to Germany. Even before then the Austrians, supported by German divisions, fell on the Italians and rolled them back broken in what seemed endless disaster—until they reached a river called the Piave.

Piave! Conan Doyle, among his large war-maps in the study, remembered the ring of that word 'Piave,' echoing through his head in an Italian hotel eighteen months before. It was curious, he thought; he could lay no claim to prevision. But this too was whirled away. By Christmas Ludendorff ordered the transport of a million German troops from Russia, to be hurled against the Western Front in spring.

These were lean times at Windlesham, where once Lord Northcliffe or Sir Flinders Petrie had sat down to eight-course dinners. In addition to the rationing, Conan Doyle put his family on half the amount of the official rations.

Heavier in the face, his forehead knotted with concentration, he found twenty-four hours a day too little. In addition to his war maps, another map hung in his study; on it were marked the towns where he had

spoken on the subject of the psychic, with a wafer
stuck at each place. His controversies—when the giant
Gothas throbbed over London he had long argued for
air-raid reprisals—went on like his correspondence with
the generals.

Nevertheless, through these haggard days, the twinkle
in his eye remained. He found his only relaxation in
arranging Indian games for the boys—small Lena Jean
called herself Billy and as soon as she could write
signed her notes, 'your loving son'—and he arranged
Indian games with such good effect that Adrian stole
Pop's revolver and fired real bullets round a besieged
wigwam.

Nor did he ever neglect his pride of creation, the
Local Volunteers or original Home Guard, whose ster-
ing military worth he celebrated in verses which were
not actually meant to be too heroic:

> "And discipline? Well! 'Eyes right!' they cried,
>   As we passed the drill-hall door;
> And left it at that—so we marched cockeyed
>   From three to half-past four."

Kingsley, too, seemed safe. Though Kingsley returned for active service, the medical board would not
pass him and he was invalided out in that fateful year
918. Adjutant-General Innes Doyle still wrote cheery
etters—with difficulty. For in the spring of '18 the full
mass of German might went all out to break through,
and very nearly did.

"With our backs to the wall, and believing in the
ustice of our cause. . . ."

Haig stopped that all-out drive against the British,
whereupon Ludendorff turned overpoweringly against
the French and British. It was daze and flash through
the summer, with casualty-lists past the saturation-

point and the Germans again near Paris. One dim flash the exhausted French never forgot: what seemed unending truck-loads of Americans—young, half-trained, crazy-keen as the French had once been—suddenly pouring up the roads towards Château Thierry.

It is an old story, how they all walked with death on the Chemin des Dames in 1918; let it sleep. Not even the Allied High Command or the War Cabinets guessed that Germany was nearing exhaustion after August 8th. It was still only a prayed-for result when, towards the end of September, Conan Doyle visited the Australian sector of the front as guest of Sir Joseph Cook, Naval Minister of the Australian Commonwealth.

Fighting was fluid, trenches gutted and wire smashed. Sitting on a disabled tank, five hundred yards from the battle and amid a gun-racket like slamming doors, he looked down a fir-tree slope like Hindhead and watched an American-Australian attack carry that section of the Hindenburg Line.

"Don't you think," he had asked Innes, as they sat the night before in a quiet, tense little mess-room, "don't you think I am out of the picture at such a moment, talking about such frivolous things?"

"For God's sake keep at it," said his brother. "It's just what they need."

Autumn rains, with the breath of the influenza-epidemic, swirled over them after that breaking of the Hindenburg Line. Much as he liked and admired the Australians, who in type were similar to the Americans, he told a great crowd of them who assembled round him to remember—and it needed to be remembered!—that seventy-two percent of the men and seventy-six percent of the casualties had been Englishmen of England. Aeroplanes buzzed overhead; the rain pelted down.

Was it nearly over? Could it possibly be?

On the night before he left London for the Australian front, Jean had come up to town to see him off. They stayed at the Grosvenor Hotel. These two had been in love for many, many years, and never more so than in the dark days. She was frightened, as always, about his going away; frightened that he wouldn't take care of himself, despite his assurances that he was still a comic civilian.

On the following morning, Kingsley called at the hotel. He knew that Jean would still be there, worried and in tears. Tactfully, he did not want to see her; but he wanted to reassure. He left her a note, with some flowers.

"As for him, I am happy," Kingsley wrote, "for I know what it must mean to him to go there and see our men at work." Jean kept that note ever afterwards, in an envelope inscribed, 'The last letter I received from darling Kingsley.'

Towards the end of October, when all the Allies' enemies had crumbled and the Italian Army had struck forward from the Piave to triumph, Kingsley was taken with influenza. Those wounds on the Somme made him too weak to resist. His father, about to go out on a platform at Nottingham to speak on Spiritualism, received a telegram from Mary—who looked after Kingsley's flat—that he was dying.

Conan Doyle showed no sign except a slight moistening of the eyes; he never did. He went out and gave his lecture, saying that Kingsley would wish it and that it was better so.

"I have no eloquence and make profession of none," he was accustomed to say, "but I am audible and I say no more than I mean and can prove."

Kingsley died on October 28th. Just a fortnight later,

when his father was again at the Grosvenor Hotel, he heard the news of Armistice Day.

It was eleven o'clock in the morning. Sitting in the foyer of the hotel, he saw a well-dressed woman of the most staid type push through the revolving doors, waltz slowly round the foyer with a Union Jack in each hand, and waltz out again. Presently the din began.

No more slaughter, ever again. No more raiding Gothas. As President Wilson had said, the world made safe for Democracy. Conan Doyle, out in the crowds—"I lost my hat," he said in a note to Jean, "or I got somebody else's"—saw a civilian in a motor-car knock the neck off a whiskey-bottle and gulp its contents raw. He wished that smug-faced civilian had been lynched.

At Windlesham, far away from the tumult, he looked round his study again. There was the mantelpiece with the pictures and decorations, with Kingsley's picture now among them. Over against the smaller windows was the polished ship's bell from the armed trawler *Conan Doyle*, which only this year they had presented to him when the *Conan Doyle*, after a running fight of several hours, sank one of the long new submarines mounted with fore-and-aft guns.

All over, now.

Alfred Wood, Major Wood, would soon be returning as his secretary. He and Jean and the children, the Ma'am at Bowshot Cottage, Innes and Clara, had all been spared if Lottie's husband, and Connie's son, and so many more had not. Christmas came with its evil influenza weather, while he and Jean sat by the fire. In February, 1919, there was another telegram.

Innes was dead too.

Brigadier-General Doyle, returning to France after a joyous homecoming, had gone down with pneumonia like Kingsley. He was bone-weary after those four years, his stamina withered. "You don't complain at all, sir," said his orderly. Innes muttered that he was an Army man, had always been an Army man; and went to join his ancestors who had been Army men too.

Innes's brother, if his knees shook under this double blow, again gave little sign of it. "Well . . . I say, don't you know! By Jove! What!" Those old words of Innes's, in a way, could still make him smile. For, thank God, the gates were not shut. They were only ajar.

Three years ago he had made up his mind on that question, and subsequent experience confirmed it.

"From the moment that I had understood the overwhelming importance of this subject," he afterwards wrote, "and realized how utterly it must change and chasten the whole thought of the world when it is wholeheartedly accepted, I felt . . . that all other work which I had ever done, or could ever do, was as nothing compared to this."

An imperative duty had been laid on him, a humanitarian duty. The world was now at peace, sitting at a ruined hearth. The pain of loss grew keener in silence, as men and women had time to remember. More than ever it became necessary to carry his message, "They are not dead."

His book *The New Revelation* had been published in June of 1918. Its successor, *The Vital Message,* was to appear just over a year later. As soon as he had finished his six-volume history of the war, for which he accepted no royalties so that it should go at less cost into the hands of ex-servicemen, he meant to devote all his time, all his energies, all his talents to the cause of Spiritualism. And there was more.

Afterwards he never forgot a night in the villa of Mr. Southey, at Merthyr in Wales. He and Jean came out of the house into the darkness, after a séance. Behind them the glare of the Dowlais ironworks lit up the sky; in front glimmered the lights of the town. His head was throbbing, his body shaken. Instinctively, as always, he grasped Jean's hand.

"My God, if they only knew—if only they could know!"

It was a heart-cry. In this, perhaps, lay the inception of his determination that this vital message must be carried farther than Britain, farther than the map pasted with wafers on the wall of his study; he must take it, with his own voice, to every corner of the world.

But the experience at Merthyr came later. From the beginning, from the time he could say he knew, he had talked the matter over with Jean. And both realized quite well what his championship of Spiritualism would mean.

Already, since his public avowal of belief in 'Light' and his sympathetic review of Sir Oliver Lodge's *Raymond* in the 'Observer' for November 26th, 1916, amazement and incredulity were being expressed. This must be a passing phase. It couldn't be serious. The feeling was much the same, but now intensified to the edge of anger, as it had been when he spoke very mildly in 1901.

"Conan Doyle, the apostle of common sense?" ran the exclamation. "Conan Doyle, of all people?"

It was that 'of all people' which showed the outrage. We, who represent the public, have minds like cartoonists. We must affix a label and keep it there, or we don't know where we are. Did you mention Crookes, or Lodge, or Russel Wallace? These were honoured men of science, admittedly; but they corresponded to the Absent-Minded Professor of the comic paper, who tipped his wife sixpence and kissed the porter goodbye. They were secluded from life, entitled to such foibles. But Conan Doyle?

This fellow had bowled W. G. Grace. He had bowled W. G. Grace; which, in America, corresponded to striking out Ty Cobb with three pitched balls. He could make a three-figure break at billiards, or hold his own against any amateur heavyweight. He had created Sherlock Holmes. For a quarter of a century he had loomed thick-shouldered as the sturdy Briton, with no damned nonsense about him.

What was wrong? What ailed the man?

All this he knew quite well. He would be the most famous convert to Spiritualism, the target for everybody, because he was the most incredible convert. Then, of course, there was the question of money.

His income must go overboard. He was now the highest-paid of all short-story writers, at the rate of ten shillings a word. An occasional short-story he might write—over there, in the window of the study, was the bust of Holmes which had been with him since Norwood days—but very few stories, and no novel unless it concerned the psychic. He must write little except psychic books, psychic articles, psychic arguments. If he lectured, he could accept only his expenses in payment.

Where does a line, to us who read, come back out of the past?

> *You hucksters, have you still to learn*
> *The things that money will not buy?*

And honours?

In 1919 he was sixty years old. He could look forward, in the ordinary course, to ten more productive years as a writer before drifting into old age and sleep. A letter comes back to us. "I could imagine a man at the end of a long and successful career," he had written in 1902, "taking a peerage as a mark that his work was done and recognized."

There had been for some time vague rumours of a peerage, not yet crystallized. It would have pleased him, and heaven knew it would have pleased the Ma'am, who now so bitterly opposed his belief in Spiritualism.

If such rumours ever became anything more than gossip, an implied condition of the peerage might be the abandonment of his mission to humanity. In that case, there would be no choice; the peerage must go. And he let it go!

But one thing did hurt. One thing was the hardest of all to face, if he could manage to face it. He would lose his friends.

"He is the man," Douglas Sladen had written some years before, "to whom the profession would undoubtedly look for a lead in any crisis. There are few people in London who do not know that big frame, that round head, with prominent cheek-bones and dauntless blue eyes, the bluff good-humoured face. He is a most popular speaker"—would they say that now?—"engaging and amusing in lighter moods, trenchant and convincing in a crisis. Of all authors of the day he merits most the title of a great man."

And only a short time ago an American writer in the Detroit 'Free Press' had recalled his visit there in 1894 as that of "a wise counsellor in the supreme issues, and a sure refuge for the friends who stand in need of his ministrations."

Well, it was unlikely they would express such sentiments much longer.

He would lose most of his friends. And not through their fault either. Who could blame them if they grew uncomfortable, or felt uneasy with him, when he spoke to them on the subject of the psychic? Gone would be the evenings at Windlesham, with the port circulating amid the leaders of law and literature and adventure.

They were entitled to their views, as he was entitled to his. But it was not a matter of viewing or deciding or theorizing. He *knew*.

"Knowing that," he said to Jean, "we must be prepared to accept what they say. Does it matter to you?"

"Nothing matters at all, if you believe you must do it."

"I cannot do anything else. All my life has led up to this. It is the greatest thing in the world."

And the old champion, loved by so many but supported by so few, girded on his sword for the last great fight of all.

XXII
THE BEGINNING

For eleven years his sword did not sleep. For eleven years, through a changed post-war world, all that incredible energy poured into going anywhere, speaking anywhere, challenging any opponent, working with scarcely any rest, seeming charged with an inexhaustible force and light.

"This can't go on forever," his medical advisers told him again and again. "A man at your age—"

At his age? To him, who somehow combined the mellowness and kindliness of a sixth decade with the driving-power of his thirties, it was not a question of his age. It was a question of what had to be done. All his work, as he said, had led up to this: he was at the beginning of his life.

"I want to speak to you tonight on a subject which concerns the destiny of every man and woman in this room. No doubt the Almighty, by putting an angel in King William Street, could convert every one of you to Spiritualism.* But the Almighty law is that we must use our own brains, and find out our own salvation; and it is not made too easy for us."

---

* It should be stated that Conan Doyle left behind him a gigantic accumulation of data on his psychic studies and experiences, in addition to his psychic library of some 2,000 volumes. These records are now in the possession of Denis Conan Doyle and would require a separate book of 100,000 words to cover their principal contents.

That was what he had said in opening his first address at Adelaide, South Australia, in September of 1920. When he lectured, now, he wore reading-glasses on a thin cord. Hear of a description of him, at Adelaide, as he faced a packed audience in the Town Hall.

"Sir Arthur had a budget of notes; but, after he had turned over a few pages, he sallied forth with fluent independence. A finger jutted out now and then, with a thrust of passionate emphasis, or his big glasses twirled in his hand during moments of descriptive ease, and occasionally both hands were held forward. But for the most part, it was a plain statement, lucid and illuminating."

His party included six persons besides himself: Jean, the three children, Major Wood, and a tireless servant, Jakeman, with her uncompromising hat and her uncompromising English ways, who had been with Jean since the first days at Windlesham. When he was lecturing, as he wrote in his *Wanderings of a Spiritualist,* he forgot the audience; forgot everything except his mission.

Thus in 1920 he toured Australia. In 1922 and again in 1923 he toured the United States. Everywhere it was the same: he found, sometimes to his astonishment, immense crowds thronging the halls and even blocking the streets outside, so that on more than one occasion he couldn't get into the hall himself until he proved his identity.

Was it his message? Was it curiosity? Was it sheer magnetism of personality, so concentrated into a cause that few who encountered it could escape his influence? You who read shall be the judge. It is impossible to doubt that something was on the march, be it message or personality, as we watch him stride from country to country in these press-reports, these interviews, these letters of commendation or vituperation.

Vituperation? It was endless and sometimes hysterical. Here is a letter addressed to, 'Chief Devil, Spiritualist Church.' It was the kind of charge which partly amused, partly exasperated him. This is the manner—taken from a letter written in Australia—in which he would reply:

"I should like to say a word in answer to the Rev. J. Blacket's remarks upon the subject of Spiritualism. In all ages those who disagree upon religious matters have endeavoured to show that their opponents were associated with the devil.

"The supreme example, of course, is that of the Christ himself, Who had this charge levelled against Him by the Pharisees, and Who answered that by their fruits you would know. I cannot understand the mentality of those who attribute to the devil the desire to prove life beyond the grave, and thus confute the materialist. If that is the devil's work, then he is cerainly a reformed character."

On April 9th, 1922, they were again approaching New York aboard the *Baltic*. It was the era of booming prosperity. As he saw the white houses on the Jersey shore grow larger, Conan Doyle's thoughts had been these:

I saw also the dangers that lay there, and how formidable they were. They have a keen sense of humour, these Americans, and no subject can more easily be made humorous than this. They are intensely practical, and this would appear to them visionary. They are immersed in worldly pursuits, and this cuts right across the path of their lives. Above all they are swayed by the Press, and if the Press takes a flippant attitude, I have no means of getting behind it.

Against this background of booming prosperity, of trap-drums and pocket-flasks, which a young man from

Princeton christened the Jazz Age, it may be as well to state what Conan Doyle did believe.

It is also as well to state this, because many persons have never heard it. Instead they have heard what somebody said he believed. In the course of years his views underwent certain modifications; but his religious philosophy in its final form might be summed up in this way:

The centre for all belief was the New Testament, with Christ and His teachings as its inspiration.

"Wherever I go," Conan Doyle once remarked, "there are two great types of critics. One is the materialistic gentleman who insists on his right to eternal nothingness. The other is the gentleman with such a deep respect for the Bible that he has never looked into it."

There was, in his philosophy, no such thing as death. When a man died, in the accepted sense, it was not his material body which survived. Nor did his material body lie in the grave to await resurrection, for punishment or reward, at Judgment Day.

What survived death was the etheric body: that is, the soul clothed in its bodily likeness at the best period of its earthly life. The etheric body—sometimes immediately, sometimes after a brief sleep—passed into another world; or, more properly speaking, another series of worlds.

Such a creed was based on seven well-defined principles. These principles were (1) the Fatherhood of God, (2) the brotherhood of man, (3) the survival of personality, (4) the power of communion, i.e., with the dead, (5) personal responsibility, (6) compensation and retribution, (7) eternal progression. The last, eternal progression, crowned it all. One might rise, through spiritual development in this other world, through a series of spheres or cycles to that highest sphere wherein dwelt the Christ.

"The revelation," he had commented in *The Vital Message,* "abolishes the idea of a grotesque hell and a fantastic heaven, while it substitutes the conception of a gradual rise in the scale of existence without any monstrous change which would turn us in an instant from man to angel or devil."

But, because the accent of Christians must naturally fall on the Christ and His disciples, this did not mean war against other faiths.

"There is nothing," he wrote at his most impassioned, in *If I Could Preach Just Once,* "there is nothing which makes the monstrous claim that God supports one clique of mankind against another. Always the teaching is that belief and faith are small matters beside character and behaviour, that it is these latter which determine the place of the soul in the beyond.

"Every faith, Christian or non-Christian, has its saints and its sinners, and if a man be kindly and gentle there is no fear for him in the beyond whether he is or is not the member of any recognized Church on earth."

In those two paragraphs he approached what might be called the fusion, the binding-together, of his religious tenets. Their actual fusion comes in the belief that man and man's spirit are not two, but one, and of this earth as much as any other.

Again to sum up:

"All life on earth is a training-ground for the spiritual. It is the womb from which the real man emerges when he dies to earthly things. The new birth which Christ preached and demonstrated can take place at any time, even in man's life on earth. . . .

"Spiritualism does prove survival of the personality, but it cannot give growth to the eternal man. One has to live in accordance with spiritual law in order to grow, as a flower must conform to natural law. The Christian Bible gives these laws. It is for the Church to interpret them as facts and advise men how to proceed, in order to live nobly and eternally. The séance room proves life after death; God alone can give that life, when man has created the cup within himself to hold and receive it."

Here was the religious philosophy. But it was the fifth article of his general beliefs—that is, the power of communion with the dead—round which controversy gathered, because he challenged it to gather there; and into these battles we must not enter. It need only be recorded that in New York in 1922, by the testimony of Lee Keedick, he broke all lecturing records. Similar records were broken when he returned in '23, crossing to the Pacific Coast with a series of lectures and concluding the tour in Canada.

"Me?" he would exclaim. "These crowds have nothing to do with me. I tell you this because it is the subject, not the man; and it is the subject which counts. They must disprove our facts or else admit them."

That was what mattered to him. When the expenses of his tour had been paid, every other penny of profit from these lectures was turned over to the cause of Spiritualism.

By the end of 1923 he had traversed fifty thousand miles and addressed nearly a quarter of a million people. Did the heart pump a little faster, in such incessant journeyings amid massed throngs and the scream of train-whistles? Was it a little harder to draw energies together? If so, he never admitted as much.

Through the middle years of the decade, '23 to '26, even a stranger—to say nothing of the worried Jean, who tried to shield him as much as possible—could have seen his labours were growing too great. His correspondence, which in America had reached the figure of three hundred letters a day, was only one item of it.

For his first three travel-books, designed more to carry their psychic message than to relate the picturesque incidents of travel, he wrote, almost as diaries during the pilgrimages. His autobiography, *Memories and Adventures,* began to appear serially in the 'Strand' in '23. Psychic books and articles, some of the latter in the 'Strand,' poured from the pen of a man who could not rest—even when he sat at his desk in the garden-hut at Windlesham, the hut he so often used as a study and had used since war-time.

Was there a meeting to be attended? A medium to be investigated? A speech to be made? A controversy to be fought, privately or in the press? There he walked, with his umbrella and his towering presence; and with him, at a few odd times in the 'Strand,' walked Sherlock Holmes.

From *The Adventures of the Mazarin Stone* in 1921 to *The Adventure of Shoscombe Old Place* in 1927, he did not abandon the old companion. But never would he publicly identify himself with Holmes.

"Why don't you tell them?" Jean would urge him, over and over. She, to whom he had confided the truth so many years ago, never ceased urging it. And yet, though he strongly hinted at it in his autobiography, Holmes's identity remained his secret joke like the identity of the real Dr. Watson. More than this, he even went out of his way to make Holmes deny all belief in the supernatural, because Holmes—whom he had set up as a calculating-machine—must click with absolute consistency, like a machine, from beginning to end.

It was different, towards the end of '24, when he wrote a novel which he at first called *The Psychic Ad-*

ventures of Edward Malone and which, in the following year, appeared in the 'Strand' as *The Land of Mist*.

"Thank God," he wrote to Greenhough Smith on February 22nd, 1925, "that book is done! It was to me so important that I feared I might pass away before it was finished."

He wrote those lines from the flat, number 16 Buckingham Palace Mansions, Victoria Street, which he had kept in town for more than twenty years; he was on his way to lecture in Paris, where, as always, great crowds gathered to hear 'the good giant' speak. *The Land of Mist*, to him, was less a novel than a stating of his own and others' psychic experiences.

We note that the central figure in *The Land of Mist* is not Professor Challenger at all. As indicated both by his own title and the story's subsequent sub-title in the 'Strand,' the central figure is Edward Malone, the athletic Irishman. But Challenger is there: a different Challenger. Old, growing grey, troubled by bereavement, he roars out with scientific scepticism until the last.

As Challenger had once guided a fundamentally serious story, now he is guided himself through the perplexities and half-lights—sometimes the dangers—of a book which the author considered so vital. He appeared less because the author liked him than because he represented a scientific scepticism, like that of Professor Hare, which Conan Doyle could understand and trust.

Well, Challenger is converted to belief in communication with the dead. Many people did not like the book because they did not like its theme. Challenger was fallen from his glory of warring monsters, when only as recently as '23 he had ramped through one of the best of all motion pictures in the film-version of *The Lost World*.

"Conan Doyle is preaching!" exclaimed so many;

and of course he was. Consider his side of it for a moment: what else could he, or any man to whom religion has become all-important, pretend to do?

Flashes of his narrative-power crackle through *The Land of Mist*; and, if anyone would read his finest ghost-story, it may be found in *The Bully of Brocas Court,* written in 1921. That year 1921 had been the year in which the Ma'am died, quietly, cherishing her beloved son though she still opposed his belief in Spiritualism. But Conan Doyle felt that she was not dead; and the intensity of his feeling for her—did the years unroll like a pageant, then?—intensified at the same time his zeal for work.

Over and over Greenhough Smith urged him to write something of more general popular appeal than his psychic articles. Here is a typical reply:

"I wish I could do as you wish but, as you know, my life is devoted to one end and at present I can't see any literature which would be of any use to you above the horizon. I can only write what comes to me."

It was as though the threads of his life were being gathered together. In 1924 he had seen an old dream take shape when he gathered together the paintings and drawings of his father, Charles Doyle, for a public exhibition in the West End. In '25 he bought a country house—Bignell Wood long and gabled, with a heavy thatched roof, amid the oaks and beeches of the New Forest—against a background from which had once arisen *The White Company*. The years '26 and '27 saw his two-volume *History of Spiritualism,* amid an even higher pressure of work and controversy, and *The Case-book of Sherlock Holmes*.

But it is written casually, almost impatiently, with its author's mind and heart turned towards other matters. In the same way he rejected the plot, sketched out and dictated, for another Holmes story: It dealt with a murder committed by a man on stilts; and the same idea, curiously enough, was afterwards used by G. K. Chesterton. "More Holmes?" all readers had been inquiring. And again:

"I can only write what comes to me."

In a matter of hard cash, which we can all understand, he devoted two hundred and fifty thousand pounds to promoting the cause of Spiritualism. As for honours, he was offered that peerage of which mention has been made. It came to the extent of discussing it, his second cousin—the Rt. Rev. Monseignor Richard Barry-Doyle, a close and sympathetic friend of the whole family since the war—came down to Windlesham to talk the matter over. King George the Fifth had been his friend for a long time, but there were others to be considered besides the king. He was prevented from receiving that peerage. In England, the country of religious liberty, a peer of the realm must not be a Spiritualist. Perhaps he deserved little better of England than this.

But to the good giant—the French journalist's phrase keeps recurring—it was of small importance. Perhaps it hurt him; nobody knows; the twinkle in his eye remained. He spent much time in the psychic bookshop, with its museum, which he established in Victoria Street and was presided over by his daughter Mary.

"Why do you go on hammering at proof and proof and proof?" Mary once asked him. "We know these things are true. Why do you try to prove it by so many examples?"

"You have never been a rationalist," he said.

He, who could command ten shillings a word if he would write about Sherlock Holmes, must now pay for the publication of his own books if he would write solely on psychic subjects. In 1927 the buried Oscar Slater, bulky and embittered, emerged from prison—innocent, but still legally guilty and without compensation. Conan Doyle, contributing both funds and support, backed his appeal for establishing his innocence, for proving he had not murdered Marion Gilchrist all those years ago, and for gaining the compensation.

And they won. In court they shook hands, figures across a gulf of years, where the suppressing of evidence and the vicious persecution of Lieutenant Trench had now been forgotten. That was in 1928; and in the autumn, when thin rains whirled with dead leaves across the lawn at Bignell Wood, he set out for an African tour which was to take him into South Africa, Rhodesia, and Kenya.

Jean went with him, and the three children who had accompanied them on all their psychic pilgrimages. The children had grown up now. Denis and Adrian, preoccupied with women and with breaking their necks at motor-racing, stood six feet high; but he still towered over them and could extinguish them with a glance. They might smile at Pop's tactics with a motor-car when something went wrong with it. Making no pretence to a mechanical mind, he would simply open the bonnet and jab with his umbrella at the engine until something happened. He was more than indulgent with them when they got into trouble. But in South Africa, in a railway compartment during that tour, occurred a different incident.

"That woman?" said Adrian. "She's ugly."

Whap went the swing of a vicious back-hander across his face; and the young man, steadying his reeling eyesight, saw his father's large red face seeming to fill the compartment with menace.

"Just remember," Conan Doyle said mildly, "that no woman is ugly."

First and last, it was his philosophy of woman.

It gave him a pang—not physical, though there were physical pangs too—when he re-visited South Africa, a land of memories since the Boer War. When he last saw Cape Town, there were fifty troop-transports in the harbour. At Bloemfontein, up country, he found himself under just such a red-and-purple sunset as he remembered from his last night at the Langman Hospital.

Old politics, old passions, still simmered a little here. But he must keep these out of his discussions, except when his temper exploded as it did of old. Never had he been more energetic, more vibrant with conviction, than in his lectures, his meetings, his journeys under that torrid sun. To his family it seemed that scarcely had he returned from South Africa to England in the spring of '29—he spent part of the summer at Bignell Wood, having celebrated his seventieth birthday—than he was off again, in the late autumn sleet, to Scandinavia.

Scandinavia? That was nothing! He meant to carry his message to Rome, to Athens, to Constantinople.

"We come back," he had written fervently, at the end of his African trip, "stronger in health, more earnest in our beliefs, more eager to fight once more in the greatest of all causes, the regeneration of religion and of that direct and practical spiritual element which is the one and only antidote to scientific materialism."

In this mood, visiting the Hague and Copenhagen on his way, he went to Norway and Sweden. In Stockholm particularly they blocked the streets and gave him one of his warmest welcomes. As at Cape Town in South Africa, he spoke over the Stockholm broadcasting system; the clear, heavy voice rose vibrantly.

According to his plans and his promise, he would return to London for the Armistice Memorial Service, to speak at the Albert Hall in the forenoon and at the

Queen's Hall in the evening. Then, quite suddenly, the good giant collapsed.

At London they carried him off the boat-train, carried him to his flat at number 16 Buckingham Palace Mansions. There were a few snowflakes in the air. In vain his doctors warned him, as he gasped a little for breath, that any further speaking might be suicide.

But, as through all his life, he would not give way. He would *not* yield, even against angina pectoris. Not only had he made a promise, but this was the Armistice Service on Sunday, in honour of those—like Kingsley and Innes—who had gone to a tune of *Pack Up Your Troubles.*

On Sunday morning he spoke at the Albert Hall, not without difficulty and a little unsteady on his feet. At the evening he spoke at the Queen's Hall; and afterwards, when a throng who could not get in demanded to hear him, he insisted on speaking to them: bareheaded, on a balcony, in the drifting snow.

And yet, it seemed, he had laughed again at bodily ills. The body might be heavier and more slow-moving, but it could be subdued. On Christmas Eve, at Windlesham, he came downstairs to dinner. Though he ate only grapes, he was in good spirits. Dr. John Lamond, a Presbyterian minister who had long been his associate in Spiritualism and who had often heard him imitate Professor Challenger, now heard him chuckle as he told of a visit to Barrie at Stanway Court.

Since they kept him quiet and warded off intrusive visitors, his health seemed to improve through the spring of 1930. Another glimpse we have, which lingers in the mind and cannot be forgotten. At Windlesham, since the earliest days, it had been his invariable habit to go out into the garden, when the weather began to clear and the flowers appear, and pick the first snow-drop for Jean.

So again, in that spring of '30, we see the weary giant going out into the garden and picking the first snowdrop for his wife.

He felt much better, or said he did, when he made the sketch of himself as the Old Horse. It amused him to put all those stages of his journey behind him.

"The old horse," he printed under it, "has pulled a heavy load a long way. But he is well cared for and with six months' stable and six months' grass he will be on the road once more."

Each day of the early summer he would go and work in his study as usual: still writing, still dealing with his correspondence. Once, on his way from the study up to his bedroom, he fell heavily in the passage. To the butler, who ran to help him, he spoke in a muffled voice.

"It's nothing! Take me gently! Don't say anything!" He must not alarm Jean.

In the same way they had often been compelled to give him oxygen, to gulp into his lungs and steady the heart again. One such occasion Denis well remembered. They were giving him oxygen in the bedroom, up there beyond the white-painted door; and the great head turned on the pillow as he looked at Denis.

"This must be very dull for you, my boy," he said. "Why don't you go and get a book?"

One of the last acts of his life had been to struggle up to London, against all Jean's and his doctors' pleading, so that he might see the Home Secretary about the law persecuting spiritualistic mediums. But the old horse had drawn its heavy load too far; it would take the road no more in this world.

At two o'clock in the morning of July 7th, 1930, Denis and Adrian were sent to Tunbridge Wells in a car driven at blind speed to bring oxygen. The galley-proofs of his last story, a Regency tale, lay on the desk in his study. In his bedroom—it faced north, with open windows—he saw the sun come up on a fine warm day.

It was characteristic, that bedroom. On the walls hung prize-fighting prints, Tom Cribb and Molyneux from the great days of the ring; and, also characteristically, drawings by William Blake. Over the dressing-table was a photograph of the armed trawler *Conan Doyle*. The wooden plaque of Gillette as Sherlock Holmes was there too. In corners lay his dumb-bells and his boxing-gloves; and in this bedroom, carefully preserved in its case, his favorite billiard-cue.

At half-past seven in the morning, though he was very weak, he wanted to get up out of bed and sit in a chair. They helped him into his dressing-gown, and he sat back in a big basket-chair facing the windows. He said little, because of the difficulty of speech. But:

"There ought to be a medal struck for you," he said to Jean, "inscribed 'to the best of all nurses.'"

It was nearly half past eight. Jean sat at his left, clasping his hand with both of hers. Adrian sat at his right, gripping the other hand. Denis was beyond Adrian, Lena Jean at the other side of the mother they called Mumpty.

The sun was up, though the lawn still lay shaded outside the open windows. At half past eight they felt a pressure of his hand. He roused himself a little, though he could not speak, and looked round at each of them in turn. Then he sank back, and closed his eyes to earthly things.

EPILOGUE

It was a scene more like a quiet garden-party than a funeral-service when his mortal remains were buried near the garden-hut, which he had so often used as a study, in the grounds at Windlesham. Jean Conan Doyle wore a flowered summer dress. Word had spread that they did not wish mourning; there was little sign of it in the vast crowd who attended on that sunlit day of July 11th, 1930.

But they missed him. And the world missed him. People at home, people in far places, saw pictures and remembered dreams when they heard he was gone. When the telegrams arrived, and the special train to carry the flowers, it seemed that all on earth remembered him.

So he was buried near the garden-hut; and the flowers that had been sent in his memory covered the whole field as though a fanciful Dutch garden had grown as high as a man's head. On the headstone over his grave Jean told them to inscribe only his name, the date of his birth, and four words: STEEL TRUE, BLADE STRAIGHT. The headstone was of British oak.

What more can be said, after that?

Nearly all else must be in the minds of those who remember. Ageing men and women who remember the pleasure his stories gave; ageing men and women who remember how he championed the helpless and the broken; those, older still, who catch an echo of 'The Bow was made in England,' and remember how all his life he served England well.

These must speak in full of him, not those of us who toil in his wake and only try to understand. For the cause of psychic religion he gave his heart, his worldly possessions, and finally his life. And, whether it be said in the spiritual sense or only the earthly influence he has left behind among us, one word may be added. Let no man write his epitaph. He is not dead.

BIOGRAPHICAL ARCHIVES

BOX NO. 1

Genealogical data and pedigrees.

LETTER-BOX, marked CHARLES DOYLE.

(Letters from Charles Doyle to his father, John Doyle, his brother Richard and his sister Annette, 1849-1869.)

LETTER-BOX, marked MICHAEL CONAN and his wife SUSAN CONAN.

(Letters from Michael Conan to Charles and Mary Doyle between 1855 and 1878. Letters from Susan Conan as late as 1885.)

BOX NO. 5

Bound typed copy of the letters of RICHARD DOYLE, 1849

BOX NO. 3

LETTER-BOX, marked SCHOOLS.

Hodder House, Stonyhurst, Feldkirch.

(Letters from Arthur Conan Doyle to his mother, with a few to his father between 1868 and 1876, when he entered Edinburgh University.)

LETTER-BOX, marked SOUTHSEA and NORWOOD.

(Letters from A.C.D. to his mother, 1882-1893, covering also letters written while he was acting as medical apprentice during student days, 1878-1882.)

LETTER-BOX, marked UNDERSHAW.

(Letters between 1897-1906. Also letters during A.C.D.'s residence in Switzerland and Egypt and his visit to the U.S. 1893-1896.)

LETTER-BOX, marked WINDLESHAM.

(Letters 1908-1920.)

LETTER-BOX, marked LITERARY.

> (About 250 letters from A.C.D. to his mother and a small number to his sister Lottie. Each letter deals with one of his stories, books or plays while he was engaged in writing it. 1882-1912.)

LETTER-BOX, marked CHILDREN and RELATIONS.

> (Letters from A.C.D.'s eldest son Kingsley, from his sisters Lottie, Connie and Ida and from his relatives by marriage.)

LETTER-BOX, marked INNES DOYLE.

> (A.C.D.'s letters to his brother Brig. Gen. Innes Doyle, mainly 1894-1918. Also a packet of letters on the death of A.C.D.'s first wife, 1906.)

ENVELOPE—INNES DOYLE.

> (Innes Doyle's letters to A.C.D. A few from boyhood, but mainly 1899-1918.)

ENVELOPE—Private letters during the war. Also Innes's, Kingsley's and others to Lady (Jean) Conan Doyle.

ENVELOPE—Early letters from A.C.D. to his sister Lottie, 1878-1892.

BOX NO. 6

NOTEBOOKS AND DIARIES

There are more than 50 notebooks and common-place books containing the notes for his literary work as well as his hobbies, his comments on life, anecdotes, and many unpublished statements. For the purpose of this biography special attention is directed to:—

SOUTHSEA SCRAPBOOK NO. 1. 1885-1886.

SOUTHSEA SCRAPBOOK NO. 2. Remarks on early psychic reading including journal of séances, 1886-1887.

SOUTHSEA SCRAPBOOK NO. 3. 1889-1890. This also includes an account of two meetings with George Meredith, written at Norwood.

SOUTHSEA SCRAPBOOK NO. 4. Generalia of all years.

NORWOOD NOTEBOOK NO. 1. At the back of this is his diary of important events between 1885 and 1894.

"ANGELS OF DARKNESS"—Complete unpublished play.

NOTEBOOK, marked—"Napoleonic soldier: the Brigadier."

POCKET DIARIES, 1891-1915, brief entries useful in verifying dates.

THE NILE:—Diary December 31st, 1895—January 20th, 1896.

"AN ALPINE PASS ON SKI," 1894.

DIARY BOER WAR, February 28th—July 22nd, 1900.
Common-place books about 1910 to about 1923.

SCRAPBOOKS

There are 60 scrapbooks. From these scrapbooks quotations
have been made from the following:—
Scrapbook titles as follows:—
  (1) *A. & L. Conan Doyle*, 1885.
      This contains press cuttings as early as 1882, as
      late as 1894.
  (2) *Miscellaneous*, 1893-1912.
  (3) *"Rodney Stone"* Reviews, 1906.
  (4) Miscellaneous, 1898-1900, mainly Boer War, and
      1900 Elections.
  (5) War controversy, press cuttings and letters, 1902.
  (6) *Panorama of Activities*, 1898-1929.
  (7) *Politics and Sport*, 1905-1909.
  (8) *"Sir Nigel"* Reviews and Hawick Election, 1906.
  (9) *The Edalji Case*, containing letters to 'Daily Tele-
      graph,' dossier sent to Home Office, reproductions
      of anonymous letters and originals of anonymous
      letters sent to A.C.D., 1907. Press cuttings in
      comment on case.
 (10) *The Congo*, press cuttings and letters, 1909.
 (11) *Odds and Ends*, 1908-1929.
 (12) *Engagement and Wedding*, two books, 1907.
 (13) *Olympic Games*, 1912.
 (14) *Sir A. Conan Doyle:* Stories, play reviews, inter-
      views, compiled by a stranger.
 (15) *"Novelist at Home,"* as early as 1892, as late as
      1913.
 (16) *New York and Canada*, 1914.
 (17) *Gt. War and Divorce Reform*, 1915-1920.
 (18) *World War Activities*, 1914-1918. Letters and press
      cuttings of his services to the nation.
 (19) *Australia*, 1920. U.S., 1922.
 (20) *S. Africa*, 1928.
 (21) *Psychic* No. 1.
 (22) *Psychic* No. 2.
 (23) *Undershaw Guest Book*, 1897-1906.
 (24) *Theatrical Reviews*, two scrapbooks, 1909-1910.
 (25) *Sherlock Holmes:* An anthology of press cuttings,
      not compiled by himself. He never compiled a
      Sherlock Holmes scrapbook.

BOX NO. 2

Contains the following:—

ENVELOPE I, marked—"Documents relating to various incidents in Sir Arthur's life."

These are not chronological.

(1) Programme of his literary lectures in U.S.A.
(2) Request to him to stand for Central Edinburgh (1900), and his Parliamentary poster for election, and letters to his mother on the contest.
(3) Grand Trunk Railways' offer of special railway coach in Canada (1914).
(4) Permission requested by Lord Fitzroy for Sir Arthur Conan Doyle to visit Italian warfront.
(5) Request to him to act as Special Correspondent in case of war.
(6) Telegram from England's M.C.C. Team touring the U.S.A.
(7) Stillwell "The Great Plan."
(8) Letter from an American claiming that later Sherlock Holmes stories are better than predecessors.
(9) Letter from Hungarian Counsellor of Foreign Affairs praising A.C.D.'s historical writings.
(10) Two or three appreciations of A.C.D.'s "History of the Boer War."
(11) Letters from Home Office re Sir Roger Casement, and A.C.D.'s vain attempt to save him.
(12) Borstal.
(13) Grateful letter from ex-Naval man for swimming collars in Great War, brought into service by A.C.D.'s influence.
(14) Plesiosaurus.
(15) Letter from a convict in an American prison.
(16) Receipt for A.C.D.'s first flight in an aeroplane 1911, and a clipping apropos his much earlier ascent in a balloon.
(17) Request to him to referee the Jeffries-Johnson World Heavyweight Championship Fight in America.
(18) Correspondence apropos Parliamentary Candidature for Edinburgh University, which he declined.
(19) The Guards' Christmas Card.
(20) Apropos M. J. A. Francis on his deathbed, saying "God bless Conan Doyle."

ENVELOPE II, marked—"In reference to his public services to the Nation and humanity" (for further reference see Scrapbooks and Biographical Photo Book).

 (1) Formation of Volunteers, 1914. (Prototype of Home Guard.)

 (2) Rifle Clubs, 1901.

 (3) "Call to the Nation for Civilian National Reserve, 1914." 1200 copies distributed at crossroads within first week of Great War.

 (4) S.O.S. appeal.

 (5) "History of Great War" (further reference, see Scrapbooks and War Dept., Biographical Archives).

 (6) "History of Boer War" (see Scrapbooks).

 (7) Channel Tunnel Appeal.

 (8) Divorce Reform League.

 (9) Attempt, at age of 55, to reach the Front in order that he might assist in rescuing wounded from the field of battle.

 (10) To revitalize system of British Medical Association.

 (11) "Crime of the Congo." (See letters to his mother, Scrapbooks, etc.)

 (12) "The Causes of the War."

 (13) Entertainment of the Officers of the French Fleet.

 (14) Vivisection.

 (15) Waifs and Strays Meeting.

 (16) A.C.D. and Union Jack Club.

 (17) Championship of old foreign waiters. (See Scrapbooks.)

 (18) Letters to his mother on Edalji Case.

 (19) Why he volunteered for Boer War, in letter to his mother.

 (20) Attitude toward his knighthood.

 (21) Address of thanks from the Artists Benevolent Institution.

ENVELOPE III, marked—"Documents relating to various incidents in Sir Arthur's life."

 (1) Account of sinking of a German submarine by the trawler "Conan Doyle."

 (2) Letter from Captain of the "Conan Doyle."

 (3) The Case of the Missing Dane. (Letters: real-life detection.)

 (4) Notes that A.C.D. made on his programme when seeing "The Speckled Band."

 (5) Letters from 2 members of the ship's company of the "Hope."

- (6) Membership List of Authors' Club.
- (7) Letters from William J. Burns to A.C.D. apropos the Frank Murder.
- (8) Copy of article entitled "The World's Happiest Museum."
- (9) A.C.D.'s personal notes on Lloyd George.
- (10) A letter from Lord Alfred Douglas, and A.C.D.'s reply to same.
- (11) A.C.D. on Courage, in an interview given to P.G. Wodehouse.
- (12) Notes on his stay with Barrie in 1929.
- (13) Envelope marked, "Letter from Barrie April, 1930" and contents.
- (14) "The Immortal Memory," A.C.D.'s monograph on Burns.
- (15) His published letters in defence of the dismissed employees of the Gordon Hotels Company.
- (16) Re A.C.D.'s letter in the 'Daily Mail' apropos conditions in the Strand.
- (17) Letters to Arthur Hardy and Hall Caine (see Scrapbooks and letters to his mother for further reference).
- (18) Article by A.C.D.'s mother on "Love and Marriage."
- (19) Notice Bill of early lecture at Portsmouth on the Arctic.
- (20) Statement on Sir Arthur's politics.

ENVELOPE IV, marked—"Various. No. 1"

- (1) A sheet of music. (He began a serious study of music at the age of 70, in the last year of his life.)
- (2) A few painting notes. (He commenced painting at the age of 70, in the last year of his life.)
- (3) A few menus of lunches and dinners given in his honour or attended by him. (Purely representative.)
- (4) Notes on envelope habit.
- (5) Verses written by a Scotsman to A.C.D.
- (6) Verses written by a Swiss visitor on A.C.D.'s first introducing skis into that country.
- (7) The Gillette Sherlock Holmes Xmas card.
- (8) A series of humorous drawings by A.C.D.
- (9) Delineation of Nativity.
- (10) A.C.D.'s Xmas card (2 years).
- (11) Burns Club Dinner. A.C.D. on Memory of Burns.
- (12) A Rhyme of the Road.
- (13) Drawing done by A.C.D. after getting his medical degree.
- (14) Menu of the 20th Division in France during his visit.

(15) Outline of a typical dinner menu at Windlesham before the Great War.

(16) List of A.C.D. MSS. sold at Sotheby's from the library of the Comte de Suzannet.

(17) Tribute paid by a clergyman in his sermon to A.C.D. and his mother.

ENVELOPE V, marked—"Various. No. 2"

(1) Letter from a British renegade (C. Pownall) in the Great War.

(2) Envelope addressed to A.C.D. from mail captured by the Germans.

(3) Letters from a Prussian Officer apropos some of A.C.D.'s war publications.

(4) A.C.D. as first guest of the Canadian Government at Jasper.

(5) Message from Oscar Slater via ex-convict.

(6) A letter from A.C.D.'s great-uncle Michael Conan containing reference to his literary promise at age of 16.

(7) Letter from Brig. Gen. Innes Doyle apropos A.C.D. at Front 1914-18 war.

(8) Letter about THROUGH THE MAGIC DOOR.

(9) Sir Arthur's monograph "An Appreciation of Sir John French."

(10) His Monograph "Tariff Reform."

(11) American magazine article in reference to A.C.D.'s handwritten MSS.

(12) The Case of Mrs. Rome. (Some of the letters are missing.)

(13) Extract from letter from Michael Conan apropos A.C.D., 1864, then aged 5.

(14) "An Incursion into Diplomacy." (Account of how "The War in South Africa" came to be written.)

(15) Two monographs by A.C.D.'s brother Brig. Gen. Innes Doyle.

(16) Picture from 'The Graphic' of A.C.D.'s play "The House of Temperly."

(17) Booklet of American codes. (Mind-reading secrets.)

(18) A.C.D.'s poem on the death of Richard Doyle.

(19) Some comments on the American race.

(20) Letter apropos request of Prince of Wales (later Edward VII) for A.C.D. as dinner partner.

ENVELOPE VI, marked—"Various. No. 3"

(1) Letter to A.C.D. from Dr. Waller, who much influenced his early life.

(2) Typical letters from his Jesuit masters to his mother.
(3) Letter apropos the gift of his watch and chain to a destitute German.
(4) Letter about his first car and training his groom as chauffeur.
(5) Controversy over George Moore's "Esther Waters."
(6) Sample letter to the Ma'am.
(7) Fight with Hall Caine (1897).
(8) The Ma'am's last card.
(9) Drawings of A.C.D. in letters from his father.
(10) Letter from Adrian Conan Doyle to Mary Conan Doyle apropos A.C.D.'s Spartan tastes and Irish Question re Home Rule.
(11) Note from A.C.D.'s writing desk.
(12) Letter re Lord Advocate in Slater Case.
(13) Motto that used to hang in A.C.D.'s study.
(14) His rough sketch of his conception of Challenger.

ENVELOPE VII, marked—"Programmes of some of A.C.D.'s Plays. Also, printed copy of the Conan Doyle-Barrie musical Play 'Jane Annie.' "

ENVELOPE VIII and attachment.—Early printed writings, and early literary efforts in MSS. Two letters to his mother and one to his sisters. An armorial drawing done by A.C.D. at Stonyhurst. Copy of his Feldkirchian Gazette and book of early poems.

ENVELOPE IX, marked—"Odd notes in A.C.D.'s handwriting." Some of them are early.

ENVELOPE X, marked—"Short scripts in A.C.D.'s handwriting."
(1) The Jews.
(2) Poltergeists.
(3) His Cornish notes—lists of words, etc. he studied on a holiday in Cornwall.
(4) His preface to James Payn's book of essays.
(5) His preface to the Rev. Tweedale's book.
(6) His notes on Atlantis.
(7) His notes on Geology.
(8) His notes on American slang.
(9) "Seasons at Undershaw."
(10) "An Alpine Pass on Ski." ('Strand Magazine,' 1894.)
(11) "On Books."
(12) Human Origins.
(13) List of a portion of his criminal library.

(14) His typed notes for a literary lecture.
(15) Satiric account of a dinner at a millionaire's house.
(16) "Edwin Drood."
(17) Jottings during his service in the Boer War. (Not to be confused with Diary.)
(18) A Prayer written in the last year of his life, and a poem composed by him in 1873 when he was at Stonyhurst.
(19) Complete play "A Foreign Policy."
(20) Fragments of an incomplete musical Play.

ENVELOPE XI, marked—"Further MS. in A.C.D.'s handwriting."

(1) On Funeral of Queen Victoria.
(2) Part of "The Lost World" written on the inside cover of an achaeological magazine.
(3) Short MS. on the Old Testament and Church of England.
(4) The Parable of the Cheesemites.
(5) A portion of "The House of Temperly."
(6) Crabbe's practice.
(7) A fragment of "The Reigate Squires."
(8) Names and descriptive notes for "A Study in Scarlet."

ENVELOPE XII, marked—"This contains typed copy of 'The Mystery of Edwin Drood,' 'Phineas,' 'Notes from a Strange Mail Bag,' 'The Dreamers,' 'Jottings from a Strange Mail Bag,' 'Maeterlinck,' 'The Power of the Ghost' (with a magazine copy of it); 'A Remarkable Man,' 'Houdini the Enigma,' 'The Alleged Posthumous Writings of Great Authors,' Photo of 'The Dancing Men,' 'The Edge of the Unknown,' 'The Flight of Dr. Curtius,' printed copy of 'The Case of Mr. George Edalji,' 'The Fool of Harvey's Sluice,' 'Spiritualist,' A page of typewriting re his first conception of Sherlock Holmes."

ENVELOPE XIII, marked—"A representative assortment of printed articles (non-psychic) from the pen of Sir Arthur Conan Doyle." Also typed copies of a number of MSS. including—
"The Man Who was Wanted" (Sherlock Holmes story never published).
"The Parish Magazine."
"The Black Hawk" (unfinished dramatization of "The Lord of Chateau Noir").
"When Truth is Stranger than Fiction" ('Strand,' 1915).
"Letters from Egypt" (his articles when he was War

   Correspondent in the Egyptian Campaign 1896).
"Plot for a Sherlock Holmes Story" (never written).
Preface to the Collected Edition (1903).
"Ether."
There is no ENVELOPE XIV.

ENVELOPE XV, marked—"Small Assortment of letters to A.C.D.
 from strangers, typical of his mail apart from the social,
 psychic, and the literary."
  (1) Letter from Indian asking A.C.D. to help him with his
   detective stories.
  (2) Letter from a peasant woman in Ireland.
  (3) Letter from surviving friend of Poe.
  (4) Typical letter from a stranger whom A.C.D. had offered to help because he had heard that he was in
   trouble.
 His daily in-mail averaged 50–60 letters per day. In
 America, 300 letters per day.

ENVELOPE XVI, marked—"Some facts relative to Lady (Jean)
 Conan Doyle" (for principal information see Letters and
 Press Books in Biographical library and Genealogical box).

ENVELOPE XVII, marked—"Copies of some of the last letters
 written by A.C.D."

ENVELOPE XVIII, marked—"Tributes to A.C.D." (For further reference see envelopes marked "Tributes" in Box 3.)

ENVELOPE XIX, marked—"Assortment of letters from A.C.D. to
 various acquaintances on various subjects." Collected by
 Adrian Conan Doyle from rare book dealers between
 1930-47.

ENVELOPE XX—very incomplete, marked—"Sport. Prince Henry
 Race. Cricket. Hunting."

ENVELOPE XXI, marked—"Story written by Sir Arthur's eldest
 daughter Mary at age of 9."
 Copy of "THE SONG OF THE BOW." In music script.

ENVELOPE XXII, marked—"Typical specimens of the extraordinary letters and envelopes that would come to A.C.D.
 through the post."

ENVELOPE XXIII, marked—"Interesting matter re the domestic side of the Great War." (Details of Windlesham between 1914-1918.)

ENVELOPE XXIV, marked—"Certain public dinner speeches by A.C.D. (For fuller details, see Scrapbooks.)

ENVELOPE XXV, marked—"A few samples of A.C.D.'s favourite paintings. He considered Norman Lindsay one of the world's unrecognized geniuses."

ENVELOPE XXVI, marked—"Politics."
LETTER-BOX, marked—"Documents relating to A.C.D. and war, 1914-1918."
LETTER-BOX, marked—"Generals' letters from the Front to A.C.D."
LETTER-BOX, marked—"War Notes, etc." Also letters from Generals and War Office, and part Diary of A.C.D.'s war work.

ENVELOPE XXVII, marked—"Letters from Officers and Men to A.C.D."

ENVELOPE XXVIII, marked—"Letters from Front 1914-18, and other data re A.C.D.'s History."
2 SMALL FAT ENVELOPES, both marked—"War."
A FLAT PACKAGE of A.C.D.'s war maps and trench maps.
A FLAT PACKAGE, marked—"Notes on the Interpretation of Aeroplane Photographs."
A FLAT PACKAGE of Sundries, marked—"To do with A.C.D.'s Volunteer work at Crowborough."
BOOK, marked—"A Course of Reading that A.C.D. chose for Jean Conan Doyle, and her comments on the books."

ENVELOPE XXIX contains:—
 (1) Drawing by A.C.D. of his mother.
 (2) Sketch by his brother-in-law, of Volunteer A.C.D. and friends, 1914-1918 war.
 (3) Map of Holmes's and Watson's Clash with the Enemy. (This is a joke, not of Holmesian relevance.)
 (4) A.C.D.'s Slater Case Appeal.
 (5) Sale List of Library of Comte de Suzannet.
 (6) List of names on Doyle dining table.
 (7) Copy of "Boer War" with statement on title page quoted in text of biography.

ENVELOPE XXX

  (1) Typescript of the Speeches of Mr. Francis Gribble, Mr. Ernest Short, Sir Gilbert Parker and Lord Gorell at the unveiling of the Conan Doyle Memorial Tablet at the Authors' Club.
  (2) Letter to A.C.D. from a Canadian Schoolmaster.
  (3) Letter from William Gillette to Charles Frohman about A.C.D.
  (4) Letter to A.C.D. from the Senior Chaplain of the 33rd Division, ex-prisoner of war, expressing gratitude for the secret code by which A.C.D. sent news to the prisoners of war in Germany.
  (5) Letter to A.C.D. from a soldier whose life he had saved in the Langman Hospital, Boer War.
      Typical of many:—
  (6) Letters to Sherlock Holmes demanding autograph.
  (7) Letter to A.C.D. from a Canadian whose only son had died in A.C.D.'s Hospital in Boer War.
  (8) Letter to A.C.D. from Edinburgh University apropos his Bursary Gift for South African students.
  (9) Letter to A.C.D. from his fellow-directors of Raphael Tuck Ltd.
 (10) Letter from Major Duval to A.C.D. apologising for his statement that the British had used Dum-Dum bullets.
 (11) Envelope found in A.C.D.'s pocket wallet: one of his last notes.

Black metal box containing the following envelopes:—
  (1) marked—"Oddments." Some of these letters are interesting; others serve to illustrate aspects of family relationships by blood and marriage.
  (2) marked—"Letters from A.C.D.'s Cousin, the Right Rev. Monsigneur Richard Barry-Doyle."
  (3) marked—"Early letters from A.C.D. to his sister Lottie."
  (4) marked—"Tributes to A.C.D."
  (5) marked—"Letters from Sir Arthur Conan Doyle to Lady Jean Conan Doyle."
  (6) marked—"Letters from A.C.D. to J.C.D. in various American cities."
  (7) marked—"A.C.D.'s letters to Charles and Charles's to him." (This is Charles Ashton-Johnson, hon. Secretary on his South African Lecture Tour 1928-29.)
  (8) marked—"A.C.D.'s letters to Lily Loder-Symonds."

ENVELOPE, marked—Sample letters from family retainers.
ENVELOPE, marked—"Letters written by friends to J.C.D. during her married life." Biographical note above.

BOX NO. 7

An assortment of A.C.D.'s playscripts, including two different versions of THE HOUSE OF TEMPERLY, BRIGADIER GERARD, THE SPECKLED HAND, THE FIRES OF FATE, Gillette's SHERLOCK HOLMES. Also proofs of his last story; 2 books of letter tributes to Lady J.C.D. and of appreciation of their home life together; also folio of letters to Lady J.C.D.; some contain reference to A.C.D.

BOX NO. 8

(1) Box of data on Slater Case.
(2) Bundle of papers and letters re Slater Case.
(3) Box of data on Edalji Case.
(4) Bundle of papers and letters re Edalji Case.
(5) Cricket and Match Cards.
(6) Billiard Break Book.
(7) Various Illuminated Addresses to Sir Arthur.
(8) Talkie Film of A.C.D.
(9) 3 Talkie Films.
(10) Charles Doyle's last Sketch Books.
(11) Prince Henry Tour, 1911.
(12) Some unpublished Sydney Paget originals.
(13) A few examples of A.C.D.'s oil paintings at the age of 70.
(14) A folio book of 500 letters to A.C.D. from famous men and women, including those to his forbears as well as his descendants after his death.

Samuel Rogers
Mark Lemon
John Leech,
    Equerry to Queen Victoria
Count D'Orsay
Mrs. Charles Dickens
Halle
Rosetti
Lord Ripon
Cardinal Newman
Cardinal Wiseman
Bishop of Westminster
Lord Aberdare
King Edward VII
George Meredith
George Bernard Shaw
Rudyard Kipling
Stanley Weyman
Sir Oliver Lodge
Ellen Terry
Lord Cromer
Winston Churchill

Mrs. Winston Churchill
J. Clynes
Theodore Roosevelt
William J. Burns
Lord Roberts
E. W. Hornung
Gen. Sir William Robertson
Sybil Thorndyke
John Masefield
Viscount Knollys,
    Equerry to King Edward VII
Lord Stanfordham,
    Equerry to King George V
Andrew Lang
J. M. Barrie
Ramsay MacDonald
Lord Northcliffe
H. G. Wells
H. Seton Merriman
Archbishop of Canterbury

Frank Bullen
H. B. Irving
Lewis Waller
Princess Marie Louise
Princess Beatrice
H. Rider Haggard
T. Hall Caine
James Payn
Lord Brampton
Lord Balfour
Joseph Chamberlain
Mrs. Joseph Chamberlain
Israel Zangwill
Franklin D. Roosevelt
Madame Caruso
Sir Lionel Lascelles,
    Equerry to King George VI
Sir Squire Bancroft
Noel Coward
Etc. etc. etc.

BOX NO. 9

Letters to A.C.D. from his mother.

BOX NO. 10

Tributes to A.C.D. from members of the general public.

BOX NO. 11

Cross-section of A.C.D.'s psychic investigations, speeches, notes, etc.

REFERENCE WORKS

Quotations have been made from the following volumes of personal (non-psychic) reminiscences:—

MEMORIES AND ADVENTURES by A. Conan Doyle.
    (Hodder & Stoughton, 1924.)
ARTHUR CONAN DOYLE, A MEMOIR by The Rev. John Lamond, D.D.
    (John Murray 1931.)

THE TRUE CONAN DOYLE, by Adrian Conan Doyle.
   (John Murray, 1945.)
BARRIE, THE STORY OF A GENIUS, by J. A. Hammerton.
   (Sampson Low, Marston & Co., 1929.)
PERSONAL REMINISCENCES OF HENRY IRVING, by Bram Stoker.
   (Heinemann, 1907.)
ECCENTRICITIES OF GENIUS, by Major J. B. Pond.
   (Chatto and Windus, 1901.)
TWENTY YEARS OF MY LIFE, by Douglas Sladen.
   (Constable, 1915.)
LIFE HAS BEEN GOOD. MEMOIRS OF THE MARQUES DE VILLAVIEJA.
   (Chatto and Windus, 1930.)
THE HOUSE OF SMITH, ELDER. Printed for private circulation,
1923.
A MIXED GRILL, by the author of "A Garden of Peace."
   (Hutchinson, 1929.)
PEOPLE WORTH TALKING ABOUT, by Cosmo Hamilton.
   (Hutchinson, 1934.)
LOOKING LIFE OVER, by Hugh Hole.
   (Ivor, Nicholson & Watson, 1934.)
CROWDED NIGHTS AND DAYS, by Arthur Croxton.
   (Sampson, Low, 1931.)
WITH THE DICTATORS OF FLEET STREET, by Russell Stannard.
   (Hutchinson, 1934.)
GIANTS IN DRESSING GOWNS, by Julian B. Arnold.
   (Macdonald, 1944.)
EUGENE FIELD'S CREATIVE YEARS, by Charles B. Davies.
   (Doubleday, Page & Co., 1924.)
THE TRIAL OF OSCAR SLATER, edited by William Roughead.
   (3rd edition, William Hodge & Co., 1929.)

FAMILY HISTORY

A HUNDRED YEARS OF CONFLICT, 1756-1856, by Col. Arthur
Doyle.
   (Longman's, 1911.)
REMINISCENCES AND OPINIONS OF SIR FRANCIS HASTINGS DOYLE.
   (Longman's, 1886.)
A MEMOIR OF MAJ. GEN. SIR DENIS PACK, by Denis R. Pack-
Beresford.
   (University Press, Dublin, 1908.)
A TRUE HISTORY OF SEVERAL HONOURABLE FAMILIES OF THE RT.
HON. NAME OF SCOT, by Capt. Walter Scot, 1688.)
   (Reprinted Hawick, 1894.)

BIBLIOGRAPHY

A BIBLIOGRAPHICAL CATALOGUE OF THE WRITINGS OF SIR ARTHUR CONAN DOYLE, M.D., LL.D., 1879-1928, by Harold Locke. (D. Webster, 1928.)

INDEX

About the Author

John Dickson Carr, the son of a United States Congressman, is the author of a long and distinguished line of mystery novels and a former president of the Mystery Writers of America as well as a member of its English equivalent. He has also written under the names of Carter Dickson and Carr Dickson. For many years he divided his time between England and the United States; he now lives in Greenville, North Carolina and writes a book review column for *Ellery Queen's Mystery Magazine*.

In writing this biography he had the full cooperation of Sir Arthur Conan Doyle's children who gave him complete access to their father's papers.

VINTAGE HISTORY—AMERICAN

A free catalogue of VINTAGE BOOKS *will be sent at your request. Write to* Vintage Books, 457 Madison Avenue, New York, New York 10022.